TAXI

The Harry Chapin Story

TAXI

The Harry Chapin Story

Peter Morton Coan

Citadel Press
Kensington Publishing Corp.
www.kensingtonbooks.com

CITADEL PRESS books are published by

Kensington Publishing Corp.
850 Third Avenue
New York, NY 10022

A hardcover edition of *Taxi: The Harry Chapin Story* was published by Ashley Books.

Grateful acknowledgment is made to the following for permission to reprint previously published material:

Pantheon Books: From *Working* by Studs Terkel. © 1982 Studs Terkel

The Richmond Organization: From "This Land Is Your Land" by Woody Guthrie. Copyright © 1956 (renewed), 1958 (renewed), and 1970 Ludlow Music, Inc., New York, NY. Used by permission.

MMO Music Group: From "There is something in the singing," by Harry Chapin, from liner notes to the album *The Chapin Brothers* (Rock-Land Records).

Goldmine: From "Harry Chapin Discography and Price Guide," by Allen J. Wiener and Neal Umphred, *Goldmine,* September 22, 1989. Used by permission.

Citadel Press logo Reg. U.S. Patent and Trademark Office
Citadel Press is a trademark of Kensington Publishing Corp.

First Citadel printing: January 2001

10 9 8 7 6 5 4 3 2 1

Printed in the United States of America

Cataloging Data for this title may be obtained from the Library of Congress

ISBN 0-8065-2191-0

───────────

For my daughters, Melissa and Sara,
and, of course, H. Forster Chapin

"Press on. Nothing in the world can take the place of persistence. Talent will not: nothing is more common than unsuccessful men with talent. Genius will not: unrewarded genius is almost a proverb. Education alone will not: the world is full of educated derelicts. Persistence and determination alone are omnipotent."

—Calvin Coolidge

Contents

Part Three

Part Four

Introduction

I was eighteen years old when I first went to Broadway previews of *The Night That Made America Famous* in January 1975 and saw Harry Chapin perform live for the first time.

I am now forty-four years old. It amazes me to think that on July 16, 2001, Harry will have been dead for twenty years!

For a great while I marked the passage of time, and the passing of people and events with Harry and his passing. For example, if a great actor, musician, or athlete retired or died, I'd think back to July 16, 1981. Would Harry have known him or her? When I realized that in many cases Harry predated most, I knew I was growing old and that my friend had been gone too long.

If Harry were alive today, the huge "We Are the World" hunger-media phenomena of the early eighties would not have died. Harry would have pressed for personal commitments from each of the stars who gladly participated in the glow of all the media pomp and circumstance.

If Harry were alive today he would marvel at the Internet and use the technology to inspire people and help eradicate hunger. At last count there were more than 105 Web sites dedicated to Harry Chapin alone.

Still, it seems to me, much more could have been done, and should have been done, to further Harry's legacy and the causes that were so important to him.

* * *

When Kensington Publishers told me they had acquired this book from Carol Publishing and wanted to print a new, updated edition I was delighted—mostly for Harry. Maybe this time, after having told so many stories of other people's lives, Harry's life story would finally be heard.

I say this because from day one this book has been a battle. Some of you may have read about it over the years. Many of you have asked me to explain it. I am not referring to the day I met Harry, nor the seven wonderful years I worked with him on this book. I am referring to the day he died: July 16, 1981.

Almost immediately upon his death, Chapin's widow tried to block publication. She claimed to own the rights to my book and this scared off my then publisher, G. P. Putnam's Sons. With a potential lawsuit attached to the book, I could not find a new publisher to print it, nor a new agent to sell it. I was young, newly married, broke, but my dream was to publish this book. Harry had already read nearly all of it before he died and loved it, because according to him I had fulfilled his only wish: "to write a balanced portrait, not a puff piece."

I could have given up on the book, and many times I almost did. But in my heart I believed that to have done so would have been to let Harry down.

Though the widow's claim to my book was untrue, I wondered what her motive was. In what can only be explained as a miracle, a friend of mine was sitting in a diner on Long Island when he overheard conversation in the next booth about a book that was soon to be published about Harry Chapin and authorized by his widow. The speaker was a man talking to a young couple about his wife, who had written the book. When the couple asked him if there wasn't already a book on Chapin, the man replied, "Oh, the widow got rid of that guy. She decided not to go ahead with it."

I sued the widow. Thankfully, another friend of mine who had recently graduated from law school was willing to take on the prosecution of the case. It was sort of like David versus Goliath because the estate had retained a powerful Long Island law firm to make sure my book never saw the light of day. I spent the rest of the eighties in litigation with the widow, all the while trying to find a publisher. A small Long Island publisher agreed to put out a hardcover edition in 1987. But just prior to its release, the publisher received a phone call from her attorneys.

I don't know what was said, but I do know that after that conversation the book suffered the fate of print and bury—meaning it received a small print run and virtually no distribution. You couldn't find it in a bookstore. (I'm now told that a copy of this edition sells for as much as $250 on the Internet).

Frustrated, angry, I mounted a personal publicity campaign as much to promote the book as to let the world know of its suppression. There was some good publicity, but nobody really cared finally, and what good is publicity—or having a book at all—if people can't read it?

The lawsuit settled in 1990 and I walked away with the rights to my book, which was soon published by the Carol Publishing Group. They put out a trade paperback edition in 1990. The book received excellent reviews, mild publicity, sold out its small print run, and was never heard from again . . . until now.

* * *

Harry had an enormous effect on my life. He was my coach. My big brother. My senior adviser. He taught me so much about so many things. His death was traumatic for me. I still don't understand why he was taken. He gave so much, to so many, so unselfishly. For years after his death, I couldn't listen to his music without crying; today, a part of me still cries.

Since the day of his passing, I've been blessed with two beautiful daughters, was editor of *World Tennis Magazine*, wrote a travel book and recently wrote *Ellis Island Interviews: In Their Own Words*. The best part of that book for me was that it found my birth family, which is the subject of my next book.

I would like to thank Kensington's Bruce Bender for helping to keep Harry's memory alive with this new edition. I also want to thank all of the Chapin fans who sent me letters and e-mails over the years from all corners of the globe about how they diligently searched for a copy of this book only to find none. Your wait is over!

On a more personal note, I thank those who have been a source of strength and encouragement: Mr. and Mrs. Robert Coan, Vicky Hayes, Arlene and Berni Rich, Jon D. Miller, Harry Weinberg, Dan Rosenbaum, Rose Lindsay, Harold Lindsay, Earl Spivack, Janis Ameduri, David McGrath, Art Lieberman, Isabelle Belarsky, Tom Carpenter, Sandy Glen at chapintouch.com and my newly found birth family (on my late father's side): Lucille, Susan-Jane, Mildred, Rex, Michelle, Jessica, Greg, Anita, Bob, Renee, Stephen and Brittany; and (on my mother's side): Larry, Gail, Jessica, Jocelyn, Julia, Amanda, Matthew, Brady, Colonel Greene, Libby, Carmen, my mother, Martha, and my late brother, Nathan.

* * *

For this new edition, I looked back at all of my interviews and research I had collected over the past twenty-five years and wondered what I could add. What would Harry want me to include? In my mind, I kept coming back to interviews I had done with two of Harry's role models: Ralph Nader and Pete Seeger.

I could think of no better people to comment about Harry's legacy than those two. Below are excerpts from those interviews which took place in 1987 after Chapin posthumously received the Congressional Gold Medal at Carnegie Hall in a ceremony that was attended by both Nader and Seeger. Let's start with Nader commenting on Chapin's legacy in citizen causes:

> Harry was a bundle of goodwill energy. I think he saw himself as a human being first, a citizen second, and a musician third.
>
> In terms of his legacy, I think Harry established a standard of obligation for wealthy entertainers to spend a little of their time and money helping the poor. I mean, that was his favorite pay-phone-at-the-airport call. He must've called up 150 entertainers that way. He got political people to take entertainers more seri-

ously because of his lobbying on Capitol Hill. And he raised the public's expectations of what wealthy entertainers should give back to society. He's also left the legacy that an entertainer can have two careers, though not many can.

In terms of time spent on citizen causes like world hunger, Harry had no peer because he was actually involved in it. He didn't just fund it. He knew the bill numbers, he knew where each congressman stood on the hunger issue. So basically, in addition to being a parent, he led two careers, one as a citizen activist—the radio hungerthons, lobbying Congress, testifying at hearings, his benefit concerts, and the second is the entertainment—and even his entertainment had a social content to it. So he was really trying to develop a unique blend of mixing the world of music with the world of citizenship. . . .

In a final sense, nobody can really take his place. He had a combination of skills that no one has now in the entertainment world. His lobbying. His articulating. His never being discouraged. The consistency in his commitment. I mean, I used to go around the country and I'd meet citizen groups and every time I'd ask "Who's supporting you?" they'd say, "Well, it's two Harry Chapin concerts a year." Nobody else helped. And since Harry died, no entertainer has helped.

Pete Seeger commenting on Chapin as a musician and entertainer:

Harry was one of those unique people who just loved an audience. When he got up in front of a crowd, right away this empathy got set up. He loved reaching out and making contact with people. It didn't matter whether it was a paid concert or a benefit. I know the most successful singing I've done in my life is when I sang for free.

Also, I would say Harry was carrying on a great age-old tradition—the story song. It's an ancient European tradition really, but he developed it in his own way. He was an expert lyricist. Harry, and I think a lot of us, learned the importance of simplicity from folk music. It's what we learned from Woody Guthrie. Woody's songs were so extraordinarily simple. Woody did something very important for Harry and me and all the rest of us.

He showed that you could learn from the old songs, but you could also change 'em.

The other key is, one of the most important things an artist can do is to give people a sense of their own worth and value, and Harry did that. He did this in concert with his stories and audience participation. Somebody once said that anybody who gets people together is a politician. In Harry's case, I would say it's because his own basic decency shined right out so that people could get together with it. He was not up there to show you how clever he was. He wanted to get everybody in there with him. . . .

Keep in mind that your book, if you do your job right, will be read by a wide variety of people. I mean, it's true, that the publisher is planning to make money out of Harry's fans. But I hope you realize there are people in distant places and distant times who could read this book and it could change their life if it's done right and be one more weapon in our race to survive. Many people think this is a useless purpose for a book, but I think it's the only purpose.

* * *

I will let you, the reader, judge whether I've done my job right.

What follows is the life story of Harry Chapin as it was originally written. It also contains an updated discography and a new list of key Harry Chapin Web sites. For those of you who knew Harry and his music, I hope you will be as pleased as I am with this new edition. For those of you who are coming to know Harry for the first time, welcome. I believe you will find his spirit alive and well in these pages.

—Peter Morton Coan
New York

Special Acknowledgments

It took me seven years to research and write this book and another nine years of torturous legal infighting to bring it to fruition. Harry Chapin would be proud, because this book is for him. And it is to him I give my deepest and most heartfelt thanks—for all his help, all his support, all the years of working together. Most of all I thank him for his friendship, the sheer inspiration that allowed me to push on when I could go no further and enabled me to write the portrait of a most complex man.

He was, and forever will be, my greatest inspiration.

My biggest consolation is that Chapin read 95 percent of my book before he died and felt I had fulfilled his one and only request—that the book be a serious, well-balanced portrait, not a puff piece. My second consolation is that Chapin liked the book. "I always knew you had the heart," he once told me. "But I never knew you had the ability."

I pay special thanks to SUNY at Buffalo professors, Leslie Fiedler and Robert Newman, who have been there for me from the beginning.

And, most important, I thank those people without whose fight and belief this book would never have materialized—in particular, Harry Weinberg, a good friend and gutsy attorney, who fought the widow's massive legal entourage with determined resolve, and successfully fended them off. Weinberg helped keep this book alive. So did my agent, Carol Mann; she deserves many thanks.

Finally, I thank God, for the words and the strength and his covering.

Author's Note

To gain an audio/musical flow to Chapin's life, listen to the songs which title each chapter as you read through the book. The discography at the back will tell you the albums where the songs appear.

Authorization to use the lyrics from Harry Chapin's songs could not be obtained from the Chapin estate.

Prologue

Harry Chapin was an unsung hero. He was an American Jacques Brel, a modern-day Woody Guthrie, and a social activist bar none. Yet Chapin never received the recognition he so richly deserved for his music, beliefs and social activism. He was shunned by the rock critic establishment, overlooked for his humanitarian concerns, and castigated for being uncool. But to his fans—millions of them, across the U.S., Canada, and Europe—he was one of the most beloved performers in pop music history. He was a spokesman of the people, the poet laureate to cab drivers, housewives and common folk alike.

Most of the world will remember Chapin for the story song. The musical genre he popularized from the best tradition of the troubadour or minstrel, who intuitively heard the whispers of the simple yet meaningful rustlings of life and transformed them into lyrics. In that sense "he was, in his own way, a contemporary poet, and his songs were ballads to our time, memorials to his own generation," wrote Clive Barnes of the *New York Post*. "His words had a certain bitterness that reflected a nonacceptance of the world's imperfections."

But more than just sing about his social concerns, Chapin tried to do something about them. For Harry Chapin was a man of ideals who lived and breathed what he believed. He was a crusader for human decency and the embodiment of the American spirit. His involvements in humanitarian causes, the arts and social organizations were nothing short of extraordinary. He created institutions, attitudes, visions. His life's ambition was not to accumulate wealth or collect creature comforts to be bordered by white picket fences; rather it was to redistribute what resources he had as the seed money, to spur others to be informed and involved and a part of the ongoing democratic process. It was a question of beliefs.

Chapin acted on those beliefs, listening to his own drummer. He was a man who spoke his mind when others remained silent, a man of courage and commitment, and his stage life (more than two hundred concerts per year) represented only a small fraction of the larger issues and involvements that preoccupied his personal time. Chapin did things not because they were popular but because they were, to him, the right things to do. He did not write his story songs for the Top 40 charts (though many of them landed there), but because he had something to say. And he wanted to say it through music.

He continued to say and do what he believed right up to July 16, 1981, and his tragic death at the age of thirty-eight. For the millions of people who knew and loved him, Chapin's passing was a bitter shock. Yet he achieved more in his thirty-eight years than some people achieve in a lifetime.

"We have a tendency when a person dies to make him appear greater in death than he was in life," wrote Congressman Tom Downey, in an article for the *New York Times*. "This is not possible with Harry. He lived Bob Dylan's admonition: 'He who is not busy being born in busy dying.'"

I first conceived the idea of writing a book about Harry Chapin when I was eighteen years old. It was December 1974, and at that point I had never heard of Harry Chapin; much less did I know he had already recorded four albums, two of them gold records, thanks to hit singles—"Taxi" on one and "Cat's in the Cradle" on the other. The latter was the number one single in America according to the *Billboard* Top 40 charts by Christmas of that year. But I didn't know any of this when I found myself driving with my father to a family Christmas dinner in New Jersey. Suddenly, "Cat's in the Cradle" came over the car radio. I loved the song. It told the story of a father and son and their estrangement, which would be an accurate description of my relationship with my father at that time.

We both sort of looked at each other.

The only thing I could think of was that I had to buy that song! I didn't know the name of it, and I didn't know on which album it appeared, so over the next three weeks—as if on some divine mission—I unwittingly bought album after album, each time failing to find *the* song—until the fourth and final purchase. By that time I had already fallen in love with the body of Chapin's work, his story-song style, the totality of what he was able to do, the moods he was able to evoke, the raw nerve he was able to strike. When I finally listened to "Cat's in the Cradle" on my stereo, the feeling was almost anticlimactic: there were at least ten songs of his that I liked better!

Then, by coincidence, in February 1975, I found out that Chapin was appearing on Broadway in *The Night That Made America Famous*, a show the people loved and the critics hated and which died after a run of seven weeks. I saw the show twice and was overwhelmed each time not only by the music and the message but now—by the man. It wasn't so much the stories he sang as the way he sang them with such passion and intensity, almost as if he singled you out of the audience and sang to you personally. His homey, easygoing stage presence transformed that theater into a living room. He had the audience mesmerized, and I was no different.

I was young and, like most young people, I was rebellious and ambitious at the same time—in search of some cause or continuity that would make the world whole. In Harry Chapin I found such meaning. He sang of youth's ambitions perversely fulfilled, fears and frustrations—all of which seemed to echo my own.

His were ballads, long, literary, and emotional, with detailed imagery and ironic twists. There were no acid-rock riffs to blur the senses, no idiomatic non sequiturs to confuse the mind. His lyrics were like fine crystal, his melodies poignant. He did not wear tight leather pants and diamond studs, just an old pair of jeans. He did not need blinding smoke and special effects, just a guitar and a microphone. Chapin had an extraordinary knack of getting at the heart of what made people tick, getting beneath the layers of posture and pretense. But what made Harry Chapin tick?

After that second Broadway performance, I walked some fifty blocks from West 45th Street to my house. I'll never forget the excitement that ran through me. That night, I wrote a three-page letter to Chapin at the theater. In it, I offered to tell his life story. Though I had no literary credentials, I had hunger and heart, two things I later learned Chapin could not respect enough, because he never forgot the days when he was young and green and filled with dreams. He had compassion.

He also had an acute feeling for the underdog, the little guys and their crazy little dreams, and often-tragic disappointments. They were the characters in his songs, the Eleanor Rigbys of the world. Chapin wrote for them. And I guess for him I was just another one of those characters. I had this crazy idea to write a book. Except, Chapin gave me the chance his song characters never had. Six months later I received a two-sentence letter from Chapin's manager, Fred Kewley. Chapin was interested and asked me to call him.

On August 18, 1975, Chapin was appearing at the Westbury Music Fair on Long Island for a double concert. Kewley arranged for me to meet Chapin between sets. I was scared to death, but Chapin was as friendly as sunshine, greeting me as though he were the fan and I the celebrity. And when I called him "Mr. Chapin," he immediately insisted I call him Harry. There was too much noise and hubbub backstage for us to talk that night, so Harry invited me out to his home in Huntington, Long Island, the following week. He told me to be there at 2:00 P.M. But as I would later come to routinely expect, Chapin was late. Two hours late. Nobody was home, but the front door was open (also typical), so finally I went inside to leave a note for him in the living room. Just at that moment I heard the front door open and slam shut. Chapin came bounding into the room. He was dressed in traditional sixties garb: work shirt, jeans and brown penny-loafers. He was smoking a fat cigar and carried what must have been a dozen records that he'd just bought at a local store.

"Ay, Pete!" he called out, somewhat winded. "I'm sorry I'm late." We spent the rest of that afternoon and evening together (and little did I know or expect then, the next seven years of our lives). I had dinner with him, his wife, Sandy, and their five children. He gave me a tour of his home and had me listen to a tape of new songs he'd just recorded. But it took only ten minutes of conversation for us to agree that I would write his biography. There was no money involved. It was strictly a labor of love. After all, what did I know about writing a biography? Chapin asked only that it be a serious writing job, not a puff piece, and he offered to help in any way he could.

An understatement indeed, because Harry Chapin and I became not just biographer and subject, but close personal friends, even brothers. During the last seven years of his life, I was probably closer to him than anyone else. I had complete access to his life. I was his confidant, privy to candid confessions and dark secrets neither his wife nor his real brothers knew.

I researched the book while I attended the University of Buffalo for my undergraduate work and Boston University for my master's. To overcome the distance between us, Harry or his secretary would call me to say he'd be in Syracuse or Portland or Providence for a weekend concert, and I'd drive to the airport and pick him up. Because of his frenetic schedule and poor driving record (Harry's driver's license was perpetually in a state of suspension or revocation), most of our interviews were done in the car, going to and from concerts. We talked and taped through blizzards and hail, from Watertown to Washington, into the wee hours of the morning.

Armed with an ordinary tape recorder and beat-up Mustang, it was always me driving and Harry talking. If physically possible, Chapin went home the night of any given concert. He was an extraordinary father and husband. His performances, usually three hours long, often prevented him from catching a late-night flight home. So rather than leave the following morning, we'd take my car or rent one and race the sun back to his home in Huntington, New York. If he was tired after a concert, he'd sleep scrunched up in the backseat while I searched for the nearest telephone so he could call Sandy and estimate our arrival time. Once we drove nine hours straight through from Buffalo. At 6:00 A.M., we pulled into his circular driveway and he staggered into bed beside Sandy. I slept in the guest room. By 7:00 A.M., he was up making breakfast so he could see his children before they left for school.

Many times I went on tour with him for a week or more. I'd quickly find a friend to cover my classes and off I'd go, carrying an attaché case filled with fresh tapes—and a pocketful of questions. Once Harry called and asked, "Have you ever been on a Lear Jet, Pete?" I hadn't, so he said, "Well, meet me in New York tomorrow. We're flying to Chicago," and we did.

Once home, I spent what seemed like endless days transcribing the tapes, organizing the material, and preparing for our next journey. Over the years, I must have waded through three thousand pages of material on Chapin alone. He used to joke that I knew more about him than he knew about himself. But my involvement did not end there. During the summers and school vacations I interviewed everyone connected with Chapin on any significant level. I did well over three hundred interviews with celebrities the likes of Robert Redford and Pete Seeger, plus intimate family, friends, fans and even Chapin's staunchest enemies, usually rock critics. From time to time I'd show Harry the material and he'd review it for dates and inconsistencies, which invariably jarred his memory for another anecdote or two. We proceeded in this manner for almost seven years . . . until that fateful day.

* * *

At six-foot-one, Harry Chapin was towering and masculine, strong and strong-willed, larger than life. His profile was that of a young Ted Kennedy with an Art Carney nose. Below his cliff-like forehead, his brow had a slight tilt aimed toward his right eye. He had a cleft chin. His eyes were hazel brown and his hair brown and wavy. When he spoke, he shouted, commanding attention. When he cleared his throat, he practically shook the room. While eating, he used both hands in rapid fire, like a Chinaman shoveling rice into his mouth.

Harry neither drank nor smoked, except for an occasional cigar or pipe during moments of personal victory, and when he drank coffee or tea, he added so much milk and sugar the brew was almost undrinkable. When he walked, he ran. "Walking with Harry always consisted of trailing five paces behind him," said his older brother James. And when he slept, he still ran, his body usually in transport by car or plane. He wrote his story songs in proliferation and scribbled them in loose-leaf notebooks. If his notebook wasn't handy, he wrote on motel stationery, backs of envelopes, torn pieces of paper, stuffing them in pockets for Sandy to find the following morning. When he sang, his face showed the emotional involvement, his cheeks swelled and his forehead wrinkled. When he was excited, his body created an effusive outpouring of impassioned energy. His eyes brightened, one hand raked his hair, one foot began a beat. He jerked, jumped, and words gushed out of him like a dam having burst.

There was no one word that best defined or described Harry Chapin. He defined himself, because he was constantly inventing himself. Robert Redford, a good friend, described him as

"Halley's Comet on a revolving cycle of once every hour." According to Chapin family lore, the phrase "two's company and Harry's a crowd" had always been a standard. But perhaps his brother James, who lived in the same room with him for seventeen years, came closest when he said, "Relating to Harry was like relating to a steam engine."

Whatever the description, the enthusiastic drive, determination and energy he radiated across a stage or across a room were always amazing to anyone connected with him, especially his fans.

For that reason, Harry's unique appeal was not as evident in his albums as much as in his dynamic concerts. For it was in concerts that the real Harry Chapin emerged. "Listening to him on records is like reading about an orgasm," a reviewer once wrote. "He has to be seen live to be appreciated." That was because of his penchant for audience participation. Unlike most performers, he did not sing at or to his audience, but rather with them. It was a Chapin trademark. "Not since Al Jolson," said Pete Seeger, "have I ever seen a performer who established such a natural rapport, empathy and involvement with an audience."

Harry Chapin was not just entertainment, he was an experience. He was a balladeer and the characters in his stories were the people in his audience—taxi drivers, tailors, students, factory workers, pretzel vendors, wives and lovers of all ages. They came to hear of themselves, for in his songs Chapin reflected their dreams, drives, ambitions, and often their failures. But always his stories ended with hope. The future will be better with his unspoken message. It was summed up best in "Circle," the "Chapin theme song" and the encore that ended all his performances, where he sang about his life being a circle: "but I can't tell you why, the season's spinnin' round again, the years keep rollin' by."

The crowds ate it up, getting the song's final note with tumultuous standing ovations; and when they quieted down, Chapin stood center stage, gave a short speech about his commitments, and told the crowd he'd meet them in the front lobby of the concert hall. There he'd autograph T-shirts, souvenir books, a book of his poetry, even hands, and the proceeds of any sales went to his personal crusade against world hunger.

Chapin's success was also aided by his "unyielding touring, performing in the small cities and towns that often inspired his songs," wrote Wayne Robins, music critic at *Newsday*, the Long Island daily. "Frequent concerts in Ohio, Indiana, Texas, Idaho, places where artists who've made the national charts infrequently wander, made Chapin a grassroots American hero." Those places were the backbone of his cult, and people often drove hundreds of miles to attend his sold-out performances, making him one of the highest paid performers in the world. He earned an average of $2 million a year.

Even so, Chapin was practically broke when he died, mostly because of his selfless humanity and his incredible interest in other people and social causes. Chapin thrived on his participation in public affairs. He called it the "qualitative side of my life." Once he was performing at a college in Queens, and after the performance he invited everyone to a charity barbecue at his house. If Pete Seeger was the prince of benefits, Harry Chapin was the king, and Seeger would be the first to admit it. Over the course of his career, Chapin performed more than two thousand concerts and more than half of them were benefits. His extraordinary largesse meant he raised more than $6 million, which helped support a total of more than one hundred organizations, foundations, charities, universities, and, of course, relatives. And he was only thirty-eight years old when he died.

On a local level, in his community on Long Island, Chapin was deeply committed to bringing arts institutions into national prominence. Simultaneously, Chapin was a board member and principal fund-raiser for the Performing Arts Foundation (PAF), the Eglevsky Ballet, Hofstra University, the Long Island Action Committee, Long Island Cares, and the Long Island Philharmonic (which, by the way, he single-handedly created by convincing the Suffolk and Long Island Symphonies to merge). Most of them depended on Chapin for survival. "He didn't just want to raise money," said David Westerman, former member of the PAF board of trustees. "He wanted to make the whole community vibrate together. With his death, I don't think anything worse could have happened to Long Island."

On a national level, Chapin will probably be best remembered for his involvement in world hunger issues. In 1975, he cofounded a hunger resource organization called WHY (World Hunger Year). Its goal was to educate the public to the root cause of the problem, suggest solutions, and hopefully spur individual concern. Toward this end, Chapin created an informational hunger magazine called *Food Monitor* and a Washington lobbying organization called the Food Policy Center. Over the years, Chapin also staged hunger-radiothons in ten cities, reaching an audience of more than fifteen million people.

But his most effective work was in lobbying Congress to endorse the creation of a presidential commission on world hunger. Like a chameleon, Chapin transformed himself from the corduroy-and-turtleneck-clad concert-giver into a sophisticated, well-informed lobbyist, complete with suit, tie and potent vocabulary. Harry always carried a verb with him. One moment, he could talk out of the side of his mouth, and the next moment, confidently rub elbows and exchange ripostes with some of the most important men in Washington. Chapin succeeded in getting congressional endorsement of his commission mostly because so many congressmen were awed by his energy and commitment, and also because some would have done anything to dispose of his badgering. It was not a coincidence, then, that the bill passed both houses overwhelmingly.

It was also not a coincidence that the day after his death, thirty congressmen and ten senators rose on the floor of the House to offer eulogies. "No other singer," wrote Dave Marsh of *Rolling Stone* magazine, Chapin's longtime adversary, "not Bing Crosby, nor Elvis Presely, nor John Lennon—has ever been so widely honored by the nation's legislators."

Chapin's world came full circle the day before. Ironically it was the automobile, the very thing that made him famous in song ("Taxi"), was the very thing that took his life. He died on the

Long Island Expressway when his 1975 Volkswagen Rabbit was hit from the rear by a flatbed tractor-trailer truck and burst into flames. The impact of the crash sent Chapin's car three hundred feet up the road before it finally stopped on the right shoulder. The accident occurred at approximately 12:30 P.M.

Almost immediately, two motorists pulled off the road and came to Chapin's aid. The car door was jammed, but the window was open, so the motorists tried to pull him through. Unfortunately, Chapin's seat belt was strapped tight. But the truck driver, who was unhurt, happened to have a pocketknife in his glove compartment. He retrieved it, cut Chapin's seat belt, and with the assistance of the motorists, freed him from the burning wreckage. The three men then carried him to a grass embankment, with Chapin still alive, moaning. Within seconds, police and an emergency medical team arrived and tried to resuscitate him. Within fifteen minutes, a police helicopter airlifted him to the Nassau County Medical Center where, at 1:07 P.M., he was pronounced dead on arrival.

At the time, authorities were not aware it was Chapin who had died, since there was no personal identification on him. In fact, Harry did not even have a driver's license. It was revoked four months earlier due to numerous traffic violations. By 2:40 P.M. his body was tagged "John Doe" and sent to the medical examiner's office for autopsy. There it was revealed that Chapin died from a "massive internal hemorrhage caused by a lacerated aorta." He also suffered numerous bodily injuries: a fractured vertebrate and ribs, and severe burns to his abdomen and back. He also suffered cardiac arrest. No traces of alcohol or drugs were found in his body. Initial newspaper reports speculated that Chapin may have suffered the heart attack before the accident. To this day, the question remains unanswered. It is this author's belief, however, that the wire which connects the accelerator on the floor to the carburetor choke snapped, causing Chapin's car to rapidly decelerate as he made what must have been a desperate attempt to reach the safety of the right-hand lane, only to find himself an easy target for that chugging tractor-trailer.

Finally, at 8:05 P.M., Chapin's brother Steve and step-brother, Jebbie Hart, positively identified the body.

"The immediate response to Chapin's death, in the media and among his fans, was truly overwhelming," wrote Dave Marsh of *Rolling Stone*. "It was as if he reached out and touched lives in a permanent and irrevocable way." His albums sold out in record stores, and throughout the country, people who had purchased tickets for the remainder of Chapin's summer tour refused to ask for refunds. Newspapers brimmed over with articles on him. Even television newscasters, hardly strangers to doom, death and disaster, expressed disbelief. In the Midwest, one Chicago newsman nearly broke down on the set, and in New York, local NBC anchors Chuck Scarborough and Sue Simmons could barely hold back the tears in order to get through the copy. Chapin knew them all personally.

When Jim Chapin, Harry's father, got the news, he was teaching a class at the Long Island Drum School. "I was devastated," he said in a *Newsday* article three weeks later. "I canceled the class and just sat around the classroom, not thinking much of anything except that there must be a mistake. You had to know Harry to know Harry was the essence of life. *Dead* was the last word you'd ever associate with him."

But the biggest shock came to a record 30,000 fans gathered in Eisenhower Park's Lakeside Theatre on Long Island to hear Chapin in concert that evening. They had not yet heard the news when an ominous voice came over the public address system with a surreal announcement: "Ladies and gentlemen, the concert has been canceled because of the tragic death of Harry Chapin."

The majority of fans remained. They huddled in small groups, numbed by the news. "He inspired me to write my first song," a girl at the concert said to a *Newsday* reporter. "I came up to him at a concert and asked, 'Will you be my friend?' He said, 'Forever friends.'" Then she paused and said something typical of most Chapin fans—"I loved him," she said unashamed—her eyes soaked with tears. "My God, how he touched me."

A few days later the theater was renamed the Harry Chapin Lakeside Theatre. Funeral services for Chapin were held at the A. L. Jacobsen Funeral Home in Huntington, New York. He was buried in a small cemetery nearby, and although Chapin's wishes were to be cremated, his wife, Sandy, on the day of his death said, "In life, Harry was scattered all over. In death, I want him in one place."

Said Robert Redford, who was never one to gratuitously hand out praise: "Harry was a rare occurrence. There was nobody like him. I haven't met anybody with the degree of energy and the degree of commitment all tied into one force like him."

It is not that Harry Chapin was a giant among men. He wasn't. But he did the best he could. One thing I learned from writing this book is that each one of us at some point buys someone's line, someone's calling, which affects who we eventually turn out to be. For Chapin it was the calling of his grandfathers. They were great men who, artistically, left something worthwhile behind. Harry wanted to be like them. And he worked at it.

If there is anything that Chapin's life can teach us, it is embodied in that wonderful Coolidge quote that is the epigraph to this book: "persistence and determination [for success in anything we do] are omnipotent." When you look at Harry Chapin with open eyes, you see a man who, at best, was a fair poet and a good songwriter, with a decent baritone voice, who yet managed to turn those marginal skills into a great success. In that sense, he is an inspiration to all of us. This is particularly true when you consider that he returned that success to society by getting deeply involved with numerous social causes.

There are, in the history of the music business, far greater stars than Chapin, people we admire professionally who've enjoyed more natural gifts and achieved greater sales, who have never returned anything to society save a good PR opportunity. And that is what Chapin's life teaches us: you don't have to be a Michael Jackson or an Elvis Presley or a Bill Cosby to succeed and do good unto others. You just have to do the best you can.

PART ONE

This land is your land, this land is my land
From California to the New York island
From the redwood forest to the Gulf Stream waters
This land was made for you and me.

—Woody Guthrie

CHAPTER I

Cat's in the Cradle

"In the 1940s, the Lower West Side of Manhattan was a schizophrenic place for growing up," Harry Chapin once said. At that time, his family lived at 353 West 11th Street in Greenwich Village, right near the West Side Highway across from Pier 48 and the Hudson River. It was a slum neighborhood tainted by youth gangs and the dirty salt breeze that came off the river, a melting pot of Irish, Italian, and some middle-class blacks. It was also an artistic community composed of humble, hard-working people. Paintings were often sold on sidewalks and rents were cheap, affording artists the opportunity to pursue their craft.

For fifty dollars a month, the Chapins lived in a small, second-floor walk-up apartment in a rundown tenement replete with barred windows. On the first floor, below the Chapins, was a longshoreman's local. And above them, on the third floor, lived a Spanish family. To one side of the building and around the back was a parking lot used by warehouse trucks for the M&M Candy Company. When backing in, they often smacked the side of the structure and left their impression by way of a huge dent and tilted staircase. The streets ran parallel to elevated railroad tracks, and at night one could hear the incessant rumble of trains. At the southern end of the block was the forbidding sight of a maximum-security federal penitentiary. The prison trucks passing along West 11th Street were a familiar scene in the cityscape.

3

Harry's mother, Elspeth Chapin, or Duchee as she was often called, was an attractive brunette of small build. She was one of three daughters born to Kenneth and Lilly Burke, Harry's grandparents. Elspeth's two sisters were France and Happy. Graduating from high school at fourteen and college at eighteen, Elspeth married Jim Chapin in 1940, when she was twenty. He was twenty-three. At six-foot-two, Jim was a remarkably handsome, athletic-looking, blond-haired man, the only child of James and Abby Chapin.

Both the Burke and Chapin families were of old American ancestry with strains of New England aristocracy. The Chapins originally came from England in 1635, and were descendants of Deacon Samuel Chapin, who founded Springfield, Massachusetts, in 1636. The Forbes family, Abby's forebears, can be traced as far back as ninth-century Scotland.

Elspeth's family, the Burkes, were descendants of the Batterham and Forster families. Harry Batterham and his wife, Eleanor Forster, were potato planters in Lancashire, England, and came to America in the 1870s after their potato crop was blighted. The Batterhams then married into the Burke family. It was from his Forster ancestor that Harry received his middle name. His was the eleventh Chapin generation in America.

Harry Forster Chapin was born December 7, 1942, in St. Vincent's Hospital in New York. At the time, Elspeth and Jim had only one other son, James, who was thirteen months old. To support his family, Jim Chapin was a jazz drummer in many of the big bands of the thirties and forties, particularly those of Woody Herman and Tommy Dorsey. Though he was a technically proficient drummer and highly respected by his peers, he never attained the standing his potential might have suggested. So, like most musicians in the era of jazz, swing and bebop, Jim was constantly on the road, especially in 1943, when he was drafted and relocated to various Air Force bases throughout the country, where he fulfilled his service obligations drumming in service bands.

Elspeth, a young mother with two children, joined her husband whenever she could, often traveling great distances by bus or train. She stayed in roadside motels or Air Force camps, and some of Harry's earliest memories were of his mother and brother James visiting his father. By the age of three, Harry had already lived six months on the road, from Oakland, California and Portland, Oregon, to eastern seaboard cities.

During one visit to the Air Force camp in Charlotte, North Carolina, Elspeth gave birth to her third son, Tommy. It was also here that Harry was first introduced to a musical instrument. "I had access to all the instruments," said Jim Chapin. "So I took out a trumpet and Harry loved to try it. He blew his first few notes when he was three years old."

The end of the war, however, did not increase the amount of time Jim spent at home. He went back on the road, and was often away for extended periods of time. He was impossible to locate, too slippery to nail down. Elspeth again was left to take care of the children. But by 1947 it meant she was raising four of them, having given birth to Steve, her fourth son.

During these years, Harry recalled very little of his father. "We saw him once a week or once every couple of weeks. He was more like a friendly uncle you'd see occasionally."

When Jim did come home, it was usually at two or three in the morning after traveling home from a concert gig. On these occasions, he often woke the boys and made them omelettes, spaghetti or his specialty, baked Alaska.

It was difficult for Jim to maintain both a marriage and a performing career. He had no time for raising a family and showed little interest in watching his children grow. Yet he cared. He loved his children and he loved his wife. But his career simply came first. Like so many jazz men of the time, he was in love with the music. During his spare moments on the road, Jim was busy writing a drum book, *Advanced Techniques for the Modern Drummer,* which eventually sold more than 200,000 copies and revolutionized modern jazz drumming.

Jim's love of music and music performance meant he took very little responsibility beyond the drumbeats of the concert stage. An incident during the summer of 1965 illustrated Jim's piquant personality and, in Harry's opinion, best summed up his father. Jim was playing drums for Harry, Tom and Steve in their group, the Chapin Brothers. They were about to begin the long drive down to Jacksonville, Florida, for a show. Jim's mother, Abby, who was wont to make emotional statements at such times, saw them off. As they boarded the van, Jim settled into the driver's seat.

"Jim! Please drive safely," she implored. "Most of my life is in this bus."

"Sure, Mom, sure," Jim said with a reassuring smile.

A few miles down the road, Jim broke into a big grin. "You know, boys, Grandma's right! Most everything that's precious to me is sitting right here in this driver's seat."

Bob Mullevaney, a friend of the brothers who managed them that summer, said, "Harry's father was a very engaging individual. He was the kind of guy you wouldn't mind being with at a party. But in real honest truth, there were times he neglected his family, his primary responsibilities, and went off and did whatever he felt like."

Since he was always short of money and short of family time, Jim's buoyant, carefree life-style caused Elspeth to reach the breaking point. Handsome and charming, on the road and in front of women, Jim found his prolonged absences from home became a source of suspicion. There was no telling where he spent his free time, or with whom. His reputation as a womanizer, then and in years following, was not a well-kept secret. "You know, Jim never went after girls," one family member said in his defense. "They were after him. He never made any move to try and get it!"

Elspeth's absentee marriage became impossible. In 1948, they legally separated. Harry was six years old.

It was the women in the Burke-Chapin families who influenced Harry's upbringing most. He was surrounded by a matriarchy of strong-minded and strong-willed women. Besides Elspeth, there were Aunts France and Happy; great-grandma Batterham; grandma Lilly, Kenneth Burke's first wife; and her sister, Libby, Kenneth Burke's second wife; Rose Housekeeper, Harry's second cousin; and, of course, Grandma Chapin, Abby. They all partially compensated for the lack of a father, especially Lilly and Grandma Chapin. They were the backbone of Harry's youth.

Both grandmothers were a rare breed of woman; resourceful, resilient, and sometimes overbearing. They were firm disciplinarians. At the same time, they could be incredibly loving and supportive. They were compulsively proud, positive, Gibraltar-like figures; battering rams for social praise and guidance, especially Grandma Chapin. She was contagiously cheerful and outgoing, and a firm believer in the best of everything. Harry was most like her, especially when it came to self-confidence, which both women injected into his personality early on, creating a foundation of high self-esteem. "You are unique, you are wonderful, you are Harry Chapin," they taught him.

"In many ways they were my first contact with the real world and practicality," said Harry. "They believed I was worthwhile long before the outside world did."

Both grandmothers were professional teachers and gave Harry and his brothers an education prior to any formal schooling. Grandma Chapin was an English teacher and head of that department at the Lincoln School, a small private school near her apartment at 50 Morningside Drive on the Upper West Side of Manhattan. Grandma Chapin first taught Harry how to read. Lilly was a math teacher who lived one block from Elspeth and the boys on West 10th Street. The brothers usually spent one night a week at Lilly's apartment. Before bedtime, she peeled oranges as rewards for the right answers to multiplication tables and math problems. By the first grade, Harry already had a firm grounding in math and English, and by junior high school, he was able to skip the eighth grade.

For the grandmothers, the Chapin boys were like young gods: "these marvelous little people." Harry walked around New York like he owned it, tearing through subways, playing ball in the streets. At the same time, doing anything short of his grandmothers' expectations or standards of excellence brought disparaging looks and words. Often on the way to school, Harry and Tom chased one another. One day the chase led across Seventh Avenue where, without looking, Tom ran into the side of a speeding car. He fell down, crying. His wrists hurt, so he was taken to St. Vincent's Hospital for X rays. "All I worried about was who was going to pay for this," said Tom. "We were broke. We had no money. Harry was devastated. All he was worried about was me."

Two weeks later, a bill for $16 arrived. Grandma Chapin, who often came by in the afternoons, found it. "What happened?" she asked disappointedly. Neither Harry nor Tom had the courage to tell her. "It was always hard to tell her anything that you had done wrong," said Tom. "Because 'You're a Chapin,' she should say. 'You don't do this.'"

Said Harry: "She had a way that you were so embarrassed. I mean, telling a lie, doing anything less than extraordinary was just unheard of. In one way, it was part of the ego building that allowed us to do things."

However, a few weeks later, a similar accident happened to Harry. This time, he was running home from school to Lilly's apartment, half a block from the federal prison (the Women's House of Detention). The prisoners there were mostly white-collar criminals, and later, during the McCarthy era, suspected communists. At one point, without looking, Harry ran across Greenwich Avenue and was struck on the forehead by the fender of a taxi cab. At precisely the same moment, a horde of reporters and photographers were milling in front of the prison waiting for the release of Judith Coplon, an alleged Russian spy. Immediately, the journalists swarmed to Chapin. The following day, photographs of Harry wound up in the center section of the *Daily News* and in the *New York Times*. It was an ironic forboding of the future, Harry and the song "Taxi," his springboard to musical success.

Unfortunately, the accident permanently damaged Harry's skull. The bone on the right side of his forehead was slightly crushed, leaving his right eye a bit more closed than his left, so when he smiled, it gave him a beguiling cockeyed grin.

As a child, Harry had numerous hobbies. Drawing and model building intrigued him, and at the age of nine, leather work inspired his first and only act of childhood larceny. There was a hobby shop on West 14th Street where Harry bought leather tools for $1.50 each. He obtained this sum by saving up his lunch money every day; thirty-two cents. If Harry didn't eat lunch for five days, he could accumulate $1.60, and with six cents tax, wind up with four cents left over.

"But finally, this started getting to me," said Harry. "So I'd buy one and steal five. One day I went in and bought one, stole fifteen." But as he started toward the door, his coat rattling, he was pulled aside by a kind store clerk. Instead of reporting him, the clerk jerked Harry's chest and said, "I've been watching you, and I think this should be the end of it, don't you?" Grateful, and perhaps picturing the hurt pride on his grandmother's face, Harry never stole again.

Like the grandmothers, Elspeth was of strong mind and soul and provided well for the boys. She was a good mother, and though she had little money, she managed even when there wasn't enough. On West 11th Street there was a combination deli-grocery store called Benny's where Elspeth often shopped. On occasion, when she was short of cash, the shopkeeper let her charge her groceries and pay for them the following day or week.

When Elspeth did have extra money, she took the boys to the movies. Harry cried during the breakup scene in *Singin' in the Rain,* his first movie experience. But when a baby-sitter took the boys to see a pirate picture, Harry became so frightened by the violence and gore he never wanted to see a movie again. So, soon after, when *Red River* played at the local theater, Harry stubbornly refused to go in unless a cartoon was showing too. "I spent the first half hour outside while everybody else was inside," said Harry. "Mother left the ticket with the usher and told him to let me in. But I was too proud to let anyone know I went in. So I snuck in, saw the movie, and when it ended, I ran out and acted like I'd been out there the whole time."

Though Elspeth maintained a very matter-of-fact surface, underneath she was a compassionate, understanding woman, and very easy to love. "I always knew that whatever I did it would be all right with mother," said Harry. "She had a calm, no-nonsense, no-pressure way of dealing with things."

Yet for all their love and concern, Elspeth and the grandmothers could not provide everything. As Harry grew older, his brothers became the bulwark of his emotional life. According to Elspeth, if she asked Harry to wash up because they were going somewhere, Harry instantly replied: "We're all going, right?"

Harry played with his brothers and rarely made friends with any of the rough-and-tumble neighborhood kids who were a direct contrast to the clean-cut, well-behaved Chapin boys. There were two local youth gangs, the 11th Street Italian gang and the Perry Street Irish gang. Less formidable than modern youth gangs, they were mostly teenagers who challenged each other with feisty words and fisticuffs. The mob had already scared away all the muggers and two-bit hoods from the surrounding neighborhood and nearby docks. Still, as outsiders, Harry and his brothers became ideal targets and were often mildly roughed up on the way to school.

"I remember going to school one time wearing an overcoat," said Harry, "and this kid came up to me with a penknife, cut off one of my buttons, and then jabbed the knife into my coat. Before the knife could land, I pulled away and charged down the metal grating of a truck-loading platform. So the kid hurled the knife after me, creating a sudden charge of sparks when it hit the grating beneath my feet."

But such street experiences did not intimidate Harry because of the love he felt from his mother, grandmothers, and his brothers, in particular James. For Harry, James was the heart of his emotional survival, and in many ways acted as a substitute father and guardian, a role each brother played for the other. For instance, Steve had Tom, Tom had Harry, Harry had James, and James had Elspeth, "who groomed him in many ways to be daddy," said Michael Burke, Harry's uncle.

James was the "brain" of the bunch, introverted and intellectual, with an I.Q. of 179. He was reading by the age of two, and by thirteen had nearly memorized the *Encyclopaedia Britannica*. His whole life was reading.

On the other hand, Harry was more athletic and sociable and became the extroverted principal of action, mainly to compete for the approval and affections of Elspeth. But like two facets of the same person, Harry and James were opposites and rarely competed. Elspeth used to say that when they grew up, they'd wind up marrying each other because they "had so much to offer each other."

James was subdued and self-controlled. In contrast, Harry always seemed out of control and liable to make a pratfall. He constantly took risks, rarely caring what others thought of him (except the grandmothers). Brash and brazen, Harry was a spectacle of unceasing action and energy, of which part was a defense against his internal doubts and fears. But he also saw that a high profile had benefits. Being loud and pushy meant that people usually stepped aside and let him have his way. As a result, over the years, certain phrases were attached to Harry by his brothers because of his boldness and bullheaded daring: "leading with his chin," "fools rush in where angels fear to tread." As James put it, "He sort of believed you could run through a brick wall. He had no finesse. Harry tried to overwhelm things."

But his brothers didn't, and so Harry was the center of the family constellation. Being the tallest and strongest, most energetic and upfront, everyone was forced to relate to him, and the typical pattern of brotherly action usually had Harry at its nucleus. "Harry was always the motor," James said, "and I was usually standing behind him telling him what not to do, while Tommy was sort of competing with him, and Stevie was a distant satellite."

For instance, in pillow fights growing up, it was always the lion (Harry) and the jackal (Steve, the youngest and weakest) versus Tom and James. All the brothers used big soft pillows except for Steve. "When Harry had everything under control," said Steve, "I'd come in there with my hard pillow and whip ass!"

Most of Harry's actions were directed at attracting attention, even at the expense of "making an ass of himself," which he was frequently compelled to do. Though never popular in school, at one point in junior high he was chosen most likely to succeed in his class, mainly because he was "the" catalyst to contend with. He always participated in class discussions, as well as habitually gossiping in the back of the room. Once his teacher, an attractive blonde, caught him and shouted angrily, "Harry! Would you be considerate for once and keep your mouth shut?"

"I bet you wouldn't be mad at me if you knew what I was taking about," Harry said.

"What do you mean?"

"You wouldn't be mad at me if you knew I was saying I love you."

Suddenly there was a rush of "woos." Everyone began chanting, "Brown nose, brown nose."

Harry's love was always unrequited. For instance, Maria Muldaur, the singer-songwriter, went to elementary school with Harry and had a deep crush on him. But Harry's crush was on her best friend, Joy Debell, who had a crush on someone else. In junior high, the situation reversed itself. Harry like a girl named Margo Wally, but she liked a guy named David Stern, who in later years became an attorney and eventually the commissioner of the National Basketball Association. Always jealous of Stern, Harry asked Margo questions, like in Truth or Consequences: "If you weren't in love with David Stern, who would you be in love with?" Margo replied, "With you, Harry." Either way, he was always second-string.

Perhaps the happiest moments of Harry's childhood were during visits to his father. Every Sunday the boys took the subway up to Grandma Chapin's apartment at 50 Morningside Drive, near Columbia University. There they got to watch television (Elspeth didn't have one) while grandma made fried chicken for dinner and one of Harry's favorite dishes, apples fried in bacon fat topped with brown sugar. Sometimes she took them out to eat at the Butler Restaurant on 120th Street, a neighborhood eatery. These were the only times Harry ever went out to dinner.

On these occasions Jim was rarely there, his career often stranding him on the road. But when he was there, "he was always fun to be with." Years later, Tom said, "I think the reason Harry, Steve and I all became musicians was because it always looked like, out of all the people we knew, Dad was having the most fun."

Besides school, visits to grandma and Jim, Lilly's apartment, and occasional movies, Harry's childhood in New York seemed mono-dimensional except for the summers. Poor in almost every material sense, Harry was rich in his one magical window to the world: Andover, New Jersey, a small country village about seventy miles west of Manhattan. There, grandfather Kenneth Burke, or K.B. as he was known in the family, owned 165 acres. The property included half of a valley and half of a big hill, at the base of which was a quarter mile of dirt access road that ran through the center of the property and on which all the Chapin relatives walked up and down. The road was lined on either side with apple, maple, oak and cherry trees whose branches joined over the road to form a shady tunnel. Beyond the road, the land sloped down to a dammed-up pond for swimming. In between there were open fields and a natural clay tennis court.

Andover was the family's summer meeting place, the congregational center. "Up the road" was the main house where Grandma Lilly, Elspeth and her sons stayed. The building was made of old chestnut beams and, at one time, was used to house loggers in the days when Sussex County was the center of a thriving lumber and iron ore industry. K.B. lived in the main house when he first bought the property in 1921, during his days as a music and literary critic for the *Dial* and the *Nation*. But in subsequent years he moved "down the road" into a small cottage and lived in Andover year-round with his second wife, Libby, and their two sons, Butchy and Michael.

Also down the road were Aunt France's "study" and Aunt Happy's house, a converted barn where Harry's cousins, the Leacock and Housekeeper families, often stayed, as well as literary and artistic contemporaries of K.B.

Ralph Ellison, Alexander Calder, Malcolm Cowley, Shirley Jackson, William Carlos Williams and Theodore Roethke were all friends of Kenneth's and frequently visited him to hear his opinions of their work. K.B. was a genius of language, a true wordsmith. He was a philosopher, poet, novelist and, most important, a semanticist, an unconventional thinker who spent much of his time trying to understand the subtle nuances and rhythms of words. He was the author of several books on linguistic philosophy, the most famous of which were *Terms for Order, Perspectives by Incongruity and Language as Symbolic Action*. The *World Book Encyclopedia* later described him as the "critic's critic" because most people didn't have the background to bring to his complicated and oftentimes convoluted writing.

"He saw things that conventional approaches missed," said Ralph Ellison, who had K.B. read his book, *Invisible Man*, before it was submitted for publication. "He approached literature, criticism and social hierarchy as it influenced communication. He was given to questioning the conventional, and was very careful not to grab a term because it was popular. He took a word and projected it to an analysis."

Another Andover visitor was Harry's paternal grandfather, Jim Chapin. Big Jim, as he was called, was a renowned American scenic painter known especially for a period of his work called the Marvin years. Big Jim was acclaimed as a painter of people—farmers, blue-collar workers, city street people—and drew on the pain and bleakness in their lives. In later years, many of Harry's story songs contained the characters and themes his grandfather put on canvas. Big Jim also sustained a thirty-year friendship with Robert Frost, illustrated some of his books and painted the poet's portrait. Big Jim was the artistic counterpart to K.B.

Of the two, however, K.B. was the central figure of Andover, the power source. He set the rules, and was essentially the kingpin of his compound. "In the country, K.B. had a very peculiar position," brother James said. "He was sort of the great genius and cartel child simultaneously. If you've got somebody who's very bright in your family, you have to shield yourself from them—not go around saying, 'Oh, this is a great man!' But the women sort of did. At the same time, he was an alcoholic and a child in some ways."

Andover's was a rural redneck kind of life, something right out of Henry David Thoreau's *Walden*. There were no telephones, electricity, central heating, refrigerators or plumbing. Instead, there was a small outhouse up on the hillside, and food was kept cool in the cellar and cooked on kerosene or woodstoves. Light was supplied by kerosene lamps and water was carried in pails from spring-fed pumps.

Bohemian in both lifestyle and dress, the family was a puzzling combination of upper- and lower-class styles, unorthodox in almost every social sense. One moment, dressed like farmers, they harvested vegetables from gardens, and the next moment they mobbed the tennis court.

Big Jim's wife, Mary Fisher, described a typical summer day in Andover: "In the mornings all the men did their creative work. Big Jim would be painting and Kenneth would be writing. At lunchtime, the mailman would come, bringing masses of material: manuscripts, the *New York Times,* etc. This was the break for the day.

"After lunch, everybody rested, Everybody. All the children had to take naps, but the adults did too. And the reason we did was because Kenneth Burke did, so we all had to. It would be quiet from lunchtime until 3:30 or 4:00. Nobody was to bother anybody—siesta. Nobody would be on the court making noise or shouting around.

"Then the delightful thing was that from rest time on, it was pure enjoyment. Nobody worked. It was swimming, tennis, croquet, etc. And it was the women enjoying their children. Purely social. Then, at dinnertime, we'd all go back to our own place, make sure the children were asleep, and go over to the Burkes' house down the road and sit around and talk. The most celebrated people in the arts and letters came out there. Some before they were famous. Alexander Calder used to come and he made a mobile for the outhouse, a wire sculpture in the shape of a hand, with an index finger, a phallic symbol, to slip the toilet paper over."

The family, then, was a self-fulfilling, self-sustaining incestual summer web. Literally incestual! At one point in time, K.B. divorced his wife Lilly, then married her younger sister, Libby, and they all proceeded to live as neighbors in Andover for twenty years. Even interracial marriages had their place in the Andover community. Ricky Leacock, Harry's uncle, was once married to Happy, Elspeth's sister. When they divorced, Happy married Jim Houten, the black labor organizer. He lived in Andover, too. For Harry then, racial mix and close family ties seemed perfectly normal. "I just felt I had more people loving me," he once said.

But that love did not come from the grandfathers. Neither one was a substitute for a father. Though they were close at hand, they were also hopelessly distant, involved in their work and egos. This was especially true of K.B. Tom explained: "It was always, 'Shhh! You've got to be quiet. He's working . . . He's napping.'"

Andover represented a world of fantasy to Harry, a place where everything was possible. It was a pastoral prism of boundless color and stimulation, not only because of its expansive physical beauty, but because of the constant traffic of people and ideas which flooded its intimate ambiance. Reborn each summer in its fresh air and freedom, Andover to the Chapin boys meant adventure and an endless stream of games: construction games, baseball games, cowboy and Indian games, slingshots, croquet, wars, bombings and tree houses. Up on the hillside the brothers built a whole city out of rocks and called it Stone Village.

Summers also meant Michael and Butchy Burke, who were Harry's uncles and an integral part of the family games. Of the two, Michael was especially important to Harry. He was his childhood hero. Though James satisfied Harry's intellectual curiosities and Tom his athletic ones, Uncle Mike was a combination of the two. He was a perfect model for Harry—active, outgoing, intelligent—and had the same pair relationship with Butchy that Harry had with James. Although Michael was technically a generation older than Harry, he was actually closer in age (only three years older, Butchy five) and had more in common with his nephew than with his own sisters; Elspeth, France and Happy. Besides his brothers, Harry's only real friend during his childhood was Michael Burke.

Despite the social interdependence of the family, there was an equally strong attitude and gravitation toward independence and the establishment of oneself as an individual. For instance, there were tasks all the boys had to perform, and with this responsibility there was an even greater sense of implied possibility. "There was a garden in back of my house and Butchy and I were told we each had to have a row to take care of," said Michael Burke. "As a result, we came along with a feeling, a really deep, ingrained feeling, that if you wanted to do something you could do it, that there were no limitations. The limitation purely effort. There was no such thing as 'I'm too dumb, or not talented enough.' These statements, by attitude, did not exist."

This ethic was indirectly inspired by the grandfathers through their life and work. Though neither was a commercial success, each set the example that a creative lifestyle and livelihood were no different from any other. That painting a good picture or writing a good book was not inherently any different from being a good banker or businessman. To the grandfathers, material concerns came second to "finding something you care about and doing it better than anybody else." In that sense, K.B. and Big Jim would always be distant symbols of success for Harry. He grew up without awe of the artistic process, but more importantly he saw that you could live by the pen and the brush and control your own destiny, be the master of its makeup.

Harry said, "I was always impressed by the single-minded dedication both my grandfathers had toward their work, that sense of almost nonquestioning. Of course, you didn't know all the internal agonies they were going through. But every day they got up and did their work and it wasn't because anybody was telling them to do it, nor was it because they were necessarily getting paid for it."

The artistic talents of the grandfathers were shared by other family members. Harry's uncle Ricky Leacock helped pioneer the cinema-vérité style of filmmaking that utilized handheld 16-millimeter cameras that eventually became standard for television news teams and documentary makers.

In addition, all three grandmothers, Lilly, Libby and Abby, were bright and talented women. And though they sublimated their artistic impulses behind the visions of K.B. and Big Jim's dreams, the next generation of women moved toward individual accomplishments of note. Aunt France became a poet, playwright, novelist and sculptress, and several years later Aunt Happy (Leacock), Ricky's ex-wife, became head of the anthropology department at City College of New York. She was also elected a board member of the American Anthropology Society, and wrote several books in her field. Elspeth eventually earned her master's degree in the history of science and became editor of the facsimile first editions of several poets, including William Butler Yeats.

In many ways, then, the family was an artistic and intellectual version of the Kennedy clan, but without their wealth or politics.

They were attracted to success and power, not necessarily for economic or political gain, but rather creative fulfillment. They were a colony of individualists, humanistically to the left. "The perspective on life was a highly conscious one," said Ralph Ellison. "Harry's grandfathers and family were certainly 'for the people.' They were not capitalists. They were not trying to impress anybody. So that children growing up in that sort of atmosphere would have certain humanistic values."

Said K.B.: "I think we all had the assumption that what you were supposed to do was to come through. Nobody was sitting around feeling sorry for anybody. Elspeth didn't raise the boys playing one against the other. We didn't say, 'He's done better than you.' Everybody was letting them go their own way."

Butchy Burke said of his father: "He was very much a put-downer when it came to the values of conventional success and making money for money's sake. I thing there was a tendency among all of us to pay lip service to the values associated with the appreciation of the plight of the human race."

Though the family set an example of celebrating life through creative work, they also wanted their children to be unafraid of death. One day, when Harry was ten years old, Great-grandma Batterham, who was in her nineties, passed away after a series of strokes. "I was napping in the boys' room on the front porch of the main house," said Tom. "Lilly always made us nap. And she walked in with tears in her eyes and said, 'You can go down the road now.' I couldn't believe it. Freedom! Harry and I went down the road, but something bothered me about it. Twenty minutes later, a hearse went by toward the main house. We were somewhere down near the pond. I don't know why, but Harry and I both went back up. Aunt Rose (Housekeeper) wanted us to touch her to show death was a natural thing. I wouldn't do it. I was too scared. But Harry did. Harry touched her."

This endless parade of people walking up the road (to the Chapins) and down the road (to the Burkes) also represented—in some subtle sense—a class distinction between the Burke and Chapin relatives. "I realized later that Libby sort of cultivated this attitude that the Chapins were the poor relations," Harry's brother James said. "Perhaps because of an undercurrent with Lilly. There was a feeling that we weren't socially acceptable in some sense, and that we were always likely to take something from them (the Burkes)."

Harry, then, was not only an outsider to the world at large, but also within the isolated community in which he grew up. Not surprisingly, the theme of the outsider, the loser, and the unlucky figured prominently in the majority of the story songs Harry later wrote.

Still, Harry longed to become part of that world community. Elspeth didn't realize the existence of her sons' social isolation until the summer she sent Harry and James to Greenwich House Camp in upstate New York. There, on Saturdays, approximately one hundred Jewish kids went to synagogue, while on Sundays, four hundred kids went to Catholic church, and six to a Protestant church. Though the Chapins practiced no formal religion, they were Protestant by birth. So Harry and James were among the six, which included three blacks and a Chicano. One day Harry decided to go to the Catholic church. "But we're not Catholics, we're Protestant," James told him. "Yeah, well, we don't go to church anyway," Harry replied.

Ever since his separation from Elspeth in 1948, Jim Chapin had not paid a penny in child support, which left her almost destitute. By the winter of 1949, Elspeth could no longer live on West 11th Street, since the apartment was in Jim's name. For lack of a better alternative, she decided to take her sons out to Andover and live more cheaply there. For Harry and his brothers, that winter was brutal. They were all stricken with the mumps, measles and chicken pox. Harry also had a bad case of whooping cough and James fell sick with bronchitis and an ear infection that permanently damaged the hearing in his right ear.

By winter's end, Elspeth was trapped in a desperate situation and decided to force Jim to pay up. Armed with the formidable presence of her mother Lilly, Elspeth took her sons and returned to the city late one night, only to find that Jim had changed the locks at 353 West 11th Street. So Elspeth and Lilly broke into the apartment, put the boys to bed, and waited for Jim to come home.

Two hours later, Jim arrived, looking dashing. He wore a tuxedo, and had a beautiful blonde in a clinging gown at his side. Her name was Norma. Norma and Elspeth engaged in a prolonged shouting match, exchanging numerous insults. Finally, at Norma's suggestion, Jim called the police to have them thrown out. "Two Irish cops came by and they saw four little children sleeping," said James. "They saw this plain woman and her mother and this guy with a tuxedo and a gorgeous blonde. If you think they were going to throw us out—no way! Not for this little blonde!"

"We can't figure this out," one officer said. "You'll have to go to court in the morning and settle this yourself."

Elspeth did. She kept the apartment and was awarded $40 per month child support.

But Jim couldn't always meet the monthly payments, and on those occasions, Grandma Chapin usually came up with the money. More important, she insisted that all the boys take music lessons, and she paid for them. Elspeth, despite getting a job at Bell Telephone, could not afford extra expenses, no matter how worthwhile the cause.

But on Saturday mornings, Grandma Chapin took Harry and his brothers to the Greenwich House Music School on Barrow Street for lessons. The school, also connected with the camp, was devoted to underprivileged neighborhood children, and as a result, fees for lessons were considerably below what most Manhattan schools charged. At Greenwich House, James and Steve learned piano; Tom, clarinet; and Harry, classical trumpet.

During the first few months of lessons, Harry rarely practiced unless Grandma Chapin or Elspeth insisted. One day, Harry arrived ill-prepared once too often and had a particularly bad lesson. His teacher, Simon Karesick, thought he had talent and didn't want him goofing off. "So Mr. Karesick got really angry," said Harry. "He popped the end of the trumpet into my lip and that scared me into practicing."

"At first I taught him simple solos," said Karesick, "melodies, some music theory, and then gradually more difficult things. Eventually I think he worked himself up into the A category. Harry was a better-than-average trumpet player."

Harry thought so, too, and was particularly upset the time he received a B instead of an A on his report card. He showed it to Grandma Chapin, who made it a point to see Karesick and clear the air.

"She was quite a lady," said Karesick. "Abby was a doting grandmother. She really wanted all the kids to get somewhere one way or another and got behind them a great deal and pushed. But I was rather impressed that it disturbed Harry because it meant he wanted to be an achiever. So I took a closer look at him, and after many weekends, I began to see a glimmer of something beyond ordinary ability. He had more than the average concept of what music really meant."

Trumpet playing was Harry's first positive way of relating to others besides his brothers and family. He began to play the instrument at Greenwich House talent shows, the first times he appeared in front of an audience. In addition, he played "Call to the Colors" and Pomp and Circumstance" at school assemblies in junior high, and soon discovered that musical performance was an ideal way to get attention, a discovery he did not forget.

At the end of 1950, after working several months for the telephone company, Elspeth took a job as a secretary to the managing editor of the newly created *Films & Review* magazine. It was there that she met Henry Hart, the man who was to become, for the next seven years, the great frustration of Harry's life. In 1951, Hart took over as managing editor of the magazine and, in 1952, Elspeth and Henry were married.

Henry Hart was a short, gentle-looking man in his mid-fifties. Cultured and well-bred, Hart was finely trained in the social graces, from his appearance to his table manners. His full name was Henry Gideon Hart IV and he came from a mainline, blue-blood, aristocratic Philadelphia family. Henry Gideon Hart I was the son of John Hart, who signed the Declaration of Independence. As a bright young man about to go to Harvard, Henry Hart faced hard times. His father died bankrupt, which forced him to go to work and support his mother and two sisters. He became a cub reporter for a newspaper and eventually worked his way up to covering big-time news events, including the Scopes trial, the Leopold-Loeb trial, and the Stanford White murder trial. He married a rich Jewish millionairess, whom he later divorced, and by the late 1930s was the secretary of the New York State Communist Party. However, Henry was more anti-Nazi than pro-Communist, so when the Hitler-Stalin Nonaggression Pact was signed in 1940, he was horrified. He did an about-face and turned all of his information over to the FBI, becoming a right-wing conservative overnight. He worked for *Fortune* magazine, among others, and eventually wound up at *Films & Review*.

Said one Chapin relative: "Henry really did seem to be a very pleasant man—distinguished, intelligent and literary, which fit perfectly into Elspeth's background. I think she felt he would really be good for the boys. She was looking for a stepfather for them."

But Henry Hart turned out to be the greatest of illusions. That became apparent in 1953, when he moved in with the Chapins on West 11th Street. Henry had a Dr. Jekyll and Mr. Hyde quality, which both irritated and deceived Elspeth. In front of guests he acted like a turn-of-the century statesman—gallant, witty and urbane. But the moment the last guest left, he became a tyrannical, paranoid and unyielding stepfather and husband. His wrath most often was prompted by what he considered the social ineptitudes of the four "ragtag" Chapin boys, and he was determined to change them, to get them into "social shape."

Suddenly the brothers were confronted with what Harry called a "scary, negative figure" and had some "real insecurities about where everything fit." Having grown up in a predominantly female environment, Henry's presence, along with his socially wayward concerns, was an antithesis to everything they had accepted as natural and normal. So, more than ever, they enfolded each other in an emotional cocoon.

"They took care of each other, and a tremendous bond came together when Henry was there," said Michael Burke. "It was for the sake of survival. They didn't know if they were going to be thrown out in the street or get through the next week. Their sense of survival was absolutely threatened. So they protected each other, trying to hold on."

"James, Steve, Tom and I used to sit on the floor at West 11th Street, Indian fashion," said Harry, "our arms around each other in a circle. We'd hold each other and moan just to feel the togetherness. James used to cry. He'd be panicking. So he wanted to make sure that everyone was close to him."

But all the brothers felt panic, and for very good reason. Henry brought home the first exhibition of physical violence they had ever seen. "When a guy hits you with a fist or a belt, all of a sudden, that's a whole different ball game," said Harry once.

Said James: "Henry was antiblack, anti-Semitic, antiwomen—a real prize in some ways."

Tom remembered: "The thing that pissed me off was how ready we were to have a good male figure. We were dying for it. But Henry was a villain. That was it. We didn't like him and we didn't want him there."

From the beginning, Henry sensed a conspiracy. He wasn't wrong, and of his four stepsons, he considered Harry his biggest threat, mostly because he was loud and boisterous and couldn't be controlled. Naturally, Henry figured that Harry was the instigator of the conspiracy. "That's funny," James said once, "because the only two devious plotters in the family were Stevie and me."

Even so, from Henry's perspective, Harry seemed to constantly challenge him, and he feared the loss of respect and control he asserted over James, Tom and Steve. Harry increasingly became a target of physical and verbal abuse. The slightest provocation of Henry resulted in violent retaliation. During Christmas of 1953, Harry was playing with Tom when James kept butting in. Uncharacteristically, Harry and James began to argue. When Henry tried to separate them, Harry yelled at James, "Why don't you leave us alone?" Henry mistakenly thought the remark was meant for him and immediately belted Harry with a terrific smash across the face.

For days afterward, Henry's handprint stretched across one side of Harry's cheek. When Jim saw the bruise during one Sunday visit, Harry, afraid of his father's reaction if he knew Henry had hit him, said he'd been hit by a kid on the street.

From this point on, and for the rest of his life, Harry became a fighter. In a sense, the coming of Henry meant the end of Harry's childhood.

In 1954, at the age of eleven, Harry, his brothers, Henry and Elspeth, and their new three-month-old son, Jebbie Hart, moved into a brownstone in Brooklyn Heights. A few months later the building at 353 West 11th Street collapsed.

CHAPTER II

Someone Keeps Calling My Name

"I would say 'Someone Keeps Calling My Name' was the song that came closest to representing those first sixteen or seventeen years of my life. I never had a sense I was going to be star-crossed, or had a destiny. But I always had a sense of hunger, of desire, that life was to be used. It wasn't so much a sense of mission as a sense of momentum that wasn't occurring. I think to the degree I later became so desirous of creating momentum was the fact that during these times there wasn't enough."

The move to Brooklyn Heights was a major change for the Chapins, both economically and socially. The Heights, a middle- to upper-middle-income district, was a quiet residential community, a charming area of Brooklyn extending from the cracked sidewalks of Atlantic Avenue to the mortar and cement pilings of the Brooklyn Bridge, a distance of perhaps one mile. Shoved up against the Brooklyn Navy Yard and the East River, the Heights had a gorgeous promenade that stared across the river to the west, to Wall Street, and the southern tip of Manhattan's imposing skyline. Its shady, tree-lined streets had a certain London flavor, a blend of brownstones, small parks and apartment buildings, ornate cast-iron fences and modest garden patches.

It also possessed the close, friendly feel of Greenwich Village, especially Montague Street, the main thoroughfare that cut through the heart of the Heights. This street was lined with bakeries, small stores, cozy cafés, and an all-night diner called Maria's. However, a few blocks to the north, south or east, an occasional run-down building, trash-filled lot or stripped car stood as reminders of the surrounding inner-city decay.

Even so, the Heights seemed to offer a new lease on life when Henry Hart bought a four-story redbrick house at 45A Hicks Street for, at that time, a hefty $11,000. It was located right next to a delicatessen-grocery store at the lower end of the Heights near the Brooklyn Bridge. On each of the top two floors was a small bedroom (the brothers slept on bunk beds), a library and living room on the second floor, and a good-sized kitchen and dining room downstairs. In the back was a small garden that Elspeth nurtured.

Despite the new and pleasant surroundings, life with Henry Hart grew increasingly unpleasant. A fastidious man, Henry aimed for an orderly life. He had a rigid value system that was rooted in an older version of social order that emphasized, among other things, good table manners, fine dress, strict discipline and social aplomb. It was a value system the Chapin boys had never known before. Henry tried to instill these values in them but instead of using encouragement, he made his points with the subtlety of a sledgehammer, establishing what resembled a militaristic regime replete with a plethora of routines.

On weekdays, everyone was to rise by 7:00 A.M., with beds made by 7:15, and down for breakfast at precisely 7:30. Tom and Steve washed dishes after breakfast. Each brother took turns helping Elspeth prepare dinner, after which Harry and James washed the dishes.

In addition, every Saturday morning, the brothers were responsible for cleaning a certain part of the house. Harry had the kitchen and dining room and James had the second floor, which included Henry's library, shelves filled with everything from film reviews to medical books on sexual problems. Sometimes, Harry snuck into the library to read them. The standing joke about James, of course, was that he dusted every page of every book.

Harry was not nearly as thorough, and many times, after playing basketball with Tom, he ran home seconds before Henry arrived from work and frantically cleaned everything up. The brothers often joked that Harry and Tom slipped in the back door one second before Henry came in the front. The reason was fear. Though Henry's strictness for enforcing his maxims varied, when he was in rare form, he checked for dirt wearing white gloves. Naturally, by Sunday, visits to Jim up at 50 Morningside Drive became momentous occasions, as much glorious opportunities to escape Henry's wrath as to see their father.

This was particularly true for Harry, who had severe problems adjusting to these routines. He could not understand Henry's pettiness and many times, at least in his mind, was ready to run away from home. "I was very nervous and insecure back then," said Harry.

But so was Henry who, in his mid-fifties, had suddenly inherited four rowdy musician sons and had not the slightest idea about how to comfortably deal with them. So he didn't. But he also had a son of his own, Jebbie, his first child and the pampered apple of his eye. So for Jebbie's benefit, Henry requested that all the Chapin boys call him father, and they did.

But of course the request was meaningless, since Henry did not treat the Chapin boys like a father. In fact, from his perspective, he saw them as almost a miniature army, constantly threatening his authority, particularly Harry. In Henry's eyes, Harry was "the general," the leader of the insurrection. He was convinced that Harry hated him, and Harry was positive that Henry felt the same. As it turned out, the two went on grinding, gritting and rubbing each other the wrong way until 1959, the year of Harry's seventeenth birthday.

During the seven years Harry lived under Henry's roof, there were numerous incidents of verbal brutality, even some physical violence. Yet all the brothers coped by developing their own defense mechanisms. Tom, who was in the process of becoming six-foot-five, tried to disappear into the woodwork. James was diplomatic, avoiding physical abuse by engaging Henry in some myopic intellectual discussion. Stevie, on the other hand, took the subtle but deadly route. He made sure he got his revenge. One Sunday morning, Stevie made noise and woke up an enraged Henry, who promptly beat him with a belt. Stevie, who was half naked, returned the favor by urinating all over him. Another time, due to some minor transgression on Stevie's part, Henry slugged him in the dining room. So, with all the form and splendor of a Hollywood stuntman, Stevie made a dramatic crash into the china cabinet, wiping out all the dishes and glasses of Henry's Philadelphia pride.

Gradually, Henry ceased to target Stevie. "For some reason, I never got that smart," said Harry. "I used to bear the brunt of everything. I always got the maximum heat from Henry. He probably hit me as many times as the other three combined."

Not surprisingly, all the brothers developed certain physical symptoms from the mental stress of living with Henry. Harry had a severe case of asthma, James rocked his head to sleep, Steve sucked his thumb, and Tom was a bed wetter until age fifteen, which particularly enraged Henry. One of his favorite subjects was discussing the fact that Tom had wet his bed. "Henry used to come up in the morning and check my bed," said Tom. "Well, one morning it was sopping wet and stinking and he put his nose right in it! Then he whipped me with his belt. I hated those days."

Henry was physical with Elspeth, too, and indeed, according to Harry, there were many times when she considered leaving him, but rejected the thought of a second divorce and putting her sons "through the mill again." Also, there were enough peaceful periods to pacify her momentary unhappiness, spurring her to "give it another try."

The same was true of Harry, who, in an attempt to please Elspeth, did try to love Henry and make Henry love him back. He resigned himself, as his mother often pleaded, to "follow his rules, stay in bounds and be a good boy." But no matter how hard he tried, it was just no good. Everything Henry was and represented went against Harry's unpolished nature and raw impulse, and that meant he rarely backed down from his stepfather's intimidations.

Said Steve Chapin: "Henry wanted a confrontation with somebody, and Harry didn't try to dodge it. He always took him head-on, so the worst thing possible was made of a bad situation. If Harry had tried to keep out of Henry's way, he could have done it. But of course you became a wimp in a lot of ways and, at that time, Harry wasn't about to give in to him. There was definitely bad chemistry between those two!"

For Harry, there were several reasons for that chemistry, not the least of which was that he felt "displaced as the male figure in the house," said James. After all, before Henry arrived, Harry was in many ways the man of the house, the vocal leader of the brothers, and he did not want to lose face. Another reason was sheer naïveté; Harry had never known anyone like Henry before. So he just kept on being himself, hoping Henry would go away and leave him alone. But Henry never did.

A lot of the problem had to do with Harry's "all elbows" personality; overt, definitive, unsophisticated. He was not innocuous—either you loved him or you hated him. And that was because he was a lightning rod, a loud burst of laughter in a silent room, a spectacle of motion. Nervous, jumpy, he was like a bumper car in an amusement park that constantly took its knocks and came back for more. Harry never seemed to learn his lesson. He didn't purposely try to annoy Henry. He just couldn't be anything other than what he was.

"Harry was not the kind of guy to just sit back, keep his mouth shut, and grin and bear it," said one friend of the Chapins.

"I suppose that was one of the secrets to his creativity later on, because he was willing to try new things, stand alone, and speak his mind."

Said Harry: "Henry was such a clear-cut scary, negative figure. Most of the time, if I had any problems with my father, I had a tremendous amount of guilt because I loved him and felt it might be my fault. But with my stepfather, I didn't have that guilt after a while. I tried to love Henry and he couldn't accept it. I didn't feel guilty about it, though. If Henry had been my real father and treated me that way, I would have had a whole guilt complex about not loving him. I ended up feeling that he really was a son of a bitch. So I didn't have that double-level ambivalence about my feelings of hatred. He just ended up being the villain. I was doubly blessed because here was a father figure I could revolt against without guilt. I mean, literally be a hero for revolting against him. He was terribly abusive. He was the guy with a black hat and a black suit on a black horse against us, the guys with white hats and white suits on white horses."

As one might imagine, suppers became great scenes when the boys in white sat opposite the man in black. They were traumatic soap-opera scenarios, comical in their absurdity, boring in their redundancy. Henry made dinners into a campaign. They were another prime opportunity "to get the boys into a social shape." He often went into long dissertations about the Court of St. James in London and the pompous mannerisms of British royalty. But that was the least of it; he often came to the table drunk. Usually, by 7:00 P.M., he arrived home from work "a little bit bitchy and hungry," and to unwind before dinner, had his customary decanter of red wine. Halfway through, he was mellow, harmless, even tame. "But by the end of the wine, he was a prick," said Tom. "He was a nasty drunk."

Even Harry knew to stay away when the decanter was near empty.

Naturally, Harry and his brothers were on guard at the dinner table. Like front-line infantry soldiers, the boys sat wincing and ducking Henry's snipings. Only Steve and James functioned actively, James trying to stop trouble and Steve trying to start it. Typically, Steve either cursed under his breath, kicked Tommy under the table, or pinched Jebbie, who was just a baby. Jebbie would let out a cry. Henry, who was hard of hearing, barked, "What happened?"

"Oh, nothing, nothing," James would quickly say.

For the most part, Henry believed James because he liked and respected him. In some sense, James represented K.B., whom Henry held in awe. But Harry represented Jim Chapin, whom Henry did not. As a teenager, James also had that stunning I.Q., a photographic memory, and played chess. Henry liked intellectuals who played chess. Besides, James could talk. Henry rarely hit James, because James usually talked him out of it. He was a master at changing subjects, usually in defense of Harry. Armed with a cross-referenced library for a mind, James could turn any Henryesque tirade about the etiquette of holding a fork into some long, complicated discussion about eating habits in southern Morocco during the Crusades. Sometimes it worked, sometimes not, and when it didn't, James found something else to talk about, diverting Henry's attention from Harry slurping his soup.

Said James: "Henry went after Harry every chance he got. Maybe it was because Harry was social and outgoing. I didn't arouse his fears. I talked about everything and anything, desperately trying to keep him off Harry."

As Harry grew older, he tried to emulate James's technique of talking his way out of corners, only he couldn't pull it off the way James could. Harry had no chance of charming Henry. No matter how valid his argument, how eloquent his explanation, Harry remained in Henry's doghouse. "Henry used to say I was going to be a politician," said Harry, "because I was trying to be a charmer, although I never seemed to charm him. He always said it in the bad sense, like I was a bullshit artist or something."

Gradually, Harry learned to sit quietly at the dinner table, his attempts at charm replaced with a brittle facial expression that gave Henry no reason for retaliation. "He'd get that look in his face like 'you're being a real asshole,'" said Tom. "And then he clenched his jaw."

But that strategy soon failed, because all Harry had to do was put his elbows on the table and Henry erupted, bellowing, "Where do you think you were brought up?"

Silence.

"Get that smirk off your face!"

Harry's jaw tightened. "I don't have a smirk on my face, Father." That was all that was needed. Henry immediately ordered Harry away from the table and gave him the choice of finishing his dinner in the bathroom or the kitchen. Harry usually chose the kitchen.

On one memorable night, Henry yelled at him for eating his peas with a knife instead of a fork. Wincing under the pressure, his hand slightly quivering, Harry picked up his fork and nervously spilled more peas. "Don't spill your peas," Henry glowered as Harry picked up his fork and spilled even more. He was ejected to the kitchen.

Even on Harry's birthday, Henry offered no mercy. The thought of celebrating Harry's birth was almost traumatizing to Henry. So on those nights (seven of them in all), he would concoct some fraudulent argument so he wouldn't have to be nice to him. Harry usually spent his birthday dinners alone in the kitchen.

In general, Harry's dinners never lasted more than fifteen minutes, and if sent to the kitchen, not more than five. Consequently, he learned to inhale his food (all the brothers did), a habit that remained with him his entire life.

Elspeth, meanwhile, was caught in the difficult position of playing peacekeeper between her husband and her children. She didn't want to have to choose between her sons and Henry, but often she did, and usually in Henry's favor. "Mother was basically bamboozled by him," said Harry. "The only bad quality my mother had was that she had lousy taste in men; first, my father, who was a charming ne'er-do-well, and then my stepfather, who was a responsible son of a bitch."

However, Harry never openly expressed his deep-seated hatred toward Henry. Instead, he held back all anger and resentment, until finally, on occasion, he broke into tears. And when he did, Henry wrenched his jaw back and forth and ordered, "Don't sniffle!" and then wrenched his jaw again. "Yes, Father," Harry said obediently, his firsts clenched at his side.

"Though Harry was never subtle, my whole life, I never saw him get mad," said Tom. "None of the brothers ever did."

Steve Chapin, who perhaps understood his stepfather better than the rest of his brothers, said in retrospect: "He was trying to give us good table manners, an old-style pride. It was very important to him. Henry talked all the time about going out in front of people and having your poise together when you're in public. There were a lot of good things he wanted us to acquire. But it was just that he had no way of relating to all these young kids. Basically, everything he was trying to do, and I know it sounds hard to believe, was in the name of trying to be a good father."

Even so, Henry's dictums were hard to accept. His own friends who sometimes came to dinner contradicted his severe social codes. One of them was Jebbie Hart's godfather, Johnny Cram. A sweet, compassionate, ineffectual man, Cram was a millionaire and philanthropist who bought shoe stores in Harlem and then gave away the shoes to the poor. He also owned a huge mansion where he gave shelter to derelicts and drug addicts. Henry fawned over Cram, yet he had absolutely atrocious table manners.

Said Harry once, incredulously: "He [Cram] poured avalanches of salt into his food. He used to unscrew the saltshaker and literally poor it into soup and on rolls. I mean, pour the salt! And then get half of it on the table. Then he slurped his soup and had a big mustache and there was soup hanging from his mustache. And he took a roll and literally pushed it through the strands of his mustache hanging over his mouth. I couldn't believe it."

Another friend of Henry's, William Everson, also had appalling table manners. But more important, he was the man who first aroused Harry's curiosity about film, an industry Harry later entered before turning to music. Everson, the curator of the United Artists Film Library, came for dinner once a month and always brought a film with him. In the living room, Harry got to see film classics by D. W. Griffith and Charlie Chaplin, with stars such as Orson Welles, Laurence Olivier and Buster Keaton. "It was one of the few good things Henry ever did for us," said Harry.

Still, more than he realized then, Henry's negative presence performed the positive function of toughening Harry up. The nastiness and hypocrisy Henry embodied were the building blocks of Harry's youth. Those stormy days and nights put calluses on his soul, until gradually, much like a boxer absorbs punches, he developed a kind of resiliency against pain. He learned to hide his emotions. Later, he revealed them in song. But for now, he was in the process of building self-confidence because somewhere, deep down, he knew if he could survive Henry, he could survive anything.

"We had an Oedipal figure who acted like a Mr. Moodstone; a villain, a strong male figure we all could hate and build self-images around from all the negative energy," said James. "I suspect having Henry around was good for us because it brought us all together and helped give us an identity."

But perhaps the most important side effect that emerged out of the Henry years was Harry's intense determination to win and succeed. Having to constantly battle Henry and then lose, Harry developed a hunger for love and acceptance he eventually found on the concert stage. But for now, it was a love he could not find at home. Elspeth's love was divided, his grandmothers' distant, his grandfathers' nonexistent, and Jim's only part-time. Of all these people, it was Jim's love and Henry's lack of it that were perhaps the most influential. While Jim gave Harry the seed of music and the stage, Henry gave him the drive to get there.

"As children," said James, "we all had rather obvious personal problems, but Harry really didn't. I don't know if that made him better or worse. If Harry took anything out of his childhood, it was an immense drive to win."

This will to win manifested itself in high school. Harry completed junior high commuting with James from Brooklyn Heights to P.S. 3 in Greenwich Village. Then, in 1956, Harry enrolled at Brooklyn Technical High School, a highly competitive, all-male school geared to mathematics and the sciences. Brooklyn Tech, as it was called, described itself as a school for "selected and superior students," of whom Harry was certainly one. He was a good student, owner of a 139 I.Q. (lowest of the brothers), and very active. He was secretary of the student court, a member of the golf and track teams, and commanded a solid B average, excelling more in math than English. However, his best grades were in world history, mostly because it was taught by his favorite teacher, David Ostraff, a young man who appreciated the same aggressive qualities in Harry that Henry despised.

Ostraff described Harry as a "bright light—a very verbal student. He had his hand up all the time. He wanted to participate in every class discussion, but never in a rude or obtrusive way. He had such a winning personality and a tremendous sense of humor. I recall that. If he could find something humorous in a situation, he brought it out. He sat in the third seat in the last row near the window. I can still see him. I see him because he was on his feet so much—there wasn't any question in class that he wouldn't volunteer an opinion on."

Harry also didn't hesitate to disagree with Ostraff, and often challenged his teaching methods. His biggest gripe concerned a ten-question quiz Ostraff gave at the beginning of each class based on readings of the night before. "I specifically remember Harry objected to this because he felt there were details on the test that were insignificant," said Ostraff. "I admitted that they were, but he made the challenge regularly."

Ostraff's real challenge, and the principal reason Harry did so well in history, was James. History was his best subject. James was in Ostraff's American History class and Ostraff was totally overwhelmed by him. "He was the most incredible student I ever encountered in my fourteen years of teaching," Ostraff said. "He was an absolute shock to a young teacher. It was the first and only time I ever came across a kid who knew more than I and could've probably taught me a great deal. I was very upset. I was ready to leave teaching. Fortunately for me, he was transferred to another class. Though Harry's conceptual grasp was first-rate, it wasn't so great I couldn't be his teacher."

James was and would always be Harry's most valuable asset for information and guidance. Intellectually speaking, James replaced the father Harry lacked. Over the years, much of the general knowledge and "lines" Harry developed as a person and stage performer originated from James. If Harry had any kind of ally or security in his childhood and teenage years, it was James.

Said Harry: "I used to ask him, 'What do you know about this?' And he said, 'Well, I don't know much about that . . .' and then for the next two hours gave me the accumulated knowledge of the universe. He was an incredible resource and has been all my life. We lived in the same room together for seventeen years, literally within five feet of each other. I could talk to James about anything. And I knew he loved me; I had no doubt about it. Whenever I wanted to know something, it's not to say he'd come up with the right solution or anything, but his mind was like a cross-collated library, so that if you looked under the Protestant Reformation, he gave you five basic theories, all the 'schticks,' and then some really wild facts about how it compared to modern jazz or something. He was an absolute wealth, the most exciting mind I ever came in contact with."

As a result, Harry hung out a great deal with James, but since Brooklyn Tech was an all-male school, he had to look elsewhere to find a social life. He found it at 254 Hicks Street, at Grace

Church, which had both a men's and boys' choir, and an organization called the YPF (Young People's Fellowship), which sponsored social functions.

The choirs were directed by Anne McKittrick, a seasoned
musician trained in voice and organ in Europe. Like Harry's
grandmothers, McKittrick was an old battle-axe, a woman of
remarkable moral fiber, who exuded pride in her choirboys: "You
are special because you're a choirboy," she often told them.
Pianist Bobby Lamm, later of the rock group Chicago, was a
choirboy. So were Tom and Steve, but not without Elspeth (at
Henry's instigation) having to literally drag them down the street
to join.

Harry and James joined the YPF, which sponsored dances and
parties every Friday night. James became the organization's treasurer. He was not interested in the choir and neither was Harry,
who was too old to join the boys' choir because his voice had
changed. Though he did join the men's choir, singing falsetto,
that didn't last more than two Sundays. "He never could sing
falsetto," said Tom. "And he wasn't particularly interested in it
anyway."

The focal point of Harry's limited teenage social life were the
weekly YPF dances and a girl he met there who lived on nearby
Grace Court. Beyond her, his other "mini love affair" was with
Antonette Kulczycki, the niece of Jim Chapin's second wife,
Manja Kulczycki. Manja had four children with Jim and became
his music manager. "She tried to book him home," Harry once
said jokingly. Harry only saw Antonette during occasional visits
to Jim and Manja's new home in Sag Harbor, Long Island, so the
relationship died as quickly as it developed.

Though Harry's romantic expectations were unrequited, he
found them in books. He did a lot of reading in high school,
especially novels by Samuel Shellabarger, Frank Yerby and Fred-
erick Van Wyck Mason. In one book he learned a strategy for
female seduction that helped open his physical floodgates to
manhood. He discovered it in a passage from a Frank Harris

book about the Victorian Age, which said, in effect, that the best way to seduce a woman was to have a tear in your eye and an erection at the same time. That, plus an incredible amount of energy chasing her, meant that sooner or later she would succumb to all the attention.

This notion, coupled with his precocious personality, meant that at the age of twelve, Harry had his first sexual experience: one "that seemingly fell out of the sky." It was with his sixteen-year-old baby-sitter, whom he seduced one night. In his song, "Babysitter," Harry told of that experience and how she was the first woman "to make my mother's son a man."

"It was strange," Harry said, "because for years after that I assumed there were two kinds of women, the kind that sort of fell in your lap in the sexual sense, and the nice girls you played games with. I didn't realize that women naturally progressed into sex. I was embarrassed about being physical. If a woman said no, I never fought. It wasn't until the end of high school that I realized that women had a sexual side as well as an intellectual and emotional one."

Harry had no male friends during his adolescence except for his brothers, particularly James, and Michael Burke. He depended on them for a feeling of belonging and solidarity. "He became a loner on the outside because he didn't know how to make friends," said James. "I don't remember Harry having any close friends. But then, none of us did."

Even among his brothers, Harry's lack of social integration was evident. In sports, for instance, Harry always picked the worst teams, convinced he could overcome the obstacles of being the underdog, and lost. "He was a terrible coach because he didn't understand his players," said James. "He didn't use them to his own advantage. It got to be a standing joke. Stevie always won because he was the only one of my brothers who understood the bad sides of human nature. Harry really didn't."

At Brooklyn Tech and Grace Church many people disliked Harry to the extent that he developed the nickname Gapin'

Chapin because of his loud and pushy personality. He often offended people because he gave little consideration to their feelings and little space for them to get to know his. Harry often did not pay attention when people spoke to him. "He was famous for that," said John Wallace, a Grace Church choirboy and later a mainstay of Harry's band. "In fact, even worse, Harry could be talking and suddenly, in the middle of the conversation, leave the room."

Said James: "I remember as a teenager I always ended up having to defend Harry. He was a central figure. A lot of people were jealous of him. He didn't get into fights, but there were people irritated at him. He was always making enemies and doing things that offended people and he wasn't even aware of it. Harry never really knew what other people thought about him."

Paradoxically, Harry thought of himself as a passive teenager, and looked much like any other. Clean-cut, conventional looking though not especially handsome, Harry had a rugged, all-American-boy kind of look: brown curly hair, a big square chin, tall and thin, with a canyon grin. However, his picture in the Brooklyn Tech senior yearbook couldn't have been more typical of the times: his brown hair slicked back fifties' style; a thin tie, white shirt and plain dark suit.

Despite his conventional appearance and antisocial behavior, Harry was the social battering ram for the brothers. "I got attention, but it wasn't from being smooth or naturally well liked, but from the pure fireworks I created," said Harry. "I would go and make an ass of myself. I would push until I got us invited to various parties. James and Tom held up their noses slightly, but then followed in the wake of what I had done."

However, Henry's presence made a difficult social life worse. All the brothers had to be in bed by 10:30 P.M. every night, including weekends. This meant that Harry and James, who often went to parties together, had to leave early. In such cases, James industriously watched the clock and reminded Harry when it was time to go. But Harry, of course, wanted to stay past the curfew, figuring that Henry was asleep by 10:30 anyway. Reluctantly, James often agreed to stay later, and then the two of them tried to sneak back into the house without arousing Henry.

James remembered: "Old clod-foot Harry! He had very big feet for his height. Harry always found a squeaky stair or else tripped over something. First of all, Harry always played with danger anyway, so even when he was frightened, he was always a klutz. I don't know if it was a guilty conscience or what, but it used to be the great frustration of my life. Because I knew if I came home myself I'd get in all right. But Harry always got in trouble. From my point of view, Harry never had any sense of self-preservation."

* * *

By 1956, at the age of fifteen, folk music became a central force, not only in Harry's life, but in the music world as well. From The Weavers and The Kingston Trio in the late fifties to Bob Dylan and Peter, Paul and Mary in the early sixties, folk music became the sound of the day, and Harry was swept up by it. In its simplest forms, folk music communicated a warmth and togetherness, and in more sophisticated forms, acted as a social mirror that reflected the cries and whispers of society through its lyric content and protest stance. In music stores, the sale of folk guitars skyrocketed. Its simplistic chordal feel didn't intimidate its listeners from trying to play.

It was Michael Burke who first introduced Harry to folk music and guitar. He had a record called *The Weavers at Carnegie Hall* and played it for Harry, who immediately became captivated by its easy, friendly feel, "like some old bannister touched by so many hands that all the rough edges became smooth."

By the summer of 1957, Harry became interested in pop rather than ethnic folk music. Grandma Chapin had an old beat-up banjo in her attic that had been in the family for generations. So

Harry fixed it and began playing. "Tom Dooley" was a major hit song, and Michael Burke had come home from Harvard with a cheap Montgomery Ward guitar Harry soon adopted. "The strings must have been half an inch off the neck," said Michael. "Pressing them gave me calluses so thick I couldn't button my shirt without looking down."

But Harry persevered, mostly because Michael, his childhood hero, was dating several girls at the time, and from Harry's perspective, was successful with them because of his guitar playing. "I switched from trumpet to guitar because girls liked guitar players better," Harry often joked years later. "I also think it was a way of him getting closer to father Jim," said James. "Music was a reinforcing factor. I suspect that was part of it."

Guitar, like banjo, was an easy switch for Harry because of all the music theory and technical training he had had on the trumpet. In addition, within the variety of all musical instruments, guitar was one of the easiest to learn. One didn't have to be a dedicated, classically trained musician to pick up a guitar and play a folk song. Given three simple chords and a basic rhythm and strum, one suddenly became an amateur folksinger. With just a nylon six-string and a song, Harry discovered that, unlike the trumpet, folk guitar "was something he could learn to be good at, fast!" In fact, within two months' time, he easily surpassed Michael on guitar and even developed a strong right hand for picking.

Folk music, particularly The Weavers (Harry's favorite group), was also a reaffirmation of his roots. Pete Seeger, one of Harry's folk heroes, was a friend of the family. Seeger's wife, Toshi, was a close friend of Judy Housekeeper, Harry's cousin, and a young Harry remembered seeing Seeger once at a family party out in Andover.

In addition, Lee Hays, another member of The Weavers, lived in Brooklyn Heights and Harry had met him once. Ever since Harry stole the leather-working tools years before, he had become quite good at the hobby, to the extent he developed a reputation for it in the Heights. One day Hays called Harry and asked him if he'd repair a couch that was bursting at the seams. Starstruck and loaded with questions, Harry, too, was bursting as he went to Hays's home. Unfortunately, Hays had a miserable hangover that day and was in no mood to talk. After a couple of stuttering attempts at conversation, Harry nervously did his job and left, very disappointed.

Folk music had also seduced Tom and Steve. Along with Harry, they often played and sang in their rooms after school. The result was a great deal of joy for a relatively small investment. A good guitar could be purchased cheaply, as could strings, capos, shoulder straps and picks. The brothers saved up their money from baby-sitting jobs to buy what they needed. Although Harry took two banjo lessons, he, like his brothers, basically learned guitar and banjo from books and records. They never listened to the radio. Harry bought the Seeger banjo book, and gradually the brothers built up an enormous folk record collection—more than two hundred albums of folk groups such as Ian and Sylvia, Oscar Brand, The Kingston Trio, The Brothers Four, and all the old Elektra and Vanguard records. The music was mainstream, apple pie, solid American.

To practice, Harry often slowed the records down from 33 to 16 rpm, looked for banjo parts, and played along. He also began experimenting with writing music, adjusting songs, and changing lyrics. Once he and Michael Burke had a songwriting contest at Grandma Lilly's apartment in the Village. They went into separate rooms for twenty minutes to see who emerged with the best song.

Harry explained: "I was a student in the sense that when something sounded really good to me, I wanted to learn why. I approached folk music pragmatically. Music was a means toward an end, not an end in itself. I was more interested in performing than practicing the guitar. It wasn't a technical exercise of running my fingers up and down the scales. I was getting good enough so that I could sing a song, or sing in front of an audience. For example, I would learn a strum that was good for a song. But I wouldn't just learn a strum. I wasn't interested in the technique of the guitar."

In contrast, Steve Chapin loved music for itself. He was the best musician of the brothers, the purist of the three. He received special attention from choirmistress Anne McKittrick at Grace Church. She took him under her wing and he was one of the few students she allowed to play the big church organ. As a result, Steve developed a strong chordal feel for music, which was intrinsic to folk, and made him a valuable member of their trio. While Tom played guitar and Harry played banjo, Steve, the "utility infielder," played a number of different instruments. At first, he played tiple, an odd, eight-string instrument, and later on the four-string guitar, upright bass and piano. Together the brothers were a kind of hip Partridge Family and began to model themselves after The Kingston Trio, who were riding a huge wave of success in the late fifties.

To Harry, the main appeal of The Kingston Trio was their exquisite three-part harmony. In fact, for this reason, Harry often said he thought the best folk record ever made was *Gibson and Camp at the Gate of Horn*. "I loved the counterpoint of their two voices," said Harry, who infused some of their vocal style into the brothers' act. "Gibson, especially, was responsible for contemporizing the tonality of folk music. He could take a piece of rough bluegrass and refine it to the taste of the time."

Harry first appeared publicly with his brothers in June 1958 at a Grace Church choir concert. They called themselves, appropriately, The Chapin Brothers. They sang three songs, two of which were by The Weavers, including "Come, Little Donkey, Come" and "This Land Is Your Land," Woody Guthrie's composition. The audience loved them and they were the hometown favorites. Their first major appearance was during a hootenanny night given every Tuesday at the Bitter End in Greenwich Village. It was an open-mike, no-pay affair where you put your name on a list and then were called up to perform. "Again we went over

positively with the audience," said Harry. "But then it was difficult to be adverse to the image of three brothers playing
together."

It naturally evolved that Harry, as the oldest and most outspoken, became the leader of the trio, at least in the sense that the
worse they did on stage, the more Harry felt compelled to carry
the ball. "Tom and Steve had a way of disappearing," said Harry.
"On a good night, Tom rattled off his lines. We worked out all
kinds of lines, some funny things. But on a bad night, when the
lines weren't going over, Tom refused to do the rest of his lines."

So Harry whispered nervously under his breath, "C'mon,
Tom, c'mon!" Too tall to hide, too embarrassed to recover, Tom
whimpered, "My brother made me say this . . ." and then recited
the line deadpan.

"Harry started pushing his brothers around before they knew
what was happening," said Phil Forbes, a friend of Tom and
Steve's who lived in the Heights. "They were really good as a
folk trio."

By the age of sixteen, Harry began sneaking over to the Village more often with his brothers, usually to the Bitter End for
hootenanny nights. "This Land Is Your Land" was their best
song. Feeling a growing confidence in their performance and
themselves, they frequently played choir concerts and occasional
parties in the Heights, but not for money, though they were once
paid ten dollars. For now, for Harry, performing music was
friendly fun, not serious business.

It was also a means of communication, a bridge to other
people that Harry was incapable of building on a personal level
without the shine and shield of a guitar or banjo. It supplied him
the self-expression he couldn't find at home. For instance, even
if he learned a new song, he might play it for Elspeth or Jim, but
as a whole the family was too preoccupied with their own creative egos and interests to pay attention to other's work. And that
was another part of performance he loved—the applause, the
instant gratification.

As Seeger once said: "Novelists have to wait months or years before they receive reaction to their books. Playwrights have to have theaters, and sculptors, warehouses. But a guitar picker can just limber the guitar, start singin' to the nearest person and make contact."

Said Harry: "It was a good social gambit. If music hadn't been tied up with social things and attention-getting, I don't think I would have done it. It wasn't purely the love of music. It was more that it was socially 'in' to play guitar. I saw it as a way of getting positive attention, a sort of antidote to Henry. I loved the way it sounded. I loved the way it felt. It felt good. I loved harmony. I loved my two brothers and me making music together. It made me feel fantastic."

"It was fun," said Steve Chapin. "It was a lark. It was different. It was something we did in the Heights that nobody else did. It was like a kid brother growing up in an acrobatic family; you became an acrobat. It was sort of inevitable. Nobody made hard and fast choices. We just sort of fell into it and people kept telling us we were good, so it just turned out that way."

* * *

Besides folk music, Harry "stumbled upon" a second new interest during the summer of 1957: architecture. Once again, the influence was Michael Burke, who was studying the subject at Harvard. For a summer job that year, Harry did construction work on Interstate 80, and the following summer, his interest was refueled when he became Michael's assistant on the construction of Uncle Robert Leacock's house in Andover.

That summer of 1958, he also discovered drinking tea and coffee. Working in shorts, perspiring and filthy, Harry and Michael took a break from their construction work in midafternoon. It was then that Grandma Lilly usually came by carrying her tea service. It was complete with a small pot of tea or coffee, a bowl of sugar, and a pot of cream. Badly in need of energy food, Michael and Harry gave each other a hungry look, then divided the milk and tea evenly, filling up the rest of their cups with sugar. This overly sweet mixture became a permanent habit of Harry's.

His interest in architecture, however, did not. As a diversion from his construction work, Harry kept a competitive running count with Michael on the horse- and deerflies. "He beat me 666 to 637," said Harry instinctively. Another time, during the construction on the foundation of Leacock's house, Harry unearthed a huge wooden beam too heavy to dispose of, yet too thick to cut in half. So, almost comically, he dug an enormous hole in the basement floor and covered it with dirt.

In the evenings, Harry and Michael shared a lot of sexual fantasies that resulted in Harry's introduction to storytelling. "Being action-oriented and goal-oriented and physical in many ways, I found that a large part of my teenage years were sexual," Harry said. "There was a cabin up on the hill in Andover, and sometimes Michael and I spent nights up there verbalizing our female fantasies. He introduced me to Mickey Spillane books. I think Mike had an impact on me in terms of the story songs because we used to make up sexual fantasies and I listened and realized you could make up stories."

Despite all the pleasant discoveries in Andover, Harry's summers no longer held the same romantic image of his childhood years. Now Henry was coming out, staying in the main house with the Chapins, and once again imposing his strict social morality. The result was a drastic change in emotional climate, from dreams and joy to a near state of panic.

In Andover, Henry Hart was embarrassingly out of place, a pathetic anachronism. The family compound, after all, was rustic, insect-infested and nearly two miles from the nearest grocery store. For a man so governed by appearance, Henry did not belong among the water pumps, outhouses and kerosene lamps. And not surprisingly, he found the entire Andover lifestyle inherently distasteful. For instance, during the day, the Burkes, Chapins, Leacocks, everyone, went barefoot—except Henry, of course. "Henry had a thing about going barefoot," recalled Michael Burke. "I mean, dress code out there was not exactly a high-priority concern. The level of dress was that you'd be wearing a pair of ripped shorts with your balls hanging out."

Even so, Henry approached it all with the swagger of a country-club guest. During the day he wore the finest tailored shorts from Brooks Brothers, a LaCoste shirt, and brand-new white tennis sneakers and socks. In the evenings he was even more elegantly attired and out of place; like a Catskill hotel maître d' directing patrons in some free-form hippy commune.

Naturally, Henry noticed the disparity of social class, and was so repelled that he tried to rearrange it to suit his own upper-class self-image. For example, in the mornings, he insisted the brothers trim the grass. "He wanted the place to look like a golf course," said one Chapin relative. But the more he tried to change things, the more tense and chaotic life became. Henry taught Harry and Tom how to use a sickle to cut grass. However, any time Henry supervised things, he created such fear in the brothers that they began to fight among themselves. "Henry felt none of them could do anything right," said Michael Burke. "And it reached a point where none of them did."

After one lesson, Harry became so nervous and self-conscious that he accidentally slammed the sickle into the heel of his own foot. Clunk! Harry recovered after minor first aid, and then, moments later, leaned down to gather cut grass, when Tom accidentally swung the sickle right across three of Harry's fingers. Chomp! Well, he recovered from that too, but not without two stitches in each finger.

Despite the mayhem, Henry's presence further united the brothers, including his son, Jebbie, whom none of the Chapins resented. As Jebbie grew older, he realized how much his step-brothers despised his father and diplomatically handled the delicate situation by separating his love for them from that for Henry. The Chapin brothers did the same. One evening in Andover when Jebbie was five, he learned the phrase *son of a bitch.* "I was up the road for dinner that night," said Michael, "and there was a moment of silence at the table and Jebbie looked up with a big smile and said, 'son of a bitch.'" Immediately Henry erupted, 'What did he say?' Stevie, with a stroke of brilliance, quickly fired back, 'Ah, Brooklyn Bridge.'"

At the age of fifteen, Harry spent his last summer in Andover as a child and young man. The following year Grandma Lilly took him to Europe for the summer, exactly one year before she died. She had already taken James two summers before, and Harry was next in line. Though Lilly possessed only a schoolteacher's income, she was a frugal woman who made soap from grease she saved in jars. She also did some translation work on the side and made extra money working for her brother, who owned an electronics store on Wall Street.

Harry and Lilly stayed in Europe more than eight weeks, touring five countries: England, Italy, Switzerland, Scotland and France. They lived cheaply, staying with family friends or in local offbeat boardinghouses, and visited mainly blue-collar sections of cities tourists rarely saw. "The trip was not significant except that it made me realize that people around the world were more or less the same," said Harry. "It also bought me time from Henry."

Chapin relatives wished they could say the same, for while Harry was away in Europe. Henry's upper-class arrogance reached a final breaking point, ending with an explosive argument with K.B. The topic of dispute was Lilly, Elspeth's mother. Of all the Chapin relatives, Henry despised her the most. In fact, Henry routinely refused to go out to Andover if she was there. To him, Lilly epitomized everything that was low class. "At one point, she looked like she was made out of leather," said Michael Burke. "She was earthy, a strong, tough woman who worked with her hands and wore baggy dungarees. Henry just couldn't tolerate her."

Finally, one night, as he often did, Henry walked down the road to K.B.'s cottage to share intellectual ripostes and a few drinks. In the past, these ripostes often turned into shouting matches about Lilly, K.B.'s first wife. "She's got character," K.B. would insist loudly. "Onions have got character," Henry would shout back. But the last conversation they had became so heated that a couple of punches were thrown. K.B. was drunk. Henry was stone drunk. "He could barely walk up the road," said Michael. "That night Henry urinated in his bed! The following morning he felt humiliated. It was too tough for him to lose face."

Henry never returned to Andover.

But Harry returned from Europe. He was supposed to have graduated from Brooklyn Tech the previous May. However, the school didn't fully recognize that he skipped the eighth grade at P.S. 3. So, to balance the credits, Harry was forced to make up one semester and had to return to Brooklyn Tech that fall. He also returned to Henry and the same impossible living situation. Only now his emotions had changed, and total confusion and fear were replaced by anger and self-confidence.

This was partly true of all the Chapin boys, who became fed up with Henry and finally banded against him. "Like all paranoiacs, Henry had that great capacity to create the world in his own image," said James. "He was convinced we were all plotting against him. After a while, we were."

Even Elspeth had grown intolerant of Henry, and much to his displeasure, began bucking his unquestioned power. "When mother started standing up to him," said James, "that really got him pissed off. As long as she was choosing him over her kids, at least ambivalently, everything was all right."

By late fall, Henry's authority began to waver, and his relationship with Harry deteriorated to an all-time low. The arguments became more frequent and serious; part of the problem was Harry. Nearly seventeen years old, he was beginning to stretch his wings. Harry was nervous about being let loose in the world, and like most teenagers, he was particularly stubborn and disagreeable. The other key factor was James, who was off at Hamilton College in upstate New York and no longer home to act as a buffer between the two. "I was also accepted into Columbia University in Manhattan," said James. "But that would've meant living with Henry. I would've gone to Outer Mongolia to get away from Henry."

With his verbal counsel and protector gone, Harry spent a lot of time eating dinner in the kitchen, sometimes three or four days a week. He was prepared for a flare-up at any moment and Henry was sensitive to any challenge of his authority. So, like two bulls, they locked horns, a final confrontation inevitable. On the night of December 7, it came.

It was Harry's seventeenth birthday, and it was perhaps the event that symbolized his first step into adulthood. That night, Henry arrived home from work at 7:30 P.M., a half hour late. Saying nothing to anyone, he headed straight for the bottle opener to uncork a fresh Bordeaux and have his ceremonial predinner drink. But the opener, one of those ordinary manual metal twisters, was slightly bent.

Henry made this his cause célèbre. "Who bent the can opener?" he erupted. Elspeth, Harry and the brothers were silent. "I will not live with liars and cheaters!" he shouted. "We're not going to have dinner or do anything until I find out who bent the can opener." Still, nobody admitted anything. He felt betrayed. "Elspeth," he ordered, "I want you to take the boys upstairs now and keep them there until somebody admits they bent the can opener."

For two hours they endured an endless stream of grilling and questioning. Finally, Elspeth pleaded with her sons. "Who bent the can opener, for Christ's sake? It doesn't matter. Just tell me who did it, because this is getting ridiculous."

Nobody admitted a thing.

At 10:00 P.M., Henry still waited impatiently in his club chair in the living room. The bottle of wine was empty. Elspeth went downstairs to report the news. Henry was drunk and nasty. He began screaming at her. Disgusted, she grabbed the can opener and slammed it to the floor.

"This is ridiculous!" she cried out. "I can't stand this anymore."

Violently, Henry grabbed her by the arm, started twisting, and despite her painful cries of protest, forced her down to the floor. "Pick it up!" he ordered angrily. "Pick it up, NOW!"

Meanwhile, Harry stood by the stairway watching, stunned, helpless. Elspeth was in tears. Anger welled in Harry's throat; but so did fear. Nobody ever contradicted Henry directly. So he just looked on as Elspeth's arm was once again jerked and twisted; her body on the floor, her voice trembling with pleas to stop. Tears welled in Harry's eyes as his mother tried to stand up. Henry knocked her down again.

Then, suddenly, almost surprising himself, Harry yelled out in an angry, manly tone, "Father, take your hands off Mother!"

Henry's face burned red. "Get out of this house, NOW! I will not live with you another instant."

Harry left. But once outside, he didn't know where to go. He also didn't much care. He felt tremendously revitalized, beautifully sorry for himself, dying to tell somebody in the family how brave he was. He had actually stood up to Henry! He called Lilly at her apartment, but she wasn't home. So, wearing a T-shirt, jeans, and no jacket, he walked through the chill December night over the Brooklyn Bridge to Aunt Happy's apartment on Horatio Street in Greenwich Village. He spent the night there.

The following morning, Elspeth called Harry and assured him that everything would be all right if he came home and apologized to Henry. Harry did go back home, but he did not apologize. He lived in a truce for two months until he graduated from Brooklyn Tech on January 30, 1960. He never lived under Henry's roof again.

Nobody ever found out who bent the can opener.

CHAPTER III

Taxi

Harry's life took on new dimensions. It seemed like the end of a war: all defenses down, fires out, artillery locked away. The smoke had lifted, the sky was smiling, and for the first time, everything around him seemed to come alive, offering new hope and new promise. It was as if he'd awakened from a long, deep sleep, and his life went from black and white to technicolor. Cocky and confident, he felt the full flush of personal triumph. He was free! Free of Henry, high school, and responsibility.

From February through June of 1960, Harry lived with Grandma Chapin at 50 Morningside Drive. He got his first job, working as a runner on the floor of the New York Stock Exchange on Wall Street. A rote job, he stuffed messages in air tubes and had to memorize a list of names of corporations. He met broker types, investor types and swindler types—to him, boring types. Wall Street seemed far more glamorous from the Brooklyn side of the river, yet for now, it didn't matter; his social life had improved. He was no longer required to be home by 10:30 P.M. He started going to dances and basically tried to fit into five months what took more than seventeen years to earn.

Still, Harry's lack of social know-how hampered his every social move. Even at a distance, Henry's nonphysical presence continued to haunt him. At one dance he met an attractive blonde named Cammy Peltz, who came from a wealthy family and invited Harry to the Gold and Silver Ball, a lavish, $50-per-ticket affair at the plush Plaza Hotel. Mr. Peltz paid. Even so, Harry needed a tuxedo and could not afford to rent one. So, in a rare moment of generosity, Henry offered to lend his, an old-style tuxedo he had not worn in years and still kept wrapped in cellophane from the previous cleaning. At first unwilling, Harry reluctantly accepted the offer.

"It was one of the few times we shared anything," said Harry, "and I should've known. The evening was a disaster. At the ball, when I was together with this girl, I was forcing a bit. Other guys were making comments and I really wasn't coming off very well. Then we went dancing and I was sweating a lot. I was uncomfortable in the clothes, and when I just had to concentrate on her, a lot of things were falling flat. By one o'clock we went for breakfast with six other couples at some fancy Fifth Avenue penthouse overlooking Central Park. We got there and it was a disaster. I felt like my whole world was falling apart. I was desperately trying to hold on. The men at one point started relaxing, taking off their jackets, unbuttoning their shirts, so I started to take off mine. All of a sudden I noticed something: my underarms were solid brown!"

Apparently, over the years, the lining of the tuxedo had rotted and, by perspiring, the color blended into his shirt, leaving a dark brown circle that extended halfway down to his waist. "I looked like I had gorilla armpits," said Harry, appalled at the memory. Luckily nobody noticed, and for the rest of the night, when everybody suggested he take off his jacket, his face dripping with sweat, Harry scoffed cheerfully: "Oh, no, I feel comfortable. Just fine. Comfortable. Thanks."

About two months later, Harry was once again disassembled by his social gaucheries. With money saved from his job, he took a rather well-endowed brunette—"one of those snobby people who knew all the social mannerisms"—to an expensive restaurant. Again, Harry called Henry beforehand, this time to ask for advice about wines. So that night, after ordering a costly bottle, the steward returned and poured a trifle into Harry's glass, waiting his approval. However, Henry had never mentioned anything about the wine-tasting part, and in an attempt at cleverness, Harry looked at the steward and said, "The lady first, please!"

Harry never saw the brunette again.

That spring, Harry applied to the Cornell School of Architecture and the Air Force Academy. Having scored in the 700s on his SATs in math and English, he was accepted at both with full scholarships. So now he had a decision to make. Coming from an intellectual and literary family, everyone naturally thought he should go to Cornell—except Henry, of course. He felt the Air Force Academy discipline would be perfect for Harry, but more selfishly, Henry knew that all academy candidates had to be cleared by an FBI security check. Harry's attendance, then, meant that Henry would be forgiven for his earlier communist leanings as secretary of the New York State Communist Party. So, with Henry's bipartisan help and encouragement, Congressman Francis E. Dorn, a personal friend of his, awarded Harry, one of 256 applicants, competitive appointment to the academy.

Said Harry: "Everybody thought it was crazy. K.B. said I was going to the 'war college.' My mother rationalized it. But I chose it. It was the first major decision of my life. I couldn't blame anybody else. In some sense, I was doing something for my stepfather. But I also thought the idea of flying was glamorous. I used to draw planes and I thought flying would be incredible. I visualized that I would be flying in a biplane over the fields of France with a chartreuse scarf, leather helmet and goggles, with mademoiselles waiting for me on the ground."

Not quite. Though the Air Force Academy certainly seemed pleasant enough—located at the foothills of the snow-capped Rocky Mountains near Colorado Springs—the physical brutality that went on below them was not. At the time, the academy was only a year old and trying to build a reputation as the most rigorous of the service academies, and in many ways, it succeeded.

The original class of 1959 had been high school graduates (underclassmen) trained by cadet officers (upperclassmen) who were war veterans and absolutely vicious in their regimentation.

This took place during the three-month basic training, which each underclassman had to complete in order to graduate and join the "cadet wing." The purpose of the training was to develop leadership capabilities by breaking people down to basics, to the loss of all self-image, and then building them back up in the Air Force mold. The academy "promotional" brochure that year read: "Through training, upperclassmen put the new cadets through many exercises of discipline to demonstrate how to think and react under constant pressure *without disputing the reasons.*"

It also said: "Because the curriculum is designed to prepare military leaders, students whose ambitions are directed primarily toward civilian professions such as medicine, journalism, the entertaining arts, or sports, find it impossible to realize their goals at the Academy."

That was Harry's first warning. The second came during the summer of 1960, when those new cadets who had survived brutal basic training became Harry's upperclassmen. From the very first moment he arrived at the academy, he knew he had made a mistake. But he also knew it was too late to turn back.

"I was flown out to Denver and put up in a hotel the first night," Harry said. "I remember a giant sense of camaraderie and excitement. Here I was going into this big, exciting, new world and the next day I took a bus from Denver to Colorado Springs, and felt really proud of myself. All the guys were joking and laughing and all of a sudden we got to the academy, and these upperclassmen started on us. They were literally screaming at us from three inches away; absolute shock technique. That first day, they cut my hair down to a quarter inch and kept shouting at me, 'You're no longer a civilian, don't act like some dumb ROTC troop.' They made us get into all kinds of grotesque positions of attention, with your chin so far back that even if you were skinny as hell, you had wrinkles in the back of your neck. Your shoulders had to be thrown back, your ass tucked in, your belly pulled in, and everytime you messed up, you started doing push-ups."

Then, later that day, Harry was ordered to run up a long flight of stairs—at an altitude of 6,000 feet. Unaccustomed to the thin air, Harry collapsed when he reached the top. Half blind with exhaustion, he heard the officer shout: "Get to your feet, Doolie! Get to your feet!" At first Harry clenched his fist and then, out of the corner of his eye, looked up at the officer in disbelief. A contorted grin rephrased his emotions.

From that day on, Harry had to conform to petty rules and regulations that made Henry's diatribes seem pleasant. The training was grueling. From reveille at 6:00 A.M. to taps at 10: P.M., relentless commands and demands breached the entire scope of individual freedom. All the new cadets had to run, jog or double-time everywhere. When they walked, they had to square corners, robotlike, and if in the presence of an upperclassman, stand and salute. They also learned to shoot M-1 rifles and .38-caliber revolvers and to tackle rugged obstacle courses, bayonet drills and hand-to-hand combat exercises.

During meals, the tension did not subside. All 1,500 cadets were required to eat "square meals" in silence at long rectangular tables in a huge dining hall. Like mannequins, they had to lift their forks straight up, shift them horizontally to their mouths, and take precisely three chews before swallowing. In addition, "gazing" was not permitted; eyes had to be locked forward while eating. And at the end of the table, a cadet officer kept a stern eye for posture and tested for "Doolie knowledge." Harry had to know, by heart, the technical qualifications of every Air Force jet, the record of the school's football team, and basic academy rules. Any mistake or slipup had him sent from the table; only this time he could not go to the kitchen to finish his meals. "There was one period, of seven meals in a row, I ate just one chili bean," said Harry. "And I was pretty skinny anyway."

For the first time, Harry felt the utter helplessness of having his life in the complete control of someone else. He couldn't believe it was real and he couldn't conform. So, as with Henry, he just keep smiling, trying to charm, and hoping it would all go away. But that tactic merely became greater grounds for harrassment. "They used to tell you jokes and you weren't suppose to smile," said Harry. "Well, I always smiled. Down for twenty-five more push-ups! There were days I probably did 500 push-ups."

Like any new cadet prone to prolonged nonconformance, Harry was put through a series of punishing drills. For instance, one time at 1:00 A.M., he was awakened from sleep and ordered to dress in full combat gear: boots, fatigues, helmet and full canteen. Bleary-eyed, he then ran two and a half miles to Cathedral Rock and back with an M-1 rifle raised above his head.

By midsummer, Harry's "Gapin' Chapin" personality became the brunt of upperclassmen brutality, whose repertoire for hazing included everything from leaning cadet foreheads on pointed pencils against walls to unlimited sit-ups. "There were times they made me do sit-ups until I literally couldn't do them anymore," said Harry. "One time I did eighty-seven sit-ups and they sat on my feet until my stomach wouldn't work."

"Finally, I decided I wanted out," he continued. "I couldn't imagine spending four years there, plus a year and a half of pilot training and then four years of service spending 90 percent of my time preparing for things I didn't want to happen: war. I thought, Holy Christ, I won't be finished with this until I'm twenty-six, which seemed like virtual eons."

So he wrote long descriptive letters home, pleading to get out, and soon became the talk of the family. Everyone was upset. After reading one of Harry's letters a few weeks before she died, Lilly began to cry. Tom remembered shouting, "I'm sick of hearing about Harry!" Henry, of course, felt the same way and did not want him home. His word was final. So Harry wrote K.B. who, for the first time, became self-admittedly "cognizant of Harry's existence." K.B. wrote back: "For God's sake, do everything you can to get out, but don't do a single thing against the law!"

Said K.B.: "This was where you saw that fella's character. It was interesting, because at an early age in his life, he had some kind of asthma attacks, and he got through that, and you'd think this would have brought them on again. You're either beaten, or you come through. And by God, he came through."

But not without a struggle. It was harder to get out of the Air Force Academy than to get in. So, in desperation, Harry went to the chaplain for advice and moral support. Years later, having returned to the academy for a concert, Harry related the conversation to an audience of young cadets.

"The chaplain was no better than anybody else. He sat me down and told me I was a quitter. He said there were hundreds of kids who would die to be in my place, kids who had sacrificed, lost their chance, and that I was being terribly selfish. He said that if I quit now, I would never be a success at anything. I guess he was right, eh?"

The cadets gave him a two-minute standing ovation.

However, at the time, the chaplain's lecture almost worked until the last bastion of his dream, the hope of flying, was shattered with the disappointment of reality. It occurred during his first jet flight. By late August Harry had completed basic training, was accepted into the Cadet Wing, and, like all new cadets after training, had an indoctrination flight on a T-33. "They took each cadet up as a reward, going through spins, barrel rolls and diving," said Harry. "But when it was all over, I remembered being up in the air thinking, Is this all there is?"

Finally, academy officials granted his request to leave, and though that Gapin' Chapin personality had some of the officers smiling occasionally, even liking him, they also hated quitters. So when they got word of Harry's departure, they made sure his final two weeks were miserable, if not memorable. At the time, Harry had just received all his personal belongings from home, a second reward for completing basic training. Among them was his banjo. So the upperclassmen, who always had a gift for utilizing a new object for some act of hazing, had Harry unpack his banjo and march up and down the hall doing the manual of arms.

"At night," said Harry, "they came into my room and tore up the place. For example, the contents of your drawers had to be perfect to the half inch, your bed had to be perfect. Well, they came in and messed up my bed and drawers. Once they made me turn my bed over and lay it on my spit-shined shoes so it cracked the wax. Your shoes were supposed to be shined perfectly. You had to add layer after layer of polish and water to build up a wax. I had to work all night to get them back in shape to pass inspection the following morning."

When Harry returned home that September to Grandma Chapin, he began bragging to Michael Burke about his great physical condition. "I can do fifty push-ups like nothing," Harry boasted. "Let's see," Michael challenged. Harry did forty-one. Michael did sixty.

With the resourceful help of Grandma Chapin, Harry tried to regain his place in the Cornell School of Architecture in time for September classes. Grandma Chapin called the dean of the school and managed to talk him into reinstating Harry on a waiting list for one of sixty possible openings. Then, daily, she battered the admissions office with questions on his status. Finally, a few days before classes began, the sixtieth person dropped out, and Harry was admitted.

But, at the same time, he was unable to regain his National Merit Foundation scholarship, without which he could not attend. In fact, the younger brothers eventually attended New York State schools because the family could not afford private tuition costs at schools like Hamilton College, which James attended, but only because he was admitted on a full scholarship. Like all the brothers, Harry also received $250 a semester from Constance Adams, Grandma Chapin's first cousin. Still, the money was not enough. So, managing another of her coups, Grandma pulled some strings and finally got Harry a full scholarship from the Union Tank Car Company.

He was off to Ithaca, New York!

"But this time, to pursue a new dream," said Harry. "I wanted to be an architect. I saw myself as a person who pointed and said, 'I visualize a giant cathedral rising in the meadows.'"

What Harry didn't see was the enormous time, effort and minute detail that went into the construction of a cathedral or any other structure; such as knowledge about how toilets flush, heaters heat, doors close, windows seal, etc. His literal mind perceived a linear sense of architecture that made it difficult for him to understand the enclosure of living spaces a good architect must intuitively sense. Harry designed walls, not space. He had no gift for design. Like the story songs he later wrote, his projects at Cornell were both literal in meaning and linear in structure. As some critics were to say about his music, so did his professors grade his architectural designs, "too definitive, not offering enough space for the imagination."

Architecture, then, was not a natural flow for Harry. At best, it was "an intellectual concept" he wanted to try. And though he loved the act of creation, giving birth and breath to something that didn't exist before, he soon discovered that architecture, for him, was too tedious. So, within a few months, he lost interest and watched another dream disintegrate.

"Once," Michael Burke said, "he had to design a house for a homework assignment. We sat down together and worked it out. I came up with an idea for a low, kind of graceful house, and Harry was supposed to draw it up. Later I took a look at it and it was the strangest-looking house I ever saw. At that point, I thought, 'Harry just doesn't have an interest in this area.'"

Harry also lost interest in the rest of his studies. He took classes in introductory English and geometry but found the courses dry, the work boring. Unlike the Air Force Academy, college presented a different challenge, intellectual discipline rather than physical rigor. This time discipline meant classes, books, libraries and the patience to study. Yet Harry could not conform to the accepted standards.

It also meant he had no concrete direction to his life. He started missing classes, became depressed, and in his depression often slept away his days. College "seemed irrelevant" and, in his boredom, he frequently went down to the local pool hall in Collegetown. He became so good at pool, he hustled opponents into fast profits. "At that point," said Harry, "I wasn't adult enough to put up with boring things for an overall long-range goal."

Even his interest in music lacked all sense of organized progression. The first two semesters, Harry lived in the college dorms playing banjo, guitar and trumpet on and off, and was "exceptional in none." He didn't belong to a band. Instead he played under the trees or in his room, usually alone, or with "some guys down the hall."

Generally speaking, Harry didn't naturally fit into the competitive "club" of an Ivy League environment, yet it was the very club he wanted to join. He was envious of other students who seemed "much better directed," such as those bent on being lawyers or doctors. For instance, to help pay expenses during his freshman year, he worked as a dishwasher at Sigma Nu, a slightly snobby jock fraternity. "I always saw those guys with the pretty girls with long blond hair. When they tossed it, it was like a horse's mane," said Harry. "The girls had fine noses, and I always thought, 'Why can't I get that? Why can't I be naturally cool so that when I held a drink, I felt natural?' Perhaps through my awkwardness, my subconscious was trying to tell me something."

Harry applied for membership in Sigma Nu, but his unpolished personality foiled him. One night, after fraternity pledging, two members of the club came to Harry's dorm room and reported the bad news. "It was the usual excuse," said Harry, "'You know, we all wanted you except for one guy. We've got a blackball rule that one person can knock you out. Well, somebody blackballed you. We tried to talk him out of it, but he was adamant. I don't know what you did to him.'"

Harry cried all night.

His lack of social smoothness was also a handicap with women. He had a tendency to come on too strong and was regularly rejected. So when the normal methods failed, Harry tried more practical attempts. As was the custom at Cornell, Harry scanned the pages of the freshman college yearbook for dates. The yearbook included pictures of the students, and when he found an attractive girl, he called her up, introduced himself, and went into a well-rehearsed monologue. The only problem was, the women used the same method to check out the caller and Harry's picture, taken as he blinked, looked more like a police mug shot.

"You could hear the sound of pages flipping on the other end," said Harry. "They'd be friendly, look at my picture, and say, 'Sorry. I'm busy tonight,' because I really looked like a schmuck—a drug addict."

But one time Harry did muster the courage to ask out one of the best-looking girls on campus—and she accepted. "Determined not to be dull bait," he took her to D. W. Griffith's four-hour silent film classic, *Intolerance,* which was playing at the university theater. Relying on what he had learned from Henry about films, Harry tried to impress her with his cinematic knowledge. For instance, during the movie, he frequently leaned over to her, pointing out the various aspects of Griffith's genius: "He invented the close-up, you know. Watch the way . . ." But the girl wasn't interested in any of this. After the first hour, she leaned over to him and politely whispered, "Excuse me, but can I go home?"

By Christmas of 1960, Harry also went home. The holiday was slated as the big reconciliation between him and his stepfather. Henry had been angry at Harry ever since he quit the Air Force Academy. He felt he had gone on record supporting Harry and had been let down. Still, Harry returned home for Christmas Eve dinner. But no sooner had he walked through the front door than it was evident that the old resentments and wraths had yet to die. After two minutes of small talk, Henry glowered: "What are you smirking for?"

"Father, I'm not smirking."

"Oh, yes, you are. Get that smirk off your face!"

"Father, look, if you're going to go after me for something like that, then this isn't going to work."

At which point Harry kicked himself out of the house. He took the subway to 42nd Street and Broadway and spent the rest of Christmas Eve alone, watching porno films.

Twenty years would pass before he would see Henry again.

The themes of loneliness, loss and broken dreams that echoed throughout Chapin's music later on had their origins in this period of his life, and specifically at Cornell. Its large campus and lonely Collegetown corners made it easy for one to feel alone. With people, Harry was always up, outgoing, contagiously cheerful. But alone he was usually depressed, and when he was depressed, he slept. Of all my discussions with Harry during the eight years I was part of his life, memories of his college days seemed like an endless pattern of somnolence and slumber. They were, by far, his most painful.

Said Harry: "I always felt the distance between my public side and my sense of loneliness. My own insecurities during the sixties meant I came on too strong with people. My first year at Cornell and most of my experiences there were very lonely. I always felt like I was wandering around the campus at weird times by myself. I might say hello to somebody, but I didn't feel I had a place, or any identity. I felt that if I disappeared, nobody would even belch. I always had the feeling there must have been places where people were naturally together and relaxing. I felt hungry. There were many damp, cold, rainy nights and shady afternoons when I was wandering around the campus wondering when the mystical lady would look at me, and accept me and hold me in her arms, fulfill my sexual fantasies and talk to me about hers. It was somewhat of a naive concept, I guess, because I wasn't willing to pay my dues in any relationship.

"Still, I had a vision that there should be some moments of absolute effortlessness where all the happy-ending movies came true. Where you were living a musical, where, at the right moment, the girl came around the corner, the orchestra struck up a beautiful chord, the camera rolled and focused on her gorgeous eyes and she smiled at you, and then, for the first time, you knew everything was right with the world. There was a crest toward that kind of nirvana."

Much of the music Harry later wrote tried to reconcile the fact that there were no such nirvanas. In the song "Mr. Tanner," a small-town dry cleaner named Martin Tanner wanted to live the movie-star life of going out, singing, becoming a big name, only to give up his dream after one poor performance. In the song "Better Place to Be," a little midnight watchman experienced a magical woman but ended up having to settle for a fat barmaid. In "Taxi," a young man wanted to learn to fly, but the closest he came was getting stoned behind the wheel of his cab. In short, most of his songs revealed that life itself, in many cases, "was just a grade B movie."

In 1974, Harry performed two benefit concerts at Cornell with Phil Ochs and Eric Weissberg's band, and thought he'd return triumphant. "But in between the two shows, I started walking around the campus by myself, and it all came back to me, how lonely I felt," said Harry. "It was a damp fall night, somewhat misty, but there were no natural smiles, no golden girls, no . . ."

* * *

It was the summer of 1961, and Harry was first able to utilize his guitar and banjo for profit as well as fun. He joined Tom as a counselor at the *Herald Tribune*'s Fresh Air Fund Camp in Fishkill, New York, a camp primarily devoted to underprivileged kids. With Tom, Harry found some sense of belonging, especially on Saturday nights, when the brothers performed sing-along concerts playing old folk songs.

But more than the music, Harry's main concern was "the women across the lake," the discussion of which became a favorite topic with him. "That was the central focus on Harry's

life for a time. A long time, as a matter of fact," said Bob Mullevaney, a camp counselor and friend of the brothers. "Harry
bragged a lot for sure. I don't think he ever said anything that
wasn't so. But he boasted about having six, seven and eight
orgasms in one night. It always blew my mind. He loved to go for
records, to be shocking, to drop lewd comments here and there and
get reactions. He had rivalries with some of the older, more established counselors, particularly over women across the lake."

The basis of those rivalries was Harry's hyperactive personality, which often created conflicts with people, especially those in
authority. "If he didn't like something they did, he told them to
go screw," said Mullevaney. "Most people found him a little
tough to take. He didn't make intimate friends because he was
the same onstage as off. He was always performing, always
center stage front. He never shut up. He was a listener only when
he wanted to be. But it wasn't a conscious habit. If he wanted to
shine or hear from you, he did. But only for as long as he wanted
and then he had to do something else. He was a guy who was
always willing to stand out and take chances. He was very bold.
In fact, a lot of people disliked him, especially his fellow counselors, because he was such a bold guy."

By summer's end, Harry received only a mediocre evaluation,
while Tom and Bob Mullevaney received outstanding ones. "It
was ridiculous," said Mullevaney, "because Harry was our
leader. I mean, anything we did was basically as a result of him.
He was the central focus of the whole camp. I think that hurt
Harry a great deal."

In the fall, Harry returned to Cornell, and in an attempt to find
the sense of belonging he'd felt with Tom and Mullevaney in the
summer, joined the Sherwoods, a twelve-man a cappella singing
group, and a form of music that had become very popular on college campuses across the country. The leader of the Sherwoods
was impressed by Harry's versatility on banjo and guitar, allowing him to sidestep the customary period of apprenticeship and
come right into the group.

As a Sherwood, Harry made several concert trips to other colleges. These were the highlights of his Cornell years, particularly during the "Fall Tonic," in which he performed a gospel medley on banjo while someone accompanied him on guitar. It was the first time he sang outside the company of his brothers.

But, of course, there were even moments in that triumph that brought him down to earth. For the concert, Harry was "scraggily dressed," and after he finished his medley to wild applause, Mike Abrams, a gifted comic and Harry's "spokesman" in the group, decided to point this out to the audience. "I'm gonna show you how hokey this young city-bred folkie is," Abrams told the crowd. He pulled up Harry's green Sherwood jacket to show his shirt sticking out, with no belt on, and then raised both pant legs, where his old socks had sagged atop his penny loafers. Finally Abrams took off one of Harry's shoes and poked a finger through an enormous hole in the bottom of the sole as the audience howled.

By the end of his third semester in architecture, Harry was kicked out of school or, as the phrase went, "busted out." He rarely attended classes, so that his grades plummeted from a 70-point average, or B, his first semester, to a failing 56 by the end of his third. "I spent an awful lot of my time sleeping and lying on my ass," said Harry. "That really frightened me. I thought the whole world was passing me by."

On January 31, 1962, the Cornell registrar printed "leave of absence" on Harry's transcript (in lieu of "busting out"), and he had no choice but to return to New York and Grandma Chapin.

There, he began rummaging through newspapers for architectural jobs. But he soon discovered they were even less glamorous than his studies. "Most of them were really horror shows," Harry said. "You sat in a room with a bunch of other draftsmen drawing up little detailed work for window casings."

Harry took one such job for two weeks, then quit and signed up as a bank trainee at Marine Midland on Wall Street, punching and clearing checks on an office machine. But by his third day at work, Harry grew hopelessly bored as he routinely punched dozens of $60 million checks. It was the high point of his banking career. On the fourth day, he did not show up.

Said Harry: "No matter what I did at the stock exchange, in the architecture office, or the bank, I was a category and had to put in a certain amount of time. I was a fits-and-starts person and there was no room for individual expression or initiative. My potential energy and imagination had no real outlet. If anything, it started making me lazy. Not that the work was tough, just boring. It was what I called my 'blessed laziness' because it never allowed me to fool myself and get into unhealthy long-term situations."

Finally, as a last resort, he called his uncle, Ricky Leacock, who was a filmmaker at Drew Associates, a documentary film company located at 166 East 66th Street in New York. At the time, the company was going through such a major expansion phase that they hired the hatcheck girl out of the Copacabana. The company was in the process of developing a new form of photojournalism using highly portable 16-millimeter camera rigs, an advance on Robert Flaherty's pioneering invention, cinema verité, during the forties and fifties. Uncle Ricky had been Flaherty's cameraman for, among others, the documentary classic, *Louisiana Story*. Besides Uncle Ricky, several filmmakers at Drew Associates were advancing the documentary art: the Maysle brothers, Don Pennebaker, Greg Shuker, Leon Brochnik, Jim Lipscomb, and owner Bob Drew. The company was producing mainly one-hour television specials syndicated for Time-Life, which produced, distributed and sold the films to television.

In March 1962, Uncle Ricky got Harry a job packing film crates for $75 a week. Despite the low pay and rote work, Harry enjoyed this job because he was thrust into an achievement-oriented environment. Drew Associates was an ambitious company. At screening time, the staff often gathered in screening rooms with clipboards, analyzing the finished products. "There was a buzz of excitement in the air," said Pennebaker. "People went in and had their reputations made or destroyed."

Harry loved that sense of challenge, the nerve to risk failure for success, to watch hard work and effort reach a perceptible end, for a perceptible goal and reward. For him, the work was exciting, an adrenalin rush that seemed far more relevant and closer to the substance of life than college. Drew was a place where his untapped energy and problem-solving ingenuity were put to immediate use. Among capable men, Harry found himself capable. He was able to do things he never knew he could and possessed abilities he never knew he had. It was the first job he enjoyed. He did not feel stifled or bored. "Once I got there, I found it was one of the last of the can-do industries," said Harry. "If you had the energy and you were excited and had ideas and were willing to call your bluffs, you could move up dramatically fast."

More important, Harry discovered a potential career that did not require an Ivy League diploma. Though partially disgusted with himself for having failed college, he took consolation in the fact that a person could succeed without it. After all, K.B. did, as well as most of the Drew filmmakers, men who accomplished much after relatively uneventful careers in journalism.

One such man, Jim Lipscomb, was Harry's working partner and a producer who came into the company in 1961. Harry and Lipscomb instantly liked each other and established a close friendship that would last for years. In Lipscomb, Harry found a friendly father figure, intelligent, patient, easygoing and supportive. Jim was a strong believer in the energy and enthusiasm of young people and gravitated toward them. He gave Harry numerous "shots" at learning the film business and frequently encouraged him to explore new ideas, take chances and "stick his neck out." Harry became a protegé of Lipscomb.

Surrounded by important men, Harry tried to distinguish himself and show that he, too, was important. "I remember," said Lipscomb, "one of the first things he said to me that sort of bowled me over was: 'You know, one of the problems in my family is that my brothers and I all have I.Q.s over 160. That's the genius level, you know.'"

Harry knew he wasn't a genius (his I.Q. was actually 139), but he knew he wanted recognition out of life. He needed a modus operandi. But as yet, he didn't quite know what that was. Once joking with Lipscomb, Harry suddenly became serious. "If you think of existence as a balloon, I want to blow it up a little," he said.

Recalled Lipscomb fondly: "Harry was bubbling with enthusiasm and excitement; a little bit overbearing and sort of pushing himself because he was determined to expand that bubble. He didn't quite know how. But he felt there was a place for him somewhere and he was going to find it! Was he going to be a pool shark? A singer? A politician? A filmmaker? He was hitting all the doors. And if a door opened, he was liable to punch through. The door that finally opened was being a singer. But if that door hadn't opened, he would've been something else. He was knocking at several doors and any one of them might have opened. I don't think he was ever satisfied with just one career. It was always: What's next? What's the next world?"

After packing film crates, Harry was promoted to syncer, which meant getting the sound and film lined up. And like everything else he did, Harry did it fast, yearning to prove his worth. "He was fantastically quick," said Lipscomb. "Though it's a boring task and takes a long time, a good syncer will do 2,000 feet of film a day. Harry sat down and did 5,000."

Harry's prolific output was mainly due to a strong competition with Lipscomb. For instance, in sync work there were often mathematical problems involving film calculations, such as the amount of footage per second. In such cases, Lipscomb was very methodical. He put the numbers on paper and multipled them carefully. Harry, on the other hand, did the calculations in his head and then rushed to come up with the correct answer before Jim. "Oh, that's 6,235," he'd hastily blurt out.

Most of the time Harry was right. When he wasn't, he and Jim got into a game of one-upmanship. "Well, you got close," Jim chided, "but of course you're working in your head and you know you can't do it quite as well as when you put the numbers on paper and take a little more time. Actually, it's 6,234."

But Harry refused to learn from his mistakes, and that sometimes bothered Jim, especially his stubborn tendency to plan too much for one day. "For instance, if we had an appointment," Jim said, "I told Harry, 'You know, we're not going to get that done in time. You've made an appointment for four o'clock and we're not going to be there.'"

"Yeah, we'll be there," Harry replied confidently.

But of course they weren't, and the next time Jim reminded him, "We weren't there for it before, were we, Harry?"

"But we will be today," he'd insist.

Harry's stubbornness was also reflected in his strong and sudden urges to play pool. Often Harry and Jim worked until ten o'clock at night. But on other days, around four in the afternoon, he would approach Lipscomb. "Now what do we have to do for the rest of the afternoon?"

Lipscomb, of course, didn't have it completely in his mind, but he knew there was far more work to do that evening than they could ever finish. "Why?" Jim would ask. "What's going on?"

"Just tell me what we need to do," Harry'd persist. So Jim would tell him.

"Well, I'd come back at six o'clock and it was done," said Lipscomb. "But not always well, you see, because he rushed through."

Finally, one day, Jim confronted him. "Harry, what is it you want to do?"

"I want to play pool," he replied.

Said Lipscomb: "That happened a lot, or he had something else he wanted to do. Pool was very important to him. And if he made up his mind that he wanted to play, he got so nervous he was like a cat, jumpin' around, flying all over the room, just so he could finish and go play."

By the fall of 1962, Harry progressed to assistant film editor and his salary doubled to $150 per week. As an editor, Harry developed the ability to tell stories, make connections, and explain complex ideas in simple ways. He saw connections that perhaps more experienced people overlooked and allowed him to gradually become a valuable asset to Drew filmmakers and, in particular, Jim Lipscomb.

Jim gave Harry the opportunity to actually edit a couple of films, the first of which was a documentary-biography entitled *Aga Khan*. The film illustrated Khan's life as heir to a fortune, member of the English Olympic ski team, and head of a religious sect of some twenty million Muslims.

The film was a success. One day, as a reward, Lipscomb took Harry and another Drew editor, Leon Brochnik, out to lunch. They went to the Forum of the Caesars, an elegant four-star restaurant in Manhattan. Lipscomb said they could order anything on the menu. So Brochnik order escargots, Lipscomb a French crepe, and Harry a hamburger.

"They both started laughing at me," said Harry. "They said, 'Christ, here you are in one of the finest restaurants in New York and you order hamburger meat.'"

Despite his embarrassment, this was one time Harry's déclassé tendencies came out ahead. When the meal arrived, the waiter performed an elaborate crepe ceremony at the table and finally put something on Lipscomb's plate that, according to Harry, "looked like a burnt dishrag." Then Brochnik was graced with a plate of escargots that "looked like a small army of miniature goat turds." Finally, Harry received his plate. It was a large wooden platter, two feet by sixteen inches, and topped with a metal cover. The waiter lifted the cover. Along the edges of the platter was a juice trough inside of which were potatoes beautifully designed with drawn butter on top. Inside that were mounds of mixed vegetables, also topped with drawn butter. Then, finally, at center stage, was a giant, juicy, oblong piece of chopped sirloin with two jumbo stuffed mushrooms on top.

Lipscomb and Brochnik's jaws dropped. Harry burst into laughter. "Would you guys like a piece of my hamburger meat?" he asked.

* * *

Though filmmaking made an indelible impact on Harry's life, it was a woman he met that summer who changed it. Tom had returned as a counselor to the Fresh Air Fund Camp in Fishkill, and Harry, accompanied by his guitar, often bused up on weekends to meet women and make music with Tom. It was here he met his first true love, a woman who would captivate his imagination and emotions for the rest of his life, a woman who the song "Taxi" was about. In the song, Harry called her Sue.

In real life, her name was Clare MacIntyre. She was an attractive, slim-figured girl, with sensuous light brown hair. Well-mannered and refined, she grew up in a rich, conservative WASP family (her father was president of Eastern Airlines) and lived in Scarsdale, an affluent bedroom community of New York. At the time, Clare was a counselor at Camp Hayden, an expensive private camp a mile down the road from the Fresh Air Fund Camp.

Mullevaney, who returned as a counselor that summer, said: "Clare was the kind of girl you dreamed of making it with, but never had the guts to go up and ask. Harry, of course, looked upon her as the super challenge of the century. He went up to her and worked his tail off in order to make it with her. He spent all summer trying to go out with her and little by little he got his way. It was a demonstration of his basic theory: 'If you want a lot of ass, you need a lot of energy.' It was something he used to say a lot."

In a social sense, Clare was the epitome of everything Harry was not, yet on the surface, she seemed perfect for him. She was bouncy and bubbly, energetic and vocal, highly competitive. She was also interested in music. A freshman at Bennett Junior College outside Poughkeepsie, she studied music therapy and worked with mentally retarded and handicapped children. She was also, like Harry's grandmothers, a dominating type who claimed attention and evoked tremendous life force. "She had a gimmick," said Harry, "where she punched you in the stomach and used to, by her own aggressiveness, take people aback."

Harry liked that about her, along with everything else, and almost immediately she became his dream girl, an incarnation of the nirvana he had fantasized at Cornell. Up until Clare, his expectations had flowed naturally—junior high school, high school and then college. But suddenly there was a drop, there was nothing. And Clare became that missing link. In her, his torn emotions had found a home, surcease, a sense of peace. The world finally made sense.

Said Harry: "There were some moments in that first year, besides all the anguish, where it just seemed like—Holy Comoly! This is what it's all about. I am so happy. I'm bursting. I love this girl. She loves me. She's everything I could dream of. I can remember the first time I kissed her. It was one of the biggest moments of my life. And the first time I was petting with her, when I was visiting her parents' home in Scarsdale, I virtually came in my pants! That's how incredibly attuned I was. She just changed my life. I mean, there were times when we made love or went walking together where it all seemed to make sense."

The change was not merely the release of emotion. Harry had become a songwriter. Clare triggered a burst of creativity in him that included his very first song, "Stars Tangled in Her Hair." He wrote it on a shirt cardboard while visiting Father Jim at some beach-bungalow nightclub in south Jersey. Clare affectionately called it "Stars Knotted in Her Mop."

Perhaps more importantly, Clare compelled Harry to improve his music performance. During weekend camp concerts, Harry and Tom sang folk songs, with Harry playing the brash, brazen, prankster role, and Tom the straight man. They were a sort of musical Abbott and Costello, but with far less identity because, despite his aggressiveness, Harry had no rapport with an audience.

An ironic fact, in that the strength of Harry's music career later on was not the sales of records but the earthy, empathetic, almost magical relationship he commanded with a crowd in concert.

Clare said: "I often told Harry, 'Get your act together!' I remember that was a very big point between us, something he really had to work on. He got up on stage and clunk! He didn't know how to talk. He was uneasy; he just went right into his songs or told a few jokes. It wasn't just nervousness. It was a real lack of professional knowledge of what you do onstage. It was just nothing. It was like he forgot that part of the performance. And learning to develop that, I felt, was very important, because his voice wasn't that much of a great thing. It had to be the song or the words."

Many nights, Clare and Harry talked for hours along the lakefront, sharing and verbalizing each other's dreams, with thoughts of the future and what could be. For the first time, Harry dreamed of becoming a music performer. They often joked about what he should call himself upon success. "We thought it was much better to use the name H. Forster Chapin," recalled Clare affectionately, "and sometimes he used to sign things that way. Have you heard the latest H. Forster Chapin record?"

Harry: "Clare also had a lot of big dreams. At one point, she dreamed of being an actress. She also dreamed of being a singer."

Clare: "Harry's feelings were more toward what was going to be. It was very evident it was going to be success. He wasn't sure at that time how he was going to get recognition. It was just to be successful and famous and have it all together and owe nobody anything. That was it! He wanted to get into the 'club' in a sense. I think he was full of pride for his family, and yet wanted to be in the mainstream of America. The kind that goes to Yale and has the good American life in a sense, but on his own terms. And I think that my background was the epitome of success to him in some ways. I think there was an idea from seeing that, that he was not only gonna beat the system, but become successful. And I think seeing my situation gave him a little impetus."

However, the differences in their backgrounds that drew them together also drew them apart. They were two high-powered, ambitious people and each had to have his own way. As a result, their personalities often clashed and their relationship became a sort of tug-of-war, a bittersweet blend of romantic incandescence and chemical explosion.

"We just came from different environments," Harry concluded once. "She represented money, Scarsdale, all the things I didn't have when I grew up. But we both wanted attention. I was not enough of an achiever back then, and she wasn't solid enough as a woman. So we were constantly threatening each other. Plus, we sure could create dynamics; there were sparks flying all the time."

For instance, Clare often visited Harry at Grandma Chapin's, planned to stay three days and, after an explosive argument, left after two. Once, Clare was driving through Spanish Harlem with Harry. They were en route to Grandma Chapin's. Suddenly their peaceful conversation encountered a difference of opinion and instantly erupted into lethal cross fire. Clare stopped the car and they both jumped out screaming at one another in front of a local bar, at which point a choir of drunks began chanting, "Go, go, go."

Said Mullevaney: "The whole relationship was constant bickering back and forth. I think she was trying to push him, mold him into doing things, bring him up to her standards, and Harry just wasn't ready. He was going to do what he wanted. And at that point, Clare really wanted a Prince Charming who was going to be a replacement for her own father, and was not willing to accept this young, creative who-knows-what."

Most everyone close to the relationship agreed that Harry and Clare were an obvious mismatch. Harry didn't see it that way at all because in a sense, he was rebelling against his background. She represented something he never had. "She represented society," said Jim Lipscomb. "She represented some deep thing at that time. He really was in love with her and one time I said something cruel to her in his presence. I didn't think she honestly cared about him. I felt she was leading him on. I said: 'What are you doing here, leading on this drummer boy's son?' It wasn't a nice thing to say and I regretted it later."

As Clare saw it, "The main problem was Harry's lack of direction. He was just all over the lot. Basically, Harry had no direction from anybody older, a father, let's say. He had a tremendous sense of love from his father, but after that, there was no help from Mr. Chapin per se. There was the problem of the stepfather. The grandfathers were involved in their own thing. And his mother was an absolutely lovely woman. But I think a son needs a kind of approach that says: 'Harry, here's the world. Here's a couple of ideas. See what you think.' A father who could help you, give you a little direction and maybe even a little money. He didn't have that. All the brothers had to make up their own minds and figure it out for themselves. I'm not saying there wasn't a lot of love and communication in the family, but it's a big world and when you step outside the door, what kind of security do you really get back? He knew he was on his own in the world and he was really going to have to just get out there and fight."

Said Jim Chapin: "Harry thought of himself as the young prince, but this girl didn't think of him as the young prince. She thought she was slumming. She thought he was going to be a loser."

Clare's parents thought the same thing and were as unenthusiastic about Harry as his father, Jim, was about Clare. "My family was very goal-oriented," said Clare. "As soon as you walked in the front door, it was 'What do you want to be?' For Harry, it was success, but it was not defined. One felt that Harry might be successful as a writer, a musician, any number of five to eight things. I knew it. But they couldn't necessarily understand that. You walk in the door at twenty-one and say, 'Gee, I'm going to be a success by the time I'm thirty,' my father would say,

'Terrific, now what are you planning on? Hijacking a plane or what?'"

Clare's father gave Harry some advice, which eventually led to his return to Cornell. They had a serious discussion about self-discipline and concentration on something worthwhile. "He suggested that I get a law degree," said Harry, "that if I learned to be a lawyer, plus knew about computers, I could become a corporate president someday."

Harry was more or less sold on the idea, but he also had a few ideas of his own. Though he liked his job at Drew, "the more savory aspects of it were beginning to wear off" and he felt there was no reason why he shouldn't complete his education. James and Tom, after all, were getting by in college, "and if they could do it," he "could too."

More to please Clare and her parents than himself, Harry reluctantly decided to major in philosophy and follow Mr. MacIntyre's advice to become a young lawyer. He wrote an essay to the Cornell admissions office about how he had really found himself, worked hard, and moved up in the company, enclosing several recommendations from the firm.

In January 1963, Harry took a Greyhound bus back to Ithaca, New York. There he secured a room at 311 Dryden Road in Collegetown, the home of Dr. Stewart Brown, dean of the arts college. The house was an old, white, wood-frame, two-story structure. It sat atop a long, winding road that led past Johnny's Big Red, a local restaurant and nightspot, across College Avenue, the main drag, and down a steep hill overlooking the town of Ithaca and the breathtaking blue waters of Cayuga Lake.

That spring, Clare was virtually everything Harry lived and breathed. Almost every weekend, either Clare drove up to Cornell or Harry hitchhiked down to Bennett Junior College. There Harry often bartered for a room at the Millbrook Manor Motel, near her school, by singing for guests. Hopelessly in love, he once hitchhiked fourteen hours in the middle of a blinding blizzard wearing only a pair of loafers on his frostbitten feet.

And Clare loved him as much. On Valentine's Day she sent him a card with a humorous picture of a smoking gorilla on the cover. When Harry failed to send anything, Clare was deeply hurt. She wrote a letter chastising him for his insensitivity. So, in passionate tongue-in-cheek style, Harry responded to her letter with his first poem:

It's gone . . . 'most a week ago now.
Why didn't I? T'would only be a quarter.
Some foolish, friendly thought; a nicety
To span the miles and get a smile.
Whimsical; a smile like mine,
As when her missal came for me.
And I? unknowing? unfeeling? uncaring? not sending?
Not so,

For I am one of love's fool dreamers,
Who couldn't let his heart ride on printed card,
With flippant quips or candied thoughts
Of thine mine love dove heart apart
(Or even a sweetheart of a smoking gorilla!)
And so I send, romantic fool that I am,
A poem, a trifle, yet MINE! to she that I love.

> a non-secret admirer
> H. Forster Chapin
> February, 1963

At the bottom of the page, Harry apologized by saying that he didn't send her anything because she already had his heart and that was all he had to give. He closed the letter in gallant Quixotic style:

> . . . Now you can brag to all the little Bennett-landers that your beau even wrote you a poem. "Beat that!" With that stick your tongue out at them and stalk proudly off. I have proved myself at long last!

During the week, Harry spent most of his time thinking of Clare and the weekend to come. He often missed his classes and slept or hustled pool at the local Collegetown billiard room. Once again, he started to drift. "And that really frightened me," said Harry. "I often said the only good things that happened to me at college were horizontal. I learned to play guitar lying on my back. I slept in a big triple bed up there and hid from the world. I probably set a record for cutting classes."

Harry's music involvements had also fallen flat. He joined "two other guys from school" in a short-lived re-creation of his brothers' folk group, The Three of Us, and unsuccessfully tried to join the Sherwoods a second time. "The people didn't want him back," said Fred Kewley, a member of the Sherwoods and later Harry's music manager. "It was a twelve-man singing group and there were already twelve people. Besides, he was the world's worst background singer. He couldn't do that. He couldn't blend with other people. He had to sing pretty much by himself. He was more of a solo guy. He just didn't fit in, and there were some personal things."

Those "personal things" were the major factor. Harry was not well liked. Once, at a Sherwood rehearsal, Harry bent down for something and, in straightening up, his elbow jolted one Sherwood with a shot square between the legs. His name was Geoff Hewitt. "It was strictly an accident," said Kewley, "but later on, Geoff said to me, 'From the day he hit me in the nuts, I never did trust the guy.'"

Witnessing the reenactment of his wandering ways, Clare, at the suggestion of her father, persuaded Harry to take a psychological test through the Johnson O'Connor Institute in New York to discover potential career inclinations. The test, a complicated series of questions for ability, brought bittersweet results. It revealed that Harry tested high in every category and, for this reason, the institute told him he was the one person they couldn't help. However, they did make the recommendation that he never get into too fixed a career because it would limit his potential. "They told him he was capable of being anything from an alcoholic dishwasher to Thomas Jefferson," said brother James. "Of course, one of the reasons Harry was so manic and never settled down long enough to do anything was the case of having too broad a range of talents. The disadvantage was that he wasn't astonishingly above average in any single one."

Maybe the test results were a factor, but during the summer of 1963, Clare disappeared to Europe, much to Harry's bitterness. He didn't believe it was her decision. He thought her father sent her away, to get her out of Harry's clutches, afraid they might get too involved. In the song "The Mayor of Candor Lied," Harry recounted his bitterness; the mayor of Candor was Mr. MacIntyre, who took "her off across the water./What a thing to do to a young man in love./And what a thing to do to your daughter."

In an attempt to forget Clare, Harry joined Tom that summer as a camp counselor again. But this time, they were accompanied by their first twelve-string guitars and took their brother act to Camp Deerfield, a rich Jewish summer spot in upstate New York. He also began dating the horseback riding teacher, Lucky Richards. The song "They Call Her Easy" was based on this relationship.

"She made no bones about sex," said Harry. "She was willing to make love to me. But I was a fucking idiot because every night after we made love, I went back to the bunk and told all the gory details to the other counselors. After about two weeks of this, she got word and confronted me directly. "'Harry, I'm being very nice to you and I'm not trying to hurt you. Why are you saying those things about me?' I felt lower than whale shit, and that's the bottom of the ocean."

When Clare returned from Europe at the end of the summer, she immediately left for the University of the Pacific in San Francisco to do an internship in music therapy. Harry, of course, believed her father had chosen the location of her new school, and that fall he returned to Cornell and tried to carry on the relationship, despite the 3,000 miles between them.

He wrote long letters and rang up enormous phone bills. "That fall, I must have spent $500 on phone calls," said Harry. One night, standing in a phone booth on a street corner in Collegetown, he talked to Clare for four and a half hours. The call cost him $119.

Harry dreamed of seeing Clare again, and he did—during summers, on and off, until she got married a few years later. Their relationship, said Harry once, became something like "a ball falling off a table," which, with each succeeding drop, bounced lower and lower until it finally sat motionless on the floor. The dream, the nirvana, was over. Yet their relationship had evoked an intensity and left a deep scar from which Harry never fully recovered. Shades, shadows and contortions of Clare would echo within a major portion of the story songs he wrote throughout his career, and especially in his poetry. He never did forget her. She remained a fascinating figure in his fertile imagination and, indeed, as in his song "Sequel" he was "Half the time thinking of what might have been, and half thinking 'just as well.'"

CHAPTER IV

Old College Avenue

Harry could not accept Clare's sudden departure. Just one whiff of Chanel No. 5 from any female passerby and her image flooded his mental gallery. Yet he knew the relationship was over and tried to forget her. At school, more than ever, he drifted away from philosophy and his appearance at any class became a near-miracle. Instead, he gravitated toward his only surviving interests: poetry and music.

That fall, Fred Kewley took over as arranger and director of the Sherwoods and was impressed by Harry's musical background. Harry auditioned a third time and made it, in part because Kewley recognized the popularity of folk music and wanted a guitar/banjo player in the group. "But mostly because comic Mike Abrams, who'd become a big deal on campus, took a liking to me," said Harry. "And although a couple of guys wanted to blackball me, he really pushed to get me in."

Said Sherwooder Rob White of Harry back then: "He always called himself Gapin' Chapin and it was true, a lot of people did at the time. He was very rambunctious. I found him hard to be with because he was always so talkative. It was impossible to have a relationship with him. For Harry, it wasn't a matter of give and take. He was not that kind of guy. You could get your words in, but you were never sure whether they were heard or not."

Despite his interpersonal problems, no one could deny that Harry had improved immeasurably as a musician, to the extent, at least, that he could carry his own weight and play alone. He had learned autoharp and harmonica, as well as fast picking, Dave Von Ronk songs, and, in particular, numerous talking-blues numbers. For that, he had sought the tutorship of two ex-Sherwoods, Alan Roth and Mack Williams, who taught him the guitar style of Josh White, the old black blues singer. But Harry had become interested in this musical genre two years before, when Tom and a friend of his named Stefan Grossman, who later became a well-known European folksinger, took Harry up to Harlem to visit Reverend Gary Davis, another old black blind bluesman and street preacher, from whom Grossman was taking guitar lessons.

Said Harry: "Reverend Gary took a real shine to Tom because he was so tall. He liked the altitude he was talking up to. Reverend Gary played a good lick and then he'd say, 'What do you think about that, Tom Cat? How's it up there, Tom Cat?' I wasn't that mind-blown by Reverend Gary's fame, because he wasn't that famous. The thing that impressed me was the energy the old man had. A vibrant man, the reverend had a delightfully ironic sense of humor that managed to prevail in his over seventy years' worth of stories, scrapes, and life on the street. It was what Father Jim called 'round shouldered'; an expression he had for people who were smart enough to get caught on every projecting surface. Reverend Gary also taught me his two-finger picking style."

Harry eventually visited Reverend Gary a second time, and both visits later became the source of his song "Bluesman," about how, according to Harry, "an awful lot of white boys learned their music at the feet of old black bluesmen to get some funk."

By the spring of 1964, Harry was able to utilize what he had learned. He began playing heavily—six nights a week at Johnny's Big Red, a Collegetown nightspot. He'd sing for meals and a small fee, performing alone Monday through Saturday from 9:00 P.M. to 1:00 A.M. with just a guitar and a microphone. His repertoire was vastly improved, and after singing his prepared set of material, Harry went around to tables taking requests. Not surprisingly, his best song was Tony Bennett's 1962 chart-topping hit, "I Left My Heart in San Francisco."

For a young folksinger, Johnny's was the only amateur testing ground in town, and it attracted numerous Cornellians willing to work their way through college, even the future chairman of the board of Xerox Corporation, who worked there as a waiter. But perhaps the most famous employee at Johnny's was folksinger Peter Yarrow, of Peter, Paul and Mary, who played for years at the restaurant-club before graduating with a degree in English in 1960, at the heart of the folk music era. Yarrow was the hometown favorite.

Harry heard numerous stories of Yarrow's reputation and the way he drew crowds, but he couldn't duplicate Yarrow's success without his brothers at his side. "Harry didn't pack 'em in like Peter Yarrow," said Johnny Patrillo, the owner. "Harry couldn't put it across like Peter. Peter got them singing while Harry was more of a quiet kid on stage. He didn't draw. When Peter played here, you couldn't get near this place. There were people jammed outside the door. Peter had pure determination and will, and the crowd joined with him. Harry didn't have that."

Performing late into the night, Harry's academic average slipped drastically again. During his three semesters in philosophy, his grades fell from 81 to 75 to 59, an almost exact duplication of his first three semesters in architecture. He flunked gym twice, four times in all six semesters, and had an 8:00 A.M. French class he never attended. "I had an infinite ability to rationalize," said Harry. "I did an awful lot of sleeping. I was good at hiding away from the realities. I didn't enjoy French, I didn't enjoy a lot of the subjects I had to take. I was not organized. In retrospect, I'm surprised I was able to spend as much time fighting and struggling in my guitar playing because I wasn't able to organize virtually anything in my life back then."

That spring, Harry would have busted out of Cornell a second time—except he voluntarily withdrew from school. Having flunked both architecture and philosophy, Harry joked years later: "It meant that no only could I not build a library, I wouldn't know what to inscribe around it."

Said Jim Lipscomb: "Harry could sit down and push himself to write song after song, poem after poem; concentrated work. He couldn't pull that together and do that kind of concentrated work at Cornell. He couldn't make it. He couldn't make himself concentrate on that level. It didn't seem as immediately relevant to push those doors as writing songs. He was studying English 101 and that was a long way from 'I want recognition as a success. How does that get me there?' I think that was it. He wasn't curious in terms of academic, scholarly subjects. That didn't appeal to him nearly as much as the whole world and finding a niche somewhere, a place where he could win recognition. And then there was that 160 I.Q. and he was a Chapin and there was a very strong sense of family."

By the summer of 1964, Harry was performing full-time with his brothers as a folk trio, he and Tom on guitar and Steve on upright bass. Sherwooder Alan Roth was impressed by a couple of demo tapes the brothers had recorded and appointed himself their manager. Roth's primary asset was his car, transportation to and from gigs. Mullevaney, who had a car, sometimes lent his services. Earning between fifty and a hundred dollars a night, the Chapin Brothers played as much as they could, wherever they could, from the Bitter End, New York's mecca for folksingers, to spot engagements at Gerde's Folk City, the Tenement, Cafe Wha, Cafe A Go Go, and Palisades Amusement Park. They also performed at small nightclubs on eastern Long Island, sleeping on the beach or at Father Jim's house, and several in Connecticut and New Jersey. Some of these gigs turned out to be disasters.

"We once played a club in New Jersey," Harry remembered. "It was almost like a Mafia club. The closest table must have been fifty feet away, with a giant dance floor separating us. The microphones stretched only so far from the band, the speakers were small, and there were these forty- and fifty-year-old Irish and Italian couples having a party. And here Tom, Steve and I came out and did a whole bunch of songs they never heard of. It was absolutely Death Valley. Literally. We were so far away from the audience and what they wanted. This was in the middle of the folk era and these people hadn't gotten the message."

The most successful gigs for the Chapin Brothers were at the Bitter End, where they played hootenannies almost every Tuesday night. They also opened for several well-known entertainers: folksingers Tom Paxton, Josh White Jr. and Jakes Holmes, as well as comedians such as Joan Rivers, Bill Cosby and Dick Cavett.

"At that time, the Chapin Brothers were being hired on almost a regular basis," said Dave Wilkes, first a doorman and later a manager of the club. "They were like the house opening band."

In the group, Harry was the energy force, "the roving maniac" always trying to stir up excitement. Tom and Steve were more laid-back. "He was always the guy to whom everybody could say, 'Harry, cut it out!'" said Jebbie Hart. This was especially true of brother Tom. When Tom sang solo, Harry was annoyingly competitive, unable to stop his cheerleader antics of clapping hands, egging on the audience, and essentially vying for center stage.

"Harry never shut up," said Mullevaney. "He couldn't walk off the stage. Sometimes he talked in the middle of Tom's numbers. I'm sure Tom spoke to Harry about it, but Harry had no ability to back off."

The group's conflicting energy forces, then, were as much negative as positive. Their drawback was youth and inexperience. "They didn't have a professional manager," said Mullevaney. "They didn't have a professional attitude. They didn't have contacts. And they weren't awfully original really. They hadn't started writing their own original material, and while they were very strong musically, they didn't have a central focus.

Everybody was so talented, pulling in all sorts of different directions, and it confused the audience sometimes.

"In Harry's own group later, there was no question what the focus of it was—it was Harry, his music, his voice, his personality, and they came to see Harry. And that put the audience at ease. The Chapin Brothers, on the other hand, were three people, all different, with different focuses, doing different kinds of music. They did a slow tune, a fast tune, a hillbilly tune, a little bluegrass. It was ridiculous. They were trying to do too many damn different things."

By summer's end, the brothers returned to school, Tom to Plattsburgh State and Steve to his senior year at Brooklyn Tech, but Harry was lost. He didn't know what to do with himself. He still felt withdrawal symptoms from Clare and now his brothers. He returned to Cornell but did not register for courses. If he had, his poor grades meant he would have "busted out" twice. "So instead, I went up there and started auditing courses," said Harry. "I had this crazy, romantic plan to audit courses, get great grades unbeknownst, be reinstated with honors, and pay my bills afterward. In fact, though I went to some courses for a while, I finally shot a tremendous amount of pool. I was living proof of Dylan's statement: 'He who is not busy being born is busy dying.' Because I was treading water."

Once again, Harry sank into a deep depression, suffocating from ambivalent drives to fulfill standard expectations: on the one hand, college and personal expectations; on the other, music. Harry wound up fulfilling neither.

"It was probably the lowest point in his life," said brother James, who was at Cornell that fall finishing his doctorate in history, having received his BA in history at Hamilton, his master's at Cornell. "But when Harry talked about how he felt, it was: 'Oh, I feel great! Isn't the world wonderful?' He was doing nothing basically. He was just chasing girls and sitting in his room playing guitar. Meanwhile, Harry had the appearance of: 'Well, I'm really busy today.' Harry was always running around like a madman, whether he was producing stuff or not. He was a remarkable spectacle of somebody working himself to death doing nothing."

But on the inside, Harry was caught in the throes of an emotional depression that soon began to affect his physical appearance. That fall, Bob Mullevaney's mother, who had met Harry several times before at the Fresh Air Fund Camp, was up in Ithaca and took Harry and James out to dinner.

"Harry didn't seem to feel well," said Mrs. Mullevaney. "He was undernourished and much thinner than I was accustomed to seeing him. He had a bad cold. I just felt sorry for him. He seemed so unhappy. I wished I had a thermos of chicken soup or something I could have given him."

In the song "Sometime, Somewhere Wife," Harry wrote of this juncture in his life as "colder than I'd ever care to make it/I had a kind of empty feeling/But no place to go where I could take it."

Harry's only consolation and comfort was the close presence of James, who took a room across the hall from him at 311 Dryden Road. Like reserve infantry rescuing a badly beaten battalion, James came to Harry's aid, offering advice, money and moral support. "I remember at the end of the semester telling him, 'Well, Christ, you've got to do something,'" said James. "It was like watching a truck spin its wheels in the mud. Harry really didn't have friends. What Harry had was lovers of the opposite sex."

The only lover who really mattered at the time was a Cornell student named Jenny Gillette. She became Harry's second missing link and the bridge between Clare and his later wife, Sandy. While Harry's relationship with Clare had more fire and desire, Jenny was more maternal and nurturing. "She made it comfortable for me to come to the inimitable conclusion that I was spinning my wheels and that I needed to do something," said Harry. "Lots of people don't realize they've screwed up until forty or fifty. But Jenny gave me the emotional strength to realize that I was a failure in school and needed to go somewhere else to make my mark. She was the first real woman I ever came in contact with."

Understanding and patient, Jenny was willing to listen to Harry and offer sympathy, not criticism. Through Jenny, Harry saw he was in far worse shape than he realized, and in her own quiet way, she put him back together, stabilizing his emotions, awakening him from his deep sleep. The songs "Old College Avenue" and "Winter Song" were all about her.

By January 1965, Jim Lipscomb was producing a film called *The Big Guy* about six-foot-eight boxer Jim Beattie, and offered Harry a job as editor. Jim's offer couldn't have come at a better time. Harry was searching for a new beginning and, with Jenny's encouragement, accepted the position and came to New York with her.

His days at Cornell were done!

By this time, home had changed from 45A to 136 Hicks Street. Elspeth had finally left Henry. But long before she did, she also gave birth to Henry's second son, John Hart. Born with a cleft palate, he was in need of speech therapy lessons that lasted three years. The therapist was Janet Castro, a warm, ingratiating woman who lived in the Heights. Over the years, Janet became close to Elspeth and was present during the breakup period. "She was so upset over the pregnancy," said Janet, "that she flung herself down the stairs and that's what caused John to be born with a cleft palate. The thing I remember was how nervous, overworked and cowed Elspeth was in that house at 45A Hicks Street. I remember going there to give speech lessons, and if any of the boys were present, she was always worried that Henry might come home."

Finally, on the advice of a lawyer, Elspeth, with the help of family, rented a truck one day when Henry was at work, moved out the furniture, and safely secured herself behind a different door. This left Henry the surprise of returning home to an empty apartment, and marked an abrupt end to ten turbulent years of marriage. Soon after Elspeth got a new job and eventually wound up at Garland Publishing Company in Manhattan.

She never married again.

Meanwhile, Jenny Gillette was about to begin a marriage of her own, but not with Harry. For several months she had been engaged to a young man in Florida, and although she loved Harry and would readily have changed her plans to marry him, Harry shuddered at the thought of such a long-term commitment, especially having witnessed a wealth of unsuccessful marriages in his own family. At the same time, Harry loved her, wanted her, needed her, but he couldn't bring himself to tell her. Years later, Harry often reminisced that "Jenny was the woman I should've married. Everybody in the family fell in love with her. But I didn't have the guts to tell her I loved her and wanted her to stay. It seemed too serious a step. So I let her go."

Jenny stayed with Harry for a week at Elspeth's apartment and then left for Miami. A few days later, Harry called her and told her his feelings. But it was too late.

Two years later, at the age of twenty-four, Jenny Gillette died of a brain tumor.

* * *

By May, Harry completed his work on *The Big Guy* and once again decided to perform full-time that summer with his brothers, who were out of school. But this time, the trio was far more professional and in tune with the changing times. For one, electronics were rapidly becoming pop music's fancy, so the brothers added electric guitar to their performances. And Harry began playing autoharp and harmonica in addition to banjo and guitar. The brothers also added a new manager. At Harry's persuasion, Cornellian Kewley appointed himself brain trust of the trio and moved in with the Chapins at 136 Hicks Street. Like Roth before him, Kewley had been impressed by the two demo tapes the Chapin Brothers had done and had wheels as well, a brand-new green Chevy van. But unlike Roth, Kewley was not merely a titular manager. He "kept the usual brotherly arguments in bounds," Jim Chapin said once, and because of his prior experience as director of the Sherwoods, improved the group's vocal balance, and wrote and rehearsed some superb arrangements of their material.

In addition, at Kewley's suggestion, the brothers added their father, Jim, on drums to give the group greater stage impact. Though Jim fit perfectly into the trio's family image, he also had a different rhythmic feel for the folk and soft rocks songs his sons performed. Being a jazz musician, Jim was accustomed to the driving tempo of a thirty-piece jazz band that played on the front of the beat, while the brothers' slower-paced folk/rock songs called for movement at the center, or a little bit behind the beat. It created some awkwardness on stage. "In certain ballads and rock songs Dad had a totally different feel," said Tom. "He understood later on, but we didn't know how to explain it to him then."

Even so, the brothers adored having Jim around and worked more or less the same clubs as the summer before, plus an occasional college concert. When Jim wasn't available, Phil Forbes, a friend of the brothers from the Heights, filled in on drums, having taken lessons from Mr. Chapin. Promoted by a brochure that promised short hair and clean-cut music, each week the foursome plus Kewley packed the Chevy van with drums, guitars and amplifiers and drove from club to club making what they liked to call "Chapin Music." Most of the material as Harry's. Many of the songs were part of a collection of thirty harmless, upbeat folk songs he wrote while at Cornell. Others were made to order for the brothers' performance. "I was writing things that fit into different categories," said Harry. "If we needed a funny song, sexy song, or lively song—I wrote it."

Like any new group, unestablished and struggling, the Chapin Brothers sometimes had to create their own opportunities. For kicks, they sang in the Vassar College parking lot once, running a power cord from the dormitory to their guitar amps. It was then an all-female school, and Vassar women, dressed in near-transparent nighties, applauded from their dormitory windows until school officials permitted the group to move indoors and complete the concert in the lounge.

But more often than not, the Chapin Brothers sang at dances and parties in and around Brooklyn Heights, often performing at Packer Collegiate Institute, a private school off Joralemon Street. Almost invariably, after concerts, they'd go over to the brownstone apartment of Manny and Janet Castro on Remsen Street, who usually threw open-house parties for them, and continued their singing there.

Harry had first become acquainted with the Castros a few months earlier, when he began dating their niece, Gail Hollenborg, a strikingly attractive, slim-figured brunette. Gail had been engaged to a man who broke his commitment at the last moment, and unable to get along at home with her parents, she went to live with Manny and Janet. At the time, Harry, too, was emotionally disenfranchised, partly over Jenny, but mostly over Clare. One day, over the phone, Elspeth and Janet got to talking. "I said, 'You know, Gail is on the rebound from a bad experience,'" said Janet. "So Elspeth said, 'Oh, that's interesting, because my son is also going through a bad time. He's sort of at loose ends and doesn't know what to do with himself. Maybe we can get them together.'"

One night Harry and Gail went on a date and afterward returned to the Castros' apartment. He brought his guitar with him. "He came in with sneakers and curly hair and his guitar," said Janet. "The first reaction of Manny and me was, 'Oh, not another amateur folksinger, please!' But one thing about him, as soon as he walked into the room, the energy was overwhelming. It was electric. I had just gotten a tape recorder because of my speech therapy teaching, and he sang a couple of songs and Manny and I were mesmerized. The first song he sang was 'I Left My Heart in San Francisco.' Manny soon brought out the tape recorder and it was out for five years after that. Harry played 'Bill Bailey,' 'Ring Tail Tom,' and many other songs he didn't write. But that first evening he played 'Stars Tangled in Her Hair' and that's the first time we heard his music and we absolutely flipped out."

At Castro parties, there was a constant ebb and flow of people: friends of Manny and Janet's; Gail; Elspeth; all the brothers, including James; David Ostraff, Harry's old history teacher; Michael Burke; Fred Kewley and his girlfriend Trika Smith; and many more.

"The thing that was neat about the Castros' was that it was a place where people could go and have a good time and listen to the Chapins sing," said Trika. "It was sort of a gathering place in the Heights. Harry always ended up singing and entertaining for the folks there. It was always fun. Harry had a way of being able to pull people with him. And we identified with his beginning success, wanting him to succeed. At that point, it was sort of a dream."

John Wallace, who sometimes joined the music making with an old stand-up bass, and who later became a mainstay of Chapin's band, said: "The Castros were fans. They thought Harry would be going places. Really nice people. I remember I went along a few times with my bass, thumping along, and I loved it. I loved the music and the harmony and playing with the brothers."

Despite the crowds, the Castros were gracious hosts. They always kept a well-stocked liquor cabinet and served whatever they had, from steak to peanut butter. As far as the Castros were concerned, the Chapins and their friends were part of the family. "It was always an open house for the Chapins and they knew it," said Manny Castro.

Oftentimes, the brothers played late into the night, long after everyone had gone home. The neighbors didn't take too kindly to this and regularly called the police complaining of the noise. "You could barely hear them sing," said Manny, "because the walls would shake."

Then, seconds before the police arrived, there was a mad scurrying about to hide the instruments. When the officers walked in, they were all talking quietly at the dining room table, sipping coffee. "We just said to the police, 'What do you mean?'" said Janet Castro. "'We weren't making any noise here.' And then we offered them a drink and that was that."

The Chapin Brothers also frequently performed at the Bitter End that summer. But from Harry's perspective, Greenwich Village had changed; it had become "commercial and contrived"— a colder place, ever since the Beatles and Bob Dylan went electric. It was no longer the lively, friendly, twenty-four-hour atmosphere I'd always known." But it was still his musical home away from home and, as a group, the Chapin Brothers developed a die-hard following around the Village. They became as polished and professional as they were to be. "The group was very, very good," said Dave Wilkes, who became manager of the Bitter End. "Sometimes Harry's father performed with them. But Harry was always the lead singer and it was mostly his material. A lot of people spoke to Harry, I know I did, about really trying to get out and make it as a group."

The primary reason was Harry's dynamic energy. Though far less musically talented than Steve, and undynamic compared to the looks and voice of Tom, Harry was still the catalytic converter, the live nerve. One night, before opening a Bitter End show for Jake Holmes (who was riding the pop hit "So Close"), Jim spotted Tom and Steve sitting on the little bandstand looking at their feet. So Jim whispered, "Listen, boys, you've only got twenty or thirty minutes out there at best. So get some energy going. Come on out there. Smile. Let something happen. Project something. Cheer up!" And to Harry, fiddling with the mikes, he whispered, "Cheer down!"

Another time that summer, Jim and the brothers went on a short tour of the South. One day, Harry was driving and took a back road in Georgia on their way to a one-night stand. As they passed a small store in the middle of nowhere, Harry decided to stop for soft drinks. "We walked in looking for all the world like a band of thieves," Jim recalled. "There were four or five people sitting around a potbellied stove. A couple of them were playing checkers. Well, Harry came bounding in and woke two regulars who were sleeping."

"Hello, brothers," Harry hollered. "Name is Chapin, Harry Chapin, and these are my brothers. We're playing a gig tonight at this small town down the road." Whereupon Harry picked up his guitar and performed a half-hour concert. His audience, now fully awake, applauded, and the shopkeeper refused payment for the sodas.

For Harry, Jim's presence was not only a marvelous recontact with his roots, but he also learned a lot, especially when it related to performance. For instance, Jim was totally against all forms of drugs and, one time that summer, gave his sons a firm lecture about it. "During the 1940s, Charlie 'Bird' Parker, the brilliant jazz musician, was killing himself on drugs," he told them. "Now Charlie thought he played better when he was blasted. He thought he needed it. He was an unhappy man. But the fact was, he played better when he was straight." Harry never forgot that.

Nor did he forget an eleven-minute story by his father called "Stonewall" about Stonewall Jackson, the Confederate general, which Jim performed one night with the brothers at the Bitter End. It was the first time Harry became aware of the story song and the potential impact of the narrative form of songwriting.

Said Gail Hollenborg of the Chapin Brothers back then: "At the Bitter End, you saw them all locked into this tiny dressing room being treated like they were there to wash the dishes. It's hard to understand the ego that's the performer. From my perception, it was 'God, you guys are working so hard and this guy is treating you like garbage and not paying you enough money.'"

Trika Smith, who was also part of the Chapin contingent in the crowd, said: "One of the things I realized after watching Harry, Tom and Steve was what it took to make it. I mean, you had to have that drive. We used to spend a lot of time listening to Jake Holmes at the Bitter End. We'd watch those people begin to make it, this incredible relentless thing you had to have to continue to have faith in yourself when nobody else did. The thing about Harry was that it was all intuitive. I don't think he even thought about it. He was just that way. Always full of energy."

By summer's end, the brothers desperately wanted to cash in what success and experience they'd accumulated and make an album. A couple of record companies had shown mild interest. Capitol Records was believed to be one. But Jim Chapin knew a man named Irv Kratka who owned a record company called Music Minus One, a small outfit that produced "play-along" records with songs that were minus one instrument, which the amateur replaced with his own. However, Kratka wanted to diversify and launch a new label for pop music.

Kratka also fancied himself a successful pop music producer. He had been a good friend of Jac Holzman, the owner of Elektra Records who was in the midst of producing such popular groups as The Doors and Love, and envied Holzman's success. With the Chapin Brothers, he saw a low-cost way to make his debut into pop music production. Kratka was impressed when he heard the brothers at the Bitter End and believed they could release an album with the material they had.

But before any record contract could be signed or a single note recorded, the Vietnam draft temporarily interrupted all their music plans. With thousands of men a month being drafted into the war machine, and conservative television reports listing not-so-conservative death counts, Tom and Steve were faced with a serious question. Should they go back to college (Tom to Plattsburgh State and Steve to Clarkson College) or should they go through with the record deal and risk being drafted?

Fortuitously, Harry faced no such decision. From his Air Force training, he received a veteran classification, without which he would surely have been drafted (with his grades, Cornell would never have accepted him back). Like any veteran, Harry was supposed to attend army reserve meetings. But somehow, in transferring his reporting place back and forth between Ithaca and New York, his file got lost, and after attending only one reserve meeting, he received an honorable discharge.

Fred Kewley was drafted immediately. When that happened, Tom and Steve's decision was made for them. "We had a big family meeting out in New Jersey with K.B. and my mother," said Harry. "It was a big, traumatic thing. They decided to go back to school, but I always thought of myself in conjunction with my brothers. That was the implicit assumption of my life up until then. Now I had to consider other careers: filmmaking, perhaps other forms of writing."

Still, a few weeks later, Tom and Steve got the best of both worlds—music and college—without having to face the draft, and Harry's "trio dream" of making an album came back to life. One September weekend, Tom and Steve came down to New York and joined Harry and Jim to record the album for Kratka. Appropriately, the album was entitled *Chapin Music!* a home-brewed, inexpensively produced folk record, with all the songs recorded live using two microphones in a makeshift jazz studio. The label was called Rock-Land Records, a short-lived subsidiary of Music Minus One that Kratka created overnight.

On the album were fourteen folk songs, most of which were arranged by Steve, and four of which were written by Harry: "Stars Tangled in Her Hair," "Someone Keeps Calling My Name" (later rewritten and rerecorded), "When Do You Find Time to Breathe?" and a song called "Blood River," the first fairly close resemblance to a Harry Chapin story song, about how some Cornell students took their lives by jumping into one of two giant gorges near the campus.

The album was a failure. It was released in late December 1966, and the folk movement had seen better days—what with the music mood of America shifting to British rockers and hard-rock music in general. Though two singles were released, a song by Steve called "Mr. Small" and Harry's "Hard Times," neither landed.

There were several reasons. For one, the record was never promoted and the music was a derivative of a bygone folk era. The songs were simplistic and unoriginal. And the lack of focus that occasionally hurt the brothers in performance was very evident on the album. There was an amalgamation of song styles: ballad, lament, protest, folk, rock, humor, story song. "The only line they drew," wrote Kratka in the album's liner notes, "was on the manuscript page or using anyone else's songs."

Still, the album had a charming innocence. On both sides of the jacket cover were black-and-white photographs of the brothers as children and young men in different poses and postures. That sense of family radiated off the album, particularly inside, where Father Jim, in a section entitled *A Dad's Eye View,* traced the musical development of his sons. And above that were two philosophical prose pieces by Tom and Steve, and a poem by Harry:

> There is something in the singing
> of other poet's songs
> that only warms my mind
> when I'm alone.

> With no one close around,
> I search inside of other's words
> and can rest in knowing
> something that they knew.

> But when you are gathered near
> I do not speak another's words
> (they should do that telling
> and gain your gathered answer).

> It is then that I make melodies
> of my own; (half our conversation)
> asking at your face and eyes
> and listening for your voice in answer.

During that fall, long before the album's release, the Chapin Brothers appeared on four network television shows; twice on Merv Griffin's show in New York and twice on Canada's hit music program, "Let's Sing Out," hosted by folksinger Oscar Brand. On one Brand show was a young, shy, blond Canadian singer named Joanie Anderson, who was just splitting from her husband. "I remembered thinking, 'She's good, but she'll never make it because she's too laid-back,'" said Harry. "She turned out to be Joni Mitchell."

Said Brand of the Chapin Brothers: "I was surprised at how good they were. I never heard of them before, aside from the fact that I listened to their record and thought it was nice. But then together live, there was a warm atmosphere, quite different from most professional groups. It really was a family."

Griffin discovered that, too, but in a different way. At the time, he owned a farm in Stillwater, New Jersey, forty miles from Andover, and in the same valley as the boys' Grandfather Big Jim, who had moved there years before, when he divorced Abby (Grandma Chapin) and married Mary Fisher. "I knew Harry's grandfather lived nearby, as did all the neighbors," said Griffin. "But we all knew never to bother him. He was painting all the time, and one day my doorbell rang and I saw this elderly gentleman in his seventies standing there. I said, 'Yes?' and he said, 'My name is James Chapin,' and we became friends. Harry's grandfather was their public relations man. He said, 'I want you to listen to my grandsons.' They had just made a tape for an album."

During the Griffin shows, the brothers, and Harry especially, acted as public relations men for their father, praising and supporting him. The family pride was in part the thrill, at least for Harry, of being close to the two things he admired most: music and Jim.

"They did a song and were interviewed afterward," remembered Gail Hollenborg, who saw one of the programs. "They spoke of Jim like, 'He's so marvelous. He's so wonderful. He's done this and that,' And I thought, 'He really didn't do that much.' For Harry, the drive was to make a name for himself, but at the same time keep the three of them together and involve Jim Chapin. I don't know why any of the three felt the imperative to involve Jim. I saw Elspeth as very much shunted aside."

The following weekend, after recording the album, Jim and the brothers performed at Plattsburgh State, Tom's home territory, and had, according to Jim, "the most triumphant concert of our career." At the time, Tom was the big man on campus, star of the basketball team, and the audience came to see him, according to Steve, "expecting little more than a lame-duck show." But professionally, the group was as tight as could be. They had a bang-up opening and a time-tested, fast-punched, high-energy presentation. In it, the three brothers began acoustically, and then, as each number built to a climax, Jim joined them on drums. By concert's end, the Chapin Brothers were overwhelmed with two five-minute standing ovations. "All four of us never forgot that night," said Harry. "What a feeling when it's all working!"

Two days later, still riding the crest of the concert, Harry, Tom and Jim headed back to New York, and Steve To Clarkson College in Potsdam. Heading south on the New York State Thruway, good fortune quickly turned bad. Tom was in the backseat, Jim in the front passenger seat, with Harry, an inexperienced driver, behind the wheel of Jim's car. As was often the case, Jim had let the tires go bald, driving until the cord was literally exposed, but this set was the worst yet.

Traveling peaceably at sixty-five miles per hour, suddenly, about ten miles south of Albany, the right rear tire blew out. What ensued was almost a reenactment of the car accident that would kill Harry sixteen years later. . . . In panic, Harry slammed on the brakes, sending the car swerving and screeching toward the grass median and opposing traffic. Instantly he wrenched the steering wheel right, then left, and skidded broadside across three lanes of traffic. The car then tipped to the passenger side, rolled once and violently bounced down a twenty-foot grass embankment, flipping two more times before landing upright.

The car was totaled: the windshield shattered, the wheel drums pretzeled, the steering column bent in Harry's grasp. Steam swelled from the engine and the air reeked of burnt rubber. No one in the car moved. From the poem "Plains Crossing":

the taut shriek
of rubber on the road,
the shattered windshield
and blood.

PART TWO

"It is about a search, too,
for daily meaning as well
as daily bread, for recognition
as well as cash, for astonishment
rather than torpor; in short,
for a sort of life rather than
a Monday through Friday sort
of dying. Perhaps immortality,
too, is part of the guest."

—from *Working*
by Studs Terkel

CHAPTER V

I Wanna Learn a Love Song

Harry lay doubled over the steering wheel, motionless. The car engine was still running, sputtering, then dying, then sputtering to life again. Jim Chapin, in a daze, slowly reached across the front seat and shut off the engine. Then, with a heavy groan from his bloodstained faced, Jim pushed open the passenger door and rolled onto the ground, half dead.

Pale and shaken, Harry felt his father's movement. He pulled himself from the wreckage and immediately went to Jim's aid. He stood over him in trancelike shock, murmuring: "Are you all right, Dad? Are you all right?" But his father lay silent. "Dad, are you all right? Are you all right?" he kept repeating, close to tears.

Meanwhile Tom, who was uninjured, joined the scene and was shaking Harry by the shoulders to break him out of it, when Jim uttered, "Yeah, I'm okay, Harr . . ." and then nodded off.

Moments later, the state police arrived and drove Jim and his sons to a local hospital for X rays. Except for minor bruises to the kneecaps and elbows, Harry was physically sound. But Jim was in agony. He could barely move his neck without flinching from a deep stinging pain that seemed to affect every nerve in

105

his neck. Even so, the doctor diagnosed only a minor sprain, and they took a Greyhound bus to New York. "Dad was in terrible pain all the way," said Harry. "After a couple of hours back, he called another doctor and we found out later that he had a broken neck. He was in traction for almost eight weeks."

"He got hurt pretty bad," recalled John Wallace, who visited Jim once in the hospital. "His head was bolted to the wall so he couldn't move it. And there was a harness around his neck."

The official diagnosis was a broken seventh vertebra in Jim's neck. His spinal cord was permanently damaged, adding further affliction to an already bad back. As a result, Jim couldn't turn his neck more than twenty or thirty degrees. Instead, he had to shift his entire body, and his curved spine left him with a stoop when he walked.

* * *

That fall of 1965, Harry got another freelance film job with Jim Lipscomb—this one about a family of drug addicts—but within three weeks' time, he quit. Cal Bernstein, the fabulous color photographer and creator of all the print media ads for Marlboro cigarettes, came to New York to interview filmmakers for television commercials he was producing in a documentary still-studio in Los Angeles. Don Pennebaker of Drew Associates, who had been good friends with the owner of the studio, Haskell Wexler, the renowned cinematographer, suggested Harry for the job as writer/editor/correspondent at $250 per week. "They wanted somebody who could write," said Pennebaker. "The money was good, he'd be working with stills, and he had enough of a background to help them. It was the perfect job for Harry."

Harry thought so too, but for different reasons. "I had never been to L.A. before and it seemed as glamorous as hell to me," he said. "I was also dreaming of seeing Clare again. Although at the time, I didn't realize she had already graduated from Pacific University in San Francisco."

Despite some mild protest from Lipscomb, Harry left for Los Angeles. Once there, he rented a ranchero-type house off Santa

Monica Boulevard, ironically, just four blocks away from the West Coast headquarters of Elektra Records, Harry's future employers.

However, Harry did not find California the glamorous paradise he envisioned, nor a very challenging job. During the six months he was there the film unit produced only two commercials, both for United Airlines, and he became increasingly depressed and discouraged. He couldn't see himself as a filmmaker for the rest of his life. "He didn't think the job could go very far," said Pennebaker, who was in Los Angeles at the end of Harry's stay. "He was writing a lot of poetry and playing music."

More often than not, Harry frequented nightclubs and porno films. With lots of free time to marinate in his thoughts, much of the loneliness he felt at Cornell began to creep back in. In his poem "Curses," which Harry later dubbed his "California" poem, he wrote: "Damn this state that drives me to discover/that curses screamed at loneliness/call only the scant comfort/of all mankind's answering echo."

Said Harry: "I wrote that poem one night when I couldn't sleep. I'd just come back from a porno film and I was doing the singles dating scene. I'd gone through a whole period of running around like a madman screwing everybody I could find out there. And although I had some ego nights with fairly beautiful women, I also had many depressing nights because there was no continuity to my life."

Still, the stark loneliness that would pervade most of his music later on had yet to emerge. One night, Harry sang his entire three-year collection of folk songs to a group called The Modern Folk Quartet, which, like many folk groups at the time, was trying to switch over to rock 'n' roll. Jerry Easter, then a quartet member and later producer of the group Aztec Two-Step, remarked after Harry finished, "I never heard so many positive songs in a row!"

"Easter didn't like them because they weren't hip enough," said Harry. "I had yet to make the transition from folk music to more synthesized forms of songwriting. I continually wrote positive songs. Not that I was happy; it just fit my mental image in those days."

More importantly, the experience slightly tarnished Harry's dream of resuming the Chapin Brothers trio, with the incomes of each tied into a neat package. Now, suddenly, the package seemed a thing of the past, an outdated concept, because popular music had shifted from folk to rock.

In February 1966, Harry packed it all in, bought a used white Corvair and drove the 3,000 miles back to New York alone. He returned to Elspeth's apartment in Brooklyn Heights and once again tried another of his short-range dreams, this time, to become a poet. Harry did little but read and write poetry, increasingly realizing the connection between his family's artistic impulses and his urge to write verse. He started taking seriously poets such as e.e. cummings and William Carlos Williams, who, at one time or another, had visited Andover and K.B. when he was a child. He bought books by numerous "beat" poets such as Gregory Corso, Allen Ginsberg and Jack Kerouac. "I was especially turned on by [Lawrence] Ferlinghetti's *Coney Island of My Mind*," said Harry.

He was also turned on by the thought of getting his own poetry published. Frequently he sent his work to the Library of Congress for copyright, and much like his grandfathers' wives, women supported the cause. Trika Smith, whom Harry had begun dating, neatly typed his poems and Elspeth xeroxed them at her office. Harry enclosed the six-dollar copyright fee and a few days later received a stamped government form and sense of self-validation that brought him a little bit closer to the posterity of the poets he read and admired. Yet, once he mailed them off to magazines for publication, they met a different fate. His poems were consistently returned, accompanied by pink rejection slips.

So Harry decided to seek out the critical opinion and approval of K.B., but the attempt was earmarked for failure. "What Harry wanted from K.B. he could never get," said his brother James. "Not because of Harry, but because nobody ever got it."

Said Trika Smith, who joined Harry for the trip to Andover: "His wanting approval was indicative of him. All his songs were poems originally and he really wanted K.B. to see them. He wanted feedback from him, wanted his approval. But K.B. was just as egocentric as Harry and the meeting between the two of them was really something to behold. K.B. couldn't accept where Harry was coming from and was very critical of the poems. Harry was extremely disappointed. But within a day or two, he was right back there fighting, trying to get his poems published."

This was perhaps Harry's greatest strength, the inability to become discouraged for any appreciable length of time. He always felt compelled to push, hustle and seduce himself into thinking that this "next thing is the next great thing." But for the moment, there was no next great thing. And it disturbed him, because everyone else around him seemed so filled with purpose and drive.

"My mother used to go to work in the mornings and many days I slept late," said Harry. "Well, the Jehovah's Witnesses had their national office in Brooklyn Heights and they sent people around to convert others. One day they knocked on my door when I was snoozing. And when this young man and woman stood at my door, although I didn't believe in religion, I wished at least I had some beliefs like them that would make everything make sense."

Harry's search for a receptive audience for his songs and poems ended with Manny and Janet Castro. For the next two years, up until 1968, the Castros would become the central focus of his life, and Harry the central focus of theirs. The Castros kept his poems and music alive, a willing, captive audience. They made him feel special, the sort of specialness he had only known from his grandmothers and the concert stage. They were enthusiastic and appreciative of his creativity since they had no creativity of their own. They gave him immediate feedback and a natural outlet for his passions. "Nobody wants to hear my poetry and music at home," Harry often told them.

"It was the first time," said Harry, "that somebody, on a personal basis, took me seriously. My family, because everyone was into artistic things, didn't make a big deal about it because they were doing it. But the Castros did make a big deal about it and gave me a tremendous amount of confidence as I was writing."

In the evenings, the Castros' brownstone on Remsen Street became Harry's retreat and second home away from home. He usually visited them three or four nights a week, either calling first or just dropping by, accompanied by his six-string guitar and his latest portfolio of poems and songs. As was custom, the threesome lounged about the dining room table as Harry spun off another endless round of song and verse. Convinced Harry was destined for future fame, Janet always kept her reel-to-reel tape recorder running. Often Harry recorded a song, played it back and they all listened, then had a serious discussion about potential improvements: change a line, rewrite a melody, alter a vocal nuance.

He also recorded his poetry, and again it was the same process throughout which Manny and Janet were always supportive, their criticisms sympathetic. With them, Harry took out his "back-closet" material without fear of rejection. And though they knew little about poetry, their intuitive opinions and mainstream taste were invaluable. "I figured if I ever did become successful," said Harry, "I'd have to please people like Manny and Janet anyway."

But the Castros were already pleased and often stayed up late into the night with Harry, then staggered to work the following morning, Manny to a stock exchange brokerage firm on Wall Street and Janet to her teaching job at P.S. 307 near Fort Greene in Brooklyn. However, neither of them minded keeping the late hours. Harry filled their lives with a certain vitality and nourishment and, in the process, they became close friends to the exclusion of everyone and everything. "Our relationship became very close because we had nothing to do in the evenings and Harry slept in the day," said Janet Castro. "He came over on weeknights and often kept us up to four in the morning and always

brought more poetry and songs. Our productivity and relationships with family, work and friends were absolutely zilch for
those years. But we loved every minute of it."

The reason was not just Harry, but all the Chapins, since the
Castros had become part of the Chapin family, "sucked into their
energy, vibrancy and family things," said Janet, who was especially close to Elspeth and often "poured out our hearts to one
another." During summers, the Castros went to Andover, and the
Chapins celebrated Thanksgivings at the Castros' apartment.
There Elspeth cooked the turkey, Janet baked the pies, Tom made
the gravy and they all watched pro football games on television.
"It was like the Waltons," said Manny. "It was all very jovial and
noisy and hard to get a word in edgewise. It was the four Chapins, the two Hart boys, Elspeth and us."

Then in the evening, Harry, Tom and Steve often sang, followed by a competitive game of Monopoly. "The way they
played the game was completely wild," said Janet. "Everything
moved fast, and if you didn't immediately recognize that your
property was landed on, you lost it! The turns went so fast you
lost your chance to collect if somebody already rolled. It was
some uptight game of Monopoly."

The evenings Harry spent with the Castros added to his personal growth and change. He gained new perspectives on his
music. Gradually he shifted his songwriting from rudimentary
folk songs to quasi-folk songs and reflective, romantic mood
pieces. "But except for the Castros, most of the songs never saw
the light of day," said Harry. "None of the songs were very good."

As a songwriter, Harry had yet to discover the use of ironic
twist and self-deprecation in his lyrics. Much of his new material was written from the distressful stance of "I am wonderful.
The world would have no problems if it were filled with more
people like myself." For instance, in a song called "Dirty Old
Man," Harry pretended to be a cool, macho, middle-aged man
about town. It didn't carry much weight when sung by a fuzzy-
faced twenty-three-year-old.

The revitalized self-confidence and egotism present in his songs grew out of the Castros' worshipful praise and support. "I remember on the way out the door one night at three in the morning, I wanted him to sign a piece of paper about Ban-the-Bomb," said Janet. "But Harry said, 'I never sign anything. I might want to be president someday. It might be held against me.'"

The only song that survived the Castro period and was later recorded was "Any Old Kind of Day." Unlike the others, the song was both universal in appeal and an honest emotional interpretation of Harry's feelings.

"Any Old Kind of Day" triggered Harry into more successful songwriting and symbolically marked the beginning of a musical transformation. But there were many influences along the way, like Bob Dylan, who had given songwriters "the courage to write about anything." Though Harry never followed the Dylan "protest" mold, he admired him for his guts and songs, especially "Like a Rolling Stone," "Blowin' in the Wind," and "Mr. Tambourine Man," the latter partially influencing "Any Old Kind of Day" and his earlier song, "When Do You Find Time to Breathe?" Gradually, Harry began to take more risks in his songwriting and developed a greater social consciousness in tunes like "Give Me a Cause," "Give Me a Road," and "Give Me a Dream." Indeed, Harry was trying to find all of those things.

Said Janet Castro: "He had a thing that he was going to change people's lives. When Manny and I were having fights, Harry came by and mediated between the two of us. He always had a belief he could change people's lives. I think that was what he was trying to do with his music."

And the foundation of that music was his lyrics. Almost all of Harry's songs were originally poems, and when he had an idea for a poem he often wrote down the verse immediately. But if he was having trouble, he used a practical trick K.B. taught him. On one pad he wrote the verse. On a second pad he wrote in prose the basic idea he was trying to communicate and then compared the two to see if they matched. "A good song is like a well-brought-up child," K.B. once told him. "You sever the umbilical cord and send it out into the world with the reflections of the parent. But it also has its own personality and that's what has to communicate."

Though most of Harry's songs were complex lyrics set to simple melodies, even his melodic writing had grown. The chords became more richly varied, the inner structure of his music showed more melodic changes. Most of all, there were glimpses of success. When Janet Castro put together a children's festival at P.S. 307, one feature was a play performed by children. It was based on a study Janet had done concerning the natural behavior of children in school playgrounds. Harry wrote for the play a song called "Springtime Is for Growing," which he wove in and out of the entire performance. Tom and Steve joined Harry in the singing. "It was one of the most exciting pieces of work I've ever seen done in a city elementary school," said Trika Smith. "Of course, the principal got rid of it the following year."

Besides the Castros, Harry found other captive audiences in the women he dated, usually older women who were attracted to his strong, aggressive male ego and his guitar playing and poetry. There was something romantic about a masculine man with a boyish charm who played love songs. In addition to Trika Smith, Harry began seeing Gail Hollenborg, the Castro's niece, again. "Harry was a charming philanderer." said Gail. "He related to women as the aggressor, with them the passive person. And when you have an ego that aggressive, it stands to reason you'll have more women in your life than men." Harry visited Gail at her new apartment on Grace Court in Brooklyn Heights and, once again, the scene of performer and audience was repeated. Except now, Gail had gone through some changes of her own. During the year Harry had not seen her, she had married, divorced, and was now the mother of a baby girl. Harry's song "And the Baby Never Cries" was based on this relationship. "We were both basically using each other and yet giving each other something," said Harry. "It was just that sense of peace we gave each other in the middle of the night that was represented by the baby in the song."

Their relationship was primarily physical, one of noncommittal companions. And since Gail was forced to be at home taking care of her daughter, she was the perfect audience. "Harry didn't share the stage very well," recalled Gail. "It was convenient for him to have a place to bop into at eleven o'clock at night. He didn't make any demands on me. Neither of us wanted much from each other. He was rarely without his guitar. I lived in a very small apartment. It was calm, peaceful, and the turmoil created was his tiger. It was his excitement, his music, his poetry and his form, and at that time of my life, I was perfectly willing to be an audience."

Harry's drive and motivations, then, were solely inner-directed. He was wrapped up in his own personal growth, gratification and state of becoming. The problem was that it created hopelessly one-sided relationships. "Harry had an attention span of three minutes," said Gail. "I used to storm, 'Who wants to see your dumb poem? I've got something to say!' Also, at that point, Harry was constantly thinking about what he was saying and how he was saying it. My feeling was that the things he'd written until then were event-caused. I don't think he had a real sense of what he wanted to say yet."

Said Trika Smith: "He was into his own self and development, and part of that self was a very generous and sincere person. He could be a very sensual, warm person when he wanted to be. Even so, he couldn't give and take in a relationship. But he never made any bones about it. He'd say, 'Look, if you want to have a good time and come with me and this is the way I am, great!' I really believe he was very straight about the way he was. But when we were together, his whole egocentric thing very often prevented him from sharing. If I succeeded in something in my own career, that didn't make a difference to him."

Harry's insensitivity was due in part to the fear of being hurt, as he had been with Clare. So he hid his emotions and remained detached, feeling the need for several superficial relationships with women. "He was just not going to show his feelings with very many people," said Trika. "I doubt if he ever shared them with anybody except somebody he really trusted. There were moments when he relaxed, let down. But he was never the kind of person you could touch on the inside."

However, one woman did, and she later turned out to be his wife. Before Harry had gone to California, he had placed an ad in the *Brooklyn Heights Press* offering guitar lessons. During the time he was away, Elspeth received a phone call from a woman who was interested. When Harry returned from Los Angeles, Elspeth suggested he call her. Her name was Sandy Cashmore.

Sandy Cashmore was a bright, classy, shy woman in her early thirties, with hair color to match her first name. She came from a middle-class Episcopalian home in Newton, Massachusetts. Her maiden name was Gaston. She had one brother named Rocky. Her father was a salesman and distributor for U.S. Steel; her mother was a dilettante artist and freelance portrait painter.

An attractive woman of small build, Sandy was the mother of three children. She was trapped in an unhappy marriage. Her husband, Jim Cashmore, was a conservative, narrow-minded wheeler-dealer, an entrepreneur and wealthy attorney who owned a furniture and decorating firm on Wall Street. He also came from an affluent family; his father was Brooklyn borough president at the time.

Sandy's life revolved around her children and the brownstone apartment she shared with her husband on 14 Monroe Place in Brooklyn Heights. She was an obedient housewife and model mother. But, she had become tired of submission. After seven years of marriage, Sandy and Jim had grown hopelessly distant, communication ceased. While Sandy had become lonely and bored, Jim had become cold and brittle. He often verbally assaulted his wife and even physically assaulted his children, especially if they awoke him on weekend mornings. At such times, Cashmore tied them to their bed and beat them.

Said Sandy: "I had three little children and I had to have the kids out of the way before their father came home at night because he didn't want to acknowledge that he had them. I assumed that was it. He couldn't stand to see me touch them. My motherhood was threatening to him."

Jim Cashmore had become increasingly antisocial. All invitations from friends and other couples were turned down on his insistence. "He constantly made me call and say I was sick, or he called," said Sandy. "He just wasn't very comfortable with people. He was even beginning to get uncomfortable with his old prep-school buddies that he grew up with in Brooklyn, who were mostly the people we got to see. I guess it was all pretty satisfactory to him and I generally obeyed him."

Deep in personal crisis, Sandy began to question the way she lived and the values of the people around her. The lack of friends was one serious problem she was forced to confront. Over the years, she had grown used to the idea that couples made friends with other couples, but now social occasions became events. The one couple Cashmore, in his possessiveness, allowed her to see were personal friends of his who lived nearby. "But I knew it wasn't going to be *me* being friendly with them," Sandy said. "For instance, they had a photography hobby, and I started to realize that sure, they had a photography hobby, but they never took pictures. They collected equipment. They had all the latest lenses from Europe and around the world. It was bullshit to me. It was a whole class of people or life I was alienated from."

In order to live with Jim, then, Sandy became someone she wasn't, someone she hated. She was a self-described "city society matron" who, for too long, had been preoccupied with materialistic splendor. She shopped at the finest stores: her shoes came from Henri Bendel, her clothing from Bergdorf Goodman, and her smile from Saks Fifth Avenue's cosmetic department.

She had creative impulses but she repressed them. She loved poetry, for instance, but was forced to become a "closet poet" because Jim didn't approve.

"He didn't approve of much of anything when it came right down to it," said Sandy. "I guess he was threatened. I think he was very seriously threatened by me in general. Every book I read he attacked. If I was reading a book by James Baldwin, he said I was on a black kick. If I was reading another book, I was on another kick. It was sick."

Suddenly the distance between who she was and what she wanted to be became more apparent. "I wanted to live a more honest life," said Sandy. "I wanted to express myself. I was the model housewife and mother; the prettiest, neatest, best-dressed, cutesy-pie thing that ever walked down a street in Brooklyn Heights. Everybody sort of admired me and I was a little sick of that. Not that I wanted to go to another extreme. I just wanted to be less of a fake."

Isolated from most adult contact, she made her children her life. With them she became immersed in the creative expression she wanted for herself. She did lots of arts and crafts projects and looked more seriously at an idea she had thought about for years: to learn folk guitar so she could sing songs with her children.

"But since I wasn't musical, I felt limited," said Sandy. "I played piano somewhat. But there was the problem of having to sit with your back to them, and that was a period for guitar anyway. My feeling was you could sit in a circle and play folk songs. I didn't think of it because I had any talent to develop. It was just something fun to do."

In search of a guitar teacher, Sandy asked friends, who gave her Harry's number. When she called, Elspeth told her "he was making a film on the West Coast" and was supposed "to be out there for a year or two." With this, the search ended, guitar lessons forgotten.

"Then," said Sandy, "I got a call from Harry out of the blue. It was six months later. 'I understand you need a guitar teacher,' he said, and then he went into his mild lecture. 'I really enjoy the guitar and I'd love to teach. But I take this very seriously and if you're not going to work hard and think of it as something important, I won't be able to keep coming.' "

Harry did keep coming, but he wasn't very reliable. Sometimes he called to say he couldn't make it. Sometimes he showed up. And other times, without calling, he didn't show up at all.

Even so, the pressure to practice was a welcome change for Sandy. She was happy to have purpose in something someone else took seriously and for the creative push she could not manage alone. As songs to learn, she chose two for her children, "Skip to My Lou," "The Fox" and two for herself, "Blowin' in the Wind" and a Joan Baez song. "Harry tried to get me to sing them," said Sandy. "Guitar lessons became singing lessons and that really finished me. I couldn't even sing "Jingle Bells." So I whispered along off-key and he would say, 'You've got to bellow it out!' "

Sandy tried and failed and Harry lectured, "Now wait! What you've got there is a noisemaker. Anybody who picks up a guitar is, by definition, wanting to make noise to attract other people. If you want to learn to sing songs with your guitar, you're going to have to learn to project!"

After the lesson was a concert period. Harry would ask Sandy if she'd like to hear a song of his, get carried away, and for the next two hours, sing his entire collection. To avoid conflict with her husband, Sandy planned the guitar lessons on the same nights Cashmore had his poker parties in the downstairs den. "It must have been really funny," said Sandy. "Because when Harry sang his songs, he didn't just sing them, he bellowed them."

In a ballad Harry late wrote called "I Wanna Learn a Love Song," he recounted almost exactly what occurred during those lessons. It was originally titled "Teach Me a Simple Song" and was as autobiographical as any song he ever wrote.

Gradually something developed between them that was more than just a guitar teacher-pupil relationship. Harry seemed almost a savior to Sandy and her isolated life on 14 Monroe Place. His youthful enthusiasm, energy and creativity were all the things Cashmore was not. As the weeks went by, Harry began to see more and more of her problems and he sympathized with her. To him, Cashmore represented another version of Henry Hart: autocratic, overbearing, villainlike. And his sympathy was not just for Sandy, but also for her children, innocent victims of Cashmore's wrath. With each visit, scenes with Henry Hart popped into his head.

More than anything else, Sandy was captivated by the romantic picture Harry created of his family, whom he often spoke of during lessons. It reminded her of another family in the neighborhood, the Kastendiecks, and specifically Mrs. Kastendieck, who was heavily involved in the community and her children. Sandy identified with her, and the clannish creativity of the Chapins reinforced that identification.

"Sandy fell in love with my family before she fell in love with me," said Harry. "I always got into philosophy, and we started talking about families and I described how I had this big, roaring, artistic family and Jim Cashmore was such a tight-fisted, tight-assed, frightened guy. This seemed like a whole different world to her."

Said Sandy: "It seemed ideal. I wished I were a second cousin in that family. I wanted that environment of artists and writers and the togetherness."

With each lesson, Harry grew fonder of Sandy and afterward headed straight to the Castros' to deliver the latest developments. "He said the husband was playing poker downstairs while she was in another room trying to find her identity and do her own thing," said Janet. "He was worried about making too much noise and kept saying to us, 'I think she's interested in something more than guitar lessons.' At first Harry said she was cute, and after more lessons, he came back and reported that she 'made a suggestive statement' or 'we touched hands' or 'we were sitting closer together.' He said, 'This is wild. I'm going out of my mind. I'm getting very fond of this lady.'"

But there was never any overt acknowledgement of their deep and mutual feelings. Instead, they both played subtle games. Harry usually sang with his eyes closed, but one time, while singing a love song, he looked directly into her eyes and said, "Don't worry if I look at you, because the song doesn't mean anything unless I look you in the eye." Another time, Harry chattered on about how well he got along with older women, when Sandy half in jest said, "I guess that's why I love you."

Sandy, in fact, was eight years older than Harry, so he often bragged of his exploits with other women, desperately trying to impress her with his carnal knowledge and veteranship. "He gave me intimate details about every girl he ever knew," said Sandy. "He loved to talk about other girls; what he did with them, to them, and so forth. At the same time, he didn't say anything about what he did Tuesday night. There were different games, different times. But they didn't necessarily click."

After weeks of this, Harry came to the front door for a lesson and Sandy, bursting with joy, rushed down the long, dark foyer like a schoolgirl in a crush, her arms outstretched and raised as if to hug him. "Then I realized, 'Hey, what am I doing?'" said Sandy, and she quickly composed herself and invited him in.

Thoughts of divorce had been brewing in Sandy's mind for a long time. It always seemed far too serious a step, but it was inevitable. During previous summers, Jim and Sandy had been apart for extended periods of time. Sandy's custom was to visit her parents at their summer home in Gloucester, Massachusetts. In addition, Sandy had been seeing a marriage counselor for months, not to patch up her "lost cause," but rather to find an out, the strength of a rationalization to leave him. "I wanted the marriage to end with the least amount of criticism," said Sandy. "I guess I wanted to convince myself and others I really tried to work it out."

But she was frightened. She wanted her freedom, but was embarrassed and threatened by all its implications of personal failure. She had never known anyone to get a divorce. Coming from a basically peaceful and happy home, she knew her parents would disapprove of any such move, especially her mother, who wanted to see her secure. Jim Cashmore, after all, was a well-to-do, solid citizen. Then there were the children and the guilt that might adversely affect their lives. Much of her reticence had to do with the times. In 1966, divorce had yet to become fashionable. Couples often stayed together, sometimes for the worst reasons, usually the children.

Still, with much trepidation, Sandy decided to go ahead with it unbeknownst to anyone, including Harry, although he was the key factor. On all levels, Harry, and particularly his family, represented an obvious contrast to her own sheltered life. That entangled maze of Burkes, Chapins, Leacocks and Housekeepers gave Sandy the knowledge and subsequent courage to accept divorce as a natural part of life. "I realized that just about everybody in his family was from a broken home," said Sandy. "Nobody ever stayed together. It was the weirdest conglomeration of people—all these kids, pieces and parts, incest and adultery, black and white, lesbians—they were all misfits. I was a misfit only in that I was more conservative. But Harry seemed pretty together to me. He was an all-American-boy kind of person."

By the spring of 1966, Sandy cemented her plans. Her husband had made arrangements to rent a beach bungalow for the summer in Point Lookout, a small town on the south shore of Long Island. Sandy decided she would make her move then. "The children wouldn't notice and wouldn't have to talk to the neighbors because everybody knew we went away for the summer," she said. "I'd tell my husband, who came out on weekends, not to bother and it would all fall apart quietly because I wasn't very good at confronting things in those days. I was much better at drifting."

In May, Jim and Sandy left on a three-week vacation to Jamaica and, upon her return, Harry inquired about further guitar lessons, but she declined. Very casually, she thanked him. She

said goodbye and left for the summer to Point Lookout with her
children . . . with plans of marital separation secretly in mind.

* * *

While Harry saw the Castros, Gail and Trika at night, he began
working days at a film company in Manhattan for $185 a week.
In March 1966, an ad appeared in the *New York Times* for a film
editor. At the time, Harry did little more than sleep, write poetry
and give guitar lessons, so Elspeth, concerned with her son's
aimlessness, saw the ad and suggested he apply for the job.

"I interviewed Harry and was very impressed by him," said
Bill Cayton, the owner of the film company, who later became
the boxing manager of heavyweight champion Mike Tyson. "He
didn't have as much editing experience as the other applicants.
But Harry had a verb with him."

The company, Big Fights Inc., was one of several small companies under the ownership umbrella of Cayton, and all were located
at 9 East 40th Street. Except for Cayton Inc., which was an advertising agency, most of the companies were involved with the production of fight films. For instance, under Big Fights Inc., Cayton
owned two companies and Harry worked for both. One was called
Turn of the Century Fights Inc., which produced five-minute
knockout shows, and the other was Greatest Fights of the Century
Inc., which produced fifteen-minute fight films in a series called
The Greatest Fights of the Century. Harry was involved with the
production, writing and editing of the films. He remained there for
nearly two years completing more than 200 five-minute knockout
films and forty-five Greatest Fights of the Century segments.

Harry's new job was considerably different from Drew Associates or the freelancing he had done for Jim Lipscomb. Big
Fights Inc. was a library film company and rarely shot on-location
in the cinema verité style Harry was used to. Instead, he com-
piled and edited new films from old film stock, and there was
plenty of it. Harry worked closely with boxing expert and champion handball player Jim Jacobs, whom *Sports Illustrated* once
touted as "the greatest athlete in the United States," and who,

along with Cayton, owned and controlled all of the major fight films in the world, well over 16,000. But for Harry, the work was more mechanical than creative. "It wasn't very swashbuckling," Harry said. "It was very logistical. Churn out the product. It wasn't quality-controlled stuff. The knockouts you just churned out. They were syndicated for television. It was almost like a presold product rather than cinema verité, which was a very exciting, very alive form of filmmaking."

At the same time, returning to Drew Associates was not the answer either. Beyond being an editor or soundman, there were very limited opportunities to advance at Drew, and Jim Lipscomb was not involved with a project. "He couldn't make the logical step to become a producer as I was and do films," said Lipscomb. "We didn't have that many going on and, in order to do that, he had to plug for treatments, get the money—which wouldn't have been easy with Bob Drew. Besides, he was a bit young to walk into a network or sponsor's office and say, 'I'm Harry Chapin and I want to produce this short for you.' What were his credits? Editor?"

At Big Fights Inc., though it was still an editor's job, at least Harry had a title and besides, he needed the money. He wanted to get his own apartment and move out of his mother's place. After working for three months, he saved up enough to rent a small apartment in a rent-controlled building at 81 Columbia Heights, just a few blocks away from Elspeth.

But by this time, Harry found his job intolerable. He couldn't adjust to a nine-to-five work schedule and felt trapped and bored in an office environment. He was not the kind to preplan, write lists and organize his days. He saw himself as an artist, independent and free to live his life as he chose. He continued to stay up to all hours of the night and frequently arrived at work late. "I hated the job," said Harry. "I was ready to quit every week."

At twenty-three, Harry was both conventional and antiestablishment in his values and appearance. In his imagination, the creative lifestyle of his grandfathers was the ideal way to live, yet establishment values dictated the necessity of fitting into certain status quo molds. "Harry was bitter about having to fit into those molds," said Janet Castro. "He was against the establishment because he couldn't express himself that way. It stifled his creativity. He was such a dynamo and so full of electricity he couldn't be contained in an office or school or anything else."

Even so, Harry was basically straight. Though he dressed in jeans, he kept his curly brown hair short- to medium-length. He did not smoke, drink or indulge in drugs. "He told us countless times that he was high on life," said Manny Castro. "And he was! He wouldn't put you down. He had orange juice while we all drank booze."

Said Lipscomb: "I don't think he was ever attracted by hippiedom. He probably smoked pot from time to time, but it was never a big thing in his life. He never gave a damn about it. I don't think Harry ever drank. If he had two highballs, he was drunk. He didn't want that kind of exhilaration. He had too much going already."

For the most part, Harry was also apolitical. Despite the disruptive social issues which altered the face of America during the sixties—the Vietnam War, civil rights, campus unrest, women's lib and the sexual revolution—Harry remained basically unaffected and so did his music. "He never went on marches or anything like that," said Lipscomb, who attended the first antiwar rally in Washington. "Harry was really taking society as it stood and trying to succeed in it with his music."

Nevertheless, Harry's unorthodox work hours frequently got him in heated tussles with Cayton. Cayton's companies employed about twenty-five people and he felt Harry's lack of discipline set a bad example for others. But Harry felt as long as he did his work, office protocol be damned! "He thought of Bill Cayton as his stepfather," said Sandy once. "He had a lot of trouble with authorities anyway and he didn't think anybody should tell him what time he should show up and what time he should leave. He felt that he could just put in his hours, like at Drew Associates, and do it on his own."

Cayton came from the era of hard work and hard knocks. He was the Protestant work ethic personified. He had started his business during the Depression, when jobs and dreams were scarce. He was a sharp, shrewd merchandiser who, besides his fight film and advertising businesses, bought and sold third-rate cartoons after finding some clever way to repackage them. "The whole construction of Bill's personality was to work hard and save," said Jacobs. "Cayton set the rules, signed the checks and insisted everyone be in by nine o'clock."

Harry almost never was.

Jacobs explained: "Our interpretation of working with Harry all day was about six hours. Harry was not a nine-o'clock guy. He was one of those unique people that came in at ten, worked 'til three-thirty and got everything accomplished infinitely better than the guy who worked from nine to five-thirty. He had a definable ability to get to the heart of the matter. Whether it was something as inane as a fight film or something as subtle as getting the character in a musical phrase, Harry always got to the heart of the problem. And if he channeled all his physical and mental energies in one direction, there was an enormous amount of activity and accomplishment."

When Harry was not at work on time, he was summoned to Cayton's upstairs office.

"Harry, you've got to get in at nine o'clock. When you came here, I told you the hours were from nine to five-thirty, and you accepted the responsibility to accept the position and you accept the paychecks. You've got to get in at nine because everyone else does. It looks bad when . . ."

Without argument or excuse, Harry shrugged his shoulders and calmly stated his case. "But what you're paying me for is to get a job done."

"I know, but you disrupt the office and you're setting a bad example."

"Yeah, but in another sense I set a great example of getting a tremendous amount of work done."

Each had a valid argument, but Harry was forced to compromise. After three or four days of obedience, Harry came in at ten-thirty again. He was fired. Two weeks later he was rehired, mostly because of Jacobs, who acted as a buffer between the two volatile, strong-willed personalities. He was also a go-between who relayed messages from Bill upstairs to Harry below. Jacobs adored Harry, "applauded him in many ways," according to Cayton, and gave him both moral and political support. "Harry had a delicious personality," recalled Jacobs. "He was contagious. He always believed that a kind word and a smart one were infinitely better than the opposite. In New York, where the veneer of civilization has worn very thin and people are angry and abrasive most of the time, Harry was a complete and errant departure. If he had a choice of looking for the good or the bad, he instinctively searched out the good."

Over the course of two years, Harry was periodically fired and rehired at least four times. His behavior was expendable; his work was not. In fact, Harry was the most productive and creative employee, far better than the union people Cayton was used to hiring, and Cayton knew it. "I was impressed with his talent," Cayton said.

In some ways, Harry's unhappiness at Big Fights represented his rejection of establishment conventions. In his run-ins with Cayton, Harry once said that he was "almost begging to be fired." He wanted to stand up and be counted. His was not just a defiance of authority but a way of distinguishing himself from the other employees by getting attention, even if it was negative attention. He felt "disenfranchised" from that vast mass of people in that work-sleep-work rut. . . . There had to be something more. "Day-to-day life situations are not set up for growth, but to feel comfortable in not growing," said Harry. "That scared me. I tried to see myself as someone unique with all my big dreams. But I realized that for swords we used ballpoint pens, and armor was cotton. And in a sense, the whole world seemed so separate from those nice clear-cut heroic encounters the cowboys had and the pioneers had and in my film work, the boxers had."

Harry tried to see himself as a "behind-the-scenes/mastermind type," but his gut instincts rejected that self-image. He wanted to be in front of the camera, waving to fans, envied and admired. He wanted to be a participant in life, not an observer. Much of his poetry at this time and story songs later hinged on that participant-observer question. In the fight films he edited into short stories, boxers were winning or losing but always participating in their own glorified self-dramatization. There were the exchanges of heavyweight titles and they emitted on celluloid the raw passion and emotion that he wished his own sterile life could claim. These were men whose livelihoods were earned feeling the push and pulse of adrenalin and in the thrill of heroic encounter; violence, sweat, blood, broken jaws—what better proof of existence? Just one scene, one splice of film, seemed far closer to the real substance of life than the totality of any nine-to-five editor's job. Harry wanted a piece of that self-drama for himself because he wanted to be a winner. Many times he felt the desperate urge to jump into the ring, knock out his celluloid challenger and be carried off on the shoulders of cheering crowds.

He actually got his chance once, but with far different results. Boxing manager Cus D'Amato was training "The Blimp," Buster Mathis, to fight Joe Frazier for the heavyweight championship, and Jacobs and Harry went to the training camp to film. Then-Yankee pitcher Jim Bouton, a good friend of Jacobs', went with them. For kicks during the filming, Bouton and Chapin got into the ring for a couple of rounds. "I remember Harry had no form whatsoever," said Bouton. "He had a windmill kind of style. He figured if he just pumped his arms quick, nothing bad could happen to him."

Said Harry: "For the first minute I felt pretty good, but at the end of the second minute I could barely keep my hands up. By two and a half minutes, Bouton was virtually hitting me at will. I suddenly realized how tiring it was just holding your fists up."

The polarity and pathos of ordinary people fighting for themselves, winning or losing in their own lives, later became an oft-recurring theme in his story songs. In his poem "Chauvinist

Prayer," also written during this period, Harry used the metaphor of the thoroughbred racehorse to illustrate his subliminal need for personal exhilaration and a taste of something larger than himself when he wrote: "But still to ride her, just once, in the Derby!"

For Harry, complacency could very well have set in, only he was a creature of enthusiasm, not habit. His catlike curiosity meant he was a jack-of-all-trades, a creative dabbler who always juggled a new song, poem, or project in his head. He wanted too much too quickly, and neither his job nor anyone or anything was going to stop him. "Harry had a fertile imagination," said Jacobs, whose friendship was the only positive part of Harry's stay at Cayton. "He wanted to produce a musical and people told him it couldn't be done. Once he said to me, 'You know, Jim, when someone tells me something can't be done, what they're really saying is that they can't do it. That doesn't mean I can't.'"

Even when socializing, Harry's mind remained preoccupied. Often he and Jacobs played handball or basketball at the 92nd Street YMHA. But always Harry brought with him a brown clipboard and pad of paper to scribble sudden ideas for songs or poems he was afraid might escape. "I always used to tease him about that," recalled Jacobs. "So many times he had that clipboard when it seemed inappropriate. We'd go to dinner, a movie, or to play basketball and he'd always have his clipboard."

"On it were all the things he was working on," said Cayton. "All these irons he had in the fire. But I can assure you, what was not on the clipboard was his film work."

Harry also socialized a great deal with Jim Lipscomb, but even with him he was preoccupied. For instance, during the summers of 1966 and 1967, Harry and Jim did a lot of sailing on a seventeen-foot Thistle sailboat. On weekends they entered regattas along the East Coast, anywhere from Boston to Maryland. The regattas usually lasted two days with two races on Saturday, a big party Saturday night, and a final race on Sunday, after which trophies were presented. At the parties, Harry became famous for his singing and guitar playing. Since half of the sailors just wanted to drink and talk, Harry gathered the other half for sing-alongs, finding a quiet corner or some empty room at the yacht club.

Though Harry and Jim were amateur sailors, they rapidly improved as a team. They entered the Thistle class, which offered stiff competition since it attracted some of the finest sailors around. Gradually they began to place and show at the regattas and eventually won a shelfful of trophies together. "Finally, we came up to the district championship, which was sailed at Nyack on the Hudson River, and my home club," said Jim. "We'd been sort of pointing to this the whole year. The first race came, and five minutes beforehand, Harry wasn't there. So I grabbed a kid off the dock and I sailed the race. I came in thinking, 'Well, Harry missed the first race. He'll be here for the second one.'"

Harry wasn't there. So Jim sailed the second race.

"That night," said Jim, "I thought, 'Well, Jesus, what happened to Harry? Maybe he got hurt or something.' I couldn't imagine him just not showing. 'He'll call,' I thought."

Harry never called.

Sunday afternoon, Jim finished the race and regatta and came in an astounding second place. But he was incensed. Where was Harry? Jim was convinced he could have won the district championship if Harry had been there.

Four days later, Jim finally met up with him. "Where were you?" he asked indignantly. "I can't believe you'd just drop me like that!"

Perfectly calm, without argument or excuse, Harry replied, "Oh, I couldn't make it."

Said Lipscomb: "There's a key to Harry there. He was very enthusiastic about sailing. He loved the competition. He wanted to be in the first crew and everything else. But at the same time, it wasn't his game. When something else happened, he was off. Maybe he was writing songs that week, or his brothers were into something. If sailing got in the way, or the friendship with Lipscomb, and the fact that he had been planning toward this race, well, the other was more important and he just forgot."

In his own mind, Harry assumed Jim would understand. Harry never realized how much that race meant to Jim. In music as well as with individuals, learning to be responsive to the needs of an audience was something he had yet to master.

* * *

Two weeks after Sandy left for Point Lookout, Harry called her at the Brooklyn Heights address. He spoke to the maid who was still coming to take care of the house, and she gave him the number at 31 Beach Street. But within weeks, major changes had taken place in Sandy's life. Her divorce plans had not worked as she had hoped. The first weekend Cashmore came out, Sandy confronted him with her intentions. Cashmore was livid. He responded by attacking her own vulnerable spot, the children, threatening to get custody of them if she left him. "Since his father was Brooklyn borough president and appointed all the judges, that seemed like a pretty valid threat," said Sandy.

In addition, Cashmore pressured her to meet him occasionally in the city, to have dinner and talk things over. But as far as she was concerned, the marriage was dead and she had already hired an attorney.

Despite the new developments, Sandy told Harry nothing. When he called, she just said she'd be in the city every couple of weeks and that they could see each other then. "I still didn't tell him I was getting separated because I had a feeling of being a scarlet woman," said Sandy. "I felt embarrassed. I didn't want him to think I had fallen in love with him and I was trying to get out of the marriage or something. We didn't talk about any of those things. We were just buddies."

And they were. Both had common interests: movies, music and poetry. But more importantly, Harry's unchanging, cheerful exterior was the perfect complement to Sandy's downtrodden interior. His boundless energy infused itself into her, recharging her with courage and confidence, anesthetizing her guilt. "He had a pretty cavalier attitude because of his own family," said Sandy. "He'd say, 'If something doesn't feel good, you don't do it anymore.' He had too much of that kind of attitude, I thought. It was mostly in the way he talked, moralistic. His attitude was very Epicurean, self-indulgent, instant gratification. He'd say, 'You only do things that feel good as long as they feel good.' That was his line. He had a lot of lines. He was really an incredible bullshit artist."

With Harry, Sandy momentarily forgot her problems and escaped to other worlds, worlds she missed in her marriage, worlds of dialogue and discussion. Theirs was a conversational relationship, cultural and nourishing. On their first date, they went to see *Doctor Zhivago,* a film Sandy always wanted to see that Cashmore didn't. They often went to movies and afterward spent hours rehashing and analyzing plot lines and characters in cozy corner cafes or late-night coffee shops. At Sandy's suggestion, they signed up for the YMHA Poetry Series at 92nd Street and frequently attended poetry readings. Gradually, Sandy discovered the intellectual and creative stimuli her curiosity craved, and finally met the family that had motivated Harry. One Saturday afternoon, the brothers and their father performed a concert on the ground floor of Gimbels department store on 34th Street. Elspeth was there along with Manja and her children.

As friends and intellectual companions, Harry and Sandy began to see each other regularly. The poetry readings were scheduled every two weeks and Cashmore had arranged for Sandy to see a psychiatrist in Manhattan, in addition to the marriage counselor. Though Jim Cashmore paid for both, he didn't take "this whole divorce business" seriously, according to Sandy. He figured Sandy was on another of her kicks and saw no reason to see the marriage counselor himself. However, Sandy did, mainly to keep her children, but also for herself. She was still searching for the "strength of rationalization to leave him."

Soon Sandy found that strength in Harry. He was her only ally and she eventually told him what was transpiring. He gave her the courage and impetus to go ahead with the divorce by giving her good feelings about herself and injecting her weakened self-image with his own youthful idealism and self-confidence. "He tended to build me up," said Sandy. "He thought I was pretty stupid to even be deliberating."

Harry and Sandy often visited Janet Castro. "She never would have divorced Cashmore without Harry," Janet said. "She'd still be married to him. Harry built up her self-confidence and supported her ego. He was able to do that with people. Despite his own enormous ego, he was terrifically able to make you believe in yourself. In a way, it was almost like he wanted to relive the Henry years by rescuing Sandy. The way he would've liked to have rescued his mother and brothers from Henry."

When they weren't together, Sandy reverted back to a state of self-shame, inferiority and fear. Though they exchanged poetry through the mail and periodically telephoned each other, talking for hours, it wasn't enough. Days between dates were difficult. Without Harry's daily presence, Sandy felt pressured and intimidated. After dinner meetings with Cashmore, she suffered unbearable guilt feelings. And during one session with the psychiatrist, after admitting she was seeing someone eight years younger, the psychiatrist replied, "So why do you think he wants you to be his mother?" Another time, Mrs. Kastendieck, whom Sandy always admired, took her out to lunch and questioned her about whether she was serious about "ruining the lives of her children." Even her lawyer did not ease matters. At the time, the only grounds for divorce in New York State were adultery. The lawyer, taking Cashmore's connections and cunning into consideration, advised Sandy to "be careful not to be seen with other men," and if eating lunch in public, "make sure at least three people are at the table."

"I thought that was nonsense," said Sandy. "Harry thought it was a bunch of bullshit."

Not surprisingly, all the negative influences caused Sandy overwhelming emotional strain. After being with Harry, she felt wonderfully revitalized, put back together and ready for battle. But on Friday nights, after seeing Cashmore or the marriage counselor, she walked out in a state of devastation that lasted for three days. "Then on Monday I had my meeting with the psychiatrist," said Sandy, "and by that time, I was absolutely carved up in pieces. If I spoke to Harry on Monday night, it got to the point where he'd say: 'You know, I'm really beginning to wonder about you. Which would you rather do, see me and hear how wonderful you are, or see the psychiatrist and Jim and hear how shitty you are?'"

Near summer's end, Cashmore finally took Sandy seriously. His halfhearted attempts at reconciliation had backfired. He joined Sandy for a few sessions with the marriage counselor, but it was too late—her mind was made up. Cashmore pressed harder, this time cutting off all financial support. That tactic failed too. Though Sandy was broke, the beach house in Point Lookout had been paid for through the summer, and by fall, she had managed to produce some income, about $70 per week.

"I had met somebody in town who started a business and I did dressmaking," said Sandy. "I designed and made sample dresses that were sold in a shop on Third Avenue. I worked hard. After I put the kids to bed I used to stay up until four o'clock in the morning with my little sewing machine. If Harry asked me out, sometimes I had to postpone the date a couple of days so I could finish my work and make enough money."

Sandy's financial salvation came in the form of her landlady, Rosemary Gomez. Sandy asked Mrs. Gomez if she could keep the house through the winter at $90 per month. But Mrs. Gomez thought she meant for weekends only. "She was making her assumptions and I was making mine," said Sandy, who was too embarrassed to tell her about the separation. Finally, when Mrs. Gomez discovered she lived there all the time, Sandy was forced to reveal her secret. And Mrs. Gomez, out of sympathy for her plight, seeing her raise three children alone, kept the rent at $90. "She really saved my life," said Sandy.

Point Lookout, though, was very Peyton Place, and that added to Sandy's sense of shame. It was a small, conservative, Catholic community, four blocks by nine blocks, located on a jutting peninsula on the Atlantic. "It was a town where you couldn't spit without having it in the village paper," said Sandy. "So I maintained the myth that my husband came out on weekends. I was partly threatened that I'd appear outrageous and the men around town might start bothering me. So I pretended I was still married. I'd go to the supermarket and someone would ask, 'I haven't seen your husband for a while.' I'd say, 'Oh, he just commutes on weekends.'"

Sandy's primary concern was for her children, who naturally needed a "daddy identification." She didn't want a parade of men in the house, afraid the children might latch on to one as their father. This included Harry, particularly because of their age difference. She promised herself she would not see him more than once a week, and only in Manhattan. "I really laid a heavy trip on myself about having made the dumb marriage, that I had been immature and stupid," said Sandy. "I didn't think too highly of myself in making decisions. I saw myself as a relatively young mother with three kids. I didn't play that I was a gay divorcée or wild young hippy and go to singles bars, run around, drink, or smoke pot. Basically, all I did was take care of my children. I led a very quiet, rather lonely, serious life."

Harry did finally come out one evening, but he, too, was concerned about falling in love with a woman so much older. "I remember walking on the beach and singing, which was pretty funny in itself," said Sandy of that night. "And then, at one point, we flopped down on the sand and he said, 'Goddamn all those birthday cakes!'"

Despite Sandy's refusal, Harry constantly tried to push and relate to her children, Jamie, Jonathan and Jason. He finally said to her, 'Well, if we're gonna get married someday, don't you think I should get to know the kids?'"

That wasn't a proposal, but in January 1967, less than one year after they met, Harry did formally propose, no matter how prematurely. Neither was prepared to handle the emotional implications of marriage and its potential consequences, Sandy for fear of making another "dumb marriage" and Harry for fear of the responsibility involved. How was he going to support a woman with three children? Still, he went ahead talking confidently of their future, at the same time terrified of the thought. They were both terrified, but they could not deny they loved each other. They decided to speed up the divorce proceedings, hedging just the same.

"Harry tended to plunge into things and think about them after," said Sandy. "At that point, I decided I really would've liked to marry him and that I was madly, insanely in love with him. But it made no sense at all. And I kept saying to myself, 'I hope it'll wear off.' I was too helpless just to break it off."

Finally the divorce settlement came through. Sandy's marriage was officially annulled and she began receiving alimony. For Cashmore, it was a crushing psychological defeat on all levels. He deteriorated. He never remarried. He became an alcoholic and gambler, spending most of his time racing horses, and developed emphysema from cigarette smoking. Ten years later, at the age of forty-four, his liver exploded. He died.

With the settlement money and some stock she owned, Sandy decided to buy a small house rather than pay rent. She had just enough to make a down payment on a cottagelike white stucco house at 69 Cedarhurst Drive in Point Lookout. Gradually, Harry began living with Sandy for days on end, commuting to and from work on the Long Island Railroad. Even so, the idea of living together permanently was never discussed. Sandy couldn't handle the emotional responsibility for herself or her children, and neither could Harry. "If he had said, 'Let's live together,' I would have said no," recalled Sandy. "I wouldn't have been able to confront that responsibility. But since he never left to go back to his apartment every night, I never thought of it, even if it happened four or five nights in a row; because he had his apartment and I had my little house."

Meanwhile, Trika Smith thought she was going to marry Harry. Trika knew nothing about Sandy and Sandy knew little of her. "The story about Trika was always that he was Fred Kewley's girlfriend and Fred was in [South] Korea and Harry was just kind of seeing an old friend's friend," said Sandy. "Harry lied like that."

What Sandy didn't know at the time was that Harry had intimated marriage to Trika also, and was essentially leading both women down the primrose path of marital bliss. He saw Trika on those nights he stayed at his Brooklyn Heights apartment. "It seemed Trika had originally been engaged to someone else while dating Fred Kewley," said brother James. "Then Harry got into a competitive situation with Fred and ended up taking Trika away from her fiancé, basically suggesting they were going to get married."

In many ways, Harry's relationship with Trika was similar to the one he had with Sandy. On dates they went to movies, the 92nd Street Y for poetry readings, and basically retraced old footsteps he forged with Sandy. And like Sandy, Trika had personal problems that were temporarily forgotten in the boundless whirl of Harry's compulsive cheerfulness. Trika's mother was dying of cancer, and dates with Harry became an escape from her emotional situation.

Trika seemed perfect for Harry, the logical choice for marriage. "Trika made terribly good sense," said Sandy years later. "He was a filmmaker but wanted to be a freelance writer, and she was an heiress. She was all the right things. She was the same age, single, free and was mad about him in a giddy way, worshipful in a sense. I was more critical, and trying to offer something serious, because it was an intellectual relationship. I wasn't gaga. If Harry showed me a poem and I didn't think it was very good, I told him so."

But for Harry there was no comparison. Sandy was *the* one. Though she was older, with three children and no money, Sandy was able to penetrate Harry's covers. She saw right through his lines and lyrics and tamed his reckless energy. She embodied a combination of qualities possessed by all the women he ever loved. She had Clare's passion, Jenny's maternal nature, and Elspeth's patience. Also like Elspeth, she was a good listener. She was supportive of Harry's ego, much as his grandmothers were with his grandfathers. "He perceived the ideal woman as a nurturing earth mother," said one girlfriend. "Noncompetitive and supportive of the genius ego."

The differences in their personalities also acted as perfect complements. While Harry was noisy and abrupt, Sandy was quiet and subtle. Her words came out slowly, precisely, and she possessed an educated thoughtfulness, while Harry talked in rambling torrents and was quick to make judgments without thinking. She was introverted and shy, which combined well with his outgoing, action-oriented personality. But having raised three children, she knew how to control and manipulate that side of him and pacify his thrashing hyperactivity.

"Sandy was the first woman who encompassed all of me," said Harry. "She kept impressing me with how she could always go deeper and have more life, love, understanding and wisdom. She energized me."

Despite Harry's emotional allegiance to Sandy, he continued seeing Trika until both women finally met each other at Bob Mullevaney's wedding in New Jersey. Harry forgot he had invited both of them. The outcome was predictable. "Trika was totally miserable," recalled James. "I remember dancing with her, and she was bitter and upset seeing Harry with another woman."

Sandy was bitter, too, and felt Harry was leading Trika on by suggesting commitments he had no intention of fulfilling.

"I didn't want to face the responsibility of making a decision," said Harry.

But in a sense, Sandy already had, and she was condemned for it. Her mother couldn't understand why she would divorce a successful man like Jim Cashmore and fool around with a young folksinger/filmmaker who had no money, no career and, as far as she was concerned, no future.

"Elspeth felt that, too," said Manny Castro. "She said to Harry, 'What are you fooling around with music for?' And K.B. also said, 'Why don't you settle down and become a physicist?' Harry didn't get too much encouragement from his own family. Elspeth thought music was just a passing fancy. She thought it was some foolishness he'd get over, then come back down to reality sooner or later. K.B. pooh-poohed the whole singing business. And they were the two people closest to him."

CHAPTER VI

Mr. Tanner

By 1967, Harry's storytelling style of writing began to emerge. Many of the poems he wrote at this time eventually developed into the story songs he later became famous for. Though he himself admitted he "wasn't consciously thinking of story songs," his poetry began to show a narrative flow and a linear sense of progression, including plot lines, climax and, finally, a denouement or punch line to bring it together. Much in the tradition of the O. Henry short story, his poems possessed a circular structure. He'd begin with a premise and wrap it up at the end, full circle, the moral of the story hanging on the last word of the last line.

One key influence was the cinema-verité documentaries Harry had done with Jim Lipscomb at Drew Associates. There, as a film editor, he had to find interesting characters going through compelling situations where something was at stake. Like a journalist who gathers facts to write a column, Harry had to create a cohesive and coherent story from bits and pieces of film. He had to cut the negatives, line up the sound and the genius of the job: know when to enter and exit a scene.

But perhaps his most practical experience came at Big Fights editing five- and fifteen-minute fight films. He had to dramatize the adventures of fighters in the ring by making logical connections and smooth transitions and telling stories in a few short minutes of footage. In those films every second was valuable. So Harry learned to cram in a lot of material, and the sheer volume of the films served as drill exercises that taught him the quick-minded discipline and precision necessary to write well-crafted songs quickly. Soon he began to write his songs the way he edited his films.

"I loved the architectural aspect of film," said Harry. "First I wrote the various elements, which were almost like the shots. Then, as I edited down, I shaved off the unnecessary words, which was like shaving off the unnecessary film and seeing the juxtapositions and how they worked. That is, how one line related to another, so that if one line had impact and another line had impact, what did it mean when you put those two lines end to end? I liked doing things that had a tangible quality."

His lyrics also began to show signs of maturity, shifting from event-caused or autobiographical writing to more developmental writing or extrapolations of personal experience. Suddenly the distance between what he attempted to write and what actually appeared on paper narrowed. He began to write with complete constructs, creating environments he'd never been in that weren't necessarily factual in detail, but truthful in emotion.

The first product of this new songwriting stage was the saga "Dogtown," Harry's first pure story song. The idea was inspired during a visit to Sandy's parents' summer home in Gloucester, Massachusetts, when she showed Harry the ruins of a legendary whaling town off Cape Ann. The town was an early settlement of the Mayflower Colony, but for some reason it was deserted, the settlers leaving wild-dog packs behind.

In the song, Harry imagined all the lonely whaling widows whose seafaring husbands left them to the company of dogs during the months the men were at sea. In particular, he imagined one Widow Cather, who mollified her physical distress by resorting to a bestial relationship with her dog. "I had strong feelings about Dogtown and I heard many legends about it," said

Harry, who once dubbed the tale as the first in a series of "perverse" songs. "But I felt there was an evocative quality about what must have been a tremendously deprived situation. Yet in this, what I feel, as in all my perverse songs ("Sniper," "Thirty Thousand Pounds of Bananas") were struggles of people toward a life force, even though they may take strange ways."

"Dogtown" was also the first and last song Harry ever wrote by piano. That fall of 1967, Harry visited Tom in Plattsburgh for a weekend. Tom was working on his master's in history and lived in a big old wreck of a house along Lake Champlain. Inside was an old beat-up piano on which, for two days, Harry banged out the notes and chords to "Dogtown," driving everyone in the house crazy. "There were a couple of college students up there who were horrified by my piano playing," said Harry.

"He sat at the piano for hours," recalled brother James, who was also there that weekend. "I hated that song and always did."

Still, Harry was pleased with the outcome and was inspired to write other story poems (later to become story songs) such as "Thirty Thousand Pounds of Bananas," his show-stopping concert piece. The poem told the bittersweet tale of a banana-truck driver who disregarded the "Shift to Low Gear" sign and plunged to his death down a steep hill that led to the entrance of Scranton, Pennsylvania. "It was triggered by my reaction to Vietnam body counts that accentuated statistics rather than humanity," said Harry. "Ironically enough, nobody ever sat down and added up all those figures because we were claiming enough casualties to have wiped out the population of Vietnam twice."

Then there was the poem "Sniper," a penetrating psychological portrait of the demented psyche of an assassin based on Charles Whitman, the young man who, on August 1, 1966, climbed the University of Texas tower in Austin and gunned down sixteen people and wounded thirty-one.

And finally there was "Better Place to Be," one of Harry's finest lyrical poems, inspired by all his travels through the lonely reaches of upstate New York to visit his brothers—Steve in Pots-

dam, James in Hamilton and Ithaca, Tom in Plattsburgh—and by
one trip in particular, when he stopped at a bar and grill in
Watertown, New York, for a couple of hours.

"I spent a week there one afternoon," Harry later teased at his
concerts. At the bar, Harry got to talking with an old night
watchman who worked for the J. R. Miller Company (Harry
called it Miller's Tool and Die in the poem and later the song).
He walked away with the sad but true story of the watchman's
magical, one-night stand with a beautiful woman, an experience
that finally resulted in his acceptance of the ugly, rotund barmaid
as a consolation for his loneliness.

In fact, loneliness was a major theme that ran through all of
these story poems. They were dark, tragic tales about ordinary
people desperately coping with their own disappointments of
broken dreams and lost lives. They were all individuals working
at their individuality. They were castaways, pariahs, people living
on the periphery of society, apart from the natural ongoing order
of all social and human activity. They were even freaks. They
were not matinee idols. Harry's sensibility was and remained
allegiant to the little guy, the underdog: the truck driver, the night
watchman, the sniper, the whaling widow, and the barmaid.
They, and dozens of other characters Harry eventually created in
his story songs, were, each in his own way, outsiders to something, rejected by someone. Yet within all of them there coex-
isted tremendous life force and an unyielding drive toward
people and love and the need for positive self-affirmation.

Harry, too, was one of these characters, and they were all, to
some degree, part of him. During the Henry years, he had
learned to hide his tormented emotions with a cheerful exterior,
something he continued to do. His characters, then, were a product of that repression, like caged creatures, who emerged both
awkward and bizarre. To them Harry attributed all the inner feelings he reserved for himself: insecurity, self-doubt, fear. And like
a vocal actor or film narrator, he played the part of each. In
"Dogtown," he was the lonely seafarer's widow; in "Better Place

to Be," he became the barmaid, the one-night woman, and, of course, the night watchman. In "Sniper," he also played three parts: the voice of public conscience, friends of the killer, and the assassin himself, who sought a reflection of his existence through a series of psychological questions.

In adapting these poems to music, Harry's melodies became more complex. As long story poems, he could no longer use the standard chorus-verse-chorus structure of a folk song. Instead, the new style demanded frequent melodic and rhythmic changes, altering patterns just when they seemed established to sustain listener interest. Often, then, his story songs had no chorus. But for now, this new style was an art form he'd yet to perfect.

* * *

Harry's job at Big Fights seemed to be on the upswing when Bill Cayton suggested he create a boxing documentary using rare black-and-white film footage and stills. It was a film Cayton first contemplated doing when he hired Harry and the first full-length feature undertaken by the company. For Harry, the new project was a welcome change. One year of editing five- and fifteen-minute fight films had become intolerable drudgery.

"I was going bananas," said Harry. "Then they were talking about making a compilation of all the changes of hands of the heavyweight title and to just string 'em together with some newsreel footage that was in such bad shape it came out of the can looking like potato chips."

So Harry wrote a proposal and treatment for a three-part trilogy entitled *The Heavyweight Championship.* The first part, called *Legendary Champions,* traced every heavyweight title defense, from the John L. Sullivan-Jake Kilrain fight in 1882 (the first official heavyweight fight) to Gene Tunney and Jack Dempsey in 1929. The second part, *The Golden Era of Boxing,* was supposed to depict the Joe Louis era. And the third part was to bring it all up to date, ending with Muhammed Ali, then known as Cassius Clay.

However, only the first part of the film, *Legendary Champions,* was ever completed. After a few short weeks of regenerated enthusiasm, Harry's artistic temperament again came in conflict with a regular work routine and the project soon ran behind schedule. "He wanted to quit," said Sandy. "But I kept telling him, 'Why don't you just finish this project? It's silly to start things and drop them in the middle.' I remember Harry had an offer to do the sound on a film that was being done as a special for television called *The Kennedy Wit.* It was being filmed in Washington and Jack Paar was interviewed and Harry wanted the job badly. He asked for time off at Cayton. They said no, so he deliberated and was going to quit completely, but finally decided to call in sick and take the time."

One month later, *Legendary Champions* was nearly one-third complete, but was taking three times longer than originally planned. In addition to coming late to work, Harry began disappearing during the day, taking extended lunch hours. Cayton was furious. "Lunch hour? It's three o'clock in the afternoon, I'd look for Harry and he's not back," said Cayton. "As a result, we ran way over budget because he was not devoting the time to it."

So once again Harry was fired and once again Jim Jacobs came to his rescue. Jacobs felt Harry had done so much work on the picture, it "would be a shame to take him off." Consequently, a few days later, Harry was rehired with the same stern warnings from Cayton and a fifty-dollar raise, partially because of his extended apprenticeship, but mostly as an incentive.

Despite the daily doldrums of Big Fights, Harry gained some sense of self-importance on weekends, visiting Tom at Plattsburgh State, joined by Steve, who traveled from Clarkson College in Potsdam. Once again the brothers Chapin were temporarily reunited. Tom and Steve had formed a rock 'n' roll band called The Beautiful People and on Saturday nights Harry performed with them, roaring from nine P.M. to one A.M. in a big beer hall on campus. Harry's visits then were purely social. It was the brothers, the music and, said Harry, "my last chances at attempting to date on Sandy before we got married."

At Plattsburgh, Harry became a special person as older brother to Tom, the resident campus hero. As an undergraduate, Tom had been the star of the Plattsburgh basketball team, an all-American who averaged eighteen points and twenty-one rebounds per game. At the end of his senior year, he received an invitation to the training camp of the then-NBA St. Louis Hawks. With Tom's self-built reputation, Harry was a cinch for positive attention. "I had an apartment then," said Tom. "Harry stayed with me. I had a room that about fit my bed. So we'd pull off the mattress, put it on the floor, and I'd sleep on the floor and he'd sleep on the springs. He came up and wenched, womanized or whatever. It was a good situation."

Harry made the nine-hour weekend trip to Plattsburgh by bus. The white Corvair he had bought in California was demolished. Steve's girlfriend, Ann Brown—whom he later married and divorced—had totaled the car in an accident in the Lincoln Tunnel after Harry had lent it to her. Often Harry took the bus ride with Phil Forbes, who lived directly across the hall from him at 81 Columbia Heights and was a close friend of Tom's and Steve's. Typically they left New York together late Friday afternoons and returned late Sunday nights.

But Harry's musical relationship with his brothers had now reversed itself. He was no longer the lead singer. After all, The Beautiful People was not his band, nor was Plattsburgh his school. "Tom felt he could assert himself more because it was his home ground," said Trika Smith, who twice joined Harry on the bus to Plattsburgh. "The brothers always had trouble off and on working together, which came from being closed in and competing with one another. But now Harry really didn't have a choice. He had to back down. He had to take a lower profile and that wasn't his style."

A lower profile meant that Harry had to fit into the secondary role of accompanist. The group included Tom on acoustic guitar, Steven on organ, and Plattsburgh students Ernie Daley on drums and Art Choker on guitar. But the band needed a bass player, so Harry filled in. The only problem was that Harry had no sense of jamming or finding his part. "I was at best a poor bass player," said Harry. "Not even a mediocre one. All I could play were the basic blues; you know, wake me/shake me and stuff like that."

However, The Beautiful People was a rock-'n'-roll band, not blues, and since Harry wasn't around during the week to practice, Saturday night concerts became free-form jam sessions, with Harry feeling his way through unfamiliar chords and songs. They played "We Can Work It Out," by The Beatles, Dusty Springfield's "You Don't Have to Say You Love Me," the Buckingham's "Kind of a Drag," and "California Dreamin'" and "Monday, Monday" by The Mamas and The Papas. Still, Harry was not a great lover of rock music. In his imagination he saw The Beautiful People as just another version of the Chapin Brothers, wanting to play only Chapin Brothers material. But it was not for him to say.

"We were in a band where we tried to sound like the record," said Steve. "But Harry was a great believer in doing original material and he came up on weekends with no time to rehearse and it was like a constant jam session. It was very loose. He tried to infuse his energy into music that he really wasn't into."

Said Phil Forbes: "I can see Harry now—carrying on, clapping hands, trying to psyche people up. He always did that kind of thing. He was never afraid to have somebody call him an asshole. Never ever. He was a great generator of excitement, though sometimes to the detriment of the whole situation. But it was that kind of bare-faced application of himself that finally made him successful."

By December 1967, *Legendary Champions* was finally completed. At Harry's suggestion, Bill Cayton hired Tom, Steve and father Jim to record the music for the film. Steve, the musical brain trust of the bunch, composed the score. "It was pretty embarrassing," said Steve; a consummate perfectionist, he considered embarrassing what many musicians would consider superb. "I really didn't know what the hell I was doing, only Harry got me the job."

Still, the music was good enough, and the film (99 minutes long) even better. Harry had skillfully made the connections between the fight game, Americana, and the history of film. The transition of scenes was smooth, the progression meaningful, the tension climactic. The documentary also brimmed over with little quirks regarding famous figures such as Jesse James, Lillian Russell, Buffalo Bill, Charlie Chaplin, Wyatt Earp, Douglas Fairbanks Sr. and Bat Masterson. It also contained Thomas Edison's 1894 film—the first film of a heavyweight championship bout that pitted Gentleman Jim Corbett against Peter Courtney. In those days, fights were among the earliest scenes recorded on film and the first to make money. *Legendary Champions* also featured Jack Johnson's famed 1910 match with Jim Jeffries (on which the play *The Great White Hope* was based) plus original photos of an 1889 bare-knuckle fight with John L. Sullivan. In all, Harry's innovations successfully gave color and dimension to the black-and-white celluloid.

Cayton thought so too, and in January 1969 submitted *Legendary Champions* for an Academy Award nomination in time for the year-end balloting. Also that month, Harry left Big Fights Inc. for good. It was a mutual agreement. He also left the nine-to-five lifestyle for dead. He vowed to himself that he'd never take another "regular job" again.

He never did.

But at the time, Harry was also unemployed, so he called Jim Lipscomb, who once again came through in the clutch, this time with a short documentary about Governor George Wallace. In fact, over the years, if Lipscomb was involved with any sort of film project at Drew Associates, he invariably called Harry to be his editor. Jim respected Harry's ideas and they worked together brilliantly as a team. Jim also realized Harry "wasn't making a dime from his songs or poetry" and "was glad to help out." Harry enjoyed Jim's company because with him he could work by impulse, not by the clock.

The film was completed a few weeks later and Lipscomb invited Harry to Ethiopia to shoot a documentary for the World Bank which would illustrate how underdeveloped Third World countries progressed to a level of respectability through

World Bank funding. A documentary had previously been shot, but the bank was very dissatisfied with the outcome and offered Lipscomb the chance to make a new, more "vibrant" picture.

Harry jumped at the opportunity. Except for his trip to Europe with Grandma Lilly, he hadn't been beyond U.S. borders, and Ethiopia seemed, to him, like "an exotic change of scenery." His only reservation was leaving Sandy, since filming would last one month. But she encouraged him to take the offer and in late January, Harry and Jim arrived in Addis Ababa, the capital of Ethiopia. They stayed at the Ghion Hotel, one of only three decent bedposts in the city. From there Jim and Harry departed for daily film expeditions. Accompanied by 16-millimeter handheld cameras, they traveled throughout the country by prop plane or jeep and filmed everything, from the unspoiled wilderness and exotic wildlife of Ethiopia's naked north country to its rugged mountain interior and half-finished cities. They even managed to film Emperor Haile Selassie, the jewel of their cinematic endeavor, whom government officials nervously referred to as H.I.M.

Back at the hotel each night, Harry wrote long letters to Sandy of his daily experiences, which read much like Bill Burrud travelogues, descriptive and carefully phrased. Sandy then passed the letters on to Elspeth and the rest of the family. The most frequent subject in his writings was the appalling level of hunger in Ethiopia. Though there were glimpses of Western influence in Addis Ababa proper, the country was primarily primitive, uncharted to many of its farthest reaches, and what scenic splendor did exist was easily offset by the cancerous poverty and venereal disease that ate at its core. After the first day, Harry wrote Sandy:

> Fifty paces from the hotel, we were accosted by about ten beggars, peddlers, pimps, joyboys, and various other types of every size, shape, color, age and infirmity possible. We were offered rugs, knives, coins, leopard skins, monkey skins, paintings, lion's claws, condoms and various brown-skinned bodies, both male and female. The persistence and various lines handed out by these

ragtag entrepreneurs actually became annoying. But when a little boy, with his eyes as big as a Keene painting, came up to you and repeated, 'I'm hungry, hungry—an orphan boy—I'm hungry'—it got to you on a far different level. The problem and solution is of course beyond generosity. You'd have to walk the streets throwing one hundred dollars bills behind you to have any effect. So you just push on.

In addition to Sandy, Harry missed his brothers and guitar and music. Normally, after a full day of filming, Harry retired to bed because he had to wake up at six each morning. But one night he had a taste of the old music glory. Along with Jim and a couple of government officials, he went to a posh nightclub replete with beautiful prostitutes. The club also had a band, and it being the slowest of a slow night, Harry popped up from the table in between numbers and headed directly for the guitar player. "I was thinking, 'Oh, no, Harry's gonna take over again,'" said Lipscomb. "Pretty soon he was up on stage, took the guy's guitar away from him and was leading the band, finding things they could play and putting on a big act. I was getting embarrassed. But there was no reason to be. The band loved it. The patrons loved it, and after a half a dozen songs, he walked down with everybody looking at him and giving him a big hand."

The proprietor of the place loved him too and even asked him to return the following night. Later that evening, Harry wrote Sandy:

> In true Chapin fashion, I played some songs that were well received. Especially because American rock 'n' roll is in much favor by the younger set here. We left about midnight (having not sampled the wares) . . .

After he finished the letter, he climbed into bed and lay back with his arms crossed behind his head, his eyes fixed on the ceiling. He thought of Sandy, his brothers, Plattsburgh and the concerts. Music and love couldn't have seemed farther away. Then, just as he was about to turn off the light, he heard music coming from the ballroom down below. It was the black hotel orchestra playing its version of the 1966 American hit, "You Don't Have to Say You Love Me," a song he had sung with Tom and Steve many times before. A sad grin crossed his face and he shut off the light, the roar of applause reverberating in his head.

By the end of February, the World Bank film was completed. As a reward, Jim offered to take Harry to Greece for a two-week vacation. But Harry couldn't wait to get home and see Sandy. "I was going completely crazy without her," he said. "I mean, I was writing her letters every day and you'd think a young bachelor with that kind of opportunity would've jumped at it. But I was so crazy to see her, I told Jim Lipscomb no and came straight home. Though I still had my apartment in Brooklyn Heights, I essentially moved in with Sandy that spring and summer on 69 Cedarhurst. She was grateful to have this young live wire in her life. She liked me being home a lot. We used to make love all day; sleep, make love, sleep, make love."

The music side of his life wasn't nearly as successful. When Harry returned from Ethiopia, he discovered—much to his resentment—that he'd been replaced as the bass player in his brothers' band by someone who could perform full-time. His name was Leon Ogdibene. With Leon, according to Tom Chapin, they "found a dependable day-to-day working situation" and began to take themselves more seriously. The Beautiful People had become a solid rock and commercial dance band. "We were a lot better with Leon than with Harry," said Tom. "Harry had been playing bass. Harry couldn't play bass. He didn't care to learn, really."

Still, one Saturday night, the brothers made room for Harry in the group, but from their perspective, it was just no good. "Stevie was the one instigating it," said Tom, "saying, 'I don't want Harry in this thing. It's just a bummer. It's not working.' Well, Stevie's not going to say that to him, so it was left to me to tell him, so I told Harry and he was really crushed."

Said Steve: "What were we supposed to do? By the time he came back, we had a band that was not only a full-time functioning band, but the most popular in town. It completely changed over to playing the latest hits. At that time, the music was very exciting to me. Jimi Hendrix songs were just coming out and Harry came back and essentially wanted to rejoin the band. It just wasn't feasible."

The reasons were as much personal as musical. For years, Harry had been the pushy, overbearing older brother and Tom and Steve needed space. They wanted to stop being bookends to Harry and work out their own identities. Where Harry's bold and reckless energy were once valuable assets to them on stage, they now infringed on their freedom. "We wanted to spread our wings," said Tom. "It was my school, our band; I don't think Harry understood that. There were musical things we wanted to do. We wanted to become a good band, and if everybody in the group was up there, we could practice in the middle of the week. We could learn some stuff. But Harry was not into doing that at all. Never was. He was perfectly happy to come up to Platts-burgh, bash away through four hours, find some girl . . ."

"I think they probably had to escape him like a son has to escape a father," said Jim Lipscomb. "They had to assert their individuality by getting out from under him. I know that hurt Harry so much I never discussed it with him."

Harry felt betrayed and suffered from internal nervous reactions. For the first time since he was twelve years old, he developed a severe case of asthma. He became morose and depressed. He began sleeping days. It was the first form of sibling rejection he had ever known, but more importantly, on a smaller scale it represented the large failure of his life. After all, he was nearly twenty-six years old. He had no job, no money, no direction to his film career and now, rejected by his brothers, no music. "The days of the Kingston Trio were over." The words finally began to sink in. "Part of the pressure also was deciding whether I was going to get married, what with the three kids, and instantly have to grow up," said Harry. "It really frightened me."

In his imagination, marriage meant relinquishing the boyish independence he loved. He could no longer use his brothers and music as a crutch for prolonged adolescence. For the first time, he had to be serious about his life, and the thought was unbearably threatening. He was about to adopt the identities of father and husband when he didn't even have one of his own. He was, after all, still dabbling, experimenting, looking for answers and disappointed at finding none. But now, if he married, there were four other lives to consider. How would he support them? As a part-time filmmaker?

"It scared the ever-lovin' shit out of me," said Harry. "I realized that I was now starting to live those serious moments in my life that I never thought would come. I realized that everything I did from then on had import. But the biggest thing was trying to accept the fact that I was an adult. I had to make money."

Sandy certainly didn't have any. She tried to get a teaching job on Long Island, but when that fell through, she decided to attend Columbia University Graduate School and get her Ph.D. in esthetic education via a National Direct Student Loan. Besides alimony support, it was her only source of income since there was some money left over after tuition expenses. But it wasn't enough, so Harry and Sandy learned all sorts of gimmicks to get by.

"One thing I often did," Harry explained, "was to cash a check in a store I knew wouldn't deposit it until the end of the week, so it probably wouldn't clear until the following Wednesday. Then I'd find some way to borrow money and cover the check and then pay the creditor back next week with a check that will bounce, but by that time, I made a little money on the outside, so there was a constant float factor."

During the day, while Sandy attended classes, Harry baby-sat for the kids, "getting more ensnared by my feelings of failure," and tried to work on a musical he wanted to produce called *Buraka,* a boy-meets-girl romance set in the fictitious Caribbean island of Buraka, somewhere between Bermuda and Jamaica. Harry wrote most of the songs for the musical during his two years at Big Fights, but in his complacency could not complete them.

Even so, his melancholy mood was only temporary. During late spring and summer, he and Sandy went to a lot of Off-Broadway theater such as Terrence McNally's *American Rah* and numerous poetry readings at the YMHA on 92nd Street. After one particular reading, Harry's creative ambitions were rekindled. "I saw a very old poet who was probably going to die in a year or two," said Harry. "He wasn't even that well known a poet, but the very competence with which he talked about life and what he'd done really inspired me to start writing again. The poet reminded me of my grandfathers and the life of 'good-tired' they had created for themselves.

"I mean, some days in my life I worked at the wrong things and yet was successful," he continued. "But they weren't the number-one priorities in my life, and even though I was successful, when I hit the hay at night it was not with the feeling of success or triumph. It was more like a certain uneasiness and it was hard to get to sleep. Other nights or days when I worked at the right things, even though I was unsuccessful with them, there was a sense of good-tired, and when I hit the hay it was like, 'Take me away!' I felt I could crash and not have any uptightness or a churning in my stomach because I fought the good fight. I wanted to lead a life that lead up to a good-tired. To fight the right battles, not necessarily win, but to have a sense of being sixty-five or seventy-five and not have regrets. Because I think the major errors we make in life are errors of omission, not commission."

When the first version of *Buraka* was completed, Harry took the script to Howard Rosenstone, an agent at William Morris. Accompanied by his guitar, Harry sang the entire musical right in his office. Rosenstone liked the music but felt the script was weak and suggested Harry collaborate with another writer to improve it. "If the writing is up to par with the music" he'd have a sale. Harry stubbornly rejected the suggestion, unwilling to accept the notion that he was a poor prose writer.

He kept writing new versions without success, then changed the setting of the musical to the slums of New York. After nine versions and still no sale, he decided to scrap the project. Many of the songs in *Buraka* ended up as the basis of his 1975 Broadway musical, *The Night That Made America Famous*.

Disappointed by the rejection of *Buraka,* Harry became lazy and depressed again. His writing production fell off to nothing, and even Sandy became somewhat disgusted with him. "He was quite selfish back then," said Sandy. "His tendency was to make himself as comfortable as possible. He would lie around things, ease out from under things, and do things as easily as he possibly could."

Sandy was beginning to have second thoughts about marrying him. She had her doubts about how long a marriage to Harry could last. She was worried about their age difference and Harry's piquant personality. "I think all the time I'll have with Harry is maybe five years," she once told Janet Castro. "Then he'll dump me."

"She thought I was going to be a lazy, two-bit songwriter," said Harry. "I was writing music around the edges but nothing that great was coming out. Then I wrote two songs for her, one called 'It's You Girl' and one called 'Sandy.' They sort of blew her away in a sense because they were just two openly emotional songs about her and even though she was disgusted at me, she had to fall in love with me a little bit again."

Well, a little bit. Sandy's "disgust" was primarily over Trika Smith, whom Harry continued to see off and on. Trika still believed Harry was her future husband, mostly because he never persuaded her otherwise. But one night he tried. It was during a farewell house party at the Castros', who were planning to move from Brooklyn Heights to Queens. That night Harry showed up with Sandy, and once again, as at Bob Mullevaney's wedding, so did Trika, only this time Harry had not invited her. She had heard of the get-together through Tom. They had become good friends when both worked as teachers for the Headstart Migrant Program that summer in New Jersey. To compound matters, Gail Hollenborg was also there at the invitation of her aunt and uncle, Janet and Manny.

So at one point during the party, in an attempt to escape the awkward bind in which he found himself, Harry decided to tell Trika his feelings. But instead of confronting her directly, he proceeded to sing the song "Sandy," looking straight into her eyes. The last two lines of the last stanza were the clincher, when he said of Sandy, "Oh yes, I see the world in her for she means the world to me."

Said Trika bitterly: "I was really pissed. I confronted Harry and he admitted he was seeing someone else seriously."

Said Gail: "I think that was Harry on one of his marvelous ego trips."

Said Harry: "All I was trying to do was survive the evening."

The predicament was not entirely Harry's fault. The family had a history of being clannish and naturally pulled people in with their warmth and togetherness and novelty of attraction. Trika too had become part of the family. For instance, not only had she been good friends with Tom, but she eventually married Michael Burke two years later.

For the moment, though, the party did not settle matters. Trika still loved Harry and refused to take the hint until the night the relationship fell apart by itself. Harry, Trika and Michael Burke had gone to a New York Knicks basketball game. Harry spent the entire evening with his eyes glued to a *Sports Illustrated* magazine, leaving Michael and Trika alone to talk.

Said Trika: "I didn't go out with Michael for a long time because both of us felt it wasn't right. We worried about hurting Harry's feelings. Occasionally Michael called me and finally I said, 'This is ridiculous. Let me call Harry and I'll talk to him about it.' Well, Harry was so relieved. He was probably wondering in his own mind how to get off the stick."

By the fall of 1968, Harry gave up his apartment in Brooklyn Heights when he and Sandy finally decided to get married. Manny and Janet Castro remembered Harry telling them the news when they drove out to Point Lookout to visit. "He said, 'There comes a point where you either have to fish or cut bait,'" said Manny. "He said, 'The relationship can't go on the way it is anymore. We either have to get married or end it.'"

Despite his fears, Harry became a better father and husband than he realized, and the changes were especially apparent to Manny and Janet. "We saw him in a new milieu," said Manny. "Now he was the daddy, the family man. We always thought of him as single with girlfriends. We were astounded. Now he was out in the backyard for barbecues, with kids running around, doing carpentry work and being the host. We always used to be the host. And I'm sure things weren't easy for him. I can remember Jaime, the oldest child, shouting: 'I hate Harry!'"

The song "Story of a Life" chronicles those changes in him.

On November 26, 1968, Harry and Sandy were married at Grace Church in Brooklyn Heights, with a small reception afterward at nearby Hotel Towers. It was a simple, low-key church wedding. James was best man. Steve provided music on the enormous church organ. There were upwards of seventy-five guests; all the Burkes and Chapins, including the Castros, Jebbie Hart, John Hart, K.B., Jim and Manja, even Grandma Lilly, who was ninety-five years old and in a wheelchair.

None of Sandy's relatives were present, not even her parents. Mrs. Gaston, Sandy's mother, had literally disowned her. One weekend, Sandy had gone up to Newton, Massachusetts, and told her parents of her wedding plans. Mrs. Gaston was furious and told her that she thought Harry was a loser and Sandy a fool for even considering the idea. Mr. Gaston, who, except for "occasional moments of stepping out," according to Harry, remained mostly under his wife's thumb and kept a muted voice in the whole affair. After a heated exchange, Mrs. Gaston kicked Sandy out of the house, vowing that she never wanted to see her again. And she didn't, at least not for another twelve years.

As if that weren't enough, Sandy faced additional obstacles to her marriage. For one, she had to appear before the Bishops' Court of the Board of Episcopal Priests and Bishops to officially annul her first marriage. She was also nearly one hour late for her own wedding, having become stuck in traffic on the Long Island Expressway, leaving Harry a bit nervous in his black tux and tie. It was almost comical, however, as Steve, who had prepared only ten minutes' worth of material, played "Here Comes the Bride" over and over.

Not surprisingly, Sandy was violently ill that day and spent most of her wedding night in the bathroom, vomiting.

In a symbolic sense, Harry's marriage to a woman with three children had familiar psychological overtones. "It was almost as if he were going to show the world he could be a good father and a good stepfather too," said James.

Finding out from Jebbie that Harry had married a woman with three children, Henry Hart just smiled.

CHAPTER VII

Greyhound

On December 31, 1968, Harry's first sweet taste of recognition became official when the Academy of Motion Picture Arts and Sciences nominated *Legendary Champions* for an Oscar in the category of Best Feature Documentary. Jim Jacobs called Harry to deliver the good news. Jubilant, but still unemployed, all Harry could say was, "Wow, what a great thing to put on my résumé."

Ironically, two weeks later, the Oscar winner, *Young Americans,* was disqualified because it had been released the prior year. Another two weeks passed before Harry, in nervous anticipation, finally got word of the official runner-up, a documentary entitled *Martin Luther King. Legendary Champions* came in second.

Even so, the film went on to win first prize at both the New York and Atlanta film festivals and received rave reviews. Henry Hart, who was still editor-in-chief at *National Films in Review* magazine, wrote a short critique of his stepson's documentary.

He panned it.

In February, Jim Lipscomb invited Harry on an expedition to Durban, South Africa, to film a great white shark, which eventually materialized into the movie, *Blue Water, White Death.* The project was financed by CBS and headed by millionaire-adventurer Peter Gimbel (of the New York department store chain), who had fired his production assistant. Lipscomb offered Harry the position. But spending six months in the Indian Ocean away from Sandy did not sound particularly appealing, so Harry turned it down. Still, it was such an interesting opportunity that Harry called Tom and convinced him to go.

"I know, it sounds great," Tom said. "But I don't know anything about film or being a production assistant."

"You don't have to," Harry insisted. "Write Gimbel a letter. Tell him you're an all-American basketball player, you're six-foot-five, you're a great swimmer, you don't know anything about diving or moviemaking, but you'd love to help if you could."

Tom did and was hired two weeks later.

As it turned out, Harry made the right decision. After six months at sea, the crew hadn't found a single great white shark, much less filmed one, and was forced to temporarily abort the mission. "We came back with three-quarters of the film," said Tom. "So Gimbel put together a rough cut to convince CBS to give them more money to go to South Australia to get the end of the film, which they did."

But Tom didn't make the second trip, although he did perform the music in the film, two traditional folk ballads along with Harry's "Someone Keeps Calling My Name."

In the meantime, during the summer of 1969, Harry cashed in his Academy Award credentials and had no trouble securing film work, this time on two thirty-minute color documentaries for IBM. Though Jim Lipscomb was the producer of record, Harry actually wrote, edited and directed both films, earning more money than he'd ever seen, a total of $30,000, or $15,000 for each film. "It was the most money anybody in my family ever made," Harry once boasted. He gave $6,000 of that sum to his father, who wanted to subsidize the publishing of the first in a series of instructional drum books he'd been writing since 1948. In exchange, Harry received 10 percent of the royalties, which amounted to a $40,000 profit in succeeding years.

By summer's end, Harry had plenty of money in the bank and decided to write music for his brothers full-time. By then Tom had returned from South Africa and teamed up with Steve, who had graduated from Clarkson College in electrical engineering, to form another rock group, this time called The Chapins. They were Tom on acoustic guitar, Steve on bass and keyboard, Phil Forbes on drums, and Phil's friend, Dough Walker (who later played in Harry's band) on electric guitar.

Harry collaborated with Steve in writing the songs. He provided the material, attended rehearsals, contributed arrangement ideas, and functioned as band advisor. Each week Harry traveled by train from Long Island and delivered parcels of music to the basement of Grace Church in Brooklyn Heights where The Chapins regularly rehearsed. Part of those parcels were songs such as "Greyhound" and "Everybody's Lonely," along with an amalgamation of song styles. Harry wrote a little bit of everything: love ballads, country rock, bluegrass, and an occasional story song. Steve then arranged and rewrote the material, tightening lyrics and adjusting melodies so as to be most in keeping with a four-man rock group.

As a new group, The Chapins needed exposure. They returned to the Bitter End for Tuesday-night hootenannies. They were far superior to any other competing band using the same showcase strategy. The Chapins had an exquisite vocal blend reminiscent of Crosby, Stills and Nash and had the strength of Harry's songwriting to back them. Within three months' time they became the darlings of the Bitter End crowd.

Said New York disc jockey Pete Fornatale: "I was in the audience one night to cheer on a friend of mine, songwriter Jim Dawson. It was like an audition night where acts were rated by audience applause. In a sense, everybody had their fans there, but I thought Dawson would easily have an edge over anyone else who might show up. And who should I see performing but a group called The Chapins and they were terrific. They made a very strong impression on me because they were the overwhelm-

". . . my life, was a Harry Chapin song . . ."

Harry Chapin during a 1972 Illinois concert, and his first major concert tour. Bass guitarist John Wallace is in the background. In those days Harry sported a rakish beard, in part to emulate Bob Dylan, but he really looked more like Abraham Lincoln. The beard vanished in 1974 after the "black book" incident. (Photo: Bob White)

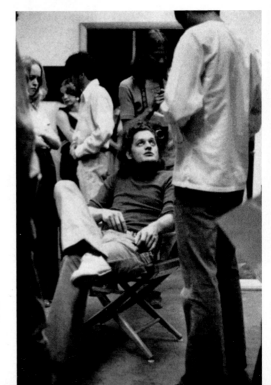

Harry backstage after that same 1972 Illinois concert. (Photo: Steve Stout)

(*Right*) The door on the right is 45A Hicks Street in Brooklyn Heights, where Harry lived from age eleven to seventeen. (Photo: Peter M. Coan) (*Below*) Grace Church in Brooklyn Heights, where Harry and brothers Tom and Steve, received their formative music training. Here Harry married Sandra Gaston on November 26, 1968. (Photo: Peter M. Coan)

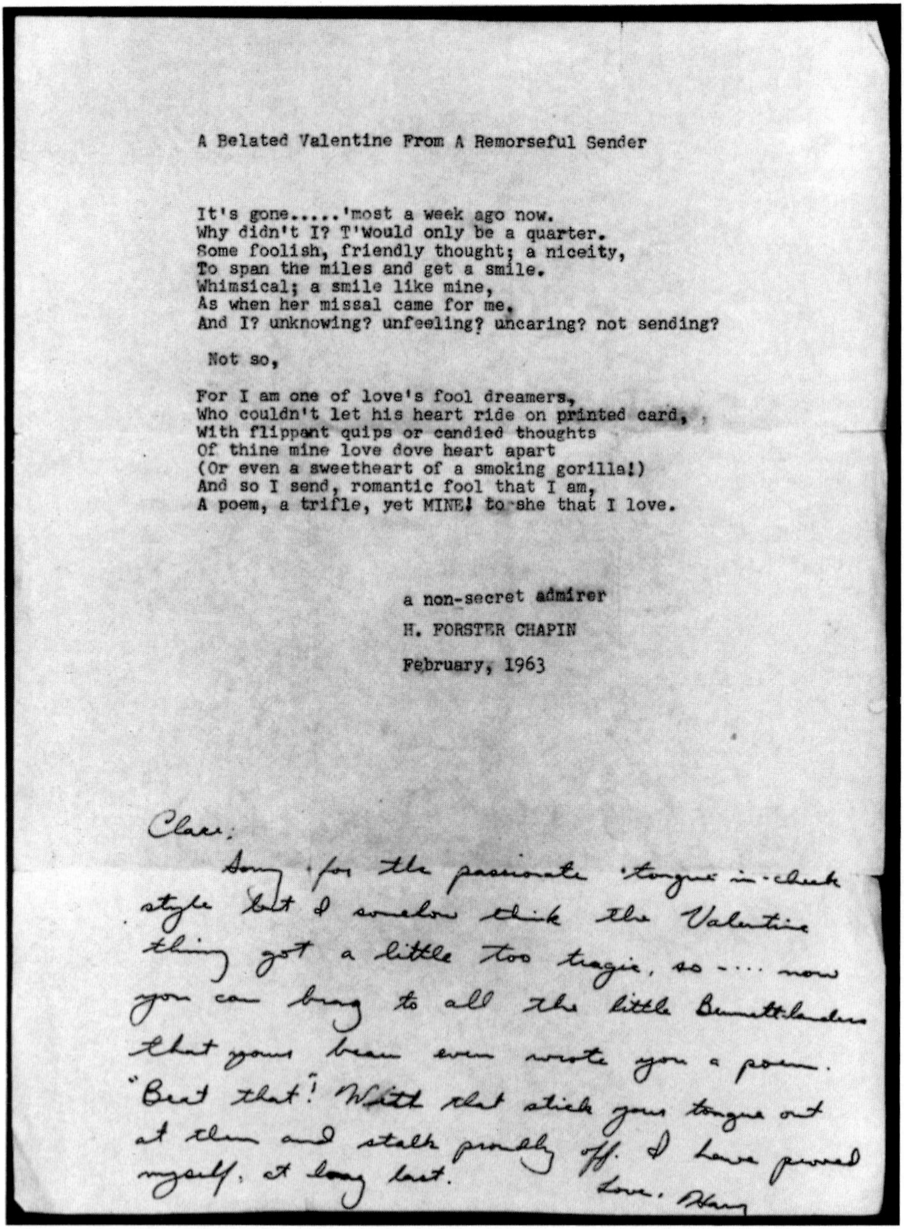

A Belated Valentine From A Remorseful Sender

It's gone.....'most a week ago now.
Why didn't I? T'would only be a quarter.
Some foolish, friendly thought; a niceity,
To span the miles and get a smile.
Whimsical; a smile like mine,
As when her missal came for me,
And I? unknowing? unfeeling? uncaring? not sending?

    Not so,

For I am one of love's fool dreamers,
Who couldn't let his heart ride on printed card,
With flippant quips or candied thoughts
Of thine mine love dove heart apart
(Or even a sweetheart of a smoking gorilla!)
And so I send, romantic fool that I am,
A poem, a trifle, yet MINE! to she that I love.

                    a non-secret admirer

                    H. FORSTER CHAPIN

                    February, 1963

[Handwritten note:]

Clare;

Sorry for the passionate tongue-in-cheek style but I somehow think the Valentine thing got a little too tragic, so .... now you can brag to all the little Bennett-landers that your beau even wrote you a poem. "Beat that!" With that stick your tongue out at them and stalk proudly off. I have proved myself, at long last.

                    love. Harry

The first poem Harry ever wrote. It was to his great unrequited love, Clare MacIntyre (who was Sue in "Taxi"). Harry wrote it because Clare got angry at him when he forgot to send her a Valentine's Day card. Throughout his career, Harry's deep love for Clare would echo within many of his story songs and poems. (Photo: Don Hunstein)

Harry, as usual, reaching for the emotion in the characters he sang about. (Photo: Steve Stout)

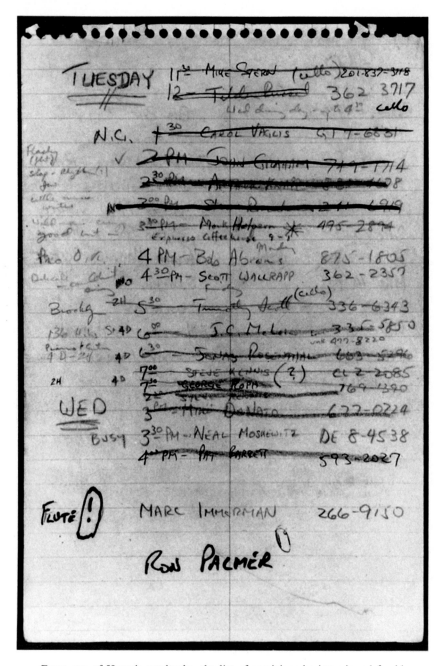

From one of Harry's notebooks, the list of musicians he interviewed for his original four-man group at his mother's Brooklyn Heights apartment in the summer of 1971. Timothy Scott eventually got the job as cellist, along with Ron Palmer on electric guitar and John Wallace on bass. (Photo: Don Hunstein)

Publicity photo (*left*) for Harry's 1975 Broadway show *The Night That Made America Famous,* and (*above*) the original notebook lyrics to the story song of the same title, the basis for the show. (Photos: Kenn Duncan (left); Don Hunstein (above))

Harry Chapin (background) and bass guitarist John Wallace (foreground) backstage prior to the Illinois concert in 1976. Wallace was an original member of Harry's four-man group and the only musician to remain in the group throughout Harry's ten-year career. (Photo: Steve Stout)

ing favorite of the crowd and even overshadowed the friend I came to see."

The Chapins became so popular that Paul Colby, the new owner of the nightclub, appointed himself their manager, signing a one-year contract with the group. A short, scruffy-looking man in his mid-forties, Colby had the perfect credentials for the job. He was a shrewd businessman with a New Yorker's wit, a veteran of the music scene with plenty of contacts: agents, record scouts, other club owners. He knew record company presidents on a first-name basis and routinely received telephone calls from television producers, promoters, or party givers to supply a band.

Under Colby's guidance, The Chapins soon became the house opening band, a cheap first act for the sake of exposure and experience. On Christmas Day they opened for a group called Rhinoceros, and in subsequent weeks, for a throng of folksingers such as John Sebastian and Tim Hardin, as well as a host of oddball comics. On occasion, during a slow weeknight, they were billed as the main act. "They didn't get much money at the time," said Colby. "But I paid them more or less what they deserved. They needed exposure, to be seen and heard in front of the public, which was the name of the game."

Part of the game was to get a record deal, so during the day, The Chapins recorded demo tapes at Media Sound Studios on West 57th Street. Afterward they sent them to numerous record labels who might be interested: Warner Brothers, Mercury, Liberty Records, among others. "We'd go up and lay down five or six tracks," said Doug Walker. "Then we'd go home and wait for the phone to ring."

And one time it did, from Stephen Schwartz, later the famous Broadway lyrist and creator of *Godspell*, who was then a staff producer at RCA Records. Schwartz adored The Chapins and pushed the group on the RCA brass, who did not. Shortly thereafter, out of correlation or coincidence, Schwartz left RCA.

However, one month later, with Colby and Harry pushing, The Chapins signed a small conditional record deal with Epic

Records, a subsidiary of the giant Columbia. Since Colby felt Harry's material "was the backbone of the group," he made sure Harry also signed the contract.

"It was one of those back-shelf record deals," said Walker. "The idea was that we were to produce hopeful singles, and if something hit, they'd release an album. There was no way they were going to release an album called 'The Chapins' unless they had something to go on."

Soon after, Epic staff producer Barry Kornfeld took them into the studio to produce the first two singles by The Chapins. Both of them were Harry's songs, "Greyhound" and one called "Lady of the Highway." Unfortunately, neither of them impressed Epic executives, so the singles were never released, and The Chapins quickly faded into anonymity at the label.

According to Colby, he unsuccessfully tried "to get on some sort of communication level" with the company, but Epic had no interest in the group, not even in Tom, whom Colby considered the jewel of the foursome. Tom was a highly visible stage performer; tall, good-looking, with a big voice and a warm, ingratiating smile that always seemed to radiate sunshine. But the strength of Tom was Harry's material, which was the only thing Colby and Epic agreed on.

Explained Colby: "If somebody else had come in for Tom, that might've brought some motivation from Epic. But the head guy at the label never even saw the act! I also felt the guy who signed the act was incapable. He wanted to find another singer to record Harry's material, which was ludicrous, but, then, some of the record companies should be shipped out to Hawaii."

At one point it was even suggested that The Chapins merge with the Simon Sisters, Lucy and Carly, and call themselves The Brothers and Sisters. During this period, large singing groups like The Serendipity Singers and The New Christy Minstrels were popular. "But we all said nix to that idea," said Harry.

Another time, Jac Holzman, the president of Elektra Records, flew in from the West Coast to take a look at Tom, unbeknownst to The Chapins. But Holzman passed. "I don't know, Paul," he said. "I believe something's here, but I can't tell. I'm not convinced about Tom. He reminds me of a Republican turned hippy."

Harry agreed. He felt Tom was "too laid-back," "undynamic," and was frustrated that The Chapins weren't advancing. Many nights Harry watched them from the audience and several times told Jim Lipscomb, who frequently came down to the Bitter End, "We need a lead singer! Tom hasn't got enough personality."

"I think the overall problem," said Walker, "was that Tom and Steve sang most of the lead vocals and never sounded funky enough. They just always sounded like the Chapin Brothers had sounded for years, too folkie, white and clean. Tom was really going through a lot of head trips about that because he wanted to 'get down' and he really couldn't. He found it hard to do."

Part of the problem was Paul Colby, who, after the first few months, became discouraged with The Chapins and never made a sincere effort to promote them. In his contract with the group, he had promised a minimum of $30,000 worth of work. But The Chapins didn't earn anything close to that figure. And even if they had, split five ways (Colby's cut included), it meant a maximum annual profit of only $6,000 per man, which gave Colby little incentive to push. "He got us only one job outside the Bitter End," said Tom. "We opened for John Sebastian, whom we'd become vaguely friendly with, at the Lambertville Music Fair in South Jersey."

The only highlight of that concert was Harry, but not because he performed. After The Chapins completed their opening set, he spotted Paul Simon backstage, who had come to see Sebastian perform. A few days earlier, Simon and Garfunkel's television special "Bridge Over Troubled Water" was drubbed in the ratings by a Peggy Fleming Ice Capades special. Harry and Lipscomb had made a presentation to Simon's manager about working on the program but were turned down. Even so, Harry had an avalanche of ideas about how the show might've been improved, and at one point backstage he cornered Simon and told him.

"Despite Simon being as big as he was, Harry had all this criticism and just started needling him about it," said Doug Walker. "But not viciously, just 'I think you could've done that...' which was Harry's approach to everyone. If you asked Harry what he thought, he let you know."

But Simon never asked. "Tom was off to the side and he just stood there with his jaw agape," said Harry. "Simon sort of looked at me like, 'Who the hell is this guy?'"

Writing for The Chapins was a formative stage in Harry's musical development. With them, he had a natural outlet to test his material, and because of this he cranked out dozens of songs. The sheer volume forced him to remain in constant contact with his craft. His story-song style was rapidly evolving now. He and Steve teamed up on a couple of long epics, most notably the song "Barefoot Boy," well under three minutes when Harry later recorded it, but then an incredible eleven minutes long that described the progressive history of America from its youthful innocence to its symbolic death.

The most important aspect of this formative stage for Harry was learning the business side of the music business: merchandising and presentation and what it took to make it as a successful act. He constantly found himself having to solve the various ineptitudes of The Chapins and cooked up numerous schemes "to make them go over." One of their major problems was a desperate lack of self-image, a hook that would leave a lasting impression on an audience.

"He was constantly pushing," said Doug Walker. "At that point, he was really behind us as a group. He was trying to get me and Phil Forbes off our asses and make the whole thing work as a unit. Some of his ideas were outlandish."

Said Harry: "I remember all those nights we talked about images. We talked about names. One time we were going to call them The Numbers and have 1, 2, 3, 4 pasted on their chests. We talked about everything. The fact was, it was constantly frustrating because people said, 'Nice guys, nice music.' We couldn't get arrested because of that lack of definitiveness, and I had learned from the film business that you had to sell projects, merchandise, and find some hooks. I started spending more nights and longer ones with them trying to push them to this or that song. I would sit out in the audience and see 'em on some nights when they had record companies come and not do a good show, when the night before or the night after they did a fantastic show. I saw them not effectively relate to an audience. . . . A lot of frustrating things."

Clean out of ideas, Harry turned to his reliable brain trust, brother James, and together they concocted the idea of turning each group member into a movie matinee idol. One night, Harry reported his master plan to The Chapins. "He said the whole sixties freak-rock thing was over and that a new trend was going to happen and we were all gonna be part of it," recalled Doug Walker. "He said that what we were going to have was a distinct image for each one of us onstage. Then he detailed it. It was like a piece of everything the rock groups had already done. I was supposed to be some motorcycle leather hood, Phil Forbes was supposed to look like a Bowery bum, Steve was supposed to look Edwardian, and Tom a cool macho stud."

But the secret of The Chapins' self-image did not lie in slick gimmicks or commercial schemes, but rather a greater belief in the songs they performed. The group relied too heavily on Harry for material. Though they performed some songs of Steve's, a couple of Tom's and a few that Doug and Phil collaborated on, it was never enough.

"That to me was the downfall of the group," said Doug Walker. "I'm sure if we'd been writing more of our own things, we would've had more of a sense of focus. I say downfall in the sense that we couldn't make the transition from Harry's material to our own. He was so prolific, there wasn't much sense in everybody knocking themselves out. All we had to do was wait for Harry to come in each week with five new tunes. Whether we liked them or not, it was something to work with. As a result, nothing was coming from within us as a unit."

Another problem was that the style and subjects of Harry's music were not always conducive to a rock format, such as "Dogtown," the song saga about bestiality. The brothers refused to perform it. Other songs, whether they were story songs, country-western tunes, folk songs or ballads, all placed an emphasis on the lyrics and their nuances rather than melody, volume or beat, which were intrinsic to rock music and to The Chapins' interest in performance. In fact, Harry always wrote his lyrics first and then tried to find a suitable melody or "tonal colors to bring across the message in a heightened fashion." Many times when Harry showed a new song to Steve, he handed him a lyric sheet and said, "Great song, huh?" and Steve bellowed, "That's not a song, Harry, that's a lyric. Give me a song!"

By the spring of 1970, Harry's role as writer for The Chapins rapidly deteriorated and he began spending less time with his brothers, writing more for himself. Part of the reason was Sandy. Though she encouraged Harry's musical ambitions, she felt "that Tom and Steve in their configuration weren't going to make it." She also didn't like the idea of him spending so many nights away from her in the city. But the key factors were his brothers, who increasingly rejected Harry's songs, to the point that they refused to perform them at all. "Some of his stuff we'd say to him, 'Get out of here! We don't want to sing that shit!'" said Phil Forbes, who was never a big fan of Harry's. "We didn't want to sing 'The Baby Never Cries' and some of his really schlocky stuff."

Part of the rejection was Harry's tendency to overplay his secondary role as band adviser. His pushy presence was a frequent source of irritation. "By this time, our relations were beginning to get a little shaky," said Steve. "Harry was trying to be like the coach, the uncle to the band, the big power-behind-the-scenes, and we weren't digging a lot of songs he was turning up with. He was getting down on us a lot because he didn't feel we were making strides. In a sense, he was right. I wasn't ready for any kind of limelight and Tom was trying too hard. We didn't push.

We didn't have a dynamic act. We were good, but no dynamic act."

"The Chapins were good," Paul Colby said once. "But in this business, you've got to be better than good. Good ain't good enough."

* * *

By the summer of 1970, Harry was short of money and briefly freelanced for Jim Lipscomb on a film called *Duel in the Wind,* a project sponsored by Alcoa Aluminum about the America's Cup sailing race. When completed, Harry decided "to take off six months and plan new projects." He spent most of his time at home in Point Lookout, occasionally writing songs, occasionally going into the city to see The Chapins perform at the Bitter End. "I wasn't a torture-genius type," said Harry. I didn't seethe. If I wanted to write, I'd write. I was more tortured by the general sense of going nowhere with my film career and all my freelancing. I was sort of treading water again."

The reality struck him late one evening after returning from Greenwich Village on the Long Island Railroad. It was a hot, muggy summer night when Harry stepped off the train at the Long Beach stop and waited at roadside to hitch a ride home. At the time, Pete Fornatale had just become the new morning disc jockey on WNEW-FM in New York and happened to be in Long Beach, having emceed a benefit at a local fire house. Fornatale was headed back to New York when he spotted a lanky, bushy-haired hitchhiker off to the side of the road. He picked him up in his little red VW Beetle.

"What do you do?" Harry asked, attempting to break the silence.

"Oh, I work for WNEW."

"Really," said Harry with bright eyes. "I've got friends there . . ." and he began naming all the people he knew.

"Yeah, well, I'm the new morning guy." Fornatale told him his name.

"Right. Sure. I know who you are. I listen all the time."

"What's your name?" Fornatale asked.

"Harry Chapin."

"You don't have anything to do with a couple of brothers, do you?"

"Sure, my brothers!" Harry blurted out. "I used to play with them. I wrote all their music and arranged all their stuff!" Then, pausing for a moment, his voice dropped one full tone. "But right now, I'm a filmmaker."

He was also a househusband with nothing to do except, according to him, "drive Sandy crazy at home." She tried to find something for him. As a graduate student at Columbia, Sandy had become interested in Congressman Allard Lowenstein, who had initiated the "Dump Johnson" movement three years before. At the time, Lowenstein was running for reelection and had a branch office in Long Beach. Sandy signed up as a volunteer and also signed Harry's name.

"But Harry didn't know I volunteered him," said Sandy. "So I said to Harry one day, 'Why don't you stop over to this office and speak to a man named Art Kaminsky,' who was running the office [and later became a top sports agent]. He did, and like anything else he did, he got involved to a point of fatigue."

Harry became literature director and worked at Lowenstein's headquarters. But he also worked in the community distributing campaign materials to all the local stores and residents and became such a valuable asset that Lowenstein himself recognized Harry's contribution.

"He was very helpful in the campaign," said Lowenstein, who died in 1980 when a disgruntled coworker gunned him down in cold blood in his office at the United Nations. "He was very committed and energetic and bright and everybody that met him loved him. He was a very special guy. But he was also in a very difficult place. Point Lookout was very heavily hawk and he was trying to be effective with people on the other side of the great division of the 1970 campaign, which was the Vietnam War issue."

As Harry explained: "The political spectrum in that town was that 95 percent of the people were for Adolf Hitler, which reflected two things. One, their knowledge of current events, and two, their political views. I was considered a communist because I had set up a coffeehouse in town where I occasionally sang. The town was isolated, on a peninsula. There was a tremendous chasm between old and young people. There was also a tremendous drinking and dope problem, and because I finally started getting the kids in one place where somebody occasionally found a beer can, I became the guy who was creating all the drug traffic and alcoholism in their children. It was like the old medieval suspicion, 'He who sees the devil is the devil.' So we had a stick sign on the front lawn that read 'Another Family for Lowenstein.' But the neighbors got a petition to make us take it down."

When Harry didn't, somebody altered the sign to read "Another Family for Lowenbrau."

Point Lookout was also the scene of the song "What Made America Famous?" which he dubbed his "farewell document" to the town when he moved away two years later.

"There was a volunteer firehouse two blocks down the road from a place in town where black families lived," he said. "It was sort of known as the welfare house. One night there was a suspicious fire in the welfare house and it took the fire department two hours to answer the call. At the same time, there were some good people in town, so I put the plumber in the song as a positive overlay and as the person making the leap."

By the beginning of 1971, the first Nixon recession had set in, and suddenly, where there was once an abundance of jobs in the film industry, now there were none. Six months earlier, Harry had rationalized that his film credits were impressive enough to assure him work whenever he wanted to return. "But now the bottom had dropped out of the film market," said Harry. "Even if I were willing to step down a notch, for the first time I found there was literally no work available, not even as a lowly editor."

So Harry tried to peddle a screenplay he had written about his brother Tom called *Thomas Forbes Chapin and the Cold, Cold World*. But he couldn't find any buyers. Instead, he decided to shift over from feature documentaries to feature films. "I figured the job potential there was greater," said Harry. "But still, there was nothing."

After six years as a filmmaker, Harry found himself out of work, on the street, a twenty-eight-year-old failure.

For lack of a better alternative, he applied for a hack license to drive a cab. Then, a few days later, he read in the *New York Times* society page that Clare MacIntyre had married a wealthy Latin businessman. Those two events triggered a whole series of memories and fantasies and fear: all those hot winter nights, summer walks, lakeside talks, camp concerts, and Clare; the innocence, the hope, her eyes; all the shine and promise of dreams of fame and fortune, of her dream to be a great actress, his to be a great singer with his pen name, H. Forster Chapin, that he'd use to autograph his albums. What went wrong?

"My head went through changes," Harry said. "I was Harry, the boy with potential, who was just goofing around and it was like a burr up my ass. I thought of myself as a total failure. I had this strong vision of picking up Clare somewhere; she getting into the backseat of my taxi and me seeing her in the rearview mirror and us recognizing each other. We would've both known right away that we had lost, that our dreams were gone, and that we had both sold out. She, to have settled down and settled in to that sort of comfortable life instead of what she'd always planned to do. And me? That all my big dreams came down behind the wheel of a cab. I imagined her getting in and saying to me, 'Hey, Harry, what happened to you?'"

He imagined that during a fifty-five-minute train ride on the Long Island Railroad when he wrote the initial concept and verse to the legendary story song "Taxi." The scene? San Francisco, of course. The place where he left his heart.

Ironically, Harry never drove a taxi. On the day he was to begin, he received three feature film offers in the mail and he took all three jobs. But the experience of having to confront his past and his broken dream of becoming a singer reinspired his songwriting ambitions. That spurred him to consider the idea of performing full-time as a solo act. That winter he wrote the songs "Sometime, Somewhere Wife" and "Could You Put Your Light On, Please," the latter of which was partially responsible for this inspiration. "I felt I wasn't writing songs with a nice mainstream feeling and beat," said Harry, "and this song made me feel like I could write other styles besides story songs."

But there were other encouraging signs. Although Harry performed once every six weeks at best, and then only for family or friends, the reactions grew more positive. Gradually, his impulse to perform began to emerge. He was like an athlete out of practice, remembering some old moves or quick fakes. "Every so often some weird thing came up and I'd get twenty-five bucks to sing somewhere," said Harry. "There were a couple of times I sang for friends and they were saying things like, 'God, you're so much better than your brothers.' And I said, 'But I can't sing as well as they can.' And they said, 'Yeah, that's true. But you can feel the things.'"

But the one event that clinched his decision to become a solo act resulted from the first positive response he ever received for his epic, "Dogtown." The song had never been a hit with audiences. Then, one weekend that winter, Trika Smith invited Harry to sing at her youth club in Princeton, New Jersey, where Judy Collins often sang and where Trika used to perform as a member of the Vassar College singing group. "Dogtown" went over fantastically. "I couldn't believe it," said Harry. "I did a double take on the audience to believe it was true."

Still, he wasn't totally convinced and decided to test his songs in a New York club before more critical and discriminating tastes. So one night he played a solo set at the Bitter End (hootenanny night) with Sandy in the audience for moral support. But the concert was a dismal failure, as Harry was hyper and overanxious and tried to "oversell" the crowd. "I really thought I had something," he said. "I sang 'Dirty Old Man,' 'It's My Day,' 'Could You Put Your Light On, Please,' 'Dogtown,' 'Any Old Kind of Day,' and 'Greyhound.' It was extraordinary, the miss. I mean, I didn't quite get it with the audience and I was up there shakin' my ass. Sandy said, 'You know, you really look obscene up there, like you're working too hard, wigglin' your ass around and you're really not graceful.'"

Harry searched for something new, an inkling or vision toward something he could try. The following week he went to see Kris Kristofferson and Carly Simon at the Bitter End, two rapidly rising stars appearing on the same bill. Harry was especially interested in Kristofferson. "Kris had a supercooled-out way of being," said Harry. "Perhaps too cooled out. But it seemed to me there were certain nice things about his relaxed attitude. When he sang, he sat on a stool and, in between songs, he talked about how he got to write them, in a very quiet voice."

A couple of days later, Harry returned to the Bitter End to perform another solo set, but this time combined some Kristoffersonian "coolness" with his frenetic gyrations. As at the Princeton Youth Club weeks before, the crowd reaction was overwhelming. "It was one of the first successful nights I ever felt by myself," Harry recalled. "I found my heavyweight material, the story songs, going over better than my lightweight. When I was bouncin' around, wigglin' my ass, it didn't go over, but when I was talking quietly and played mellowed-out thought songs, they were going over much better than the hyper thing. For me to say I was cooled out compared to Kristofferson was a joke. I was still about three times more energetic than he was. But at least it made it into something palatable and I wasn't so frenetic and anxious. And I resolved that that would be the new tonality I would have, one of revealing myself rather than trying to be cool or hyper."

More importantly, Harry developed a clear vision of what he had to offer as a performer. During the past two years, having witnessed the various successes and failures of The Chapins,

Harry had formulated his own ideas about the requirements of a successful performer. He had to be a merchandiser, a hustler and, above all, have a definable image. Now, he had it.

"It was the story songs," Harry explained, "and an open, positive way of relating to an audience. Besides, Paul Colby was managing another group at the time called Gunhill Road. And I kept saying to myself: 'If they can make it, I can.'"

One weekend in May, Harry performed as the opening act for The Chapins at the Village Gate, then the other nightclub bookend to the Bitter End. And once again, replete with his new "mellowed-out, stool style," the crowd fell in love with him. "That's when I started believing," said Harry. "At that point, I realized I didn't have it all by myself, but I could be a leader. I didn't need to get back with Tom and Steve. I was my own act!"

So Harry decided to give up filmmaking and commit himself to music, partially because of an idea Fred Kewley had conceived. In the summer of 1970, when Colby's contract expired as manager of The Chapins, Kewley, who had returned from Korea, appointed himself their manager. But except for the one Village Gate gig, Kewley was no more successful than Colby in booking The Chapins. So he came up with the idea of renting the downstairs room at the Village Gate to showcase the group.

"I worked out a deal," said Kewley, "where we could rent the downstairs room after the show *Jacques Brel Is Alive and Well and Living in Paris* finished. I could have them performing in New York seven nights a week and I could get the press down. The Chapins could work out new songs and get some noise going because when they were sitting over in Brooklyn, nothing was happening."

Kewley signed a five-week rental at $400 per week beginning June 29, 1971. Art D'Lugoff, the club's owner, was more than happy to accommodate him. The rental meant guaranteed income for generally slow midweek business, and for the money he was paid, D'Lugoff supplied nothing. The Chapins received no sound system, decorations or help, just an empty room filled with small cocktail tables and chairs. They had to supply everything, including tickets, drinks and paid advertisements. After the Brel show finished its two-hour performance at 9:30 P.M., the stage belonged to The Chapins, with only half an hour to set up before their ten o'clock show.

Suddenly a convenient forum emerged for Harry to test his music on a regular basis. The Chapins needed an opening act, and although Harry was aware he "didn't have it all himself" as a solo performer, he knew that if he could—as he wrote in the song "Six String Orchestra"—put a group together around his acoustic guitar—a bass player to keep the beat; a cellist to add a sweet, feminine counterpoint to his masculine, raspy voice; an electric guitarist to add some funk—and essentially surround himself with more competent musicians than himself, he "could make some of these story songs come alive."

Harry said of his thought at that time: "I was turned on by the cello in one of Judy Collins's songs. I figured if I could put a group together . . . But if everything fell through, I knew I was going back to filmmaking. That was the fall-back, solid position. I felt I was getting more out of music than I ever had before, and it was time to return to the field in a more committed way. I had just been paid for three feature films ($3,500). So I had some money to try something really far out. I knew I only had a short shot at making it, which meant I had to be more hard-assed about things, much more goal-oriented. And actually that was a comforting thought. Because I was Gapin' Chapin for a lot of my years and I had stuck my neck out a million times and made an ass of myself about 999,999 of those. I had the great security of knowing that I had to go pretty damn far to top some of the boo-boos I'd already made in my life. Which gave me a kind of security . . . why not take some chances? It became a personal philosophy of mine, the Chapin credo, 'When in doubt, do something.'"

Harry told Fred and The Chapins of his "opening act" idea. "We didn't give a shit," said Phil Forbes. "We could've had anybody opening for us. We didn't know whether Harry was going to make it or not. So for us, it was just another of Harry's everyday activities."

Nobody took Harry's idea very seriously. They believed he was just going to make a fool of himself. "When Harry said he wanted to be the lead act, everybody was sort of cringing. 'Oh, God, it's gonna be really awful,'" said brother James. "There was always the feeling that Harry was going to make a pratfall. That's why he always joked about Gapin' Chapin. Harry always wanted to be accepted by the 'in' crowd, and never was."

With more faith in Harry, K.B. once said: "I think Harry had a greater range of improvisation than any of the other boys. Harry could turn up overnight and decide to be a nuclear physicist or something."

Meanwhile, Fred Kewley found himself straddling the fence as titular manager for both Harry and The Chapins, with the knowledge that he'd pursue the winning operation. Fred had no contract with Harry, but then there was nothing to lose. Around this time, Harry told Fred, "What the hell, Carly Simon is doing what I do. She got a record deal, maybe I can. I'll try to get a half-assed record contract, get some songs around and some publishing going. We'll split the whole thing five ways, every dollar we make, and we'll all take twenty percent."

Deal!

But now he had to form a group. Only three weeks before opening night, Harry placed an ad in the *Village Voice* for a cellist and guitar player, and on his own began the search for a bass player. Tom suggested he call Leon Ogdibene from The Beautiful People. But Leon, who never took Harry very seriously, turned him down. "To him, Harry was always a little bit of a joke," said Tom. "He couldn't see Harry as a single act."

So Harry called John Wallace, who used to play bass with the brothers at Castro house parties and who always loomed large in the Chapin's lexicon. Wallace was also the "hot" voice in the Grace Church Choir with a five-octave range, from low bass to high falsetto. But Harry hadn't seen Wallace in seven years. In 1965, Wallace had moved to Florida, gotten married, then divorced. He had moved back to New Jersey and become a truck driver, drifting from Bloomfield to Newark to East Orange and finally East Newark, where he lived with another truck-driver friend.

"I had driven for a company for three years, so I went out and bought my own used tractor-trailer," said Wallace. "I ran it for seven months and then the engine blew out. It blew a hole right in the side of the block. It wasn't me either. I knew how to drive them, but the guy who owned it before me was pretty much of a madman. Anyway, the truck was laying up in the garage. I was broke. Overhaul would cost at least $3,300, maybe $5,500 dollars. Meanwhile, I drove my friend's truck because he had a contract to haul fuel to Newark Airport. I was twenty-seven and not doing much with my life. And then one day Harry called me. I hadn't seen him for seven years. Somehow he got my number."

Harry laid out the proposition.

". . . . Look, I need you to sing background vocals and play bass. All I can pay you is twenty bucks a week. I can't promise you anything, but we'll split whatever money we make five ways, and I'll give you a place to stay at my mother's. Hopefully we'll get a record contract and try to do an album."

"Harry, I'd love to. It sounds great," Wallace said. "But I haven't touched a bass since the last time I saw you."

"Don't worry," said Harry confidently. "I remember you were a good musician. You'll learn quick."

"Well, shit, if he wasn't going to worry about it, why should I?" Wallace said. "I never played bass to begin with. I just fucked around with the thing. I wasn't a bass player. I had it in the sense I was in the choir for years. I had a natural feel for music that way. I always listened for bass lines and I knew what bass was supposed to do. I had a concept. And I got the feeling that Harry knew what I could do more than I did at that point."

Harry had his bass player.

Pressed for time, one Tuesday afternoon, Harry auditioned all respondents of the *Village Voice* ad at Elspeth's apartment on 136 Hicks Street. Beginning at 11:30 A.M. Harry tested twenty musicians every half hour on the hour: fifteen guitarists, four cellists and one violinist. He had them all play their version of "Could You Put Your Light On, Please." All the guitarists failed miserably. One of them was a nine-year-old boy.

"I discovered an incredible variety in guitarists," Harry once said to the Associated Press. "Some could hardly play a C chord and others were quite good. All four cellists were very good. Anybody who takes up cello has to be serious about the instrument. I picked a guy named Tim Scott because he had the most flair."

Tim Scott was a twenty-one-year-old Brooklyn boy who, for lack of anything better to do, answered the ad after his mother discovered it in the paper. "That summer I wasn't doing much," said Scott. "I was going to City College in the fall and looking for something to do for the summer. My mother always read all the ads in the *Village Voice* and she saw one that said a rock singer-songwriter was looking for a cellist to open in a Village club in two weeks."

Scott, like Wallace, was told the proposition and accepted.

Harry's fourth and final addition, an electric guitar player, was eventually discovered via a demo tape that was circulating around the music industry and somehow wound up in the hands of Fred Kewley. The guitar player was Ron Palmer, a thirty-six-year-old small-time musician who lived in Syracuse, New York. Since 1959, Palmer had performed in every conceivable type of band, from country-western and rock 'n' roll to jazz trios. As a result, he had developed a unique "café" guitar style. He was a master of harmonics, with a knack for finding guitar licks, riffs or hooks.

"I used to work in a place called the Barge Inn in Syracuse," said Palmer. "I did a demo tape of a couple of songs I wrote and some guitar music. The guy who used to own this Barge Inn had a friend he thought might be interested in hearing it. I was looking for an agent who could get me some gigs instead of just playing in one joint all the time. This friend turned out to be Fred Kewley."

Kewley played the tape over the phone to Harry, who liked it and gave Palmer a call.

Said Palmer: "He asked me if I'd like to join the group and laid out what the proposition was. I went down to New York for a promise of twenty bucks a week and a place to stay. I mean, that's how down I was. He said there's a possibility of getting a record contract. He was very low-key about it. He tried to give me an honest outlook about the potential. He told me about the story songs, but it was hard for me to visualize from his explanation what they were all about."

On June 22, just one week before their debut at the Village Gate, the entire crew met at Fred Kewley's office in a dingy, downtown section of Port Chester, New York. They were a motley crew indeed, a mixed bag of men, from their ages to their personalities. Tim Scott was quiet and conservative. John Wallace looked like the truck driver he was, big, burly, overweight and a terrible dresser, with a wry, deadpan sense of humor. Ron Palmer was the wandering backwoods musician with a down-home country charm and glibness. And Harry was the riotous, rebel ringleader. The only thing they had in common was their hunger to make good and, except for Scott, all were married men with children, including Kewley.

As a musical collective, they were as limited as their backgrounds were diverse. The musical capability of each man was pretty much one-dimensional. "There were four lame-os there," said Tom Chapin. "Each one did one thing very well. Harry had the songs and the vision, Wallace could sing great and play bass adequately. Palmer played one kind of guitar style, but other than that was very limited. He couldn't sing very well. Scott was a cellist of the medium rank, pretty good, not great."

Realizing their limitations, Harry and Fred arranged all the songs for the strength of each member, seven tunes in total:

"Could You Put Your Light On, Please," "Dogtown," "Baby Never Cries," "Any Old Kind of Day," "Greyhound," "Sandy," and "Sometime, Somewhere Wife." Harry was still in the process of completing "Taxi." The group rehearsed in a loft Kewley used for some theatrical business he had on the side, and spent what seemed endless hours arranging, shaping and tailoring each song to each member by finding parts each could play, all to set up and emphasize Harry's voice and acoustic guitar.

"We spent five or six days, hours on end, arranging those first seven songs," said Kewley. "We wrote cello parts for Tim and background vocals for John Wallace, and structured the songs, trying to make something out of them."

The day before debut night, Harry moved the entire operation to Brooklyn Heights and Elspeth's apartment. Then, precisely as planned, the four strangers—armed with seven songs, a few gag lines, and nervous hope—opened at the Village Gate on June 29, 1971. They called themselves Harry, not Harry Chapin, to avoid confusion with The Chapins.

That night, the concert was a completely home-brewed family operation. After the Brel show finished at 9:30 P.M., both bands plus family, friends and friends of friends helped set up the drum platform, wire guitar amps, hook up microphones, and straighten chairs, all in a frenzy of last-minute preparation. Wives and girlfriends took admission tickets ($2.50) at the door and also functioned as cocktail waitresses. Ex-Cornellian and Sherwooder Rob White helped man the lights along with Jebbie Hart. And prior to the performances, Kewley had posters printed and strategically placed throughout Greenwich Village. He also put a huge banner outside the front door that read THE CHAPINS. There was no banner for Harry.

Even the audience of approximately fifty people was filled with home stock. The brothers and Fred had invited everyone they knew "within a two-hour distance of New York." Among others, there was Elspeth, K.B., the Castros, David Ostraff, Jim Lipscomb, and Michael and Trika Burke. Sandy Chapin was there also, suddenly finding herself in personal crisis, trying to assimilate her husband's new "performer" role, a role that, for years, he promised he would not play.

"I really married Harry with my eyes open, knowing who he was, and he had said he'd never be a performer," Sandy explained. "He had said that for years, so I absolutely knew it was true. He would *never be a performer*. He said it had broken up his own home life and there was no way that you can have marriage and family and travel. And he said that so many times that when I was sitting there watching him perform at the Village Gate, I said to myself, 'Is he trying to tell me something?'"

PART THREE

But the battles are of small concern
Mere looks and words and smiles
It's the war he fears he loses
You can see it in his eyes.

—Unknown

CHAPTER VIII

Same Sad Singer

For better or for worse, Harry's life had come full circle, and he was determined to see his music dream through to the end. If he failed, he wanted to blame no one but himself. So he left nothing to chance and bore down harder than ever to make things click—the group, the songs, the performances, the lines—and to make them all "sell." He paid close attention to every detail, like a ship's captain attempting to steer a steady course through the rough waters of anonymity. His course was simple: attract favorable press and send the reviews to record companies, who then would get excited enough—hopefully—to come down and see his act. Without good reviews, the journey was hopeless. No record company would bother to send a representative, much less offer a contract.

The first two weeks at the Village Gate "were not very promising," said Harry. "In fact, it looked bad." Many nights, the group Harry and The Chapins outnumbered the customers. One evening they played to an audience of four. The club held 225 seats. On a good night, usually weekends, they attracted perhaps one hundred people, but the average crowd was more like ten or fifteen.

And even on the "good nights" there was no cause for optimism, since most seats were filled with Chapin family or friends to impress a journalist or critic who was thought to be in the crowd. Harry had a list of all the local newspapers and record companies and, each day, during rehearsal breaks in the basement of Grace Church, he called them to generate interest. Even a vague promise by some callow concert reviewer had him phoning friends and relatives to ask them to come and clap. "I still remember packing that damn place every time some record or press guy came down," said brother James. "We'd call on family and relatives and suddenly there would be a roaring crowd of eighty-seven."

On those nights, for good measure, Harry stood outside the front door before showtime, to bring people in off Bleecker Street, but with little success. One time John Lennon and Yoko Ono passed by. "I went up to them and started walking along," said Harry. "I told Lennon how much I admired him and that we had rented this club and that it would be a gigantic thing for us if he could come over one night."

Lennon, in an attempt to rid himself of this annoying intruder, nodded a grudging yes, but, needless to say, he never came.

The small audiences, though, were a positive force. Harry played under minimal pressure that enabled him to gain self-confidence and work out performance snags. It was very important to him that everyone in the group have his role, so his concerts were carefully packaged, leaving little room for spontaneity. "Up until then, I made it a point to be well prepared," said Harry. "We had to have our schtick down, our lines."

Said Ron Palmer: "Harry was into being a serious performer and very seldom cracked any jokes or anything like that."

But sometimes, with a rough audience, Harry had to reach down for something extra, and gradually the gutsiness he displayed offstage began to emerge in performances. He did anything to win over a crowd and often made a "complete ass" of himself. "Man, there were times I wanted to slink offstage when he didn't recover well from something he said," recalled Palmer. "But for the most part, Harry was a helluva performer because he was ballsy. He plowed through anything."

In the meantime, Harry's music career took on new dimensions when he began writing songs for a new ABC children's program called *Make a Wish*. Tom had become host of the show a few weeks earlier. It was a half-hour program slated for 11:30 on Sunday mornings and created to compete with other popular informational children's shows such as *The Electric Company* and the number-one ratings rival, *Sesame Street*. Like its competitors, the program was designed, according to producer Lester Cooper, to provide "an educational experience for children between the ages of six and twelve." But unlike them, *Make a Wish* originated in ABC's news department, not the children's programming department, and therefore had a larger budget for on-location filming, instead of the usual in-studio approach.

Cooper needed a host who could sing, perform and write original songs. The host also had to be warm and personable, alive and happening, very American and very moderate. "I decided I wanted somebody who was kind of clean and pure and non-extreme," said Cooper. "I was looking for a guy who could perform, but also relate."

Several candidates who fit this description were considered, a cavalcade of singer-songwriters from veteran folksinger Oscar Brand to new names like David Pomeranz, who later wrote Barry Manilow's smash hit, "Tryin' to Get the Feeling." And then there was Tom Chapin, who heard of the job through Paul Colby on the day Colby's contract expired as manager of The Chapins. All of them were put through a careful grilling of screen tests and interviews. "I went up and met two twenty-five-year-old girls who were production assistants," said Tom. "And they did everything short of checking my teeth for some horse infection."

Despite the promising crop of candidates, Cooper was not convinced, and one week before the first filming, he decided to go for broke and get James Taylor, at the time the hottest name in pop music. One year earlier, Taylor, the twenty-one-year-old phenomenon, had become almost a legend with one album and his trendsetting hit, "Fire and Rain," and graced the covers of *Time* and *Newsweek*. "I went up to see James Taylor on Martha's

Vineyard," said Cooper. "But he turned us down. He just decided at that particular moment in his career that he didn't want to do anything. He just wanted to stay up on Cape Cod and live in his house and be left alone."

Apparently, Taylor was heavily into drugs at the time. The following day, Cooper told one of his ABC associates: "God, he's almost autistic. He could barely talk!"

When the final day arrived, Tom edged out Brand, in part because of his "youthful," "visible" appearance, but also because of Harry. Nepotism scored again! Cooper needed a songwriter, and during interviews Tom had told him about his brother's musical abilities and specifically how Harry wrote songs for The Chapins.

"That's what clinched it," said Tom. "They took Harry sight unseen. Cooper felt that if Harry could do the job, a brother duo would make for a good working relationship."

However, on the first day Harry met Cooper, they had an explosive argument. Cooper had given Tom four versions of a theme song from which to choose for the program. The lyrics were written by Cooper, the music by a young songwriter named Bernie Green. Tom didn't like any of the versions, but Harry found one with possibilities and rewrote the entire middle section of the song. When Harry showed the rewrite to Cooper, Lester was delighted, but not enough to pay Harry for his efforts. He felt that Bernie Green "wrote most of the original music," but, more precisely, he had prearranged that Green receive credit and royalties for the song.

"So he just started hollering at Harry," said Tom. "Cooper was like a bear. He hollered and yelled at you. He was known for a nasty temper. I don't like to get into yelling arguments, but I stood up and started yelling because he was yelling at Harry."

Harry lost the argument, but his aggressiveness won Cooper's respect and the job, which for Harry was perfect: no office or nagging boss, only a small sacrifice of his time (about two months per year); between royalties and fees he earned hefty money (approximately $40,000 per year). Now Harry was being paid to do what he loved most, write music. Before summer's end, he wrote thirty-two songs for the sixteen slated programs.

After concerts at the Village Gate, Harry often stayed up until early morning writing songs, usually on the Long Island Railroad back to Point Lookout, scribbling verse in spiral notebooks. Other nights he took the subway to Espeth's apartment, and on occasion he spent the early morning hours at Maria's Diner on Montague Street, his boyhood greasy spoon and the only all-night restaurant in the Heights. There he'd grab a late-night bite and write his one-word songs for the show: "Press," "Fish," "Ball," "Wall" and "Circle," which later became the Chapin theme song, used to close all his concerts. In fact, of the 160 *Make a Wish* songs Harry eventually wrote during the show's five year run, only "Circle" was later recorded. "I wrote it at three o'clock in the morning," said Harry. "It took me about a half hour. I was sitting there bleary-eyed, with my guitar in my lap, a cup of tea in front of me, and saying to myself, 'Circle, I've got a word . . .'"

Then, around 6:30 A.M., Harry gave the songs to Tom, who had less than four hours to learn them before the live 10:00 A.M. recording session at ABC's Manhattan studios. If Harry was in Point Lookout the night before, he called Tom and either played back a tape recording of the music or sang his last-minute creations over the phone.

Either way, the time pressure was enormous, but it served the positive function of sharpening Harry's composing skills. He learned to write to order, and write well. Although *Make a Wish* was a children's show, Harry was told to write "adult" songs.

"Ordinarily, a children's song is thought of as nothing more than a bad adult song with simplistic ideas," said Harry. "But I found this wasn't the case because adults, if they're approached on some kind of premise, such as antiwar songs, will be polite and listen for a while because they're supposed to hate war. But children are the ultimate tough audience. You could be God, you could be Stevie Wonder, and if you go and sing for six-year-olds, it doesn't matter. There has to be something funny in it, something strange, something happy or something sad."

With steady income from his songwriting job and the increasing involvement of his band, Harry, for the first time, began to "feel a sense of direction" in his life. After three weeks at the Village Gate, his group had developed a complex live sound and possessed all the finesse and subtlety of a fine string quartet. John Wallace's five-octave-range voice began to sound like "a one-man choir"; Ron Palmer's riffs, haunting; Tim Scott's cello lines, enchanting; and Harry's stage manner had become more poised and refined.

At the same time, despite the progress, Harry knew The Chapins were eagerly waiting in the wings. He had to offer something shocking, even lewd, to distinguish himself from his brothers. Once when Harry called a newspaper and introduced himself, the reviewer said, "Oh, The Chapins, I've already seen them." Harry knew that he had to differentiate himself from his brothers, but he also knew he could do little to improve upon the seven songs already arranged. "However, I could stage my material better and create more impact, mystery and theatricality," said Harry.

For dramatic effect, he began to "gross people out with a wild introduction to 'Dogtown,'" opening his sets with the houselights down, the audience in total darkness as he belted out the opening lyrics to "Could You Put Your Light On, Please."

Harry also began to involve his band in performance with more clowning and wisecracks in between numbers, playing off the catcalls of the crowd. To add further humor and counterbalance Harry's melancholy melodies, Palmer, midway into the performance, sang a series of thirty-second compositions he called "Experiences," off-color joke songs sung in a sexually suggestive style. Palmer's deep country drawl boomed out "Lesson Eighteen," a lighthearted ditty about a sleeping bag, or "Nine," about getting a rupture on a bicycle, or "Lesson Twenty-One," the showstopper, a tune about catching the clap.

Gradually, the group Harry began to overshadow The Chapins, and, in fact, became such a powerful act that by the time they finished their set, any subsequent performers would have seemed almost anticlimactic. When The Chapins came on, half the club had already emptied out. "Occasionally, on a Friday or Saturday night, Greenwich Village tour buses unloaded tourists and filled the club to capacity," said Doug Walker. "But after listening to Harry's set, most of them left before we came on. People who were interested in hearing Harry would leave, not knowing and not caring what we were going to be doing anyway."

Said Steve Chapin bitterly: "It was weird, because a lot of people came down to see us and left after Harry performed. I got a little testy about that. The place cleared out. All the noise and buzz and hubbub changed into a normal club when we came on."

During the day, Harry continued to try to attract press people to his performance, but it wasn't until July 22 that his "honcho-hustling" paid off. That night, Mike Jahn, a music critic for the *New York Times,* planned to review Harry's group. A good review in the *Times* was worth a dozen in any other local paper. So once again, Harry went back to the phones to make sure the house was papered and, half an hour before showtime, he resumed his familiar position outside the front door of the Gate. Everyone else manned their posts: wives and girlfriends took tickets, the brothers and band members set up the equipment, Rob White and Jeb Hart manned the lights. And just as they had practiced the past month, the houselights went down, the music came up, and Harry's voice bellowed out the first verse of "Could You Put Your Light On, Please."

In the meantime, the packed house played its role admirably, offering wild applause right on cue at the end of each number and a final standing ovation when the last note died. All of this left Mike Jahn in head-shaking wonder at his small cocktail table. "It was all just very family blood," said Jeb Hart. "We got everybody down to make a lot of noise and make it sound full and spontaneous. And Jahn walked in and saw a room of people going bananas. Once that ball starts rolling, it's very quick."

Very quick indeed. Two days later, on July 24, Jahn wrote a glowing review in the *Times,* and by a stroke of brilliant luck, the piece was perfectly placed in the newspaper. That day, there was a major airline hijacking story on the front page which carried over to page 16, and right under the article was the headline of Jahn's review: HARRY CHAPIN SINGS GORGEOUS BALLADS.

"I remember Harry the first time he saw that review," said John Wallace. "Tim was buying papers all the time to see if something was going to happen. He came running down the stairs of the Gate and yelled out,'Hey, it's here, right here!' And Harry grabbed it right out of his hands."

With Jahn's review in hand, Harry shifted gears and accelerated his strategy. He had a giant blowup of the article made and placed it in the glass showcase out front. He xeroxed dozens of copies and sent them to record companies, then followed up each mailing with a telephone call. More often than not, he called as his own manager. Typically, he'd first reach a secretary who refused to put him through to the president of the company. So Harry would try to charm her until she finally gave in and put him through to some lower-echelon record executive. Then Harry would go into an aggressive monologue:

> *"Hi, my name is Fred Kewley. I'm a manager and I found this guy—he's absolutely unbelievable. He'll blow your mind. He's going to be the next Bob Dylan. Right now, he's playing at the Village Gate and he's been favorably reviewed in the New York Times.*
>
> *"You really have to hear this guy! His name is Harry Chapin. He's a former filmmaker. He did cinema-verité documentaries and won an Academy Award nomination and has developed a unique storytelling style that's almost like mini-movies. He's got a cello in the group and a sound like you've never heard."*
>
> *Skeptical, the record executive would ask, "Has any other company seen him?"*
>
> *"Sure," Harry would lie. "We've already got strong interest from Ampex, but we'd really like to see if you guys would be*

interested because we respect what you do as a company and feel that you've got more clout."

When Harry called Ampex, he used another record company name.

Calling Epic Records, with whom The Chapins were still contracted, he couldn't use Fred's name, so he announced, "Hi, this is Irving Schlegel . . ."

Harry later said of this time, "I felt like an ass, but to make it you have to push."

But once he got caught. He called Vanguard Records and asked for the A&R director. He reached Dave Wilkes, who had managed the Bitter End a few years before. But Harry didn't know it was Wilkes, and midway through his sales pitch, Wilkes interrupted the familiar-sounding voice. "Fred Kewley? Is that you, Harry?"

"What amazed me," remembered Tom Chapin, "was what a sure sense Harry had that he was going somewhere. We were sitting at the Village Gate doing our music and we expected the world to come to us. But Harry just went, 'Fuck the world!' It didn't matter. And it struck us as being cold and hard and calculating, but that's the way the world was. We were insulating ourselves. These nice boys playing nice music . . ."

In fact, The Chapins were floundering so badly that Kewley shifted his attention to Harry and became an ideal manager for him, not so much for business reasons as personal ones. While Kewley was laid-back and reserved, Harry was a steamroller whose personality could easily manipulate and control Kewley. Though Harry didn't like being told what to do, Fred didn't mind taking instructions. It made for a very pleasant relationship. "Fred was sort of a yes-man," said Jebbie Hart. "Harry basically was his own manager. He was out front, making calls, running around making sure things were happening. Fred was more an assistant to Harry's wishes and concerns and very rarely initiated any strong ideas of his own."

"The biggest strength I had at that time," Harry explained, "was really being a hard-ass. I expected to do everything myself and solve everything myself. Fred was a good arranger and helper there, but I was very willing to do all the hard-ass horsing through: figuring out an angle, pushing with the audience, calling up newspapers, calling up record companies. I had been a behind-the-scenes merchandiser with my brothers. I knew what I had to do if I was going to make it. I probably had more experience working behind the scenes in the music business than Fred Kewley did."

Indeed, Harry so continuously hustled and schemed that he paid more attention to the business side of music than the music itself. "In fact, John and Tim and I would get disgusted," said Ron Palmer, "because we were supposed to be in rehearsals and Harry showed up late. He was just running. Trying to make all these contacts click and work."

But Harry's frenetic behavior was not without justification. He was trying to succeed in an industry where failure was the norm, success the exception. He was also nearly twenty-nine years old and, having discovered the work ethic late in life, he had reached a point where sheer effort, not talent, would dictate his destiny. He had no rich uncle in the music business; no natural tie-ins to make the going easier. Harry had to create his own market, and the competition was tough.

"You got thousands of tapes from individuals," said Wilkes of Vanguard Records. "Usually you got them from producers, lawyers, or managers that were respected and well-known. But the average kid with a tape off the street didn't even get heard in 85 percent of the cases."

And Harry was no different, until Ann Purtill, a talent scout at Elektra Records, became fascinated with his music. A short, rotund woman with light brown hair, Purtill possessed both a quick wit and a sharp eye for detail. She was an urbane, sophisticated New Yorker with a delightfully subtle, sarcastic sense of humor. Formerly a music staff photographer at *Vogue* magazine, she had joined Elektra only a few months earlier to cover night-clubs, find artists and screen material. The night Purtill first saw Harry perform, she was overwhelmed. As usual, the place was packed. "I thought, 'Gee, this is an unrecorded guy and he's fill-ing a club,'" said Purtill. "People with contracts can't fill clubs."

However, it was the magnitude of Harry's performance, not the multitude of patrons, that impressed her most. In less than five weeks' time, Harry had a finely honed act. He had cleverly stitched together bits and pieces of performance. Now it was a truly dynamic act, so emotional in intensity that his performances went from a mere show into the realm of an "experience." The latest and final addition to that "experience" was a song Harry sang for the first time in public that night, his ode to Clare Mac-Intyre, "Taxi."

"He did 'Taxi' as an encore and it was terrific," said Purtill. "He opened with 'Could You Put Your Light On, Please' in the dark. I mean, when people were unrecorded, they usually sat there with a guitar and hoped, but this was very well staged. At that point, to sign somebody, you had to get the president of your record company to agree."

After the show, Purtill told Harry that she liked what she saw and needed a demo tape of his music, but made no commitment. "She said there was no way he could get on the label," said John Wallace, "because Elektra already had thirty artists and they weren't looking for any more."

But that was merely a ploy. From Ann's perspective, Harry "seemed too good to be true." So unbeknownst to anyone, she secretly went to the Gate three more times, and each night she walked away with the same terrific reaction she had on the first.

"I thought, as an entertainer, he was the best live act I'd ever seen," said Purtill. "His songs were totally different from any-thing anyone else was doing. There was nobody like him. He was purely one of a kind."

Purtill wasn't the only one to make that discovery. By August, six major record companies had shown mild interest in Harry:

RCA, Capitol, Atlantic, A&M, Bell and Vanguard. Harry and his band were ecstatic. "We were like little kids," recalled Kewley. "We couldn't believe it! We had been at the Village Gate, playing seven nights a week, with maybe thirty people coming in and not making a dime—and all of a sudden . . ."

"For the first time in my life," said Harry, "I believed in capitalism."

Meanwhile, when the five-week rental expired, The Chapins were no better off than before and embarked on a cross-country tour to promote a single they had recorded for Epic Records. Both songs on the disc were Harry's. One was called "Lady, While You're Working on My Life" and the other was called "The Only Thing You Ever Have to Do." The single was promptly pressed, released and went out to radio stations nationwide.

"But nobody wanted it," said Doug Walker. "Tom, Steve and Phil left on a cross-country driving trip to personally promote it, splitting up the country into three geographical regions, and went to various radio stations. But they didn't get any real good reaction."

So The Chapins recorded a second single, this time two songs by Steve Chapin, "Hard Workin' Man" and "You Deliver Me." But once again, there was just not the response they expected, and The Chapins disbanded.

In the meantime, Harry extended the Village Gate rental five more weeks. Only now Harry appeared as the main act, with other groups opening for him, such as Gene Pastilli and the Mann Act. Outside the club, The Chapins banner was replaced with one that read Harry Chapin, and the marquee read the same. But despite his brothers' absence, the rest of the Chapin machine remained well-oiled and intact. "It was still a very home-brewed situation," said Jebbie Hart, who continued as light man. "It was devotion time to help Harry."

Of all the record companies, Harry first tried to get a contract with Vanguard Records because of his longtime acquaintance with Dave Wilkes. Wilkes hadn't seen Harry perform since the days of The Chapin Brothers, more than seven years before.

"Harry had grown tremendously," said Wilkes. "He was writing better, he was much more dynamic and dramatic. He was much better by himself, or with his new band, than with his brothers."

And as with every other record or press person who came down, the papered house went undetected. "If there was any hype," said Wilkes, "you didn't feel it."

But Vanguard was indecisive about Harry "because they didn't know what to make of his storytelling style," Wilkes said. "They—the top brass—felt it was a little too contrived. But they didn't say no." Instead, they offered Harry a singles deal much like the one Epic Records gave The Chapins. But Harry wanted no part of that arrangement.

Instead, he pursued Elektra Records. Of all the labels concerned, this one interested him the most because during the fifties and early sixties Elektra and its enterprising owner, Jac Holzman, recorded many of the folk artists Harry emulated and admired as a teenager: Hamilton Camp, Bob Gibson, Oscar Brand, Erik Darling, Phil Ochs and Josh White, among others.

Holzman was one of the great entrepreneurs of the music industry, a Horatio Alger child of the Great Depression. Holzman started Elektra Records in 1949, with $600 and a small tape recorder in a Greenwich Village storefront. In 1970 he sold the company to the multinational conglomerate Warner Communications for $10 million and then stayed on as Elektra's president. But by this time pop music had already felt the enormous popularity of hard rock. Elektra adjusted to the times by signing numerous "folk-rock" acts such as The Doors and Love. And by 1971, the company held two of the genre's hottest names, Bread and Carly Simon. From Harry's perspective, his music was similar to theirs, and he felt Elektra's "soft rock" reputation would perfectly complement his story-song style.

Harry followed Ann Purtill's suggestion and recorded a demo tape of seven songs (for approximately $2,000) at Media Sound on West 57th Street in Manhattan. The tape included Harry's sleeper, "Taxi." Naturally, Harry sent a copy to every company interested in him. Purtill received hers one evening at the Gate when she came to see him perform again. Over that summer, Ann had grown to take a strong personal interest in Harry, and since she had yet to sign her first artist, she hoped that "Harry would be that one." But that night she learned of the interest from all the other record labels and immediately reported her finding to Holzman. As was custom, Ann dealt with Jac in writing. On August 27, 1971, she sent him this memo:

Jac, here is a tape of Harry Chapin. He's the older (28) brother of The Chapins and, incidentally, writes much of their material. I saw Harry several weeks ago and again this week at the Village Gate. I think he is a premier artist, and I urge you to listen to the tape and perhaps try to see him in person.

He told me the other night his group has been together since June. The instrumentation is different and both interesting and effective. Harry sings lead and plays acoustic guitar. There is a Fender bass and amplified lead guitar, both of whom are fine musicians and both of whom sing harmony lines. The special thing of this group, however, is a cello. The player is a bitch and the mellow mixture is a marvelous complement to Harry's occasionally rough voice . . . Harry does, in person, occasionally get a bit too grating of voice for dramatic emphasis.

My other complaint about his material is that it is too long; sometimes this is okay, but sometimes it seems to me not necessary. In person they seem to hold the audience's attention. I find—both times—that Harry himself reminds me of James Taylor of 1968, with a lot of the same warmth, if somewhat less magic.

I really think he can be very, very major, and that he shouldn't slip by us because too many are pending. I will be heartbroken, of course, if you pass on him, but I'll feel better knowing you've seen and heard him.

At first Holzman did not share Ann Purtill's enthusiasm. Commuting on business between Hawaii, Japan and California, Holzman was in New York one week, read Ann's memo and went to see Harry at the Gate with Bruce Harris, his new advertising and publicity chief. "Jac didn't like him," said Purtill. "Bruce Harris didn't like him either."

Ann felt Harris influenced Jac's impression, and a few weeks later, she convinced Holzman to see Chapin a second time. Still, his reaction remained unchanged, so Ann hammered away: "You've got to sign him! she wrote him in one memo. "There's nobody who writes like this. He can be great. There's all kinds of potential."

Holzman remembered, "It was the first time I ever saw Ann go out on a limb for an artist."

Though Holzman had yet to listen to Chapin's demo tape, he grudgingly gave in to Ann's better judgment. As was often the case, Holzman gave his employees considerable responsibility. Although it was true Ann was new to Elektra, she was also a veteran of the club scene and Holzman respected her intuition, believing she was "a member of the golden ears club," an oft-heard cliché used in the music business. Holzman offered a $3,500 advance. Ecstatic, Ann relayed the message to Harry and Fred. "We were looking for $5,000 maybe, if we were lucky," said Kewley. "We were looking for anybody willing to sign Harry."

But with all the sudden interest from other record companies, Harry held out and told Ann he'd think it over, primarily because Columbia, the largest record company, decided to enter the contract derby. This occurred when Columbia A&R man, Paul Leka, was alerted to Chapin via Buddy Robbins, a friend of his at Chappell Music. Like most A&R men, Leka's job was to find talent and produce acts for the label.

One evening, Leka went down to the Gate with Robbins to see Chapin, and he loved him. A few days later, Leka met with Harry and Fred at CBS and listened to the demo tape. Leka was impressed again. He sent an office memo to Columbia president

Clive Davis, as well as Kip Cohen and other top brass at the label. He wanted them to see Harry perform and a date was set. In the meantime, Robbins felt he had stumbled onto something big and he tried to arrange a quick record deal with Chapin before the numbers got too high. The deal fell through.

On the night of October 12, 1971, Davis showed up at the Village Gate along with a string of Columbia cronies, and by evening's end, he adored Chapin. The story songs, the cello, the drama were all something new to Davis, and he liked that. Davis always had a penchant for original talent. Over the years he had signed Janis Joplin, Bruce Springsteen, and later on Patti Smith. He had also signed Bob Dylan. Ironically, Davis had been in Dylan's Village apartment minutes before Chapin's performance, selecting songs and sequences for Dylan's *Greatest Hits* album. "I thought Harry was as original as you could get," said Davis. "I was enormously impressed by him—in the material, as a person, as a potential writer-performer. I was very eager to sign him."

Said Leka of that night: "Clive loved Harry. He definitely wanted him. Kip Cohen wanted him. So they just used their old CBS policy of, you know, 'cool it, show you're excited, but be careful so you don't get killed later with figures.'"

Ann Purtill also showed up and watched the enemy camp from the sidelines. She found out about it through Fred Kewley, who had called her about Clive Davis's sudden interest, with the hope of "baiting" her affections and increasing Elektra's meager offer. Kewley's tactic worked. The following day, Purtill wrote Holzman:

> I saw Harry again last night. Clive came with a huge entourage. The group was its usual fine self and the audience reaction again was insane. For your information, as of preshow time, Harry and manager Fred Kewley were still leaning toward us if they have a choice.

After the show, Davis offered Chapin $5,000 and then left on a business trip, as did Jac Holzman. But before Holzman left, he got word from Ann of Davis's offer and countered with $7,500. "That's absolutely it," Holzman told her. "That's what I paid for Judy Collins."

Harry was exuberant. Holzman's offer was double Carly Simon's original advance ($3,500) and greater than the average advance for a new artist (then $5,000).

"I loved the challenge when Clive and Jac and other record company people were coming down," said Harry nostalgically. "I loved those nights. It put requirements on me to perform and push and feel my adrenalin flow. I felt alive. The fact that I could persuade these important people to spend hours on me was tremendously exciting; the same people who spent hours with Bob Dylan, Paul Simon, Judy Collins . . ."

"Harry was in heaven," said Rob White. "So was Fred. They were both laughing about it a lot behind the scenes."

In the meantime, the band was broke. By September, Harry could no longer afford to pay the $400 per week rental alone. So he rented the Gate for a week at a time—and only when a record executive wanted to see his act. In addition, Tim Scott arranged some concert dates outside New York to help bring in some money. They played Sarah Lawrence and Bennington College for $300 a pop.

"We got really frustrated," said Tim Scott. "All of us wanted a contract, especially so because no one in the group had any money. Harry and Fred kept putting it off, waiting for a better contract."

Ron Palmer said of that time: "We played occasionally on weekends that fall. That gave me a chance to go home to Syracuse for a while and see my wife and kid. But every time I took a bus down to New York I was wondering, What the hell is this? Is it over? What's happening?"

Finally, on a bright, sunny October morning, Jac Holzman was driving down the California coast from Monterey to Los Angeles in an expensive rental car. During the trip, he listened to Chapin's demo tape wearing headphones connected to a stereo cassette on the front seat. The volume was high as he raced down the empty highway against the splendid backdrop of the sun rising over Big Sur. By the time Holzman reached L.A., he had fallen in love with Harry's music. "It might have been the setting, but the songs really hit home," said Holzman. "I was impressed by 'Taxi.' But I was also impressed by the totality of what he was able to do, the emotional moods he was able to evoke. They hung together in a way that said appropriate to me, appropriate for its time."

When Holzman returned to New York a few days later, he told Ann the good news. "He came back and said, 'Oh, Jesus, that song, that "Taxi," it's just a wonderful song,'" recalled Purtill. "He said, 'I've got to have him. He can have $15,000, that's my top offer.'"

Deal!

Clive Davis, who was still away on business, could not be reached for a counter offer. But as far as Harry was concerned, it didn't matter. His heart was with Elektra and he was particularly excited about the possibility of becoming the number-one artist on the roster, a spot held at that time by Carly Simon via her hit song, "That's The Way I've Always Heard It Should Be." Harry was convinced he could topple her.

"He had a terrible competitiveness," said Purtill. "He once said to me, 'I want to knock Carly Simon out of the box.' Harry's way of connecting to success at that moment was to replace her."

On November 4, Harry officially ended his thirteen-week stint at the Village Gate and verbally agreed to a contract with Jac Holzman. Holzman made arrangements for Harry to record his repertoire in Elektra's studios at 1855 Broadway and pick the best ten or twelve songs for the album. Then, within a week's time, the contract papers would be printed and ready for signing. "They got together and shook hands," said Ann Purtill. "I was in Boston. I called in and they said, 'It's done.'"

Holzman was proud of his new acquisition and gave Chapin a sense of the place by inviting him to an executive lunch and a grand tour of Electra's modern East Coast office high atop the Gulf & Western Building at Columbus Circle. The office, built in a circle, had plush carpeting, mahogany tables, lots of chrome and glass and lithographs of rock stars on the walls. From the windows one had a breathtaking view of Central Park, the Manhattan skyline and, off in the distance, Brooklyn Heights.

Harry loved his new home, so Holzman invited Harry to his: a converted barn in upstate New York elegantly furnished with a spacious living room, sunken sofa and a waterbed in front of a nine-foot-high fireplace. Holzman also had a recording studio on the premises, along with approximately thirty speakers pumping music from different directions all over the house.

On November 8, a Monday, Ann Purtill returned from Boston and found a tape of Harry's songs on her desk along with a note that read: "I'm coming to you! I'm coming to the people who first believed in me. Let's make music!" Ann promptly sent a memo to Jac, saying that she liked "the whole tape" and was "ready to do the album." Ann then tried to call Harry, but couldn't get hold of him.

"Sometime over that weekend something happened," said Purtill. "For the rest of that week I couldn't find Harry. Everyone I called said something like, 'He's at a rehearsal at Steve's house.' So I called Steve's house in Brooklyn Heights and he'd be at a rehearsal at Tom's house. And apparently I was calling where he was and he just wouldn't come to the phone. So I called Jac and said, 'Something's the matter. I smell a rat.' He said, 'No, no, you're imagining things. It's your first signing. You're nervous. He's probably just resting somewhere.'"

Ann's intuitions were correct. Over that weekend, Clive Davis entered the picture again. Since no contract papers were signed yet with Elektra, Harry was still legally free to up the ante. With Elektra's $15,000 deal in his pocket, Fred Kewley called Paul

Leka of Columbia that weekend and told him they were about to sign with Elektra.

"Kewley asked me what he should ask Clive Davis for," said Leka. "I said, 'Why don't you ask Davis for $25,000 up front.'" Fred did. Clive did better. He invited Harry to his luxurious Manhattan penthouse and doubled Holzman's offer to $30,000.

Harry was both torn and in heaven. Each company had its advantages and disadvantages. With Elektra, Harry could demand the personal attention he craved because it was a small company. But small companies also mean small money, and money was something that Columbia had plenty of. At the same time, Columbia possessed a huge roster of more than 200 artists and they could never offer a personal spotlight. For instance, though Epic was a subsidiary of Columbia, Clive Davis never knew The Chapins were on his label.

Then there was the matter of the company presidents. On a personal level, Holzman was far more committed to Chapin than Davis. Jac was the kind to make a personal investment in every one of his artists, and after his long drive down the California coast, had memorized the lyrics to every one of Harry's songs, and that impressed Chapin.

Davis, on the other hand, was more aloof, businesslike; a musical version of George Steinbrenner, the New York Yankee owner, who sat pretty with a dynamic roster and a murderers' row lineup, not caring so much about individual players as team production. One of those individual players was Bob Dylan, whom Harry worshipfully admired, and that meant a chance to challenge a legend. Columbia had prestige.

Harry didn't know what to do and sought the advice of everyone close to him, Sandy, James, his father. He even called Manny and Janet Castro, whom he'd spoken to several times in the previous weeks to keep them abreast of his building triumph. "We felt he should take Elektra's offer and make up his mind and have the deal set," said Manny Castro.

Said Janet: "He would listen to what we said and then say, 'You know, you're right, you're right!' And then go out and bargain with the other record company. He didn't seem to be surprised or confused. I think he thought it was his just due. We couldn't understand his coolness."

Steve Chapin, bitter at his brother's sudden success, said: "Harry turned out to be a real heavyweight dude. Tom and I sort of resented him at the time. It was kind of hard to take. We'd been paying our dues a long time when Harry was making films. We were rehearsing very hard and he got a band together in two weeks and was blowin' out these record companies with these fuckin' fantastic contracts. He made it look easy, you know? That made for a little pain."

In the meantime, Harry's solution to his indecision was to run on the beach behind the house in Point Lookout, or disappear to Andover, New Jersey.

Ann Purtill finally tracked him down when she called the house in Point Lookout and reached Sandy, who could no longer hide her growing feelings of anxiety. "Sandy couldn't cover," said Purtill. "She blew it. There was some kind of distress in her voice and she hinted that he was out in Andover. I thought the whole thing stank. So I called Jac. I said, 'You better get in on this one.'"

"We finally got hold of Harry in Andover," said Holzman. "It was a Friday night and I was about to get on a plane for California. I was on the phone with Ann, who was on the phone with Harry and Fred. I told her that if they met me at Kennedy Airport, I'd talk to them. Meantime, I delayed my flight three hours and they met me. Harry told me that he was going to sign with Columbia. I don't remember what their offer was, but it was more a matter of his wanting to be on the same label as Dylan. He was really wrapped up in that. I said, 'Well, I know you want to be with me. You don't want to be with him. So I'll give you $25,000 because I'm a better record company.' Meanwhile, I went out to California and for a week pursued him through his manager every day by telephone."

But Purtill was angry and hurt, and would be for years. And though Harry dutifully thanked her for her loyalty in the liner notes of every album he ever recorded, for the moment he had lost his staunchest supporter. "At that point, I wouldn't have signed him," said Purtill. "He didn't believe me when I told him, 'You reneged on a handshake and I wouldn't sign you.' As far as I was concerned, he could've been on Columbia and I didn't care. I never forgave him for that. But apparently, in the record business, a handshake doesn't mean anything. Neither does a signed piece of paper. You just renegotiate!"

Said John Wallace in Harry's defense: "Actually, he was kind of caught. I think he started to feel bad about it because I'm sure he wanted to say, 'Hey, you guys fight this out. Leave me out of it.' Because it really got nuts, you know? It got very emotional."

Tim Scott remembered: "I don't think he was playing one against the other. He was just trying to see what they'd do. He got caught up in the momentum of it."

Steve Chapin agreed. "It was more like Harry sitting there saying, 'Oh, good, great! Now what are you gonna give me, dad?' He was very kiddy at the time. There was no heavy thinking."

Much to Harry's disbelief, he found himself caught in a bidding war between Jac Holzman and Clive Davis. The reasons for it went far beyond the appeal of Harry's unorthodox story style. At the time, Warner Communications was locked in a bitter battle with Columbia Records to overtake them as the industry giant. Besides Elektra, Warner's corporate umbrella included Atlantic Records, Warner Brothers and Nonesuch (the classical label). Warner had also just purchased Asylum Records from "boy wunderkind" David Geffen, who had accumulated a small roster—and a small fortune—signing the likes of Jackson Browne, Joni Mitchell and The Eagles. Within this industry competition a kind of personal competition flourished between Holzman and Davis. Clive had recently beaten Jac out of numerous record contracts. All forces combined, Harry suddenly became the plum of the land and the prime object of the egos of two very powerful men.

Though Holzman firmly denied it, the competition with Columbia became so intense that, according to Chapin and Kewley, Jac broke down in tears when they met him at the airport. "Jac said he wasn't going to have Clive beat him out of an artist again," said Kewley. "That's the reason the whole thing went sky high."

"Yes, I was emotionally upset," Holzman conceded. "I was a vegetable when I got on that airplane. Having to sit next to Mayor Sam Yorty all the way to California didn't please me too much either. But I was extremely upset and down and had some sleepless nights. It was rough for me. I could safely say that week to ten days I spent trying to get Harry ran me down quite a bit."

Kewley called Clive Davis, told him Jack's offer, and said they'd "have to go with Holzman," that $25,000 is close to $30,000," that "Elektra is a smaller company and that's what we're looking for."

Clive countered with an offer of $50,000.

Said Kewley: "We went back to Jac and said, 'You know, you offered twenty-five and Clive is saying fifty. We've got to go with Clive.'"

Jac said, "Forty thousand dollars."

They told Clive.

Clive went to his limit, sweetening the pot to a stunning $80,000.

"Finally," said Davis, "after vacillating back and forth, Harry called me and said, 'Look, I've decided on Columbia.' I said, 'Well, great.' He said, 'This is my final decision and I'm not going to take any more phone calls from anybody at Elektra. I want to be with you. I know that you will give me the personal guidance even though the company is large. I believe our relationship can be very special.' I said, 'I'm sure it can be.' Then, the following day, he called me again to say he felt obligated to talk to Jac personally because Jac spent so much of his time with him, rather than do it through attorneys, which I well understood."

So Kewley called Holtzman in California to tell him of their final decision. "We had a long conversation. I told Jac, 'Listen, we don't want to screw you guys. But we can't take $40,000 when Clive is offering $80,000."

There was no way Holzman could match a cash advance for that big a sum. When he hung up the phone, he was dejected. Clive had won again, or so it seemed. "I refused to let it go," recalled Holzman. "I could not separate business and my personal feelings about artists that I wanted. The reason was that they had excited something in me personally that was important. Harry moved me. His songs moved me. I would say he was one artist I didn't want to lose."

The following morning, Saturday, November 14, Holzman, out of blind perseverance, took the red-eye flight from L.A. to New York. He stayed up all night plotting and planning a way to hook Harry. At six A.M., Holzman's chauffeur picked him up at Kennedy Airport and drove directly to Fred Kewley's home in South Salem, New York, where Harry was staying.

"I just walked in the door and told Harry about how we were going to make the record together," said Holzman. "I told him about the recording plans and that I would produce his songs. I just acted as if that's the way it was going to be. I promised him whatever it would take to get the job done and get him to sign and it all just clicked. I pulled out every idea I had to make that deal go through. Harry kind of caved in. I guess the sheer gall of it was what changed his mind."

"It turned my head around," said Harry. "It really did."

By the time the morning ended, Harry had agreed to sign the biggest contract (for a new artist) in Elektra's twenty-two-year history. It was an exclusive multiyear deal worth (at the time) more than $600,000, but in succeeding years it turned out to be worth several million. The contract called for nine albums over five years, plus a $40,000 advance to sign. Chapin was guaranteed a $20,000 advance on his second album, $25,000 on his third, with $5,000 interval increases on every album to the ninth.

But that was only the beginning. The "unprecedented offer" included numerous perks and bonuses no artist had received before, at least not publicly. For instance, Harry received free studio time, which meant he paid no recording costs, a savings (then) of approximately $25,000 per album, which multiplied tenfold in subsequent years with the advent of twenty-four-track studios and general inflation.

"No artist on Elektra or any other label had such privilege," said Clive Davis. "This was simply unheard of. There was no such thing as free studio time."

Holzman also promised that the month a Chapin album was released, no other Elektra LP would be distributed. In this manner, for four weeks, the entire Elektra promotion department would give maximum effort to having Chapin heard. "Now obviously a company like Columbia that released twenty-five to thirty albums per month couldn't possibly do that," said Davis. "So that really was very clever."

Harry also received the right to terminate his contract six months after the release of the second album. This was Elektra's way of giving themselves "a vote of confidence" to convince Harry they'd "do a good job."

"This was unusual, too," said Davis. "It was an unheard-of weapon to hold over a record company."

The deal was further improved by Chapin's attorney, Monte Morris, one of the finest legal minds in the entertainment industry. Morris was the guiding force in Harry's newfound venture and gave important advice regarding money, contracts and royalty rates. For instance, one out of every seven records sold was considered "free goods" given away for promotional purposes and for which the artist received no payment. But Morris made sure Harry was paid.

"Monte saved a lot of money," said Fred Kewley. "Some of his suggestions paid off one-hundred-fold over the years."

"But the clincher for me," said Harry, "was Jac Holzman's personal commitment to my music." For instance, Holzman promised to produce Chapin's first album himself, something he had not done for nearly seven years, since the folk days, when he was producer of The Doors and Tim Buckley, among others. In 1965, Holzman stopped producing when heavy metal and rock music came to the fore. But with Chapin, Holzman rediscovered his roots; enough to make him come out of his executive closet. From Jac's perspective, Harry was a unique artist offering a unique art, the story song. "I produced most of the records here for the first ten years," said Holzman. "Then, whenever we moved into a new area, I produced the first album in the field."

For Holzman, the most appealing part of Chapin's artistry was his soft-rock sensibility, reminiscent of Jac's past. In all the old Elektra albums, Holzman emphasized the singer and the voice, precisely the emphasis of Chapin's music. Holzman didn't bury the performer in the noise.

"I've always tried to keep things simple," Holzman told *Billboard* magazine. "And I've always said, 'Less is more.' I have certainly had my share of rock-'n'-roll artists. But I probably recorded fewer rock-'n'-roll bands that were noise-oriented than anybody else."

Clive Davis, on the other hand, was not a producer. But then, few record company presidents were, and Chapin liked that about Holzman. He was the last of a vanishing breed.

But most importantly, with Holzman as producer, Harry was guaranteed the kind of push and promotion his brothers never received. "A producer serves many functions," wrote Barbara Lewis of *Chicago Today,* "but probably the single most important factor is the ability to convince the record company that THIS record is THE record." Because Holzman was president of the record company, that hardly seemed a problem.

Said Harry once in an interview with the Associated Press: "People often forget there is a very torturous path between an unknown artist and the public. If the middlemen are not working for you, it is very hard."

The day after Holzman's dramatic visit, Harry called Clive Davis and told him of his new deal and that it was "irrevocable, irrevocable." Davis was stunned by Holzman's concessions and backed down, ending the conversation: "Well, just make a good record."

Said Davis: "We had reached the zenith where I was not prepared to go any further. I mean, I really wanted him. I wasn't complacent at all. But Jac could do certain things I could not. It was one of the few times we did not prevail in trying to attract an artist. The vacillation was unusual. When someone says they'll sign with a company, they usually sign. But Harry was really legitimately torn."

* * *

On November 18, the ten-day bidding war officially ended and Harry signed with Elektra. That afternoon, in the company's Gulf & Western office, there was an important meeting of all the record presidents within the Warner Communications group. "So at one point I excused myself to sign contracts with Harry, who was waiting in another room," said Holzman. "Then I brought Harry in and introduced them all to him. They all knew about it. They were all watching from the sidelines because Atlantic was in there for a while. Ahmet Ertegun, president of Atlantic, felt that Harry was probably more appropriate with me than he was with him. And all of the people from the other record companies really patted Harry on the back and made him feel good for having made the decision."

During the bidding war, Clive and Jac, despite being good friends, never spoke to one another. "In the record business," said Holzman, "company presidents can go after the same artists with hammer and tongs, but that doesn't mean they didn't go out for dinner together two nights later."

And they did, but when it came to the subject of Harry Chapin, Davis said, "Jac, you must have really wanted that artist." To which Holzman replied acidly, "Yes, I wanted that artist," and immediately changed the subject.

Throughout the music industry, word spread that Jac Holzman had outbid Clive Davis for this hot new property named Harry Chapin. From music critics to record executives and their secretaries, there were high expectations of Chapin, the new phenomenon whom Holzman had taken under his wing. That December, Harry and Sandy, the band and their families (including Harry's first child, three-month-old Jennifer) were flown out to L.A. on Elektra's Kinney Lear Jet (otherwise known as the "Wicky Bird") to record their first album. Except for Chapin's brief film stint in California, none of the group had ever been to the West Coast. So, once there, Holzman showed them the town and introduced his "prize boy" to all the heavies in the business. Holzman also limousined them to Las Vegas, but not before stashing some cash in each of their shirts.

Despite his triumph, Harry's time in Los Angeles brought back painful memories of the past. Elektra's studios were just a block away from the apartment Chapin had lived in when he was a struggling filmmaker, and being in L.A. brought back old feelings for Clare MacIntyre. Not surprisingly, his first album, *Heads and Tales,* was filled with stories of lost loves and broken dreams.

"The irony of that part of my life was I lost the woman I loved, which was the reason I was being successful: 'Taxi,'" said Harry. "And then the fact I was suddenly going to be hitting the airwaves, which I hoped would make me reach out to her."

One song, "Same Sad Singer," was about Clare and was written in the studio as a last-minute addition to the album. It was one song, in later years, Harry never sang in concert, saying, "It's too personal and too hard to tune up." Mostly because his love for her persisted, for a woman who never thought he'd be a winner, and who never could understand his blind chase of music and fame. But now H. Forster Chapin was about to become famous, about to hit the airwaves. Harry was speaking directly to Clare in "Same Sad Singer" when he wrote:

> They're bringing in the strings
> To melt your heart somehow
> You couldn't hear me then
> But maybe you can hear me now.

CHAPTER IX

Changes

For Harry, the Los Angeles recording studio was a new world with a new language. He wanted to learn every inch of it. It was a modern sixteen-track studio packed with instrument panels, buttons, mixers, flashing lights, all of which looked like the cockpit of a supersonic jet; the latest in recording technology. Being the first one to use the studio, Harry made sure every track was put to good use.

"Harry went apeshit in the studio," recalled Jac Holzman. "He saw there were sixteen tracks, and if there was one spot on a track that wasn't filled, he would figure out a little banjo over-dub. . . .

Holzman, however, was no more familiar with the studio's technology than Harry. He had never stepped inside a sixteen-track studio and couldn't have cared less if he had. He viewed them as "technically impractical and unnecessary." All those early Elektra folk records Holzman recorded were on four- and eight-track systems and even plain tape recorders, with one microphone held in front of a voice and guitar.

So Jac had to learn, and at first it wasn't easy. There were many retakes as he groped through this modern maze of piled-up sophistication. Chapin, meanwhile, just played along, and wisely so, doing nothing to offend Jac and perhaps jeopardize his support.

As Fred Kewley explained: "Harry always flattered his ego because the guy was in a position of importance. There was a time in the recording studio when Jac was trying to be the producer and all of us took a break for dinner. Jac said to Harry, 'I'd like you to go in there and sing one more time and I'll guide you through because I know exactly what has to be done.' Well, Harry knows how he's supposed to sing it! But he pampered this guy for forty-five minutes while Jac was trying to figure out how to work the board and how to get the mike working. Harry was in an embarrassing situation. But he played him like a one-string violin. Harry had all the phrases for how he played people. He doused his ego, sang the song and it was embarrassing. Jac couldn't even work the machines or any of the equipment."

Finally, Jac did learn. It took a couple of days, but after he did, the first album went like clockwork, taking only three weeks to record. In fact, *Heads and Tales* turned out to be the most smoothly produced album Chapin ever put to vinyl. The songs, after all, were the same ones the band had played for months, with Ron Palmer on electric guitar singing low harmonies, John Wallace on bass singing the higher registers, Tim Scott on cello, and Chapin on a six-string acoustic guitar. For added impact, only two other musicians joined them in the studio: Steve Chapin on piano and famed L.A. studio musician Russ Kunkel on drums.

Once the album was completed, the promotion work began. It started on January 11, 1972, at Elektra Records' first national sales convention in Palm Springs, California. As part of the many bonuses in Chapin's contract, Holzman promised that Harry would be featured at the event. The company-wide convention boasted an audience of some three hundred salesmen, distributors and branch personnel of Warner Communications, the middlemen responsible for an album's sudden takeoff or sudden death. Elektra's strategy was simple: instead of merely sending sample copies of *Heads and Tales* to their promo people in the field, they could bring them all together to hear Chapin live. The salespeople would then solicit radio stations throughout the U.S. and Canada to help the fever catch on. In addition, Elektra was also trying to impress its parent company, Warner Communications, with its growing stable of stars, past, present and future. So, besides Chapin, the convention featured Holzman's baby, The Doors, as well as the hot, new sensation, Carly Simon.

Chapin's performance was thoroughly successful, highlighted by a four-minute standing ovation. Though he was virtually unknown, the salespeople walked away convinced they had a winner to work with. "Harry just killed 'em," said Ralph Ebler, the Elektra PR man assigned to promote Chapin. "His warmth, his one-on-one kind of situation. All the new releases were featured. But when it came to a tune called 'Taxi,' the audience went crazy. After that, he had everyone in his back pocket."

The convention performance paid immediate dividends and was a solid springboard to stardom. Thirty thousand copies of *Heads and Tales* were ordered for the Los Angeles area alone. And by February, total sales rose to $75,000, which meant the album was now out of the red and into the black.

It also meant that Elektra touted Chapin as a shoe-in superstar and made certain that other label performers, such as Carly Simon, helped the cause. Simon's manager, Arlene Rothberg, arranged for Chapin to tour with Carly as opening act. Rothberg also managed comedian David Steinberg and made plans for Harry to appear with him for a two-week engagement at Mister Kelley's in Chicago. And when Bill Lockwood, who booked the Great Performers Series at Lincoln Center, heard a tape of Chapin's music, he was so impressed, he signed Harry immediately, as did Doug Weston, the owner of The Troubadour in L.A.

More importantly, the distributors' euphoric reaction to "Taxi" convinced Elektra to release the song as the B-side single off *Heads and Tales*. "Could You Put Your Light On, Please" had already been chosen for the A side. But that was not to say Elektra wasn't reticent about releasing "Taxi." For one, the song did not have a chorus and was not geared to teenyboppers. Instead, said Harry, it was about "this old guy and this old married woman." More importantly, Elektra was concerned about the length of "Taxi." Most singles run 3:05 to facilitate radio programming. But "Taxi" was more than double that running time at 6:44, and the original, unrecorded version was over eleven minutes long.

"I remember when Harry was working on 'Taxi' out in Andover," said brother James. "I said, 'Well, it's sort of interesting. But, my God, the song goes on forever.'"

But "Taxi" wasn't the only long number on *Heads and Tales*. Of the eight others, seven exceeded the standard length, and one song, "Dogtown," was even longer than "Taxi," running 7:30.

"I do create problems for myself," Harry often said. "I write eight-minute songs and an album should only have forty minutes' worth of music on it to have a good sound. So for me, that's five songs."

As Ann Purtill once said, "Harry's got to write songs with a break in the middle so they can do commercials."

She once wrote a memo to Jac Holzman, after hearing one of Chapin's shorter songs, "Sandy," saying, "I'm afraid his bigger numbers just knock me out so much I can't get used to these 'lesser' efforts. . . . He showed that to me just to prove he could write a song under five minutes."

But long story songs were the basis of Chapin's stardom, particularly "Taxi." Its melodic variations and engrossing lyrics justified its length. Unlike most pop songs, the story line of "Taxi" demanded more than just repetitive beats and chorus. It grabbed the listener's attention, for every word had its purpose and place. "'Taxi' was the kind of song you just couldn't edit without ruining the story," said Ralph Ebler. "It had a punch line, and a build to that punch line which was the hook. There was no way it was going to be cut."

Mel Posner, then Elektra's general sales manager, said: "We took a chance releasing 'Taxi' as a single. It was the most difficult thing we had done to date as far as trying to promote a single because the programmers don't want a seven-minute cut; that's two and a half songs practically."

By February 1972, Elektra's staff was putting all promotional gears in motion. Test pressings for Chapin's album and single were mastered and approved for printing. Then came the media blitz. Sales, promotion and art departments prepared a massive merchandising campaign to guarantee maximum exposure in record stores, radio and print. With "Taxi" as the album's central theme, the cover was cleverly packaged with a double gate-fold jacket designed like a Checker cab: yellow with black and white trim. At the center was a color photograph of Chapin behind the wheel and a picture of the band on the back. Inside was a beautifully designed six-page color lyric folio to give special emphasis to Chapin's words and his storyteller image. Not surprisingly, his songs were copyrighted Story Songs Limited.

In addition, slick promo booklets, or "samplers," were sent to radio stations throughout North America. They contained a copy of "Taxi," glossy fact sheets, bumper stickers and a big, four-by-eleven-inch photo of Chapin. The sampler served as a preview of albums soon to be released. Normally, Elektra might promote as many as six artists in one booklet, and a larger company such as Columbia even more. But Harry was alone: he had a booklet to himself.

It did not end there. Press parties were held on both coasts. For print ads, a new concept in mini-glossies was created whereby the album cover, logos, headlines and quotes were stylishly reproduced. For the record stores, Elektra supplied a three-dimensional, color stand-up display as well as four-color posters and two-color banners.

In a phrase, the campaign was exhaustive, but Harry made sure it was. He was involved in every step, from packaging to promotion. He spent hours picking the brains of George Steele, head of marketing; Stan Marshall, East Coast sales manager; Ken Deteze, head of promotion; and Jerry Sherrel, head of artist development. Facts, figures, sales, the psychology of the business—Harry wanted to know it all, even their opinions of his new songs.

Said Ann Purtill: "From the moment Harry came into the company, he demanded more personal attention than any artist I ever saw. He had a lot of Jac's personal time and he wanted everybody's opinion of a song when he wrote it. He often came running into the middle of an executive luncheon conference, sat down and said, 'Hey, I wrote a new song.' Then he played it and later walked around saying everybody loved it. I mean, what did he expect them to say except, 'Fine, Harry, see you later, get out of here?'"

Other times, Harry called Purtill at her office and said, "I wonder if I can come over and play a new song for ya?" After he did, he then ran across the street to Jac Holzman, who always respected Ann's musical opinion, and said, "See, Ann likes it." However, Ann was not fooled by this, so as soon as Harry left her office, she called Holzman and said, "Ah, Jac, Harry's on the way over. . . ."

"You had to be involved with Harry Chapin," said Posner. "It was not just a matter of being there. And it was great. There were very few artists who took the time, effort and energy to get involved with all these people."

By the end of the month-long promotional campaign, an exhausted Jac Holzman told *Billboard* magazine: "I've never worked so hard or been so intensely involved in a project during my entire twenty-one years in the music business."

But Harry's work had only just begun, and during the spring and summer, he embarked on a promotional tour, the standard circuit traveled by anyone who yearned to make it in the music business. He played small colleges, but mostly club dates: the Bitter End in New York; the Cellar Door in Washington, D.C.; The Troubadour in L.A.; The Boarding House in San Francisco; Mister Kelley's in Chicago; and others. The idea was to develop a following in each town by playing the "in" places.

But most of them were hardly "in," such as Chapin's first concert stop in Rochester, New York, at a pizza joint called The Nugget. "It was one of those places where, as you were singing, they called out your number to say your pizza was ready," said Ralph Elber.

Another time, Harry performed in Bloomington, Indiana, at a movie theater that staged concerts on weekends and showed porno films during the week. That week, he played opposite *Deep Throat*.

The tour, a low-budget operation, was hardly the glamorous world of Lear jets, limousines and beautiful people one connects with a rock star. Unlike most popular entertainers, Chapin traveled by car or van without an entourage or fanfare. Stolidly independent, sometimes he even traveled without his band, catching up with them later at concerts. Their lodgings were mostly cheap, musty motels, the kind where if a fan spun from the ceiling, it would have been the perfect setting for a Clark Gable flick about a hard-driving journalist in Southeast Asia.

The main reason, of course, was lack of funds. Royalty checks were still in the offing, and although Elektra allocated expense money, it was a modest sum at best, sufficient for a band of four, manager Fred Kewley, plus a road crew of two: Jebbie Hart and the Chapins' friend Rob White, who were both seventeen years old and had volunteered for the job without pay. Meanwhile, it was Kewley's job to plan the tour, make motel reservations, deal with promoters and essentially, according to him, "make the whole operation go." Kewley was good that way. He kept expenses to a minimum, refusing to be extravagant until "we get on our feet."

But then Kewley had no choice, because concert money was as bad as the motels were musty. For instance, the group made $250 for one week's work at the Bitter End ($50 per man). And at The Boarding House in San Francisco, they earned $300 per week appearing with an unknown named Pamela Polland.

"The best place we played," said Ron Palmer, "was at Mister Kelley's in Chicago" for a two-week engagement opening for comedian David Steinberg. But even there, with a four-dollar cover charge that included Chapin, Steinberg and two trios, the band made a paltry $500 per week.

Even so, Chapin rarely became discouraged and never stopped hustling. He became a shrewd businessman, always conscious that art alone wasn't worth a damn without an audience to witness it. For instance, his long story songs had a difficult time getting played on both AM and FM radio. So Chapin pushed harder. He visited radio stations and personally promoted himself to disc jockeys. He performed for record chains at their retail sales conventions and never missed a press conference. Once, at a Long Island club called My Father's Place, Harry went on four nights in a row with a fever of 102 degrees. His blind persistence meant that in 1972 he performed more than 200 concerts. "And that's a lot of traveling," said Ebler to *New York News* magazine that year. "If he was in town he'd call the local promotion man or branch and say, 'Is there anything I can do, anyone you want me to see?' There are very few artists willing to put themselves out the way Harry is."

Said Chapin, in that same magazine article: "I'm in a business and I realize the business aspect. . . . There are just different ideas about what being smart is. Any artist realizes there are commercial aspects to it. You need singles. You need ways of getting out to the people. . . . There are nuts and bolts decisions about ways of presenting yourself. The whole kick in my songs is look at reality. Look at the facts. So many of the young writers and people of my era like to think they are in a pure art form. All they're worrying about is just the art and nothing else. That's bull! Because just about the only reason they are getting a chance—and the only reason I'm getting a chance now—is because some people thought that on the bottom line, I was going to make them some money. It's a sad reality, but a true reality."

Concerts were business too. Despite any personal or professional problems that may have existed within the band, showtime was showtime. "Backstage in the dressing room it was all small talk," said Ron Palmer. "We all felt that was no time to bring up heavy stuff within the band. It was an unwritten law that everybody stayed cool in the dressing room and went out and did a good show."

Then, after shows, Harry and his band spent hours in local interviews, usually at radio stations. Once there, Harry did most of the talking. He talked about everything from himself and his music to the latest movies. He always spoke philosophically, in the second or third person, never praising his abilities, mostly because "it gave me instant authority when I spoke." He learned that from his songwriting. Privately he called it the "put-down game," the art of self-deprecation or debunking. For instance, he'd say he wasn't intelligent and had no talent. Then he would speak about his family ("artsy-fartsy," he termed them) and say, "Everybody is brilliant, has a degree, or is awesome," he told *New York News* magazine, as if to exclude himself.

But part of that "demystification" process came from the true belief that Harry saw himself as just "an average guy" who made good. For this reason he debunked the star syndrome, the creative process, and his two favorite targets, filmmakers Mike Nichols and Stanley Kubrick, for their "dark, inchoate sense of humanity"; Nichols for his then controversial blockbuster *Carnal Knowledge,* and Kubrick for *A Clockwork Orange.*

He also lambasted T.S. Eliot, whose poetry, he felt, was "riddled with fancy code words and over-intellectualizations that were unavailable to the masses." But that was not to say Chapin felt art should be commercial, just definitive so that "it offered new perspectives on life." As a result, he often praised the genius of William Shakespeare "because he wrote for people in the cheap seats" and Johann Sebastian Bach "because he wrote gorgeous music all day, then came home, drank beer and screwed his wife." (Bach had ten children.)

Meanwhile, night after night, John Wallace, Tom Scott and Ron Palmer sat silent in the radio booth, contributing a phrase or two whenever Harry seemed to be lost for words. Then, suddenly, Harry would start up again with the same level of enthusiasm and intensity. He spoke so passionately that the interviewer was left more a spectator than a participant in the one-sided conversation.

At the end of interviews, when asked of his future plans, Harry spoke faster than ever. He spoke of films, writing a novel, a musical, and the possibility of doing an album with his brothers.

His ". . . probably won't be the history of your basic garden-variety singer-songwriter," wrote newspaper music critic Phil Van Huesen. "That's one of the things you sort of absorb from the buckets of conversation Chapin can pour across the table in an interview over supper—more like a monologue, really, with Chapin's views on music, politics, the quality of life, and things in general punctuated by elbows, legs, hands and french fries."

And one very potent arsenal of a vocabulary. *Crawdaddy* magazine once described him as possessing "a twelve-string vocabulary to match his beautiful twelve-string guitar."

Once, on the way to a concert, Harry was asked if he was nervous and would like to postpone an interview with a reporter, who happened to be former Cornellian Geoff Hewitt. "Hell no," Chapin replied instantly. "I'm fine. I'll just go onstage and do my stuff when it's time. I can talk like this right up to the show."

Chapin's first major show was on February 12, 1972, at Symphony Hall in Boston, opening for Carly Simon. The timing of the performance couldn't have been more perfect, since just a few days before, "Taxi" had been picked up by WRKO in Boston and given heavy airplay. It was also the first time Harry heard his music played on the radio. He and Tim Scott were driving to the concert up Interstate 95 when "Taxi" suddenly came over the radio.

"For the first time," said Harry of that moment, "I realized that all of these mysterious processes were now working for me. What a charge!"

Ironically, Chapin, who was notorious for being late, nearly missed his own debut. At one point, right outside Boston, the car ran out of gas. The concert was to begin in an hour. There was no gas station in sight, so Harry jumped out of the car and hitchhiked a ride to the nearest one, returning with one-gallon gas cans in each hand. To compound matters, when they arrived in Boston, they pulled up to a large redbrick building adjacent to rows of parked cars. They thought it was Symphony Hall. But unfamiliar with the city, they found themselves at Boston Garden, where the Celtics were having a home game. Finally, they got directions and rolled into the backstage entrance of Symphony Hall literally seconds before showtime.

The concert was a smash. As usual, Harry opened with "Could You Put Your Light On, Please" in the dark, while offstage to one side, a camera crew, whom he introduced as old friends and holdovers from his film days, recorded the action of his first big-city appearance in case it was his last. But that was unlikely. The concert was heavily hyped by local newspapers proclaiming "Elektra unwraps its hottest new property," touting Chapin as the new "wunderkind." At the end of his one-hour set, Harry left the audience starstruck, receiving a thunderous standing ovation that even overshadowed Carly Simon.

The following day, Ernie Santosuosso of the *Boston Globe* wrote: "The spirited reception saw him stroll off the stage ten feet high. He, in fact, stole Carly's thunder."

The Symphony Hall concert not only marked the official start of Chapin's music career but the beginning of a hostile relationship with the critical rock press that remained constant throughout his ten-year career. Chapin's primary denouncers were Robert Christgau of the *Village Voice,* John Rockwell and Robert Palmer of the *New York Times* and Jon Landau and Dave Marsh of *Rolling Stone* magazine, all of whom disliked Chapin's modern folk sensibility. Landau drew first blood. Though local Boston press lauded Chapin's performance, Landau (an editor at *Rolling Stone* since its first 1967 issue) wrote a malicious review attacking Chapin personally, from the way he smiled to his habit of "slapping palms" with the boys in the band between songs. He also saved a few select jabs for Carly Simon. Though years later Landau admitted being wrong about Chapin and regretted having written the piece, at the time he had no such perspective.

Said Jon Landau: "Chapin was unappealing to me. He was intelligent. There was a cleverness to his music. But I found him pretentious, self-important and exploitive. He seemed to think with a song like 'Taxi' he was somehow baring his soul, but he really wasn't. . . ."

Harry burned. He felt Landau took cheap shots, or "zingers," as he called them, and for weeks afterward was deeply resentful. During subsequent interviews, Harry did not fail to mention Landau's lambast and one time even told a reporter, "If I ever meet the man, I'm going to punch him out!" One month later, after a concert in Stonehenge, Massachusetts, he met a reviewer between sets and immediately asked, "Are you a Landau stringer?"

Said Ann Purtill: "Landau came out of the Boston intellectual group. It was a well-known thing out of Boston writers that the more arcane you were, the better off you were. They liked to kick people in the rocks."

Understandably, Harry became highly defensive and sometimes read unintended meanings into rock reviews and feature articles. This was true of all the Chapins, who suddenly found their private lives opened for public dissection. This invasion of their privacy became a highly sensitive issue. In one incident, Manny and Janet Castro suggested a friend of theirs, an editor at the *Daily News,* do a story about Harry and the Chapins. The editor sent over a young woman. For one full day, the family graciously took her in. She interviewed all the brothers and Elspeth, and wrote her piece, which was published two weeks later. "We thought the article was great," said Janet. "There was nothing negative about it, and I called Elspeth to see how she felt. I expected her to be quite pleased, but she was furious."

Apparently there was an inference in the article about Elspeth being a "Jewish mother," and that upset her. Harry, of course, loved the Castros and held no grudge, but after the story, the Castros' relationship with Elspeth and the Chapins died. "Somehow I got the feeling Elspeth was mad at us ever since, because it was our friend that sent the reporter," said Janet. "I thought they all got sort of paranoid about the press. Tom, Elspeth, Harry, Steve—everybody got paranoid. The stuff they read into the paper, we didn't see. They felt it was a terrible invasion of their privacy. I went over and met Elspeth for lunch one day at her apartment and she was cool. She wasn't the same old friend."

However, most record reviewers raved about Chapin and his debut album. *Cash Box* magazine hailed *Heads and Tales* as "... the arrival of a completely original, clear-sighted talent of major proportion." Of "Taxi," *Record World* said, "Spellbinding. ... A classical ballad ... the ultimate in musical storytelling." And one rock writer of the *Blade-Tribune,* Oceanside, California, said that Chapin "has the sweet smell of success about him, that star quality which you'll discover in an unknown once or twice a decade." And concerning the album's production, the same critic wrote that it was "as close to perfect as you can get, having no discernible flaws of any consequence. It is low-key, interesting, tasteful. ..."

Chapin's debut also sparked the expected gamut of comparisons with other artists. Some found his full-throated baritone reminiscent of Hamilton Camp and Gordon Lightfoot, while others found his "soul-baring" themes and "naked despair" similar to those of David Ackles, Tim Buckley, Peter Rowan and particularly the Belgian balladeer, Jacques Brel. Still others compared him to Jonathan Edwards and James Taylor. This was especially true of Taylor, whose 1969 appearance on the rock scene signaled the start of the singer-songwriter boom, of which Chapin was a part.

"My first tendency was simply to poor-mouth Harry Chapin as just another downer rock troubadour riding the tattered coat-

The February 3, 1978, White House meeting which realized one of Chapin's dreams: a Presidential Commission on world hunger. In addition to President Carter and Harry Chapin directly across from him, Dr. Peter Bourne, members of the White House staff, and thirteen senators and representatives attended. Senators present were Dick Clark (D-Iowa), Richard Stone (D-Fla.), Robert Dole (R-Kan.), Henry Bellmon (R-Okla.), Patrick Leahy (D-Vt.), George McGovern (D-S.D.). Representatives present were Donald Fraser (D-Minn.), Thomas Foley (D-Wash.), Richard Nolan (D-Minn.), Anthony Beilenson (D-Cal.), Paul Findley (R-Ill.), James Weaver (D-Ore.), Benjamin Gilman (R-N.Y.). (Photo: Jimmy Carter Library)

Harry conducting the audience in their singing of the four-part harmony ending to "30,000 Pounds of Bananas." (Photo: Steve Stout)

(*From left to right*) Robert Redford, Harry Chapin, and PAF artistic director Jay Broad, backstage at Nassau Coliseum on Long Island for a gala benefit for the Performing Arts Foundation in April 1979. (Photo: Courtesy Chapinfo)

Harry singing "Circle" during a 1976 barbecue-concert in his backyard to raise money for the Performing Arts Foundation. Everyone joined in the fun by holding hands in a large circle. (Photo: Peter M. Coan)

Harry Chapin (*right*) and Pete Seeger (*left*) performing a benefit concert for PAF at Huntington High School in January 1976. Besides Ralph Nader, Pete Seeger was Harry's biggest idol. (Photo: Peter M. Coan)

Harry autographing his poetry book and souvenir books for two fans after a 1976 concert. All the money from those books went to support his antihunger organization, World Hunger Year (WHY), something he continued to do right up to his death in July 1981—and long before the hunger cause became chic among entertainers. (Photo: Steve Stout)

Harry backstage after the 1976 Illinois concert, caught in a rare moment of exhaustion. Though Harry gave much of himself in concert, he had a bottomless well of energy that permitted him to sign "one more" autograph, make one more phone call, grant another long interview. (Photo: Steve Stout)

Harry's younger brother, Tom Chapin, Andover, New Jersey, 1976. (Photo: Peter M. Coan)

tails of Taylor and forget him," admitted one record critic. But other critics felt he was the most important singer-songwriter since Taylor.

No matter what performer was mentioned in connection with any aspect of Chapin's artistry, it was only one aspect; he could not be buttonholed. His style was neither purely folk, rock, country, nor classical. Rather, it was a unique synthesis of all four. Most critics, then, were left perplexed by Chapin because he was somewhat of an oddity, an aberration. He didn't write like anyone else. He didn't sing like anyone else. He wrote and sang like—well, Harry Chapin.

However, these were comments directed at Harry Chapin the artist, not the performer. In concert Harry was as unorthodox as his story songs were unique. His secret weapon was audience participation, and for that he soon developed the reputation of being a great showman who could transform any large concert hall into a living room, or some Irish pub. Chapin looked for any opportunity to involve a crowd, and once he did (usually by the second song), he was in full command, the distance between the stage and front row as close as breath. "Chapin's ability to make an audience sluff off their inhibitions and feel like a part of the performance makes his shows more of an experience than just a concert," wrote columnists Dewey Blanton and Rob Shepard in the *Hatchet*. "Solo artists like James Taylor and Van Morrison have been criticized in the past for singing at their audiences rather than to them. Harry Chapin does neither; he gets them to sing along."

Though "Taxi" was released in early February, the song's success had a delayed reaction and, in part, fueled the common misconception that the song was a number one hit and *Heads and Tales,* a gold album. Actually, the highest "Taxi" ever rose on the Top 40 Charts was 24 in *Billboard,* 22 in *Record World* and 19 in *Cash Box.* After WRKO in Boston picked up the song, several months passed before the rest of the RKO radio chain (the largest in the country at that time) gradually added it to its playlist. As a result, it wasn't until May that "Taxi" had filtered its way to the West Coast and was being heard regularly in Los Angeles. Another factor was that "Taxi" was the number one request song in the country for ten weeks, or a "turntable hit"; meaning the single sold the album (approximately 250,000 copies) more than the single sold itself (less than half that figure). In addition, the song had "cross-chart" success and was played on easy listening, rock and some country stations. It also penetrated both FM and AM airwaves, the latter a highly unlikely place for a song of its length. And all of which meant that Harry earned royalties, another unlikely thing for a new artist with a new album.

On the other hand, the song's dark-horse success was not without precedent. Two years earlier, Arlo Guthrie garnered Top 40 fame with the song "Alice's Restaurant," as did Richard Harris with Jimmy Webb's "MacArthur Park" and Bobby Gentry with "Ode to Billie Joe," all of which were contemporary folk ballads that far exceeded the length of the standard pop song. But the real groundbreaker was Don McLean's "American Pie," a national hit just six months prior to the release of "Taxi." In content they were all "noncommercial" tales that told a story with a message that went far beneath the shallow veneer of the average AM single. And though, like "Taxi," none of them was a blockbuster seller, each was an "event" song whose uniqueness transcended time. "Some songs are big sellers and others are events, which involve more than volume and numerics," wrote *Cash Box* magazine that year. "'American Pie' was this year's first 'event.' In quite another way, Harry's 'Taxi' is driving in that direction, with Chapin behind the wheel."

As a result, Chapin learned early that quality, not sales, was the goal to shoot for. When "Taxi" was on the charts, there was a hit single called "The Lion Sleeps Tonight" by a new artist named Robert John. The song was the third version of "Wimoweh" first done by The Weavers in 1952 and then by The Tokens in 1960. But Robert John's version was the most successful. It was number one on the charts and sold over two million copies, twenty times the amount "Taxi" did. However, once "The Lion Sleeps Tonight" disappeared from the Top 40 charts, Robert John found himself playing rock in a roadhouse outside Philadelphia at $1,000 a week. Chapin happened to be in Philadelphia at the time and performed five concerts for $2,500 each. "Immediately I realized that Rod McKuen, in a certain sense, McDonald's hamburgers, or Robert John were only as hot as the specific need in a specific time," said Chapin. "I want to depart from that. I want my audience to perceive that what I'm offering them is quality."

Still, there was no denying that a major part of Chapin's appeal was the novelty of "Taxi," not only because of its style and length, but because of an explicit drug reference in the last line: "I go flyin' so high when I'm stoned." Coming out of the sixties, that line was likely to become radically chic, and it did. It made Chapin an underground folk hero much as Don McLean was for "American Pie," or Billy Joel later on for "Piano Man." During Chapin's first six months of touring, crowds everywhere were enthusiastic, calling "'Taxi!' Sing 'Taxi!'" Throughout his career, the song became the anthem of his die-hard fans. When Chapin delivered that last line, roaring ovations shot up from young audiences.

Ironically, the line's implication was totally antithetical to Harry's nature. He could not have been less an advocate of drugs, escapism or self-destructive protest. He only used "stoned" as a metaphor to illustrate the driver's frustration at not becoming a pilot and how "dreams come true in strange but unexpected ways."

"It's an antidrug song," he frequently insisted to reporters. "The guy's a loser. It has nothing to do with being on drugs. It's a song about the ironies of life. 'Taxi' is really about two people with broken dreams. You'd be surprised at the varying ideas people read into the lyrics and the number of letters I've received from people in my past asking me if the song is about them. Actually I've never been high in my life and I've never been drunk. But when you're writing a song, it becomes a reality away from your own experience. You use your emotional basis for a song to be right. But after that, the facts of a song only have to be true in the context of the song, not in the context of yourself."

By late summer, Chapin was rapidly becoming a headliner, with "Taxi" his identity. He received top billing at small clubs and occasionally performed before large audiences with established stars such as Blood, Sweat & Tears (10,000 people), Bread (16,000), and Melanie (22,000). Finally the money was beginning to roll in and Chapin could now afford to buy a bigger house and move out of Point Lookout, a place in which he never felt comfortable. Sandy began looking for possible homes. And for the first time, the road crew got a piece of the action.

"We worked for free for about thirty weeks," said Jebbie Hart, referring to himself and Rob White. "But then, all of a sudden, we had an operation going. There was plenty of money going down. So we went on salary."

But for Chapin, other opportunities emerged from his success that meant as much to him as, if not more than, the money. "I've been wanting to write a screenplay for a couple of years and I'm going to get a chance to do that now," he said to reporter Salli Stevenson of a midwest newspaper. "That means more to me than a fancy sports car. Theoretically, when the royalty checks come in, I could do that. But I'm not interested in that. I wish I was. It would make life simpler."

Chapin's main interest was to compound his success; to feed his mounting machine. For years, his spiral notebooks were filled with unused dialogue and ideas for screenplays, films and Broadway musicals. Now Chapin was getting offers to write feature scripts he didn't get when he was a full-time filmmaker. One of his ideas was for a film/musical called *The End of the World,* a story about a young journalist who follows and reports on the star of his favorite rock group; one reason, among others, I believe Chapin let me into his world three years later. Warner

Brothers contracted him to write the screenplay, although nothing ever came of it. Harry also worked on the score for a documentary, *Cutting Loose,* about Jim Lipscomb's travels around the world in a sailboat. "When you're successful at one thing," said Harry, "people automatically assume you're going to be successful at the next thing."

Indeed, with just one song, Chapin was in instant public demand. Fabergé, the beauty products company, was promoting its latest line of toiletries called Music and chose Chapin to pick the winner of a sweepstakes prize. And when the Greyhound Bus Company heard that Harry wrote a song with their name, a phone call to Chapin soon followed. "They had visions of a new song turned commercial," said Harry to the *Home Reporter and Sunset News.* "Maybe something like, 'I'd Like to Teach the World to Sing—on a Greyhound Bus.'" But when the bus company found out that one line in the chorus described the Greyhound as "a dog of a way to get around," the matter was quickly forgotten.

Chapin now found himself on the Johnny Carson, Dick Cavett, Merv Griffin and Mike Douglas shows, singing "Taxi" and rubbing elbows with America's famous. He also performed the song on the first "Midnight Special," hosted by John Denver. By the end of the year, "Taxi" was selected on Sam Riddle's Big Record of 1972 called *Superstars of Rock.* And in his book *On the Campaign Trail '72* (about Senator George McGovern's presidential bid), Dr. Hunter Thompson quoted a few lines from the song.

Despite all the good fortune, Chapin's marriage began to shake, tremble and dislodge. It started sometime before the promotional tour. Suddenly, Sandy was confronted with a husband more successful than she ever dreamed, and in a business antithetical to any kind of normal family life, the only life Sandy ever wanted or needed. Now she had to confront the reality and the fact that her husband would be spending the majority of his time away from home. What would this mean for their marriage? The children?

At the time, Sandy was still in graduate school at Columbia University, needing only a thesis to earn her doctorate in esthetic education. But with four children, and pregnant with a fifth (Harry's second child), she had to decide how much she could handle.

"I could see the handwriting on the wall in terms of his schedule," said Sandy. "At that point, I suggested we kind of separate. Not a legal separation, but that we say to ourselves we are going our separate ways. I was going to work out my thing and he was going to work out his thing. But Harry would hear nothing of it. He got so terribly threatened anytime I mentioned it. He got apoplectic. He just wouldn't discuss it. That's what usually happened to him. Sometimes he could not confront something going on at a certain level. I suppose by me putting it into words, it became terribly threatening.

"But, either out of loneliness or fear, I also felt terribly threatened. There were a lot of adjustments to make. First of all, I thought of Harry as somebody totally fantastic who was going to be a freelance writer, never make any money, but be posthumously famous. And in the meantime, I was going to support him through his years of struggle and keep us all together and get the next meal on the table. I would work at a teaching job and Harry would always be working at the great American novel or something and would be greatly acclaimed after he died. That was my assumption. My fantasy.

"But suddenly, he was off in areas I didn't understand, meaning music and recording studios and all those buttons and mixes and so forth. Whereas before we were both in the same world. A world of dialogues and articles and throwing around existential philosophy. Suddenly we were in two different worlds and we couldn't communicate. I couldn't talk to him and also I was used to having him around. Not in any organized way like somebody who goes to a nine-to-five job. But in some kind of controversial relationship. I felt threatened in that sense. But also by the fact that I had made the decision to have all these kids and marry Harry. Suddenly I realized it was a solo trip. I was going to have all these kids, sit home, raise them myself, and I thought, how the hell had I gotten myself into this?"

Even someone as headstrong as Harry, for whom success had come late, could not avoid the corruption of self-importance. He had peddled himself for years with no result. But now Chapin had joined the winner's circle. He went to parties and became the focal point. The spotlight was finally his and now Gapin' Chapin was listened to whenever he spoke. People hung on each word, the same words they used to laugh at. His mailbox became filled with offers, fan mail and fat royalty checks. Backstage at concerts he met people from his past, some of them old enemies, who now suddenly called him "Harry my old friend." Others were those Chapin "super-admired" in high school and college who now "super-admired" him.

"They came up to me and said things like, 'Harry, what happened? I'm so lost!'" said Chapin. "They had a wife and kids and everything else; their lives were organized. But they didn't feel like they were living. Yet I, who had fouled up and made some real mistakes—they seemed to see me like I could solve the world."

After a while, Harry began to believe it himself and it showed when he came home from touring "perhaps one or two days in a month." During those times, he was forced to confront the life he left behind; a life of parenthood, husbandry and domestic chores, a life very different from his new one.

"I treated my family like a promotion man," said Chapin. "I was going through a star trip feeling like the all-time hot shit. I'd get exhausted on the road living a life of self-indulgence and then come home expecting everybody to nurse me. It really was a double standard. I'd stay home for two days, make a stew and go off again."

Said Sandy: "For the first two years in the music business, he went through a period where he was terribly glib to the extent he didn't know who he was with. It was all the same. Glad hand! He'd walk in the house and paw the kids the way he pawed the girls in the line after the concert. He had absolutely no sense of relationship or appropriateness or where he was or who he was. It was ghastly!

"I went through periods of living with Harry where it was like screaming in the dark to try and make any contact. He should have been free to live as he wanted to live, like a seventeen-year-old, footloose and fancy-free with no responsibilities, no concern for anybody but himself. For instance, he was going through a thing where he'd get up in the morning and go out and make certain appointments and I would ask him if he would be home for dinner and he would say, 'I'll be home when I get home,' which was something typical of that period, but not typical of him."

Jim Lipscomb recalled the first time he saw a change in Chapin. "It was after the first tour in 1972. I went out to meet him at a Ramada Inn in New Jersey and Sandy and I went into the room. When he was talking, I suddenly sensed the difference. He spoke with greater assurance, almost in a deeper, more resonant tone of voice. The boyish, uncertain quality was lost. There was a respect for his own opinion, I guess. He knew what he thought and had an idea that other people were going to respect it. It came with recognition."

But along with recognition came the fear it would disappear, that this great dream he was living might end at any moment. After all, he knew only a thin line existed between success and anonymity; between the song that got him there and the lack of one that might bring him back.

"So he lived in constant fear and fought with a nightmare of inadequacy," said Sandy. "He didn't know who he was, and there were so many things threatening about that. First of all, he was doing something that was not in the family tradition, a public and commercial kind of thing that would generally not be considered 'artistic' in terms of family tradition.

"At the same time, another part of him wanted to be a super-star on the covers of *Time* and *Newsweek*. Harry never accepted anything less than the furthest reaches of his imagination. He wanted to be thronged on the streets, he wanted to be universally loved. He wanted to be a phenomenon and nothing else would please him. So he lived in constant fear that this wasn't going to happen, that he started something that would not turn out to real-ize his dreams or his imagination about it. But it was even worse than that because it wasn't happening. Harry could not go into a place like The Troubadour in L.A. and have people not recognize him. He would have to push himself forward into a conversation and aggressively confront somebody in such a way that he could get to where he could say, 'I'm Harry Chapin. I wrote the song 'Taxi.''" And force them to say, 'Oh, yes, you're Harry Chapin. I should pay attention to you,' when they were at The Troubadour to see somebody else. He had to fight for every crumb."

In fact, even promoters, D.J.s and record store clerks still greeted his name with, "Harry who?" It got so bad after a while that Chapin began doing jokes about it. Once that fall he even had trouble getting into his own concert. It was his debut at Lin-coln Center's Avery Fisher Hall, his biggest concert to date. But when he arrived at the backstage entrance, the security guard wouldn't let him in. For one, Chapin's attire did not befit a star. He wore his usual ensemble of old brown corduroys, beige turtleneck, beat-up Hush Puppies, and his curly hair was unkempt. In addition, the Lincoln-like fringe that ran around his jawbone was scraggy and knotted. So the cop, of the abrasive New York variety, responded, "Harry who?"

"Chapin. Harry Chapin. C-H-A-P-I-N."

The cop began flipping through the pages of the backstage guest list. "I'm sorry, but your name's not on the list. I don't know what to tell ya. I can't let anyone in whose name . . ."

"Look," said Harry, perturbed. "Do you have a program of tonight's show?"

The cop pulled one out from a desk drawer.

"Okay, now open up to the third page. The one with the picture . . ."

Embarrassed, the cop apologized and let him through.

"Suddenly," said Sandy, "Harry found himself in a whole new world where I don't think he would've said he didn't belong; but once Harry started something, he rode it through to the end."

CHAPTER X

W*O*L*D

During the summer of 1972, Chapin went into Elektra's Los Angeles studios to record *Sniper and Other Love Songs*. It was his second album and a very important one. Though *Heads and Tales* sold impressively, Chapin had yet to establish a solid sales trend. If Elektra was going to promote his second album as heavily as his first, Harry had to come up with a blockbuster.

Chapin was still thoroughly caught up in his newfound fame and spent much of his time on self-promotion and personal projects, some of which created "bad vibes" in the studio. Within the band, it became a bone of contention that Harry was "spreading himself too thin." There was always that "one last interview" and writing scripts for movies. He also began work on a book of poetry and, since it was an election year, started doing an occasional benefit for political candidates such as Ramsey Clark and Presidential hopeful George McGovern. In addition, Sandy and the four children came out to California to join him and Harry couldn't resist showing them the town, with lunches and dinners and Disneyland. All of this meant there was little time for group rehearsal. In fact, before Chapin flew out to L.A., the band rehearsed together only one week so that they were unprepared in the studio, arranging songs and changing lyrics at the last minute.

Said Ron Palmer: "I felt that as a group the four of us had tremendous potential if Harry concentrated his talents on writing good songs with plenty of rehearsal so that all of us felt comfortable with the songs. John, Tim and I wanted to put our very best down on record. In addition, I was apolitical at the time and didn't like being dragged into political benefits that were more or less Harry's personal interest."

Bad vibes were also fueled by the band, for whom success had also rubbed off, along with a strong dose of self-importance. In the beginning, they were all just "bum friends." But now the home brew had bittered, and once friendly minds had become unfriendly egos. Their camaraderie suffered from cash and crowds and living at close quarters on the road each day.

"It became a bit of a status thing between the group members and the road crew," said Rob White. "I'm thinking specifically of Ron Palmer and John Wallace. They went from bum and truck driver, respectively, to all of a sudden making money as big rock musicians nationwide. I think it stuck in their heads a little bit."

Part of the pressure in the studio was because Chapin wanted to make *Sniper and Other Love Songs* a double album. This began the first of what turned out to be a near-annual struggle with Elektra Records as he tried to convince them of his passion. It was all part of Harry's urge to succeed beyond success and, in this case, follow up "Taxi" with not only a hit record, but a double one. So Chapin recorded twenty tunes, including new story songs such as "A Better Place to Be" and "Sniper," a couple of revised pieces like "Barefoot Boy" and "The Baby Never Cries," as well as several old numbers that had been stashed away in his notebooks for years: "Dirty Old Man," "Pidgeon Run," "Mrs. Hart," "Songwriters Woman," "She Was a Mother," "Companions," none of which was ever recorded, but most of which would resurface three years later in his brief Broadway show, *The Night That Made America Famous*.

As a collective, the songs formed a concept album, meaning they were all held together by a thematic thread. That theme centered on city people and city life and Chapin's attempt to reverse the common preaching heard in many sixties songs of escaping to the country. For this reason, the album was originally entitled *Sweet City Suite,* then *City Suite,* but, unfortunately, Chapin could use neither name. He had previously written an article for a rock magazine mentioning the title. Soon after the publication appeared, the music duo Cashmen and West called one of their albums *City Suite.* Coincidence or not, Chapin was convinced they stole it from him. He finally changed it to the bittersweet *Sniper and Other Love Songs.*

"The album was about a young man who comes to a city, any city, and the kind of people he meets," said Chapin. "One, he tells of their stories and conditions; two, the things he wants; and three, his relationships with women."

On the day Chapin's songs were considered for a double album, Jac Holzman held a private, closed-door conference in his Gulf & Western office. Attending were Bill Harvey, Elektra's general manager; Mel Posner, general sales manager; and Ann Purtill. Harry didn't want to take any chances with the fate of his record, so he and Fred Kewley, who always traveled in tandem, decided to show up at the meeting, hoping their presence would influence Jac's decision. But when they arrived, Holzman asked them to wait outside his office until the end of the conference.

Said Purtill: "The four of us listened cut by cut through the album, making no comments until the entire album had been listened to. At that point, Jac wanted to hear everyone's opinion: a short, one-sentence critique as he went down the list of songs such as 'Yes, I like it,' 'No, I don't like it,' or 'It doesn't belong,' and then a brief comment explaining why. . . . It was a totally unusual process, and the fact that Harry was outside the door was even more unusual. Most artists never heard what the record company felt about their work. But Jac's way was the old way."

In the meantime, Chapin nervously paced the sitting room like a caged cat. Two hours later, he heard the last note of the last song die to silence. No longer able to stand the anticipation, he barged into Holzman's office and took a seat near the door. Harry perched silently atop a shelflike air-conditioning unit that ran along the base of the window.

Holzman let him stay. He knew Harry wouldn't go home unless he heard the consensus for himself. So he proceeded down the list of songs, and in regimented fashion, Harvey, Posner and Purtill made their comments on cue.

"It was just like that," said Purtill. "We gave no consideration that a song was probably good, but didn't belong on the album or whatever. So Harry was not only getting the judgment, he was getting the machinery of the judgment as well. On the other hand, he had no right being there. But that's how he was. He was pigheaded and bullheaded and kept barging into things that were not his concern. It was a unique Harry situation."

For Chapin, the situation did not feel good. He was as much surprised at their rejection of his work as at the calculating terms they used to discuss it, like a contingent of mechanics bending over a broken Buick. As the critique progressed, so did the negative comments, which, for Chapin, had the effect of a boxer's punch. His shoulders began to slump to one side, and the setting sun at his back turned his figure into a hunched silhouette. By the end of the commentary, it was clear he had lost. His broken spirit advertised itself like a broken pinball machine flashing Tilt.

Purtill vividly recalled that moment. "I thought, Oh, my God, what are we doing to him? Here he's done all these songs and we're talking about them in the crassest terms, as though it took no creative effort to make them. It's the only time I ever saw him look down. I think his first surprise was that he was back to a single album, which he rationalized by saying, 'They didn't want a double album.' So we were ganging up on him, which, of course, would not be true."

Elektra's rejection of his double album also had more subtle, psychological undertones. Chapin had begun to make a nuisance of himself with the record company staff, and in the process he lost some of their respect. It was reflected in less eager promotion. Backstage one night at a concert, Jebbie Hart unleashed his mounting frustration at his stepbrother, shouting, "You know, sometimes people would have more respect for you, Harry, if you came into a room, sat down and listened for once."

Said Jebbie: "Harry was up there almost every afternoon saying, 'Did we pick up that station in Seattle? Did we pick up that station in Detroit? What number?' It was a very high-pressure question-involvement thing. And I think that hurt him because after a while the record company would say, 'Oh, Christ, Harry's here again. What's he want now?' In one sense it was good because he was involved and concerned. But in another sense he was alienating people. Judy Collins, who was also at Elektra, walked up there once every six months and the place was buzzing. After she left, everybody was saying, 'Oh, wow, isn't Judy nice, man? Let's push her record some more. Let's help Judy out. . . .'"

In the final analysis, it was the bizarre nature of Chapin's material that really did him in. His twenty songs were, for the most part, long, sad, emotional tales about outcasts struggling with personal trauma. Paul Rothchild, former producer of The Doors, called the songs a "threshold of pain." And brothers Tom and James, after listening to the album, described them as dripping with "doom, doubt and despair." The song "Burning Herself" was a true story about a woman Harry had once seduced at Vassar College who scarred her body with cigarette burns. Another, "Woman Child," was about teenage abortion. "Sniper" was a portrait of a mass murderer and "A Better Place to Be" was about a lonely, alcoholic midnight watchman who has an unrequited love affair. Not exactly the stuff of which pop songs are made.

Naturally, Elektra thought twenty songs of this variety were not conducive to repeated listening and made for "too heavy" an album. After the album's release, Stan Marshall, head of Elektra's East Coast sales, said at a press party, "How do you put that on and have it play for people? It's something you either have to absorb and get a message from, or you can't listen to it."

Said Chapin once, in retrospect: "They were painful impact statements. They were like watching a mugging. They had a tremendous amount of dramatic impact, but weren't things you'd listen to over and over again."

Sniper and Other Love Songs was released in September 1972, but within one month's time, it became obvious the album was a commercial failure. Record store reorders were down, and the album was poorly promoted, nowhere near the effort of *Heads and Tales*. The album also lacked a hit song. "Sunday Morning Sunshine" was the single, a tender, offbeat love song inspired by a line from a William Carlos Williams poem which said, in effect, that the smallest town or place takes on a different face if it holds the one you love. The song was selected mostly because of its "friendly, mainstream feel," the only one of its kind on the album. The only problem was that when Harry tried to sing happy, he was not very believable. His style was built for sadness. In addition, "Sunday Morning Sunshine" was not a story song, and when placed next to "Taxi," it seemed almost a letdown. Not surprisingly, the song received limited airplay. And the album sold poorly, approximately 100,000 copies.

Said Fred Kewley in a 1973 article by former Cornellian Geoff Hewitt in the *Cornell Alumni News:* "What we have found is that many people really like and appreciate these songs artistically and are willing to pay attention all the way, but without AM airplay, and without a hit record, a large number of people will not become aware of the artist, or his album, or buy it, or attend his concerts. The record companies, with the help of their computers, are keenly aware of the single and album sales, and, most importantly, the bottom line—net profit. The music, the art be damned."

However, most music critics agreed that *Sniper and Other Love Songs* was an artistic tour de force. The inside jacket cover was proof enough, with surreal, black-and-white sketches to match the bizarre portraits of people in Chapin's songs. The artwork was done by Rob White, Harry's road manager, whose real talent lay as a brilliant sketch artist. White's illustrations deftly captured the grotesqueries Chapin sang about, which verged on the poetic. They were mural-like etchings of people, both horrifying and intriguing in detail, with arms fusing into rifles, heads into breasts, fingertips containing city buildings—a marvelous collection of cameo collages (one for each song) designed and modeled after the style of *New York Magazine,* and all to make Chapin's musical messages sink a little deeper.

The album further perpetuated Chapin's image as the maker of long story songs and contained perhaps the best writing he ever put to vinyl. The classic of the collection of nine songs was the ten-minute pièce de résistance "Sniper," which many Chapin buffs and music critics consider Harry's finest musical composition. In fact, ever since 1966, when Harry first wrote the song-poem, he had added eighteen melody and tempo changes to dramatize the horror and terror associated with an assassination attempt. A major influence was Jethro Tull's *Thick as a Brick,* which Harry admired for its musical complexities, textural richness and shifting time sequences. "Sniper" possessed all of these characteristics and, for this reason, was more like a movie or rock opera than a pop song. The story was equally potent, as it probed the pathos of Charles Whitman and other assassins who needed guns to obtain recognition and a reflection of their existence.

The portrait Chapin painted was so believable and emotional that the psychological makeup of psychotic killers like Charles Manson, James Earl Ray, Sirhan Sirhan and Arthur Bremer (who shot Governor George Wallace) became instantly perceptible. "In fact, Bremer's diary, revealed at his trial," wrote the *Morning Star News* of Pasadena, California, "could be translated into 'Sniper'!"

The album also contained "Circle" and "Better Place to Be," which went on to become Chapin classics and prompted several music critics to compare Harry's lyrical work to Bob Dylan's. One Indiana newspaper, the *Daily News,* on December 21, 1972, ran the headline CHAPIN—BEST SINCE DYLAN, saying of the album: "It is the best thing anyone has done since Dylan at really getting into someone else's head and explaining it to us." But there were also large national publications such as *Record World* and *Cash Box* that lauded Chapin's story-song artistry. One local New York publication, the Brooklyn *Spectator,* summed up his artistry best when it said: ". . . few have the perspicacity and imagination to create a prose story line set to music. Thanks to this singer, a new term joins the musical glossary: Chapinesque."

Throughout his career, Chapin rarely received lukewarm reviews; critics who disliked his albums were as strong in their abomination as those prolific in their praise. Over the years, the most scathing reviews came from what Harry termed "the cool-school rock press, that small consortium of five to ten pseudo-intellectuals who turn inarticulate child prodigies such as Alice Cooper and David Bowie into musical messiahs and see truth and deep meaning in non-sequitur phrasings."

One of the people Chapin was referring to was Stephen Holden of *Rolling Stone,* who gave a ripping review of *Sniper and Other Love Songs,* writing, "No singer-songwriter, not even Rod McKuen, apotheosizes romantic self-pity with such shameless vulgarity." Holden called "Sniper" a "maudlin sensibility," "Better Place to Be" a "Saroyanesque barroom soap opera," and his only positive comment was: "Chapin has the courage of his convictions, and the sheer insistency with which he advertises his case of emotional diarrhea does carry some energy and invoke some sympathy."

Said Pete Fornatale, then a disc jockey with WNEW-FM: "Harry was a target, no question about it. And I think I understand why he was. Harry spoke from the gut and not necessarily from the head. Critics almost always do the reverse and, as a result, there's a conflict. For the most part, critics are posers of sophistication. Once, in the *New York Times,* John Rockwell reviewed Crosby, Stills and Nash and Neil Young in the same column. He tore Crosby, Stills and Nash apart and praised Neil

Young to the skies, for the very three albums I found to be the most narrow and self-indulgent of Neil Young's career. Now I love Neil Young, but to praise him at the expense of Crosby, Stills and Nash was really unfair. Harry was exposed to the same kind of treatment. He touched a chord in record buyers and concert audiences on the most basic human communication levels there were. Either from jealousy, misunderstanding or lack of sensitivity, critics tended to lambast performers like that."

Rockwell once explained: "What defines Chapin for me are the words, the story songs. Now, I suppose, you've already got a problem there because what I like in pop music is the music. In a lot of my favorite pop songs I don't even know the words, and the fact that Harry doesn't interest me musically is already a strike against him."

As Ann Purtill put it: "Rock critics such as Stephen Holden, John Rockwell and Robert Christgau all detected a phoniness about Harry. But then someone like Christgau intellectualized three-chord rock 'n' roll too much perhaps. So he didn't like any kind of pretentiousness brought to common music. He also didn't like fair songwriters. He called Harry self-important. Well, talk about self-importance. Didn't Christgau once write an endless diatribe about how five writers were responsible for making Bruce Springsteen? He wrote that in the *Village Voice*. I thought, this guy is in bad need of an editor. Critics would like to think they have an influence. They tend to deal from personal prejudice rather than objectivity. The whole musical criticism thing is just shuck!"

In fact, music criticism rarely affects the sale of an album or the artistic appeal or popularity of an artist. Unlike theater critics, whose reviews are usually published two or three days after the opening of a play and before the general public can form its own opinion, music reviews are published weeks, even months, after the release of an album. The music critic, then, is a nonfactor, the proof of which came in the fall of 1972, when Chapin won a Grammy nomination for Best New Artist of the Year. In addition, *Billboard* magazine presented Chapin with its Trendsetter Award "for devising a storytelling style of songwriting with a narrative impact rare to popular music."

There were also the negative music critiques that bruised the artist's ego, and Chapin was no different. In fact, over the years, Harry called his staunchest critics on occasion to find out why they felt as they did. But for now he was only beginning to feel their full wrath, the latest of which was Stephen Holden's review of *Sniper and Other Love Songs*. Two weeks after its publication, Harry was backstage at The Troubadour in L.A. during the sound check. He was alone, disconsolate. He bristled for days over Holden's remarks. He was also disappointed that Carly Simon, his Elektra rival, received huge promotion efforts for her single "Anticipation" while "Sunday Morning Sunshine" slipped by unnoticed. On his lap was his trusty spiral notebook. He began to scribble thoughts at the top of an empty page:

> *Rolling Stone* review—absolute demolition job by Stephen Holden. Feeling low—slightly put upon—Carly's single just went on WABC after only four days—wondering if it's all worth it . . .

At that point Chapin paused, as Jebbie Hart came into the room to tell him he was "on" and that "things look good." The Troubadour was filled to capacity. So Harry picked up his guitar and was about to head for the stage when he returned to his notebook and wrote: "*—Of course it is!*"

* * *

The financial disaster of *Sniper and Other Love Songs* was a humbling experience for Chapin. He had slipped in standing at Elektra and realized, more than ever, that despite his artistic ambitions he could not overlook the harsh realities of record company economics. At year's end he was no more than a figure in Elektra's profit-loss statement.

To compensate for dismal record sales and lack of exposure, Chapin doubled his concert schedule, relying on his strength, the live show, to regain momentum. It was there Chapin felt most comfortable and could create the magic that eluded him in the studio. He needed audience excitement to produce his best. In fact, by late 1972, Chapin's dynamic performance qualities had crystallized. He had become an engaging homespun raconteur, knowledgeable in the making of good drama and good comedy. He routinely received standing ovations and often moved audiences to tears.

"There were few dry eyes in the house," wrote *Newsbeat* after one Bitter End concert. "It was a powerful display of emotion and feeling as the Bitter End has rarely seen in a performer."

On occasion, Chapin, too, became deeply moved by such audience reaction. Once, during a concert at Bananafish Park in Brooklyn, Chapin sang "Taxi" and "Sniper" as an encore and was greeted by an overwhelming standing ovation. He came down the steps at the side of the stage, his eyes glassy, his legs shaky. A freelance photographer, Ruth Bernal, who later supplied many of the photographs for Chapin's songbooks and album covers, remembered that day: "Everybody was so moved. Harry came backstage and was so humanly touched he was practically crying. He was jumping around. He didn't know what to do with himself. So he just came up and hugged everybody. And frankly, in all the times I saw him, I always flash back to that night."

Chapin also had his share of disaster concerts. He was, after all, still relatively unknown and, aware of this, he accepted every conceivable concert offer to make money and make himself a name. "If somebody said, 'Hey, Harry, there is an interview here, a concert there,' I'd be off and running," said Chapin. "Even if a radio station promised to play one extra record, even if it was somebody's birthday, I'd go charging off. In fact, for my first year in the record business, I probably worked harder than any other white male singer in the country." And if there was a free night in between towns, Chapin somehow found a booking, often as a last-minute addition or to fill a cancellation. This meant he sometimes subjected himself to disrespectful crowds who neither knew him nor cared if they did.

For instance, one evening Chapin was tacked on to a performance at a high school in Amsterdam, New York. The concert was in a gym where the acoustics were built for echo. "It was one of those gyms," said Harry, "where if twenty people were screaming it sounded like the whole Hessian Army." To compound matters, the stage was only six inches high and bleachers made of loose boards lined the sides of the gym. The speakers echoed violent shrills, like some strangled goose, and since there were no spotlights, the gym lights had to remain on or else the performance was in total darkness. But the worst part was the audience, a group of rowdy high school students who were half stoned, throwing beer cans and wandering aimlessly in the aisles. One student had a tennis ball and was having a game of catch with his friend a few feet away from Harry. In short, everything possible was working against Chapin, a performer whose lyric-based songs required intimacy and attentiveness in order to achieve their full dramatic effect.

Into the first number, Harry began, "Hey, man, it's great to be here! Absolutely wonderful! I'm glad everybody's having a good time! We're gonna do some music for ya . . ."

Pandemonium. Catcalls, jeering, the two friends continued their catch.

Introduction to the second number: "Hey, man, it's great to be here, we're glad everybody's feeling good! If you listen a little bit, maybe you might even get into a couple of things. We have some good songs here we've been working on . . ."

Pandemonium. The kid playing ball threw a spectacular pass to his friend, who caught it.

Introduction to the third number: "Hey, guys, would you give us a break! We're really trying! And, kid, can you please sit down. I mean, if you're gonna play ball at least go outside."

Fourth number. Absolute pandemonium. "For Christ's sake, we played thirty-eight concerts in the last two months. We played for all kinds of audiences and this is one of the toughest situations to work in, but, by God, we're gonna do a good job, just give us a break."

Fifth number. Pandemonium still. "Look, we'll get off shortly. I want to do a couple more good numbers." The ball goes sailing by, narrowly missing Harry's head. "Listen, buddy, for Christ's sake, would you go outside? I'm really starting to get ticked at ya."

The kid didn't move.

Chapin finished the sixth number. The gym was in chaos. Harry was flabbergasted. He bristled. "Is the term 'asshole' still used in this part of New York State?"

The kid in front of Harry turned and shouted, "Hey, man, what do you want, a fight or something?" He slowly marched toward Harry with his fists clenched, but his ballplaying friend quickly interceded and held him back.

"I was convinced Harry was going to get into a fight with this guy," recalled John Wallace. But then, as calm as can be, Harry lowered his head to the microphone and said in a forceful tone, "Buddy, you don't want to mess with me."

The kid backed off. After three more songs, Chapin left.

A couple of months later, a big Top 40 radio station in El Paso, Texas, was doing a promotion and scheduled The Temptations and a couple of boogie bands to perform at the local civic center. But at the last minute one band canceled out and Chapin agreed to take its place. That night the crowd consisted of approximately 8,000 people, of whom 5,000 were black, 3,000 Chicano, and about 17 white.

Said Chapin: "The radio station had just passed out 8,000 Frisbees with the station's name on them. We were the opening act of the three and we got out there and Ron Palmer was late. So it's me, Tim Scott and John Wallace. I started singing 'Sunday Morning Sunshine' and all of a sudden a noise went up from the crowd that must have been roughly analogous to the noise the Romans made when the Christians and lions were led into the Colosseum, 'rrRRRaaahhh!' Within the next couple of minutes, a good half of those 8,000 Frisbees came flying in our direction."

When Palmer finally showed up, Harry tried to charm his way out by making a joke that compared Palmer's lateness to his sex life. But the crowd wanted no part of it. "These people were there to boogie," said Chapin years later. "They didn't want a little white boy with his group and a cello."

Chapin was constantly on the road now and he lost touch with his roots. Every night was another show in another city, the same twenty-two strings playing their familiar patterns to cheering fans and greedy promoters. Backstage after concerts there were the weirdos, the women, and the sincere people. After a while, the faces and places began to look the same: a Holiday Inn in Denver, a Ramada Inn in Dallas, the rooms all looked alike, as did the rent-a-cars, the highways, the audiences. "Is Kansas City tomorrow?" "No, we played Kansas City two days ago. Tomorrow is Kalamazoo."

Living out of a suitcase often brought sudden urgent longings for a good home-cooked meal, a plain, comfortable living room, and some ordinary conversation with good friends. A place to go where there was no spotlight, no performing, no selling oneself; just some cold beers, raunchy jokes and talk of the latest sports playoffs, particularly basketball and the New York Knicks, Harry's favorite team. Essentially, his was a longing for many of the things he had before success, when life was simpler.

But now life had become complicated with jet planes and credit cards, and every move he made had a financial relationship to someone else: to promoters, the record company, and the people he hired—the band, his manager, lawyer and accountant. To take off two weeks from a tour in Texas meant a loss of thousands of dollars out of the pockets of each of those people. Such were the dangers of being "the product," placed on a pedestal of admiration and worship that defied all logic or merit, even for a "third-rate rock star," which Chapin often called himself. But sometimes, just sometimes, Harry wanted to come down from his contrived pedestal and be Harry. In many ways he forgot who Harry was, and that was because "he had no base or security for who he was," said Sandy. "He lost complete sense of himself. I think he lost touch with the real roots he had with his family."

Harry rediscovered them in Boston with another family, the Marsdens. Several months earlier, during his first promotional tour, Chapin appeared at a small club outside Boston called Lenny's on the Turnpike, a roadhouse on its last legs and since closed. It was a cold, rainy night, the perfect setting for a Chapin concert. For some reason, the white noise of rain had a cathartic effect on Harry and inspired him to perform better. And that night he did, before an audience of one hundred people at best, most of whom had never heard of Harry Chapin. Except, that is, for Zeke and Peachy Marsden, who specifically came to hear Harry, having fallen in love with his first album. After the show, Zeke and Peachy approached Chapin and struck up a friendship that lasted the rest of Harry's life.

Zeke told Chapin he was a big fan—something Harry did not have many of then—and agreed that the next time Chapin was in Boston they'd get together, which they did. In September 1972, Harry was booked for a one-week engagement at Pall's Mall, another Boston club (since closed). After each evening's performance, Harry and the band went over to the Marsdens' apartment and indulged in one of Peachy's delicious corned beef and cabbage dinners, which soon turned into tradition. In succeeding years, any Boston concert meant an evening visit to the Marsdens, and they became not just good friends, but Harry's adopted family, his home away from home.

Zeke Marsden was a short, pudgy fireball of a man with dark brown hair and glasses. He was a fun-loving, salt-of-the-earth-type guy who spoke in a thick Boston-Irish drawl. A brakeman on the Boston and Maine Railroad, Zeke had a marvelous gift for gab and a glib sense of humor that was always good for a risque story or two. He never held back a verb. In many ways, he was like Harry: bold, brusque, abrasive, but without the intellectual refinement. Harry liked that about Zeke. He was a straight talker and straight shooter who was unconcerned with what others thought of him. "He has brass balls," Harry said once. "He's like me. He's willing to do anything."

Part of Zeke's appeal was the entire Marsden clan and their strong sense of family togetherness. They reminded Harry of his own family. The Marsdens transmitted a deep warmth, we-stick-together attitude much like the Chapins. Besides Zeke and Peachy, the Marsden relatives—Zeke's mother, Mame; his brother, Jay; his sister, Mary, and her husband, Paul Rizzo (another old Boston family); as well as numerous friends, aunts, uncles and cousins—all lived within a few blocks of each other in the old Irish Catholic neighborhood of Charlestown, a lower-working-class section of Boston.

It was a section that reminded Harry of Brooklyn Heights, with its narrow, hilly streets, cobblestone roads and old three-story buildings. Charlestown also overlooked Boston's downtown skyscrapers, and nearby, just like the Brooklyn Navy Yard, was the Charlestown Navy Yard, where the U.S.S. *Constitution* was moored in the green waters of Boston Harbor. Even Zeke and Peachy's redbrick apartment house (built before the Civil War) reminded Harry of the one on 45A Hicks Street.

But more importantly, the ambience of life in that house was somewhat reminiscent of his days and nights with Manny and Janet Castro. Zeke and Peachy's home was the gathering place in Charlestown for all their relatives and friends. Anyone could drop by, say hello, no telephone calls required. Weekends, the Marsdens' home became a joyous open house with parties and beer and good times. Leaving their home after a concert and dinner, Harry once triumphantly called out to Zeke, "This is where it's at! This is roots!"

Harry returned to those roots every time he was in Boston or near it, which was fairly frequently in the early part of his career. Zeke invariably waited at the airport, drove Harry to his concert, invited him home for supper, and made sure he caught his return flight back. In addition, Sandy's father was in and out of Massachusetts General Hospital for treatment of a malignant brain tumor and Harry often called Zeke on weekends to pick Sandy up at Logan Airport so she could visit him. Then, afterward, she had dinner with Zeke and Peachy. "The Marsdens were important to me in that they made themselves important," Chapin said once. "They went out of their way for me."

Zeke didn't mind, nor did the rest of the family. Just knowing Harry and being able to call him a friend gave them a sense of specialness they returned to Harry by always making him feel special.

"To Harry, I represented people here in Boston," said Zeke. "I represented them in Omaha. There were lots of places where he didn't get to meet people because the record company isolated you. They got you here, got you there, to the radio station, into a limousine. But he knew that every place he went there were a whole bunch of Zeke Marsdens, a whole bunch of little fat guys. To be a number-one fan, this was what I had to offer him."

But to Harry, Zeke offered more than that. To him, the Marsdens were "special people." With them, he was "one of the boys." And with Zeke, for the first time, he could say he had a friend outside the family, something his brothers had plenty of and never failed to remind Harry of during arguments. Though Harry was hardly a model friend, he showed his love and generosity in other ways. During the summer of 1972, he performed an outdoor benefit in Boston's City Hall Plaza, sponsored by WRKO. The place was jammed, some 35,000 people parked everywhere: in the trees, on the ground. There were no chairs for anyone. Of course, the whole Marsden crew came along, including the family matriarch, Mame, Zeke's mother. Harry adored her. She was a plain old Irish woman who more than compensated for her lack of worldly sophistication by a charismatic charm and wit. Mame had the art of jest by its throat. She was also sixty-two years old with a bad back and needed a place to sit. At the beginning of the concert, Harry was on his stool at center stage when he noticed Mame standing off to the side.

"Where's Mame gonna sit?" he asked into the microphone.

"She could sit up on the piano and flip pages for me," said Steve Chapin, who had joined Harry for this one concert. The crowd cheered.

"No, no, she's gonna sit down," said Harry, determined. He motioned toward a big Irish cop at the base of the stage and asked for a chair.

"We can't put a chair up on stage," said the cop. "It'll be in their way. The people will start yellin'. Anyway, there's no chairs."

"Look, all we want is one chair," Harry persisted, the crowd egging him on. The policeman shrugged his shoulders.

"Look," said Harry, pointing to Zeke. "This is my best friend in Boston and I want a chair for his mother. Because if I don't get one, you ain't getting any songs."

The crowd roared its approval.

With that the cop disappeared into City Hall and reappeared two minutes later with a chair for Mame. She received a standing ovation.

Meanwhile, as Harry took on different sides to his life, Sandy took on different sides to hers, and their marriage continued to strain and falter. In September 1972, she faced emotional and domestic troubles of her own. Not only was her father ill, but she was five months pregnant with her fifth child. In addition, that month the Chapins left Point Lookout and moved to a new home in Huntington, Long Island. Beyond basic essentials such as some furniture Grandma Chapin sent over, everything was in makeshift order. Cardboard boxes were piled in corners, and painting, decorating and carpentry work still had to be done. Harry was on the road so Sandy supervised the move alone and adjusted both herself and her children to their new home. It was quite an adjustment.

The new Chapin residence was an eighty-year-old, three-story, seventeen-room house that sat along Huntington Bay (Long Island Sound) with lots of backyard, about one hundred yards worth between the back porch and waterfront. The house was the former homestead of a bootlegger, complete with zinc-lined bathtub in the attic, and the only "ramshackle" structure in a neighborhood of modern exclusive homes—Harry liked that. In fact, when Sandy first took Harry to show him the house, she drove down the long private road which led to it, passing a multitude of manicured lawns and estates that so revolted Harry that he asked her to "please turn the car around."

Once they reached the end of the road, Harry fell in love with his new home, which he soon called his "Make a Wish House." It was paid for ($100,000) with his songwriting royalties. To go with the house, Elektra Records donated a regulation-size pool table as a housewarming gift and Harry bought a Technics sound system for his small, paneled workroom/study on the second floor, which he built himself during spare days over the years. The windows of the study opened to a veranda-ledge that ran along the north side of the house and overlooked the waters of Long Island Sound. In the room were two giant blue-foam stereo speakers below a shelf holding dozens of records, old and new, with a handwritten sign scotch-taped to the shelf: PLEASE PUT BACK IN ALPHABETICAL ORDER. There was also a small oak secretary desk with lots of compartments and an old, black, manual typewriter for Harry to compose his poems, scripts and story songs.

By November, there was a new addition to the "Make a Wish House," a precious, blue-eyed shiny boy named Joshua, Harry's first son. On the day of Joshua's birth, Sandy drove Harry to Kennedy Airport to catch a plane for a one-week gig in Atlanta. After she dropped him off at the airport, she experienced terrible labor pains and went directly to the hospital and had her baby. But there were complications. Joshua was two months premature, losing weight and in need of special care. Later that day Sandy called Harry at his Atlanta hotel to deliver the bittersweet news. And every night after concerts, he commuted home to be with her, catching the last flight out of the city.

There were further complications. Ever since the move to Huntington, Sandy found herself entertaining huge crowds of people, fans from Chapin's concerts. When Harry felt pressured enough by certain people who gave him more attention than others, he invited them as guests for dinner or weekends, often without telling Sandy. It was Harry's way of dealing with fans. He could not say no. The only problem was that Harry was rarely home to welcome his invited patrons, which placed Sandy in the awkward role of hostess to a melange of strangers who suddenly appeared on her doorstep.

"The thing I thought was strange," said Sandy, "here Joshua was premature and in pretty serious shape and Harry was having huge crowds of people at the house, even staying over at the house. He was inviting all kinds of people to be entertained. And I was going around the clock entertaining and he wasn't there, you see. Because he didn't like to socialize. He didn't like to deal with people. He got really crazy if he had to be in a social situation. So he left or locked himself in a room with a hockey game on television. I couldn't understand how I got caught in this situation and I said, 'No! I won't have it anymore.' But it didn't do any good. There were just more hordes of people."

To vent her frustrations while Harry was away, Sandy kept a book of poems she called her "Fuck You, Harry" poems about his star trips. But some of her poetry was also an attempt to plug into Harry's world. For instance, Sandy's poetry rarely rhymed, but she started writing lyrical poems with the intention of giving them to Harry as potential songs. One of her poems turned out to be the lyrics to the song "Cat's in the Cradle." Several months earlier, when Harry was gathering material for his second album, he asked her to "come up with a concept for a song." Sandy told him she thought a story about a father and son was universal. But Harry quickly rejected the idea. "I guess it didn't have sex appeal," said Sandy. "It didn't sound like an AM single."

So Sandy decided to write the lyrics herself in her own groping attempt to communicate with him, to awaken him to the alienation his stardom had created between himself and his family. The poem was about a son, forced to grow up without fatherly attention or love, who rejects the father years later when the father needs him. In detail the father was not Harry but Sandy's ex-husband, Jim Cashmore. But she began to see startling parallels between the two, which included Harry's relationship to Jim Chapin. He was becoming more like his father every day, and that frightened her, particularly for her children and specifically for Joshua, whom Harry later called "The Cat's in the Cradle Kid."

A few weeks later, when Harry returned home for one of his two-day visits, Sandy showed him the completed lyric of "Cat's in the Cradle." But he was not impressed. He also missed her message. Perhaps he chose to ignore it.

In April 1973, Sandy's emotional troubles compounded when her father was readmitted to Massachusetts General Hospital in Boston at the very time the Chapins were making plans to have him stay with them in their new home. Then, on April 15, Sandy got a call that her father was in bad shape; she should come "right away." At the time, Harry was in Philadelphia cohosting the *Mike Douglas Show*. Sandy called him but there was no way he could leave. "Call Zeke," he told her.

"She did call me and I ran to the airport," said Zeke. "I picked her up and, needless to say, five minutes before we got to the hospital, her father passed away."

Before April ended, Harry received his share of disappointing news when cellist Tim Scott decided to quit the group and chase down his dream of playing classical music in a symphony orchestra. Part of his decision stemmed from his "general unhappiness" in the band, not the least of which related to Harry and their differences in artistic temperament. Scott, like most cellists, was a special breed of musician: meticulous and finicky and dedicated to an instrument that required years to master. Naturally that kind of disciplined personality conflicted with Chapin's free-wheeling approach to life and music. And not surprisingly, over the course of Chapin's ten-year career, the cellist position was the one part of the group that saw the greatest turnover, five musicians in all. Scott also had "a bitter taste in his mouth" from the previous recording session of *Sniper and Other Love Songs*. And since Chapin's third album, *Short Stories,* was only a month away from recording, Scott decided to expedite his decision.

"There were things I didn't like about Harry," said Scott. "Up until that time he had been pretty fair to work for. The money was fair. But I didn't like the lyrics to some of his songs and sometimes he was too aggressive. He could be very friendly, but he just pushed himself too much. If we were recording, he tried to go fifteen hours straight."

Said Ron Palmer: "Tim didn't like all the holdups, the hap-hazardness of everything. Tim was a funny dude. He didn't have much patience. He didn't like it when schedules were upset and he was inconvenienced. I think he got fed up with it. He especially got turned off when we recorded the second album."

Scott's departure was amicable. He wrote Harry, Fred and the band a long letter explaining his feelings and said that he'd stay as long as necessary to train a new cellist, but come June, he was gone. "He gave plenty of notice," said John Wallace. "Harry figured he could change his mind, but it was set. Tim went out to Portland, Oregon, and joined the symphony orchestra there. He made a hundred and fifty bucks a week and was happy as a clam."

Scott's replacement was Michael Masters, a tall, brown-haired man in his late twenties who wore a thick beard and glasses. Masters was a fine cellist, superior to Scott, with seven years of Juilliard training behind him. Equally important, Masters loved the limelight and travel and, for the moment at least, had no trouble fitting into Chapin's freewheeling ways. In fact, once Masters learned the music, the band became tighter and more polished.

"It happened one night after a performance in Texas," said Wallace. "It was rock 'n' roll on the road from then on."

In the meantime, Chapin wanted to forget past disappointments and embark on a new beginning. He spent the entire summer of 1973 recording *Short Stories*. In his attempt to organize things, Harry spent one month rehearsing his new collection of story songs and authorized Fred Kewley to find a professional producer because of the "commercial failure" of *Sniper and Other Love Songs,* which Kewley produced. Chapin wanted somebody who could give him a hit record and reestablish his good standing with Elektra.

Kewley called Paul Leka, the producer at Columbia Records who originally introduced Clive Davis to Chapin and who probably would have produced Harry had he signed with the company. Though Leka was a relatively unknown producer, his short list of production credits included the songs "Green Tambourine," "Nay, Nay, Goodbye" and the hit soundtrack from the movie *Summer of '42.*

Leka accepted the offer immediately. It was not a difficult decision to make. "I couldn't stand working for Columbia anymore," said Leka. "I couldn't touch the control board there due to the bureaucracy of the company. In addition, I owned, in partnership with a guy named Billy Gross, an eight-track recording studio up in Bridgeport, Connecticut. We had enlarged it to sixteen tracks. So when Fred called me, I decided to leave Columbia and go it alone as an independent producer. Fred said he couldn't handle producing Harry, that he was too busy managing him and that Harry just wanted to go back to the original day."

Part of Chapin's want was a complete change of scenery, and since Leka's was a quality studio located close to home, Bridgeport it was. There was no way Sandy could spend the summer in a California hotel again with a new baby and four children. Recording would last at least a month. In Bridgeport, Harry was only a two-hour drive away from his Huntington home. He was also away from Los Angeles and the bad memories of recording *Sniper and Other Love Songs* in Elektra's studios.

Said Ron Palmer: "Harry tried to blame the failure of the second album on a lot of things it shouldn't have been blamed on. For the third album, he tried to justify this and that. He thought if we recorded the album someplace else, it would be a big hit. Maybe it was the studio that was buggin' us? That's when he shot for a new producer and went to beautiful downtown Bridgeport, Connecticut."

With this decision Harry passed up the free production time he would have received in Elektra's California studios. Now all rental fees came out of his pocket, approximately $35,000. To defray cost, Chapin recorded the album from midnight to noon—at lower rental rates—for six straight weeks. Typically, after each session, Harry drove home, slept four or five hours and had dinner with his family. Then he went right back to Bridgeport. It was grueling for the band as well.

"Let me tell you, Harry and I were sometimes the only guys awake," said Leka. "I was practically walking over dead bodies. We consumed Dunkin' Donuts and coffee and watched the sun come up every morning. People were sleeping underneath the piano. It was crazy!"

But Harry loved every minute of it. He was all pumped up, consumed with purpose. During recording breaks, he was either on the telephone (Harry loved the telephone), holding magazine interviews, or playing pool on a regulation-size table Leka had in the studio.

"He was a fantastic pool player," said Leka. "He came in with his own personal cue stick tucked under his arm. Other times I watched him eat hamburgers and french fries, stuffin' 'em down his face with two hot coffees, never one, and always Sweet 'n Low. Then he ate a couple of donuts and with his greasy fingers played guitar. In the meantime, to the left or right of him, he had thirty-two songs he had to write for Tom Chapin's TV show. And he'd be writing them down with a cassette going, and then he'd be on the phone again."

In the studio, Harry, according to Leka, was often flanked by women and occasionally disappeared for an hour when some female visitor stopped by to say hello. Many of them were included in a black book he kept that contained names, addresses and telephone numbers of various women he met while touring throughout the country. But Harry wasn't the only one.

"They all kept books," said Leka, referring to the band and Fred Kewley. "And they had it in codes. Who did what. Who was good at what they did. They all had this crazy thing."

Said brother James: "Harry was not a Don Juan. But he could surround himself with a hundred and fifty women. Every woman he ever slept with he had to have an investment in. He liked to keep them all around, which I could never understand. It's hard enough to have one woman in your life."

One time in the studio, Leka, astonished at Chapin's exploits, said to him, "You're with a chick in the morning, then a different one in the afternoon, another one before you go on stage, another one when you come off stage—it's so crazy! You're gonna get caught!" Then Leka grabbed a crayon and inscribed on the glass of the control room window: *Live by the sword, you die by the sword.*

Chapin also lived by the sword artistically. In the studio, Harry had the incorrigible habit of changing verse at the last moment. His mind worked like a dictionary of synonyms, always redefining and creating a better way of saying the same thing, out of fear that what he put down for posterity was not good enough. Often he attempted to record songs without the standard practice of testing them in front of a live audience first. Naturally this irritated the band members, who were forced to record a song they had yet to adequately learn. But whatever changes Chapin did make, if he was sold on them, he stuck with them. Frequently he stopped right in the middle of a song and said,

"Hold it! Hold it! I wanna change this line. What do you think, Paul?" But before Paul could answer, Chapin shot back, "Well, I'm gonna use it anyway."

It wasn't so much that Chapin was a perfectionist as that he understood perfection. One part of him wanted to produce the very best album he could. But another part of him wanted to crank it out, get it done, mindful that another album was another mark and further proof of his existence. He looked at life as a series of achievements. He was what he produced. The only problem was he had a habit of winging it, relying on his initial gut instinct to be correct without paying enough attention to rewriting and trimming off the excesses. His brothers Tom and Steve often served that function and Harry made sure they were around. This was especially true of Steve who, either directly or indirectly, had a hand in almost every Chapin album. In many cases, Harry's most successful melodies were partially the work of Steve's smoothing and improving them.

Besides his brothers, Chapin's saving grace was his bottomless well of energy, drive and concentration. "He was a lift for me in the studio," said Leka. "He proved the fact that most people worked at forty percent of their talents because he used a hundred percent of his. He used everything he had. So when he was in the studio, he just poured everything out, and it was either one giant mistake or it worked."

Before *Short Stories* was completed, Fred Kewley convinced Chapin to renegotiate his contract with Elektra since a new regime was about to take over at the label and Kewley was unsure of their promotional commitments in light of the poor push accorded *Sniper and Other Love Songs*. David Geffen, the former owner of Asylum Records, was to become chairman of the board at Elektra/Asylum. But the most threatening change was the soon-to-be-announced resignation/retirement of the president, Chapin's chief supporter, Jac Holzman.

According to Chapin's contract, Harry had a guarantee of three albums but had the choice of renegotiation after the second if he was dissatisfied with the company or if Holzman, for some reason, left. Kewley's logic was that if Elektra didn't give him the promotional guarantees he wanted, he would shop Chapin's contract to another label, knowing full well that even if there were no takers, Elektra still had to produce *Short Stories*. The record company had no bargaining position. However, Harry wasn't crazy about the idea of leaving Elektra and when he told this to Holzman, Holzman said, "We like you Harry. We really do. But Fred loves to renegotiate."

Finally, Chapin went along with Fred's idea and, once again, there was a crisis meeting in Holzman's Gulf & Western office, Ann Purtill, this time between president-elect Mel Posner, Chapin and Kewley. However, Kewley's idea didn't go over very well and the meeting ended unresolved, with a stern warning from Holzman threatening Chapin with something Jac couldn't do: if Harry shopped himself around to other labels while they were trying to settle their differences, Elektra would not produce his third album.

Naturally, Harry disregarded Holzman's threat and shopped *Short Stories* to several record companies to gauge interest. But the reception was far from overwhelming. ABC Records and a couple of other companies turned him down. One of them was Warner Brothers, which, being under the same corporate umbrella as Elektra, had access to the same computer sales figures and declined. But it also meant that Mo Ostin, the president of the label, worked for the same company as Holzman. So after Chapin left Ostin's office, Mo naturally called Jac for an explanation and Holzman blew.

Chapin was unofficially gone.

Harry instructed Leka to try to sell *Short Stories* to Leka's longtime friend and former Columbia crony, Kip Cohen, who had become vice-president of A&M Records. Leka met with Cohen and had him listen to the nearly completed album. Cohen loved *Short Stories,* especially the song "Mr. Tanner," Chapin's evocative tale of a Midwest dry cleaner who dreams of becoming a singer and, at the persuasion of friends, gathers his money and his prayers and leaves for New York. But after his debut appearance in a concert hall there, he receives horrible reviews, gives up on his dream, and returns home.

The song was a true story, based on a review Chapin read in the *New York Times* that dismembered a young amateur named Martin Turbidy, whose name Harry changed to Martin Tanner in the song. Chapin's sensitivity to Tanner's plight grew out of his own hostile feelings toward music critics.

As Cohen and Leka listened to the song, Leka noticed something strange about Cohen, who once dreamed of becoming a singer, and was well acquainted with the occasional cruelty of music critics. "I was looking at Kip and he was making funny faces," said Leka, "Then all of a sudden, he took off his glasses and he was crying like a baby! I couldn't believe it! The song moved him that much."

Kip Cohen and A&M, of course, were more than willing to pick up Chapin's contract, but Harry decided against the change, much to Kewley's chagrin. Harry had a long, emotional talk with Jac Holzman and David Geffen that settled matters. But in the process, Kewley became very bitter, in part because Harry had "undercut" his position at Elektra, but mostly because he felt Chapin made a mistake, that they should have gone to a "fresh company" who'd be willing to work harder. Over the years, Kewley's judgment turned out to be correct. But for now Elektra did meet Chapin's promotional demands, and it was a sound decision.

Of the eleven albums Chapin eventually recorded, *Short Stories* was perhaps his best "listening" album, as opposed to *Sniper and Other Love Songs,* which was his worst. Leka's production was masterful and, much like *Heads and Tales, Short Stories* went neither platinum nor gold, but it had a single, "W*O*L*D," a sad, sensitive saga with a driving, syncopated melody, about an aging disc jockey trying to hang on in a business geared for the young, hiding his age under a toupee and contrived voice that sounded "forty-five going on fifteen."

"After 'Taxi,' I met all sorts of disc jockeys," said Harry. "The guys saw the world as their apple and there were those in their prime. The older guys were hanging on by their fingernails, especially those at WMEX and WRKO in Boston, the two stations most instrumental in bringing 'Taxi' to life. One disc jockey at WMEX, Jim Connors, claimed the song was about him. Actually it was about dozens like him. I flashed on what it would be like to be forty-five going on fifteen because the disc jockeys had to keep young listeners while they were getting older. It seemed to me there were a lot of analogies to be made between performers and disc jockeys. The frightening thing I started to realize was that as you get older, many times your audience stays the same, especially for D.J.s. But I was finding it wasn't true with me. People I picked up from the 'Taxi' album were sticking with me. I brought in new fans who weren't necessarily going to leave because I wasn't the kind of performer who was as hot as his last hit record. But also, Sandy and I were going through some tough times and I realized the kind of pressure put on a relationship by this kind of life-style."

Chapin didn't want to take any chances with "W*O*L*D." He wanted it to catch fire the same way "Taxi" first caught fire in Boston. The strategy was simple: bombard radio station WRKO with requests until the song got on the RKO playlist nationwide. Harry called Zeke Marsden and asked him to help out. Within one week, the entire Marsden clan was inundating WRKO with telephone and letter requests for the song. To guard against station suspicion, they alternated the use of pens, stationery and handwriting styles, signing the letters with false names, many out of the local Charlestown telephone book.

Within two weeks, "W*O*L*D" went to number nine on the RKO playlist. Some time after that, Chapin went up to the station to promote the single and was greeted by the manager, who said, "I've never seen so many calls and letters for one record in my life." At that point Harry let out a burst of laughter and, unable to restrain himself, confessed the truth.

Though "W*O*L*D" never attained the cult popularity of "Taxi," it, too, was a turntable hit, similar in style, length and sales. The song remained in the *Billboard* "Hot 100" more than thirteen weeks, mostly because disc jockeys played it for themselves, and rose to 36 on the charts. The song rose to 34 in Great Britain and stayed on the charts for five weeks. It was also a "minor" hit in Germany and Holland.

All of this meant that Harry was no longer a "one-song artist" and he found himself back in good standing with Elektra. At the time, Judy Collins was in a sales slump, so Chapin regained position as one of the top five artists on the label, behind Bread and Carly Simon. "W*O*L*D" also earned him financial security for the comfortable life-style "Taxi" created. His concert fees rose dramatically from an average of $1,500 his first year to $3,000 his second and $5,000 his third. In succeeding years, Chapin was always quick to credit his renewed success to Zeke and all the Marsdens and, in fact, told him at the time, "I couldn't have done it without you."

By Christmas 1973, Chapin's star trip came to an abrupt and unexpected end. Everything changed: his career, his marriage, his personal values, even his songs. It happened when a woman called the house in Huntington to find out if Harry was appearing on Long Island. At the time, Chapin was in Bridgeport recording his next album, *Verities and Balderdash*. Sandy answered the phone. "I don't know exactly where he'll be tonight," she said matter-of-factly. "Can you call back later? He should be home in a few hours."

Four hours later, at dinnertime, the woman called back. Harry was still not home.

"Well, wait," said Sandy helpfully. "I think I know where his appointment book is. Let me check." She went upstairs to the bedroom to find it. She looked in Harry's brown leather shoulder bag where he kept all his papers, spiral notebooks, credit cards and his appointment book. Inside was also his black address book.

Sandy discovered it. She stood in trancelike disbelief, slowly flipping the pages, her anger mounting with each page she turned.

After disposing of the female caller, she called Harry at the studio and confronted him with her find. She told him not to bother coming home . . . ever.

Harry hung up the phone, shaken and dejected. The worst thing he'd ever thought could happen had just happened.

"It was quite a blow," said Leka, who didn't find out what happened until two weeks later. "We were recording at the time and I remember Harry left a little different. He went straight home after that, saying nothing."

On the control room window, Leka's crayon inscription from four months before, *Live by the sword, you die by the sword,* was still visible, only partially erased.

PART FOUR

Won't you stop your locomotive
Release the steam of who you are
No character portrayals you write
Will tell you who you are.

You say listening to the whispers
Is the way to write a song,
But when the whispers you're not listening to
Come from you,
Who are you?
When the music's moved along.

—Peter Morton Coan
Buffalo, 1976

CHAPTER XI

Star Tripper

Sandy never wanted to see Harry again. At least, that was her immediate reaction. Filled with anger and hurt, she inwardly scolded herself for being duped by suspicions she had never bothered to investigate.

When Harry returned from Bridgeport, Sandy had already called her lawyer, the same one who had handled her divorce from Jim Cashmore, her first husband. Within a week's time, she got an injunction preventing him from coming to the house and essentially locked him out.

The marriage was over!

The thought paralyzed Harry. The ultimate sobering situation crushed him. A panic and fear unlike any he ever felt began to inundate him. His personal life was sinking with no visible means of rescue. After all, Sandy was his whole world. She comprised his entire emotional universe. She was his confidante, the keeper of some of his deepest secrets. And she was the oasis that always yielded water; a lifeline, who, during times of crisis, was always there. After two years of Chapin's distorting success, she was still there, his only remaining contact with reality. That included his brothers and family, who, for the first time, had diminished in importance in Harry's life. She remained, the lone survivor of his success; the only intimate fixture among a scattered assortment of superficial relationships.

For Harry, Sandy's exit from his life meant not only personal loss and failure, but a kind of emotional death. He tried to imagine life without her, but all he could feel was a dark sense of aloneness. "It was the first time in my life I really understood that you could blow something good that you couldn't go back to," said Harry.

He began to experience the deep depression he had not felt since his college days. Life-scripts, patterns began to emerge. He had visions of becoming a forgotten man like Cashmore, whom Sandy rarely spoke of during their marriage, almost as though he had ceased to exist. There was Mrs. Gaston, Sandy's mother, who, by disowning her daughter, had become a totally forgotten figure as well. Harry was concerned his name would be added to the list. How could he have allowed success to create such terrible consequences?

But he also had memories of Cornell and the day he quit school. He felt proud. After all, he had come a long way. And just as he felt the momentary satisfactions of personal triumph, the bittersweet image of Jenny Gillette, his old college sweetheart, shot into his head. She had gone to Florida, became engaged and totally forgot him. The pristine face of Clare MacIntyre swept into his mental gallery—the amatorial scare who dropped him flat.

For the first time Harry thought of his children and the kind of father he had been. He thought of his own father, Jim Chapin, whose genes, on some levels, had become apparent, potent. He was disgusted by the realization that he offered his children no more than his father had offered him; just a friendly visiting uncle. He didn't want his children to grow up alone.

And at some point in this montage of thoughts, feelings and images, he decided he wanted his wife back, his kids back, and would do anything to have it so.

"The bottom line was very simple," said Harry. "I was doing a whole bunch of things to reject her and she got the message. I didn't know what I was doing. I wasn't purposely doing it. When I saw I was going to lose her, it scared the shit out of me. I grew up. Relationships alternate from each being a parent to companion to lover to child, and I was only acting as a spoiled child. I wasn't giving her anything."

Sandy wasn't alone in her disappointment of her husband. Over the past two years, Harry's relationships with Fred Kewley, the band, road crew and record company had become strained. "A lot of people were fed up with him," said Sandy. "But he was also pretty fed up with himself. Something had to happen. I think he began to feel somewhat disintegrated. If it had been anybody else, they might have gone off on a long trip somewhere to find themselves or something. But that wasn't Harry's nature. His nature was to come out with fists flying and try to change. I don't think he knew how. He was just desperately grasping at anything in order to somehow put his world back together again. He started talking on the phone about fixing his schedule and planning more time at home."

Sandy didn't believe it. She had heard those words before. Living apart, Harry called her several times each day from Elspeth's apartment, pleading her forgiveness, telling her that he needed her and loved her. But Sandy remained unconvinced. Finally, Harry decided a third person was needed to help them patch up their differences. Sandy grudgingly agreed to this because, despite all that had happened, she could not deny she still loved Harry.

She loved him so much that, even in her pain, she remained understanding of him, believing, correctly, that although Harry was no longer the same man she had married, it was the corruptive nature of his business that temporarily transformed what was a generous, loving, sincere man, and that it probably would have happened to anyone. In quite another way, she also saw him as a child, just one of her children badly in need of growth and change. So, as long as Harry was willing to change, she was willing to listen.

The "third party" Chapin sought came in the form of Father Bill Ayres, who also lived on Long Island. Father Ayres was both a priest and a disc jockey. Harry had met Ayres a few months earlier on a radio talk show broadcast by WPLJ in New York. Ayres hosted a weekly program called "On This Rock" and on the show he played contemporary rock music and interviewed performers. When he interviewed Chapin, Harry talked about his personal beliefs, and they instantly became friends. Chapin appeared on the program two more times. Then Harry invited Ayres to a concert on Long Island, and when they were alone backstage, he told Bill of his marital problems and asked if he would help.

Ayres agreed. In many ways he had all the right qualities for a marital moderator. Kind, soft-spoken, gentle, Ayres possessed great patience and was a good listener. He was also a composer and writer, his songs appearing on an album called *Where's It All Going*. In addition, he was a friend of Steve Chapin and Pete Fornatale and, from Harry's perspective, was already part of the "Chapin family." But Ayres was also a man committed to solving social problems and tried to achieve his social goals through his work as a minister and broadcaster. "It wasn't because he was religious," said Harry. "I just respected him and liked him and he wanted to help."

During the sessions, Harry and Sandy had numerous philosophical dialogues as part of Chapin's attempt not only to rebuild his marriage but to do so by rebuilding himself first, by redefining his value system and developing a more responsible attitude toward his fame. This attitude, and his eventual involvement with humanitarian causes, grew out of their discussions, many of which centered on the concepts of commitment and community involvement. Others related to the music business that Sandy disdained, believing it had "nothing to do with quality" and that a large part of it was "hype" and "bullshit" and "counterproductive to living a sensible life."

But the most frequent topic concerned the "illusions of stardom" and the "true meaning of success."

"What would you rather do," Sandy would ask Harry, "be a color picture on one issue of *Rolling Stone,* or get the Nobel

Peace Prize? It's a huge contrast, but I think the former is so superficial and self-serving. You have to have larger goals! I think being a superstar can be very destructive because something like that can only go down, and who wants one's life to go down?"

Sandy believed those "larger goals" had to be geared toward benefiting humanity and using one's fame to improve society, not just take from it. Helping others was, in and of itself, the reward of such goals that she called "enlightened self-interest." This belief often led them into discussions about "engagement versus example theory." As a teacher, Sandy would say, "Nothing is worthwhile unless you are involving other people in an experience where they are stimulated to have an experience of their own."

Harry would disagree. "Example is important. You do a thing and show how it should be done and people have an example."

"That's wrong!" Sandy would protest. "It's detached. You've got to bring others in. You must remember where you came from. Draw from your roots, your basic resources. I believe in Jonathan Livingston Seagull. I believe that because you learn to fly doesn't mean that you go off on your own trip. You have the personal responsibility to turn around and reach out your hand to teach somebody else to fly too. Otherwise, there's no point in living."

Meanwhile, Father Ayres played marital mediator. "If one of us was bullshitting," said Harry, "he would say, 'Hold it a second . . .'"

From these sessions, Harry and Sandy managed to recreate some kind of working relationships and Harry moved back into the house in Huntington. The injunction was stopped. It was also agreed that "Harry was going to have to find something to care about," and he immediately began looking for ways to relate to Sandy, to get closer to her in any way he could. Instead of asking her to plug into his world, as he'd done in the past, he made every effort to plug into hers.

"Sandy was chasing me up until the Christmas of '73," said Harry. "I mean, there's always the subtle sense that one person is the seducer and the other is the seductee. But then, from the beginning of 1974 on, I've been chasing her in the truest sense of the word. I'm very grateful she's in my life."

Said Sandy: "It wasn't like I clearly outlined a program that if he did certain things I'd take him back. It was much more abstract. He tried to figure out ways that would make me admire him."

The first thing Harry did was to eliminate all long concert tours, particularly those on or near the West Coast. In this way, his absences from his family were no more than three or four days at a time. However, for bookings east of Chicago, Harry tried to be home the night of any given concert. His performances were usually three hours long, so this meant he did not leave the concert hall until after midnight. Then he would catch a direct commercial flight home such as Northwest 222, the title of a song about a late-night mail-run flight; a near empty jumbo jet on which Harry could sleep, stretched out across three seats, cuddled up with a pillow and a blanket. Many times, he took two or three commuter planes to get to the Northwest one. Other times, depending upon the city, there were no flights at all, so rather than stay at a hotel and leave the following morning, he sometimes chartered a plane.

But more often than not, he rented a car and drove as many as eight hours from cities like Buffalo or Baltimore, racing the sun back to Huntington to have breakfast with his children before they left for school. And for good measure, no matter where he was, he called Sandy an average of three times a day, reporting his latest location and reassuring her of his love. This manic routine, and in a sense self-punishment, became a permanent part of Chapin's life-style.

The key reason was not only Sandy, but her poem, "Cat's in the Cradle." One day she showed it to him again. "But this time," said Sandy, "he was very interested and enthusiastic and said, 'Wow! I'm gonna put music to that.'" When he did, using a melody based on "some old berserk eastern Kentucky banjo tune," the message of Sandy's poem finally sank in.

"It scared the shit out of me," said Harry. "It said when you're gone, you cease to exist to your children and they don't expect you back. So if you don't show them they matter to you, they'll show you that you don't matter to them."

Chapin's newfound sense of responsibility was reflected in other ways. For one, he adopted his father's fifteen-year-old daughter, Dana, his half sister, as a result of Jim Chapin's second marriage to an "exotic dancer." Dana immediately moved in with the Chapins, making Harry a father of six. Also, the richest member of the Chapin clan (for years, according to Harry, no one in the family earned more than $10,000 a year), he began to help pay the bills of several relatives and planned to give his family (all thirty-two members), plus his band, a summer vacation in Australia, but that plan fell through at the last minute.

At the same time, Chapin also became heavily involved in the Long Island community. "Sandy was interested in it and there was nothing else I could do to show that I was sincere about her," Chapin said once. For instance, Sandy had recently become a member (later vice president) of the Huntington Arts Council. The council was badly in need of funds, so Sandy came up with the idea of creating what came to be known as the Lively Arts Festival, a full weekend of outdoor cultural activities sponsored by the council's sixty member art groups and located on the grounds of a local school. The festival featured, among other things, workshops in drama, dance, poetry, fine arts and crafts, as well as a children's concert. Chapin volunteered to perform. He also taught a workshop in songwriting. For a nominal charge, residents from all over Long Island enjoyed the spring event, which eventually became an annual tradition in Huntington.

More important, Chapin began to immerse himself in Sandy's primary community concern, the Performing Arts Foundation of Long Island (PAF). His involvement began in November 1973, when Sandy volunteered him for a performance at a benefit concert for the foundation at Huntington High School (which also became an annual tradition). In January, he performed a second one, pledged a third, and eventually found himself as PAF's number-one financier and chairman of the board.

PAF was a progressive arts organization headquartered in Huntington that featured its own playhouse for theatrical productions as well as a unique arts-in-education program that was the only one of its kind in the United States. The program comprised young artists, actors and actresses who assisted teachers in classrooms throughout Long Island (and also performed in the playhouse) to show how art and acting techniques can be used as learning tools. For instance, if the topic in class was circulatory systems, the artist might have two students stand up in front of the room, with one pretending to be the heart and the other a blood vessel, and then act out what happens. Or if the subject was mathematics, the children attached numbers to their shirts and performed exercises of subtraction, addition and multiplication. The goal of such techniques was to personalize the educational process based on the assumption that children will learn more if they're playing a little. "But many times, what they were really interested in was talking to the artist," said one teacher. "They often asked, 'Do you really do this for a living?' It opened up a whole new world."

Sandy first became associated with the organization six months after the move to Huntington when she was feeling isolated and bored. Although she still had her thesis to write for her doctorate in esthetic education, she'd grown tired of school and fed up with long pointless papers on "theories of political action and community development." Instead, she wanted to find something in the real world, not for money, for herself, and she wanted to be in the community. "I wanted to meet other grownups and get involved," said Sandy. "I wanted to talk to someone else besides children."

Then she read about PAF and their arts-in-education program, "an actual living program in the area I had done my doctorate work." So Sandy volunteered herself to the organization and became coordinator of esthetic education for teacher training. She started out with the idea of working two half days a week, enough time to feel a sense of purpose without neglecting her family, but pretty soon she was at it full-time. Like any arts organization, PAF was constantly in the throes of financial crisis. But Sandy loved it. She enjoyed working with actors, artists and new ideas, and the feeling of heroism associated with a cause always on the verge of self-destruction.

And it was. PAF had accumulated a $50,000 deficit over its seven-year history, primarily because playhouse subscriptions and ticket sales did not cover the cost of its productions. The arts-in-education program, however, was completely subsidized by the wealthy Huntington school districts. There was talk of dividing the foundation in half and even abandoning the theater altogether. But meanwhile, there were heavy bank loans to repay, so Harry was asked to join PAF's twelve-member board.

Said Chapin: "They figured, 'Aha! We've got a soft one here who raises money.' I was expecting to find myself a new, exciting learning situation surrounded by heavyweight ideas about education, kids and community. Instead, I realized the organization was drifting. At the first meeting I attended, the board spit out their creator and visionary, Clint Marantz, partially because they disagreed with some of his philosophies, which was wrong, and partially because he hadn't been a good financial manager, which was right. It was one of those gray areas."

A few days after Marantz's departure, Chapin went to speak with him to probe what he knew about this "whole new area," the concept of arts-in-education, professional theater and its role in a child's education.

Said Marantz of that conversation: "I realized Harry was a cellmate. We discussed the importance of art in the total development of the child. We talked about the kind of world we were moving into, the transformation that was taking place."

"The problem," Marantz told him, "is that schools are not educating kids to be able to be successful in the new age. Having a child memorize thirty-two facts is naive. What we really need now is for kids, at a very early age, to begin to grapple with paradox; that there is no one way. How is a child able to cope with constant change? Education in the schools today doesn't prepare the kids. The great artist is always on the vanguard. He perceives ways the average person doesn't. So his responsibility is to go into the schools, open up the windows, open up the doors and begin to be a catalyst."

"Well, how can I get this thing off the ground?" Chapin asked earnestly. "Harry, you've got to take the leadership," said Marantz. "They're waiting for someone strong to come in. Until you, or somebody, take over that board and set the tone of what this professional theater can be, it's just going to dribble, drabble and die."

Chapin took Marantz's advice and regularly began attending PAF's board meetings, trying "to find a way of keeping both sides of the foundation together." He began raising funds for PAF by giving occasional benefits with his band. But more often than not, he sang alone in auditoriums of Long Island high schools and colleges as an "artist-in-residence" for PAF. Then, after concerts, Harry held "rap sessions" with the students, talking with enthusiasm about everything from life, goals, music and education to genetic engineering and Watergate.

"Look at Richard Nixon," he'd say typically, occasionally stroking the brown, scraggy Dylan-like beard that ran like a fringe under his jaw. "Here is a man without any talent or imagination who got to the highest elected office in the land when, at one time in the early 1960s, he couldn't have gotten elected dog-catcher in California. He got what he wanted out of sheer determination, and in that sense, he's an inspiration to us all."

These rap sessions were all part of Chapin's self-evaluation, his effort to stay close to reality and go back to the "inputs" and "innocence" which, he felt, were the source of his stardom in the first place. "I don't want to be a phenomenon," he told *Newsday* in a feature article called "Rich Little Poor Kid, Back From a Star Trip." "I want to be a human being." Toward this end, by Chapin's own estimates, he spoke to more than 75,000 young people in forty-two high schools and ten colleges between 1974 and 1976.

"I believe he started doing this to help PAF," said Kas Bendiner, the head of the arts-in-education program. "But I also think he got a lot out of it himself, close to the roots."

During these rap sessions, Chapin also started talking about a new topic, world hunger. The subject first came up during Harry's marital meetings with Father Ayres. And soon the world hunger issue emerged as Chapin's second major social commitment and, subconsciously at least, another potential venue to prove to his wife that he was a worthwhile human being who cared about other people.

At the time, March 1974, the entire sub-Saharan region of Africa (Sahel, Somalia, Chad, etc.) was in the throes of a severe drought, with hundreds of thousands of people starving and millions more faced with the same fate. The covers of newspapers and magazines illustrated the hunger crisis with a photograph of a dying woman robed in black, holding a naked skin-and-bones baby with a swollen stomach. "It flabbergasted me," said Harry. "I wanted to learn more about the problem. Hunger seemed like such a gigantic issue that I knew so little about and Bill Ayres was interested in it, so we started having these meetings to figure out what we could do."

The meetings took place at Chapin's home, on and off, during the spring of 1974. Harry and Bill invited anyone with an interest or background in hunger issues to openly discuss the subject, from Long Island Congressman Tom Downey to Harry's brother

James, who was a professor of American diplomacy at Rutgers University in New Jersey. In addition, Father Ayres was interviewing hunger experts on his radio shows and reading books on the subject, which he then passed on to Harry. One of them was *Bread for the World* by Washington economist and hunger expert Lester Brown, which temporarily became their hunger bible.

"Neither Harry nor Bill had solid backgrounds in hunger issues," said Geri Barr, who was a participant in these early meetings and later became a codirector of World Hunger Year. "But they were very interested and willing to ask a lot of questions of other people."

As Chapin learned more facts, he gradually grew more committed. The data from the U.S. government was startling. It read like wartime death statistics: "Nearly thirty percent of the world's population is near the starvation level and survives on an annual income of less than $220 dollars . . . Ten thousand people die every day from hunger-related causes . . . In several Third World countries, half of all children die before the age of six from diseases that have a foothold in malnutrition."

Chapin was not the only one awed by these statistics. Several months earlier, Bob Dylan, George Harrison, Ravi Shankar and others held a Bangladesh concert at Madison Square Garden in New York and raised $400,000 for hunger victims of that country. After one meeting at the Chapin home, Bill Ayres read that the World Food Conference was coming up in Rome in November and said to Harry, "You know, I think it's time for another Bangladesh concert."

"Yeah, you're right," said Harry. "But I'm not George Harrison." To raise the same $400,000 Harrison et al did in a single night, Chapin would have to perform perhaps fifty concerts.

So Chapin and Ayres solicited the United Nations with their benefit idea. They spoke to John Scali, the U.S. ambassador to the U.N., who agreed to subsidize the search for performers provided that his aide, Michael Viner, who had arranged for the entertainment at Richard Nixon's 1972 inaugural, spearheaded the search. Chapin agreed. Viner certainly seemed impressive enough, especially when Harry first met him and Viner boasted he could "bring in The Beatles for a concert." Chapin was further satisfied when one U.N. colleague said of Viner's influence, "Are you kidding? He's got so much clout he could get Ray Charles a driver's license."

But Viner, according to Chapin, "turned out to be a blowhard." During the summer of 1974, Harry took Sandy to Greece for a badly needed second honeymoon. While he was gone, Viner was supposed to book performers and set up the November benefit. The United Nations Association, a U.N. booster organization partially funded by U.S. business, put up $30,000 for the effort. But when Harry returned from Greece, the money was spent and nothing was accomplished. Viner had not booked a single performer.

"He spent all that money within two months, didn't do shit, and blamed me for not getting performers," said Harry. "In addition, I had a promise of support from Bill Graham, the concert promoter, but that fell through."

The fiasco forced Chapin to reevaluate the seriousness of his hunger commitment. Once again, he learned that nothing was accomplished by leaving one's personal concerns to others. It was clear to him that the hunger problem went far beyond the mere donation of dollars or "one-shot deal, flash-in-the-pan concerts," which Chapin described as the "event psychosis" of American culture. The hunger problem, much like PAF, required administrative involvement, fact-finding, attending meetings; all the nonglamorous sides of the issue Chapin was just beginning to understand.

"If we'd done a Bangladesh concert every night of the year, making $2 million each night, it would have meant $760 million," said Harry. "But that's only a drop in the bucket considering there are one billion hungry people."

So it was back to Chapin's house for more meetings until Harry and Bill came up with an effective approach to the problem. According to their new analysis, the primary causes of world hunger had nothing to do with the scarcity of food and land, or even overpopulation. Proof enough was the United States, which had near zero population growth and enough food to feed four times its citizens, yet twenty-five million Americans went to bed hungry each night. Nor did it have anything to do with lack of charity from rich nations or hunger-relief groups such as UNICEF. Instead, the problem had everything to do with big business, multinational corporations, international politics, dictatorships and oligarchies. These power structures made the distribution of land and wealth so terribly unbalanced that people could not produce enough food for themselves. Consequently, the equitable redistribution of land and wealth, combined with teaching people how to farm, and thus, feed themselves, seemed to be the only long-term solution to world hunger.

"We decided to set up an organization on step two of the hunger question," said Harry. "That is, a change of life-style and values through the use of the media, education and political awareness. The goal was to create a constituency of concern in the country so that people became involved in the issue."

"The hook," said Bill Ayres, "was that there were a lot of hunger groups, but none who had access to the media as we both did."

This was especially true of Ayres, the Director of Radio and Television for the Diocese of Rockville Center on Long Island. He ran the diocesan television center and, besides his Sunday night radio show on WPLJ, had a Sunday morning show on WABC and did some radio work for WNBC. All combined, Ayres broadcast more than 250 radio and television shows a year. His radio interviews were almost exclusively with wealthy and well-known rock stars who possessed megabucks and media access.

So Chapin and Ayres tried to enlist their support for hunger benefits so that an initial kitty could be created for the organization. "Every group I talked to was interested," said Ayres. "Some actually came forward and said 'I'd like to work with you,' such as Don McLean and Crosby, Stills and Nash. They wanted to do a little bit here and a little bit there. But they really didn't want to change their lives. Harry once said to me, 'I will change my life because of this.'"

And he did.

No one else committed themselves to hunger benefits, so Chapin went out and raised the money himself. He set up a slew of concerts, including some in which his brother Tom and their father Jim and his trio, Jazz Tree, participated. Harry's new non-profit hunger-resource organization needed a name. He chose the acronym WHY, which stood for World Hunger Year (which was every year), or more figuratively, Why hunger?

Still, Chapin needed expertise to set up such an organization, and the first name that came to mind was Ralph Nader. Harry had always admired and respected him. Nader was a man whose history preceded him, an undaunted social activist who became a legend fighting private self-interests for the public welfare, achieving positive social change with limited means. He was the creator of the PIRG's (Public Interest Research Groups) that had branch offices on almost every major college campus. He also founded Congress Watch and, in 1969, brought the giant General Motors to its knees with a lawsuit.

He was a man of commitment who, more often than not, operated from the position of underdog and, more often than not, made good. He was a visionary, that rare breed of pioneer much like Chapin's grandfathers, and a workaholic. Once, when one of the lawyers in Nader's litigation group wanted to take the weekend off, Nader glowered, "Do I take the weekend off?"

Chapin met Nader through Art Kaminsky, the young lawyer Harry worked with when he was literature director for Allard Lowenstein's 1970 Congressional campaign. Kaminsky knew another young lawyer named Mark Green, who worked for Nader. Later Green became Ramsey Clark's campaign manager in the 1976 Congressional race and ran for Congress himself in

1980, but lost. Kaminsky made an appointment for Chapin to meet Nader at Green's apartment, a beautiful brownstone in the Georgetown section of Washington, D.C.

That day Nader looked exactly as Harry had seen him on television and in the newspapers, a perfect caricature of himself: very slim, somewhat stoop-shouldered, about six-foot-three, with a five o'clock shadow and cavernous cheeks. Nader wore his customary dark conservative suit and thin tie. Prepared with a pocketful of questions, Chapin immediately began pumping Nader for advice.

"But in his inexorable way, Nader changed the subject to some of the things he was interested in, like his public interest research groups," said Harry, "and how he talked with other performers and never got them to realize how impactful these things can be."

Nader already had met quite a few "concerned stars" who promised to support his causes through donations or benefit concerts and then backed out at the last minute. He described his dealings with Marlon Brando, Linda Ronstadt and Bobby Lamm (of the rock group Chicago), who, according to Chapin, "had not been able to get beyond the point of doing a big splashy publicity thing and making a long-range commitment."

However, these were big stars with big bank books. So from Nader's perspective, Chapin's altruistic sincerity was immediately suspect. "Harry who?" Nader had vaguely heard the name before and instantly envisioned another "go and hide" performer.

Sensing this, Chapin was quick to sympathize with him, explaining that he, too, had been disappointed by his peers and that his music really did reflect social concerns.

"Well, I don't know anything about your music," Nader told him. "I really don't listen to anything."

"I wish you had a guitar," said Harry, "so I could play you something just to give you an idea, because I do lyrically oriented stuff."

Fortunately, Mark Green had a guitar, an old, beat-up six-string. Chapin picked it up and began playing "Cat's in the

Cradle," a mellow ballad with an infectious melody. By song's end, Nader's skeptical countenance had altered, his foot tapping to the beat.

Said Chapin of his thoughts at that moment: "I was proud of the fact that my music wasn't just bullshit, you know? Like, I love you, woo-woo-woo, love me too. I think he seemed to respect me."

"Well, that's something I could listen to," Nader said after the performance. Then he asked Harry what he thought about Food Day. He got the answer he wanted.

"Well, I think it's a great idea," said Chapin. "But we've got to get away from what I call 'event-psychosis.' I mean, half the country thinks we solve our environmental problems on Earth Day, or racial problems with Peter, Paul and Mary singing on the steps of the Lincoln Memorial, or hunger with a Bangladesh concert. You have to be working in the process. Students ask me when world hunger will end and I tell them it'll be decades before we really see a difference."

But the inquisition into Chapin's sincerity did not end there. Harry recognized that Nader wasn't going to be cooperative unless he made some concessions of his own. So at meeting's end, with many of his questions still unanswered, he promised Nader he would perform a few PIRG benefits; that eventually became a commitment of fourteen. Chapin also agreed to perform at the national convention of the PIRGs in Washington, D.C., a few weeks later.

Much to Nader's surprise, Chapin followed through on every promise he made and became the one shining light in a sea of unfulfilled promises. Thereafter Harry had direct access to Nader and was able to consult him regularly for advice. But Nader was not the only one. During the rest of the fall of 1974, Chapin sought the expertise of several politicians and hunger groups, making numerous fact-finding flights to Washington, D.C.

WHY was on its way!

* * *

But Chapin's sudden benefit binge had a chilling effect on relations between himself and his band. Concerts that were once paid became donated (nearly one-third). The group didn't particularly like giving their money away for Harry's personal projects. Part of the problem was the benefits themselves. Many times they took Chapin and his band to small towns with poor concert facilities run by small organizations that had no experience in promoting anything. They provided no transportation, dressing rooms or food. (For paid concerts, dinner was always provided.) Chapin didn't mind; he placed no value on creature comforts. But the band did, and so, many times, Chapin had to perform alone.

Once, when Harry did a benefit for the Hartsdale Mother's Lunch Program, north of Manhattan, he noticed a lack of facilities when he arrived and asked, "Is there a stage?"

A woman pointed to a table.

"Where's the microphone?"

"Here." She pointed to two tape recorder microphones taped together, one for voice and one for guitar.

"Well, at least have you got some lights?" Chapin asked.

"Sure," said the woman. She walked over to a wall and flipped the light switch on and off.

"It was incredible!" said Harry. "But by concert time, I explained the problem to the two thousand or so people who came and it turned out to be one of the best concerts I ever did."

Chapin's rocky relationship with his band and manager was also, in part, fueled by himself. He had grown cold and aloof with them, operating more on a business level than one of old friendship. Sandy was the main cause. Harry had adopted her thoughts and feelings on many things, including personal philosophy. She intensely disliked the "road lifestyle" that she considered "totally irresponsible" and of which Fred Kewley and the band were a major part.

Kewley explained: "Harry started disliking everybody in the band. It was no longer a family. Ron Palmer told me with misty eyes, 'I'd give anything to get this thing back to where it was six months ago.' I mean, it used to be that I wouldn't make a major move without talking things over with Harry first, and he was the same way with me. We would talk for hours on the phone about everything. But as soon as it hit the fan with his wife, there was a marked change in him. He sort of made a transition from trying to become a star and have hit records and make a lot of money to getting adulation from the public. His career suddenly became a function of saving his marriage and not brilliant career moves. It became much more important to him to prove to his wife that he had feelings, that he was a worthwhile human being. That's not a bad motivation. I think the secondary motivation was the Nobel Prize thing, a way to tie the two together and head in those directions. That's when he started going crazy with all the benefits, and if you didn't like it you were out. He never sat down and said that. But he'd say, 'We're doing this thing and we'll give it to PAF.' So if John Wallace said, 'I'm not giving it to PAF,' then he was out. Harry would get rid of him for a lot of reasons. His wife really hated John. She thought he was a bad guy."

But what Fred and the band didn't understand was that Harry needed to do this for himself, not just Sandy. He had to bolster and refortify his sagging self-image, reconstitute his self-respect. Harry was fighting the success, so he pursued his newfound philanthropic urges as passionately as he once pursued his more self-serving ones. "I started doing not just an occasional benefit," said Harry, "but trying to articulate both verbally and in my actions a more responsible attitude toward my success."

Even his songwriting was affected both in content and proliferation. At the time, he went on a productive writing streak, composing many songs and poems not only about his children, but mainly his wife, a trend that would continue throughout the rest of his career and albums. It started with "I Wanna Learn a Love Song," the nostalgic autobiography of how he and Sandy first met, and the beautiful ballad "Shooting Star," about the relationships of his grandfathers and their wives, but also partially about

Sandy. Harry saw a great deal of his grandmothers in her. She had the same supportive, nurturing, omnipotent aura. The whole concept of the mythic woman behind the mythic man, the silent guiding light behind the pampered genius, was most clearly seen in "She Sings Her Songs Without Words," in which Harry described Sandy metaphorically as a poetic, almost angelic being. He even began work on a twenty-one-minute song (which he never completed) based on the true story of a plane crash in the Peruvian Andes and a rugby team that turned to cannibalism to survive. But in Harry's song there was only one survivor, a man. At the end of the song, that man cries out: "God is a woman."

He also finished work on a story song called "Star Tripper," a recapitulation of his first three years in the music business and his subsequent life-change. The song started out telling how good he felt about making music and made an analogy between astronauts and performers and ego trips.

During the spring of 1974, Chapin went back into the Bridgeport studio to complete *Verities and Balderdash* and, overstocked with a fresh supply of material, naturally started thinking again about a double album. "He was full of piss and vinegar," said Paul Leka. "His idea was to put out a double album for the price of one. But Elektra turned him down."

However, unlike his preceding albums, Chapin recorded *Verities and Balderdash* without his band. It was Leka's suggestion. Chapin left a large part of the work to Paul, confident in his "winning production abilities," and recorded the album instead with New York studio musicians, "hookmen," the unsung heroes of hit records. They included some of pop music's best: Alan Schwartzberg on drums, John Tropea on guitar and Don Payne on bass. Leka felt Chapin's band lacked the "grooves," the "big sound" necessary to produce the "big single." Chapin also wanted horns, strings and a piano to add a little jazz and funk. (An oft-repeated criticism of Harry's music was that his band could not provide either.)

"We couldn't cut the singles with the guys," said Leka. "They just didn't have the kind of licks to make it work. Harry's think-

Harry in Andover, New Jersey, at the family's country house, with his children Joshua (*left*) and Jennifer (*right*) in January 1976. (Photo: Peter M. Coan)

A typical Harry pose—on the phone. He was a compulsive caller. This time he was phoning his wife, Sandy, during an intermission in a concert. When on the road—and especially after the 1973 "black book" incident—Harry called home at least three times a day, a custom he followed throughout his career. (Photo: Steve Stout)

The Dr. Pepper Music Festival in New York's Central Park, August 4, 1976. Steve Chapin is on piano. Others (left to right) are John Wallace, electric guitarist Doug Walker, cellist Michael Master (his last concert as a member of the band), and the man himself. (Photo: Peter M. Coan)

The cello made Harry's story songs distinctive and emotionally evocative. From left to right in this 1978 photo are bass guitarist John Wallace (partially hidden), Harry, drummer Howie Fields, electric guitarist Doug Walker, and cellist Kim Scholes. Scholes was fourth in a line of five cellists who played in Harry's band. (Photo: Steve Stout)

The Chapin home in Huntington, New York, a seventeen-room mansion. Harry called it his "Make a Wish House" because he was able to put a downpayment on it from his songwriting earnings from the children's program *Make a Wish*. To the right of the circular driveway (not in the photo) is a steep gully leading down to a basketball and tennis court. Harry built two of the rooms in the house himself. (Photo: Peter M. Coan)

The backyard of the Chapin home in Huntington, New York. Approximately a hundred yards long, the backyard reaches down to a small stretch of beach on Long Island Sound. Harry's writing room—where he wrote most of his vintage story songs in 1972, 1973, and 1974—is on the second floor behind the white porch railing. To the left is the master bedroom. (Photo: Peter M. Coan)

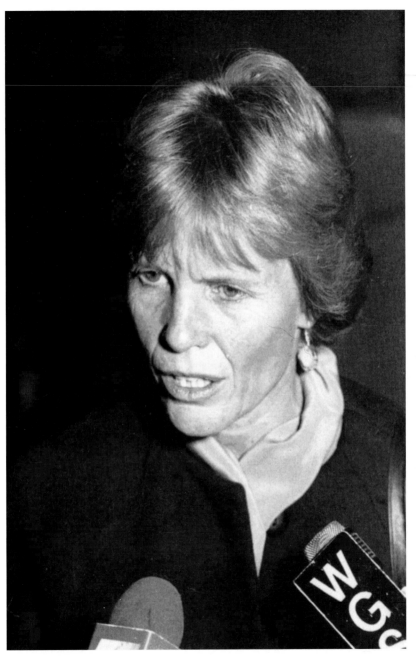

Sandy Chapin at a New York press conference in October 1986, announcing that she had won $7.3 million from a negligence lawsuit she had filed against Supermarkets General, Inc., the company that owned the truck that killed Harry Chapin. With interest, the award totaled more than $10 million. (Photo: Ken Sawchuck/New York Newsday)

Harry at a 1981 concert. (Photo: Steve Stout)

ing was, 'Why take chances, spend big bucks and find out another failure? Let's use the guys that do it everyday!' That was his rationale for bringing in hired guns and putting his own band aside. It was a tough blow for them."

Chapin spent very little time in the Bridgeport studio, partially because he was preoccupied with his personal life and new-found social commitments, but also because many of the songs on *Verities and Balderdash*, such as "Thirty Thousand Pounds of Bananas," "Six-String Orchestra" and "Halfway to Heaven," were culled from earlier albums. Harry recorded only four new songs including Sandy's "Cat's in the Cradle," and for these, he merely recorded rough tracks and conferred with studio musicians. One of them was his father. Jim Chapin played drums on a couple of selections, as did brothers Tom and Steve on banjo and piano, respectively. Leka then arranged Chapin's compositions, put together a final mix, and mastered the album in his Bridgeport studio.

Harry's favorite song on the album was the seven-minute saga "What Made America Famous?"—his "farewell document" to Point Lookout and his personal choice as the single off *Verities and Balderdash*. He knew the song was too long for AM airplay, so whenever he did interviews at radio stations, he personally promoted it to program directors by singing it for them in their office. "I wrote a new song and I'd like you to tell me what you think," he'd say, in typically unassuming Chapin fashion. The reaction was always the same: "Oh, terrific, Harry. Just great. Real winner."

He reported his findings to Ann Purtill. "He'd come back and say, 'I've played this song for all the program directors and they loved it. We've got to cut it right now and do it!' Well, what does he expect them to say? Harry could've played 'God Bless America' on chopsticks and they would've told him the same thing."

Even so, by the fall of 1974, Elektra released *Verities and Balderdash* and its single, "What Made America Famous?" To ensure its success, Harry reverted to his old reliable formula: WRKO in Boston and Zeke Marsden. Almost immediately, the gears were set in motion as hundreds of requests for the song began bombarding the Boston station. But this time the station manager was not fooled and the song died in its tracks.

"I cared almost too deeply for that song," said Harry. "I loved it. I wanted it to be a hit more than anything I ever wrote." He felt the song made an important social statement about America and the American Dream, which embodied everything Chapin had learned to become, a social activist and humanitarian. On a symbolic level, the song said that the only real source of fulfillment and the only true solution to social injustice was social involvement, and Harry wanted to let the world know it. To him, America seemed to have forgotten the passion for life it had in the sixties: the marches, the music, the ability to dream. But now, from his perspective, his once vocal "love-child" contemporaries had become the new middle class in leisure wear. They had grown conservative and apathetic, like the high school and college students he spoke to, dismayed and discouraged by the humiliation America absorbed in the wake of Vietnam and Watergate. Chapin felt it was time to reintroduce some hope into that great dream of ours.

In the spring of 1974, Harry had approached two Broadway producers with the idea of building a musical around "What Made America Famous?" along with twenty-nine of his other songs. Part of Chapin's inspiration was not only to pursue a long-forgotten dream, a musical, but to stay near his home and Sandy. According to Chapin, the theme for the show, which later came to be known as *The Night That Made America Famous,* was an emotional musical history of America from the sixties into the seventies. It was synthesis of theater, rock concert and multimedia effects (one-third each), including the latest in television, film projection and lighting techniques—in short, Broadway's first multimedia musical.

The two producers were Edgar Lansbury and Joseph Beruh, whose list of credits included such celebrated hits as *Pippin, Gypsy, The Magic Show* and their latest success, *Godspell.* Both men, known for experimenting with new ideas, heard the body of Chapin's work and liked it.

"After *Godspell,* we were looking around for a show about America," said Beruh in a *New York News* magazine article by Penelope McMillan. "We felt that was the next big thing. Harry came over and started talking about doing a show with his songs that fit in with our idea."

For the musical, Chapin signed a one-year contract with a one-year option. He would receive 10 percent of the gross receipts as its author and star, with rehearsals beginning in January 1975, and opening night at the end of February. Meanwhile, Chapin worked on the concept of the musical with its director, Gene Frankel, a highly respected though eccentric avant-garde theater veteran of twenty-five years who helped found the Off-Broadway movement. He was a production-oriented director known for his staging of *Volpone* (the first Obie ever awarded for best director); *Machinal* (his second Obie and the Vernon Rice Award winner for best production); and *The Blacks* (his third Obie). Frankel was chosen by producers Beruh and Lansbury at Chapin's urging. Harry had become familiar with his work several years before, back in the days of *Buraka,* when he and Sandy attended numerous Off-Broadway productions, one of which was Frankel's play *Indians,* Harry's favorite. "It made quite an impact on me," Chapin said. "Frankel had a berserkness and a powerful conceptual feel."

In October 1974, Elektra stopped sending "samplers" of "What Made America Famous?" and released "Cat's in the Cradle" as the second single off *Verities and Balderdash.* Almost immediately the song shot up *Billboard*'s Top 40 chart. Ironically, a week before its release, Chapin wanted to rerecord the song and told Fred Kewley, "It's terrible, just terrible. It's much too fast a tempo."

But by December, the matter was irrelevant. "Cat's in the Cradle" went to number one. The day it did, Chapin was fast asleep. He had yet to hear the news. But Susan and Bill Gensel did. They were close friends of the Chapins through their association with PAF, Bill as lighting director and Susan as Theatre Guild vice president. Susan immediately called Harry to congratulate him.

"Hey, star," said Susan proudly.

"What?" said Chapin, drunk with sleep.

"We know a person on the hit parade," she teased.

"What are you talking about?"

"'Cat's in the Cradle' made number one, dummy!"

"No shit!"

Harry dropped the phone, jumped out of bed and, in his boxer shorts, ran downstairs and out to the front lawn to get the newspapers, *Newsday* and the *New York Times*. Half naked, he stood there in the freezing cold, rapidly turning the pages until he verified the fact. There it was! The number-one song in America, "Cat's in the Cradle," and next to it, the composer's name, Harry Chapin.

"I remember him coming to our house later that day," said Susan Gensel. "He was so thrilled. He was bouncing up and down on the couch in our den, clutching the newspaper and yelling childlike, 'Look at this! Look at this!'"

Music critics across the country raved over *Verities and Balderdash,* except, of course, the critical rock press that continued to snub Chapin. A *Village Voice* review was the best example. Under the headline PITY FOR SALE, Stephen Holden wrote his usual diatribe attacking Chapin's overall artistry, calling his albums "greeting cards"; his music, "patronizing pity mongering"; his characters, "cartoons of pulp magazines and TV archetypes"; and finally terming the whole thing "nauseating." *Rolling Stone* didn't even bother to review the album. "The previous reviews read like you would substitute the album titles," said Jon Landau of the magazine. "It just got to the point of, why bother? It was not very enlightening or interesting. It just became repetitious."

Nevertheless, the quantum effect of "Cat's in the Cradle" on Chapin's career was enormous. For one, it presented the public with a new image of Harry: Mr. Family Man. In his first three albums, his image was more rugged, rakish and counterculture, with offbeat love songs and tragic portraits of people with broken hearts and broken dreams. They were torn threads of America's social fabric, both common and uncommon folk alike, from the barroom lush in "A Better Place to Be" to the assassin lusting for attention in "Sniper." Everything about Chapin was unorthodox and, in that sense, he was counterculture, from the style of his music to the subjects of his songs.

But with "Cat's in the Cradle," the more conventional side of Harry Chapin emerged, moving him more to the mainstream of American music. Suddenly people's assumptions of Chapin changed. A song about parenthood and children was an extreme departure from the kind the public had identified him with. He cut off that brown scraggy Dylan-like beard.

Chapin said, "Now, after concerts, people were approaching me saying things like, 'Oh, what a sensitive man you are to be so concerned about your children . . .'"

"After it started," said Sandy, "Harry began to realize he was getting just as much if not more admiration for this new image. And he was perfectly willing to go along with it as the 'world's best daddy.'"

The Chapins received a flood of mail about how the song changed their lives. So much so that Harry hired a personal secretary named Judi Parker to handle his new wave of popularity. Sandy, of course, was overwhelmed by it all. Being a teacher, and interested in changing lives, she found the response inspiring and began writing more lyrics for Harry to put to music. Naturally, Harry welcomed her reinforced ambition because it brought them closer together. But they weren't the only ones.

"We were really surprised to find out that it had been used in church services and marriage counseling," said Sandy. "That was the kind of song people bought to deliver to other people. American parents seem to think they can buy out their relationship with their kids. I guess the song proved them wrong."

"Cat's in the Cradle" also made Chapin a millionaire and a household name. *Verities and Balderdash* sold over 600,000 copies and became a gold record (Harry's first) within four months of its release. "Cat's in the Cradle" stayed number one for two consecutive weeks, remained on the Top 40 charts for nineteen weeks and sold a colossal (by Chapin standards) 1.3 million copies. The song was chosen for all the spun-gold record packagers. Conventional artists such as John Davidson, Wayne Newton and Andy Williams added the song to their Las Vegas acts. And Muzak companies began piping its contagious melody into dentists' offices. Suddenly, Chapin was inundated with requests for interviews. His concert fees rose into the $10-$15,000 range and he began receiving all kinds of television appearance offers, from Johnny Carson to the Smothers Brothers and Mac Davis shows.

The only problem was that Chapin couldn't take full advantage of all the opportunities because he was already contracted for his upcoming Broadway musical. It was a case of bad timing and bad luck. Many people close to him suggested he postpone the Broadway project and capitalize on what would have been a highly lucrative concert market. Instead of performing before 2,000 people in a Broadway theater (earning perhaps $7,500 a night or less), he could be playing before ten thousand people for twice that sum.

Chapin didn't accept the advice. He felt Broadway would add another dimension to his career, and although many performers had been to Broadway with concert shows—Neil Diamond, Alice Cooper, Liza Minnelli, Bette Midler and her *Clams on the Half Shell Revue*—Chapin believed the musical would distinguish him from his peers. "As a songwriter, it put him on Broadway, which neither Dylan nor Paul Simon could claim," said Ann Purtill. "They were the two people he was most fond of comparing himself with."

Said Elektra's president Mel Posner, years later: "I don't think it hurt his career. In fact, if anything, it helped because he now had those credentials. Harry was so multitalented you couldn't just say he was a recording artist or a concert artist. You had to think of him in terms of career."

In December of 1974, after nearly 700 concerts over three and a half years, Chapin's four-man band disbanded. Only John Wallace and Michael Masters joined Harry for the thespian venture. Jebbie Hart and Rob White had already packed it in as road crew six months earlier, Rob to return to his real passion, artwork, and Jebbie to become road manager of a group called Mount Airy which featured, among others, stepbrothers Tom and Steve. Jebbie and Rob were replaced by two new road-crew members, Michael Solomon (for audio) and Jeff Gross (for lights), both of whom were responsible for those functions on the Broadway show.

Ron Palmer left partly because his relationship with Chapin had soured, but mostly because he had musical ambitions of his own. "For a while, I looked at playing with Harry as a stepping-stone," said Palmer. "I wanted to leave and try it on my own. I thought I had some writing ability and wanted to try." But that didn't last very long. Almost immediately, Palmer returned to his wife and son in Syracuse, New York.

Years later, Palmer said of his decision: "It was fun to have a taste of it. But, man, I'm glad I ain't there now. I wouldn't go back to the business. It's just too phony. Basically, I'm playing for my own enjoyment and that's it. I realized that it's not talent as such, that when you get success in the business it's all politics. The record company—some top-echelon people decide what records to throw the money behind. They more or less dictate hits, and they hold a lot of good people back for their own reasons. It's a false success. Part of the upper for me was to travel around the country and meet other musicians. Stardom in the business is created and it doesn't necessarily start with talent. It's all hype. There's a lot of glitter there and false imagery being projected that I don't think is healthy for a lot of heads. The irony for me was, here we struggled for three and a half years to get to number one, and the next week I was out of a job."

One of the last concerts with the old four-man group was at the Music Hall in Boston. As usual, Chapin happened to be in the area around the time of his birthday (December 7) and, as usual, spent it with the Marsdens. A week before the concert,

Chapin was in town one day to do promotion work. That night, Harry, Zeke and the rest of the Marsden crew went out to dinner at The Tradesmen, an old warehouse converted into a restaurant and not yet officially open for business. The owner was a friend of Zeke's and brought out the red carpet for Chapin.

Harry fell in love with the place. "Next week when I come up here," he told Zeke, "I want to hire the place! Every time I come we eat at your house. The whole gang's at your house. Now it's my turn. So I'm gonna have the party for a change, and it's gonna be on me."

Zeke made all the arrangements, but turned it into a surprise party instead. The Marsdens invited 125 people—Elektra executives, radio people, promoters, friends, relatives—and asked everyone to bring some kind of ball as a gift.

When the night arrived, after his performance at the Music Hall, Harry went directly to The Tradesmen to find, much to his surprise, the restaurant jammed with people. After dinner Zeke brought out a birthday cake. Chapin made a small speech, a silent wish, and blew out all thirty-two candles. Then came the gifts, presented one by one. There were footballs, tennis balls, basketballs, gum balls, Ping-Pong balls, and so on.

"You know, Harry," Zeke bellowed, "you've got a lot of balls writing those long songs."

The last present was a small, thin box. It was from Zeke's brother, Jay.

"Well, there can't be any balls inside this one," said Harry. He shook the box next to his ear. Slowly he took off the wrapping, opened the box, and pulled out a jockstrap.

"That's to carry the balls home in," Zeke called out.

Everyone roared, Harry especially.

"You son of a bitch," said Chapin, "It's the wrong size. You gave me a medium. I take a large!"

* * *

In January 1975, musicians were selected for *The Night That Made America Famous,* and, like most everything else Chapin did, he turned the show into a family project. A nine-piece orchestra was slated for the musical, so Harry hired his brothers.

After the breakup of The Chapins at the Village Gate, Tom and Steve had teamed up with a friend of theirs, Bob Hinkel, to put together a studio band called Mount Airy and record an album by that name. Mount Airy included Ralph Denafio (also known as Cash Monday) on drums, Rich Look on piano, and Eric Weissberg on guitar. But there wasn't much national interest in the album or the group, except for Weissberg, who recorded a single, the theme from the movie *Deliverance,* which was at the top of the charts, with Weissberg in great demand. As a result, Mount Airy toured heavily and built a small following, though they never got a major recording contract. "It was a great fun band," wrote the *Village Voice* of the group. "Always playing around town someplace with an enthusiastic and devoted audience on home territory, but little else."

Finally, by late 1974, after almost three years, Mount Airy folded, and Tom and Steve hooked up with Harry. For the musical, Tom played acoustic guitar, banjo, harmonica, and was Chapin's understudy (though Harry never missed a performance). Steve became music director and hired all the musicians. One of them was their father, Jim, who played percussion (kettle drums, traps, wood blocks and bongos). Steve also hired a string player, violinist, reed player and a man who played three instruments: flute, saxophone and clarinet. But he also needed an electric guitarist and immediately called up his old friend, Doug Walker, who played the instrument when he was a member of The Chapins.

Like Tom and Steve, Walker had experienced an eventful three years. After the Village Gate stint, Walker and Phil Forbes, the other half of The Chapins, formed The Performing Band, a rock group. It was mildly successful for a while, but, like The Chapins, The Performing Band lacked that same critical ingredient for success, a definitive identity, and by 1974, with the rise in popularity of disco, the group lost its commercial appeal and died. Steve Chapin called Doug and offered him the electric guitarist job.

For Walker, there wasn't much to think about. "All I was thinking," said Doug, "was, 'Wow! I've got a gig.'"

Steve Chapin also needed another drummer and, at Walker's suggestion, hired Howie Fields, who played percussion for The Performing Band. Fields, a Brooklyn boy in his early twenties, was a smooth, versatile drummer capable of playing almost any music style. Along with Steve and John Wallace, Walker and Fields became the permanent mainstays of Harry's band for the rest of his career.

For the cast, director Gene Frankel made sure everyone had a big voice, an essential element for singing Chapin's material. Since most of Harry's songs originally came from the play *Buraka* and were written for female singers, Frankel hired two of the best available female voices on Broadway, Kelly Garrett and Delores Hall. He also chose a second male lead singer (besides Harry) named Gilbert Price. "Chapin had to have guts just to go out on stage with them," Martin Gottfried later wrote in the *New York Post.*

And it was true. For one, Price was a gifted black actor-singer and ten-year theater veteran who possessed a five-octave-range voice much like John Wallace, but softer, with a Paul Robeson-like resonance. In fact, Merv Griffin was so impressed by Price that he once hired him as a weekly performer on his show.

"I've never heard a better voice in my life," Chapin once told Frankel. "But he thinks with his throat," Frankel replied. "If he could ever think with his mind, it would be truly extraordinary."

Then there was Delores Hall, a black gospel singer with an incredible voice who was in the original L.A. cast of *Hair* and left the cast of *Godspell* to join *The Night That Made America Famous.*

Of the three, Kelly Garrett was the most impressive, a small, attractive brunette who had a potent voice and commanding stage presence. Her claim to fame on Broadway was her appearance in *Mother Earth,* for which she won a *Theatre World* Award. Garrett was mainly a nightclub performer and a frequent talk-show guest, particularly on *The Tonight Show*. Garrett was a favorite of Johnny Carson. In fact, three days before . . . *America Famous* opened, she got a call from Carson, who invited her to open for him at Caesars Palace in Las Vegas for one week. Garrett turned him down.

Chapin's six-member supporting cast was not too shabby either. There were expert dancers in Bill Star and Ernie Pysher; plus Alexandra Borrie (who appeared in *Follies* an *Over Here*); and Mercedes Ellington, granddaughter of the Duke. They were "well chosen, . . . good singers and good movers all," Clive Barnes later wrote in the *New York Times*.

On January 13, 1975, rehearsals began at the New York School of Ballet on 82nd Street and Broadway. On that day, choreographer Doug Rogers, who was chosen for the job having worked with Gene Frankel in the past, asked the entire cast to take some steps to see who could dance, including Chapin.

"Manfully but clobbily I clomped along," said Harry. At one point Steve Chapin, who was accompanying the dancers on piano, leaned over to Doug Walker and asked, "Well, how's he doin'?" Doug replied, "Anybody got an elephant?"

Said Chapin, "I suddenly knew I was not the next Rudolf Nureyev."

The *Village Voice* also noticed this when they later wrote in a review: ". . . watching him attempt to move through a few of choreographer Doug Rogers's simpler steps with people who are used to doing such things is a discomforting experience."

It took almost six weeks and $400,000 to prepare *The Night That Made America Famous* for opening night. The money came from six backers, something Beruh and Lansbury arranged and Harry despised. "It was like performing for Mount Rushmore," he told *New York News* magazine. "Backers don't cheer like fans."

The backers' auditions were a success. Listed under "general partners" was the Shubert Organization, which invested $150,000 in association with Beruh and Lansbury, who put up $75,000 each. Then there was Lansbury's actress-sister Angela, who tossed in $8,000, along with thirteen other partners who wrote checks for anywhere between $4,000 and $8,000. Chapin also spent $5,000 of his own on props and scenery.

The Night That Made America Famous opened for its first preview on February 26, 1975, at the Ethel Barrymore Theatre. As usual, it was another impressive display of Chapin nepotism. Just like at the Village Gate, Harry invited everyone he knew, from the Marsdens and Castros to New York Mets shortstop Bud Harrelson, whom Harry had met at a Long Island party a month earlier. Even Mel Posner, Elektra's president, flew in from California to see the show.

For Manny and Janet Castro, it was a particularly moving experience. They had hardly seen Harry since the days when he tested his songs at all hours of the night in their Brooklyn Heights brownstone. Eight years had passed. Now, suddenly, that same kid with the curly brown hair and the big grin was, of all places, on Broadway!

"It was a funny feeling," said Manny Castro. "We parked our car on Ninth Avenue and walked along 46th Street toward Eighth Avenue and there was this big Broadway sign: HARRY CHAPIN . . . THE NIGHT THAT MADE AMERICA FAMOUS. We just dissolved."

After the show that night, there was a backstage party, Chapin old home week, as Harry blindly circulated the room hugging everyone. He was ecstatic. Another dream had come true. "I don't think he even knew who we were," said Janet Castro. "Tom and Steve were relaxed. But Harry was out of it."

Chapin was under enormous pressure, however self-imposed. During the four weeks of daily rehearsals and production meetings, Chapin gave benefits for PAF, WHY, Ralph Nader, as well as paid concerts in Trenton, Buffalo, Milwaukee, Scranton, Brooklyn and Manhattan. He also continued writing a book of poetry *(Looking, Seeing)* as well as songs from Tom Chapin's *Make a Wish*. In addition, he made numerous flights to Washington, D.C., to set up World Hunger Year and made several all-day high school appearances. He even had time to appear in anti-drug ads for television.

"Harry needed that kind of schedule, being in two cities the same day," said Elektra promotion man Ralph Eber. "He enjoyed it. He thrived on it. It also gave him material for his songs."

"I function best in times of crisis," Harry once said. "Probably one of the reasons I have too busy a schedule is I like to be forced into situations where I have to come up with things."

Once the Broadway show began, Chapin's schedule continued at its frenetic pace despite eight shows a week, including matinees on Saturday and Sunday. On one typical day, Harry had a breakfast meeting in Manhattan with Steve Spinola, the director of World Hunger Year and a friend of his brother James and former PR director for Off-Track Betting in New York. Harry was half asleep, having performed the night before. Afterward, Chapin and Spinola went to Long Island for an afternoon high school benefit for PAF. Spinola drove while Harry slept in the backseat.

"I thought to myself, how is he going to put on another show?" said Spinola. "How is he going to put out for a bunch of high school kids when he's got Broadway to worry about?"

Still, once they arrived, Chapin sang for two hours, "holding nothing back," according to Spinola, and then spoke for another hour about world hunger.

"He talked about why he was there," Spinola said. "He talked about the hunger problem and why something needed to be done about it and it got across to the kids. Clearly. It wasn't crap and he wasn't speaking down to them. It was really very direct conversation. He answered all their questions."

At four o'clock, Harry left for the one-hour drive back to Manhattan and another performance of . . . *America Famous*.

Like most people, Spinola was amazed by Chapin's nonstop energy. "Surely at that point," he said, "Harry didn't need World Hunger Year. *The Night That Made America Famous* could've been a smash success, but WHY was only time-consuming. It was a big burden on him. But he was going ahead with it anyway."

Indeed, Chapin's once-struggling career had begun to blossom on all fronts and he wanted to maintain the momentum without sacrificing anything, except himself. After his Broadway performances, Chapin either went home or directly to Paul Leka's Bridgeport studio to record his fifth album, *Portrait Gallery.*

"He was running himself ragged," said Doug Walker. "He was singing himself hoarse on Broadway. Then he went to Bridgeport and sang himself even hoarser. And came back the next day still cranking it out."

By March 9 (the official opening of the musical), and in the days that followed, the critical reviews began to trickle in and they were mixed. "We didn't get very successful reviews from the more standard critics," said Chapin. "All the major critics over forty bombed it, all those under forty loved it. And Clive Barnes, who was about forty, wasn't sure. It seemed to be a Roschach test for the age group that listened."

Most of the confusion was created by all the stage innovations Chapin brought to Broadway, such as well-produced studio sound. "There's no such thing," Gene Frankel once told him. "You can't improve the sound. A theater is a theater. It's not a studio." But Chapin disagreed. He felt that modern Broadway shows lacked musical impact on stage. "You go to a Neil Diamond or Elton John concert in a fairly decent hall," Chapin told him, "and you'll see that the actual sound impact is better ten to one than on Broadway."

Chapin installed a modern quadraphonic sound system and used microphones (unheard of on Broadway), and although no one could deny the sound was superb, Chapin could not quite make the equipment look right. Instead, it looked like "spaghetti with wires and cords," wrote John Simon in a scathing *New York* magazine review. They were "literally sprouting from large tin containers." In fact, on the first night of previews, when Gilbert Price was singing "Mr. Tanner," he accidentally tripped over the microphone cord and pulled out the plug. At that point, Chapin, who was standing off to the side, bounded forward in his contagious homespun manner (replete with work shirt, khaki pants and army boots) and motioned to Price to stop singing. Harry then plugged the cord back in the socket and the show resumed, turning a highly awkward moment into a sort of triumph. The audience generously applauded him.

But for some critics there were too many awkward moments, largely due to a barrage of unusual costumes and the intricate set design. For one, the musical employed a plethora of multidimensional light and visual effects created by Joshua White of the famed Joshua Light Shows. Chapin sang several songs high atop a diving board platform, while his image (and that of other cast members) was projected onto a giant-sized closed-circuit TV screen via cinema-verité handheld cameras worked by the stage crew. The set was covered with modules and yards of cloth, and in one scene a group of singer-dancers slithered on the floor wearing glitter masks and fright wigs. There were also numerous flashing lights and a revolving band shell for the nine-piece orchestra. In short, the musical was a highly dramatic stage show best summed up by Martin Gottfried of the *New York Post,* who wrote, "It may be dressed up, but its heart is beautiful and it sure is alive."

But there was a problem. The show had no plot or story, only a theme. Act one depicted the 1960s, the Kennedy Inauguration and the idealism of young people. The second act covered the 1970s and tried to show how young people coped with the disillusionment of reality, Vietnam and Watergate. This theme was supposed to be communicated through the interrelationship of Chapin's music and stage effects. For instance, news clips of the Kennedy assassination were projected onto the TV screen during the performance of the song "Sniper."

Unfortunately, only a handful of Chapin's thirty songs related to recent historical events, which further compounded the show's lack of focus and perplexed the audience of predominantly older theatergoers. "They expected a straight book show," said singer

Kelly Garrett. "If they don't understand what it's about, they're not going to go. I don't think having that hit record ["Cat's in the Cradle"] really helped because we didn't have that many young people in the audience. We had theater parties and subscription people and they would say, 'Gee, what is this? Yeah, I liked it. But I don't understand it.'

"You have to realize what kind of music we were dealing with," Garrett continued. "By the time I got through with each performance, I was emotionally drained. You couldn't sing his lyrics and not mean it. You were dealing with your head and it was pretty heavy stuff. He was talking about the war and political issues. I think Harry had to get it out of his system. He was ahead of his time. But people don't want to hear about that. People go to the theater to forget. They don't want to be reminded how repressed our country is. They'd rather hear 'moon, spoon, June.' At the same time, you couldn't help but get hooked on that show once it started. But we couldn't leave it open long enough for word to get around."

The title of the musical didn't help because it read like an incomplete sentence. "Every time I was doing publicity, nobody could remember the name," Garrett added. "We used to laugh about it. I mean, you want to make money for your investors. So you want to make it as feasible as possible. Call it *January.* Call it *Pie in Your Eye,* something that's catchy that people are going to remember. But *The Night That Made America Famous?*"

"It was too glorified," said Gene Frankel of the title. "I think what basically went wrong with the show was that no matter how we went with it, it was basically a Harry Chapin concert, a glorified Chapin concert. If the show would've been called *Harry Chapin: A Musical Revue* or *An Evening With Harry Chapin,* it would've been a lot closer to what it was."

The show picked up steam at the end when Harry was allowed to do what he did best: sit on a stool and sing. It was the free-form part of the performance when Tom, Steve and Harry each sang a song closing with "Circle." The result was a standing ovation every night. "If you put Harry by himself with an acoustic guitar before a group of people, he had tremendous impact," said Frankel. "He didn't need all the staging."

The best example of this came one day when Harry, Tom and Gilbert Price were returning to New York from a Long Island concert and stopped at a local diner for dinner. As usual, Harry had his guitar with him and, at one point, struck up a conversation with the waitress, whose daughter had recently gone through some personal tragedy.

"I'm going to sing a song for you," Harry told her, and he placed himself on a stool at the counter and began singing "A Better Place to Be." Tom and Gilbert harmonized in the background. Everyone in the diner turned around to listen.

"It was like a fairy tale," recalled Price. "I'll never forget that in my life."

At song's end, the diner erupted with cheers and applause. The waitress began to cry.

"That was Harry's power," said Price. "He was able to make people feel. And that's what we tried to do in the show. The producers should've sat back, taken more time, another year, found a script and put his songs to life—the people to life—and show exactly what happened in that diner!"

By April 2, after five weeks of performance, the demise of . . . *America Famous* seemed imminent. At the bottom of Earl Wilson's gossip column in the *New York Post* he wrote: "The cast of the musical *The Night That Made America Famous,* trying to keep the show alive, took salary cuts to scale minimums. Composer Harry Chapin waived his royalties."

The following day, producers Beruh and Lansbury were castigated by a Tony Award spokesman for having run a misleading ad for the musical in the *New York Times.* The copy read, in small print, that they had gathered seven Tony nominations "during the current season." What it failed to mention was that five of the awards were for other shows.

With all going poorly, Chapin decided to perform regular concerts on Mondays (the only off-day of the week), which the band referred to as Monday Night Football. Chapin's new group was now Steve Chapin on piano, Doug Walker on electric guitar, Howie Fields on drums, along with holdovers John Wallace on bass and Michael Masters on cello. Except for Wallace and Masters, none of the new members had performed in large concert halls and were unaccustomed to smoothly run shows and good public acceptance.

"You could count on one hand how many big concerts we'd done," said Walker.

However, Monday Night Football did not last long. Their first—and last—concert was at the McCormick Performing Arts Center in Chicago. The following day, prior to showtime, a closing notice was posted for . . . *America Famous* by the producers.

That day, Chapin was on a flight to New York with Steve Spinola, having completed another of their fact-finding missions for WHY in Washington, D.C. Harry looked tired and beaten, like a racehorse that had seen one too many quarter poles. His eyes were bloodshot, his voice coarse. He leaned back and turned to Spinola. "It's really been rough, you know? I think the show is going to be closing soon."

"Where did you hear that?" Spinola asked in surprise.

"Well, it's picking up attendance, but we're hitting a point on Broadway where it usually drops off. Which means that financially we'll be hurting for a couple of months, and Beruh and Lansbury don't want to go through with it . . ."

While Harry was talking, Spinola was thumbing through the *New York Times* and suddenly noticed the ad for the show with big black print over it that read: LAST FIVE PERFORMANCES.

Spinola turned to Chapin. "Ah, Harry, you're closing on Sunday."

In a way, Chapin was glad it was over. The show had hardly been the huge success he expected and had already cost him the national exposure associated with a number-one record. So, by his way of thinking, Harry wanted to forget his failure and go on to the next thing.

At the same time, he also had plenty of reasons to feel proud. A few weeks earlier, World Hunger Year officially became incorporated in New York State as a tax-exempt nonprofit organization and the program *Make a Wish* had just won Emmy and Peabody Awards for best children's show on television. Ironically, the program was canceled a few weeks later. In addition, Chapin won a Grammy nomination for Best Performance by a Male Vocalist for "Cat's in the Cradle." That award had special significance for Harry.

It was March 1 at the Grand Ole Opry in Nashville, and Harry was about to go on and sing "Cat's in the Cradle." But just before he did, his guitar was accidentally broken by a stagehand. Harry was headed back to his dressing room to get his backup when he spotted two little men in front of his door.

"They were huddled so close, about a foot apart," said Chapin. "I didn't know them and I thought, 'I wonder who they are?' It was sort of freaky the way they were standing there."

Ironically, they turned out to be two disappointing figures from his past: John Lennon wearing a black beret, and Paul Simon with a cowboy hat. Neither recognized Harry. So with great pleasure, Chapin politely asked them to step aside from the door, got his guitar and paused for a moment, wondering whether he should say anything to them. But pride welled in his throat and he walked out the door saying nothing.

"You goin' on?" Lennon asked.

"Yeah."

"Good luck," both men chimed in.

"Thanks," Harry said, "but I don't need it anymore."

Chapin looked out the window of the plane. There was a smile on his face.

On April 9, after seven weeks, fourteen previews and forty-five regular performances, *The Night That Made America*

Famous closed at an estimated loss of $400,000—ironically, the same amount needed to bring the show to opening night. In the final performance Harry introduced Michael Burke from the audience: "He's the person who started me on the guitar in the first place," Chapin said, as Michael sang a chorus of "Circle" to wild applause, and then the final punctuation, when a cast member smothered Harry's face with a whipped cream pie.

In the weeks that followed, Chapin returned to the road, taking his Broadway band with him. This meant the addition of drums and piano, something Harry had always wanted for greater stage impact. It also meant that his brother Tom joined him in concert for approximately six months with his acoustic guitar and smooth baritone. Harry also brought along his Broadway light- and soundmen, Michael Soloman and Jeff Gross, who remained as the road crew.

"It was almost like everything fell right into place," said Doug Walker. "Harry said, 'I like what I'm hearing. Let's go out and be a concert band.'"

One of their first stops was at Massey Hall in Toronto, and the following morning, Harry, Tom and Steve paid a visit to their grandfather, Big Jim Chapin, and his wife, Mary, who had moved to Toronto several years earlier to be near their son Elliot, who had escaped to Canada to avoid the Vietnam draft. Big Jim and Mary lived in a beautiful brownstone on Monteith Street in a fashionable downtown section of the city.

However, Harry's memories of his grandfather remained in Andover in the fifties and early sixties, back in the days when Big Jim, an athletic man, used to play tennis, his favorite sport. "He always had problems with his hips and feet," said Harry. "So he'd have to cut out the toes of his tennis sneakers to play."

But now, at the age of eighty-four, it was obvious that time had taken its toll on Big Jim, who had suffered from a severe case of gout the past two years. At one point, he came slowly down the steps to greet his grandsons, and when he reached the bottom, moved to a chair so he could rest. Then, with Mary's assistance, he hobbled to a second chair near the couch in the living room, which Mary had set up as an art gallery for her husband. At that moment, he looked at her.

"His eyes lit up with such pride," Harry recalled nostalgically. "Because she was taking care of him so well, like he was getting everything he could ask for, because she'd completely taken over. It's like in the song 'Shooting Star.' She made him holy."

In the past, Big Jim always had wide, eagle eyes, very alive, glowing. They were like a small falcon's or a New England hawk's; even his nose was rounded like a beak. But now there was a mist over those eyes. "You felt his whole body was in pain," said Harry. "It used to be that after a long day of painting he'd get that mist as he got tired. But this was early morning. The sense of purposefulness was gone, like he'd finished all the paintings he wanted to finish, like his business was done."

On that day, Big Jim was in a nostalgic mood. A few weeks before he had seen Harry on television cohosting *The Mike Douglas Show*. He felt a tremendous sense of pride, as though a kind of richness had passed down through the blood, and that he, along with K.B. (whom he always respected), had sired this entire family of big strapping boys who were energized, accomplished and a credit to the family name.

At one point, with deep serenity in his eyes, he looked at Harry. "I've never been a big success in the marketplace," Big Jim began slowly. "But ever since I was a little boy, I wanted to be a painter, and that's what I've done all my life. I guess you could say I've had a truly happy life. I've known very few people who've been able to do as much of what they wanted as I have."

Said Harry a few months later: "To me the sense of peace that he had while facing the inevitability of death was one of the most enviable things I could ever think of. His life and words still speak to me. He reminded me of the poet I heard nine years ago at a poetry reading at the YMHA on 92nd Street. From the poem "Changing of the Guard":

> A life progressed so competently
> up to its end stands
> ready to encompass death.

Two months later, on July 19, 1975, Big Jim Chapin peacefully passed away.

CHAPTER XII

Old Folkie

By June 1975, Harry Chapin, to the surprise of no one, had been elected PAF's chairman of the board. Since becoming an active board member the previous year, Chapin had proved his worth to the organization. He was the only energy source, its problem solver. "The minute Harry became involved in something, he could not be second fish," said Sandy once. "He had to be top banana, so that people could turn to him and say, 'What do we do next, Harry?' And Harry gave them an answer. He solved each little problem in its own isolated container."

PAF's main problem was a lack of funds, and Harry was routinely relied upon to go out and get it and that meant another benefit! Chapin had to raise anywhere between $10,000 and $20,000 each month just to keep the organization and its playhouse alive. The majority of the money went to pay past debts such as back taxes and bank loans. The rest of the cash was used for daily operating expenses of the theater so that Chapin was totally responsible for the livelihoods of twenty-five full-time employees.

"To my thinking, Harry was chairman before he took the chairmanship," said one board member. "He came in like a ball of fire. He was looked to for leadership before it became official."

It finally did, at PAF's annual board meeting on June 29, and there was no contest. Except for one board member, nobody else wanted to be chairman with all its attendant responsibilities, and the one person who did was an alcoholic. Chapin won by default and was elected to a three-year term. "I knew what it was going to mean and I was not looking forward to it," said Harry. "It was going to be tough."

More than anything, it meant that Chapin had to become more involved than simply fundraising. It meant a total commitment to rebuilding the organization. PAF was nearly bankrupt. To save Long Island's only year-round professional theater company, Chapin made a major commitment to personally raise a minimum of $50,000 a year during his three-year term as seed money to revitalize the organization. And during that time, Chapin would have to convince major Long Island businesses to accept their corporate responsibility of supporting the arts in their communities through PAF.

The latter part of Chapin's commitment was based on something Pete Seeger told him at a benefit for PAF at Huntington High School in January, the first of what turned out to be six such benefits they performed together over the years. "Pete said to me that if Clearwater Sloop (the Hudson River cleanup project) ends up being Pete Seeger's boat, then it's a mistake, it's a failure," said Harry. "The idea is to essentially be the seed money to make something that's viable, that had a life beyond my life. PAF's health can't be based on the health of my singing career, or even me. If I get hit by a car and PAF dies, or WHY, then it's a terrible mistake. Essentially, it's wasted effort, because it's supposed to be integrated in the community and in the participatory democracy."

So, in addition to Chapin's personal commitment, he established the rule that every board member be responsible for $10,000. "Either you've got it, you get it, or you get off," was his dictum. That was Chapin's chief responsibility as board chairman: to make his trustees understand that they were not there to lick stamps, but to raise funds. He also authorized job descriptions for all PAF positions as well as a host of fundraising initiatives, such as a subscription campaign.

But within one month's time, Chapin saw that his board of trustees was hopeless. As one PAF'er said, "It was sort of like Dwight D. Eisenhower becoming President. He sat there behind his desk and one month later he said, 'Goddammit! When I was in the army and I gave an order it was carried out. Here I give an order and nothing happens.'"

Said another PAF trustee: "There was an impatience in Harry with other people's values. If people weren't as enthusiastic as he was, I think he had trouble accepting that. He had moved mountains himself, and kind of expected other people to do the same."

Even so, the trustees were uncommitted, uninterested. "We bulldogged them, pushed them, and massaged them," said Susan Gensel, who was appointed PAF's secretary by Chapin. "We played games with them, and finally decided they were absolutely worthless. They weren't going to get out and hump for this. So what do we do? We had to build a new board, a power board. Harry could not see where there'd be any time to do this. But it had to happen."

Said Chapin: "For the moment, I had to achieve step one of the PAF equation, to bring the quality of the plays in the theater up to the level where we really did have a story to tell."

Poor reviews and mediocre productions bothered him more than anything else. But there was also a limited supply of top-notch talent and artistic personnel in the organization. "If PAF is going to have a professional theater," he said at the time, "then let's find someone to make it a damned good one."

Chapin went on an active search for a big-name producer who could turn around PAF's artistic mudslide and, most importantly, give the organization an identity. "PAF was still not sure whether it was a community theater or neighborhood theater, or whatever," said one trustee. "It was trying to do a little bit for everybody."

By August of 1975, Chapin had found his professional producer in Jay Broad, a handsome, burly, blond-haired man who was an innovative stage director and playwright. Broad first established himself at Theater Atlanta, a repertory company in Georgia, as production director from 1965 to 1969. In his last year there he directed and coauthored a musical with composer Don Tucker called *Red, White and Maddox,* a controversial political lampoon about the governor of Georgia, Lester Maddox. The production was taken to Broadway for only thirty performances, but subsequently became a television special. In addition, Broad wrote *The Killdeer,* which was produced by Joe Papp at the Public Theatre in New York.

Chapin found out about Broad through John Voss, a member of the New York State Arts Council who had made himself available to PAF in an advisory capacity. Voss was well aware of PAF's search for a producer and was good friends with Broad, so he called him.

"I said no," Broad recalled. "I was on my way to Maine to work on a play. But Voss said there's this interesting situation going on here and he told me about Harry. 'Why don't you call him?' he said."

Broad did, and after a local concert, Chapin met him at his Upper West Side Manhattan apartment. They talked for hours, until Chapin finally sold Broad on the idea of becoming PAF's producer, but not without numerous compromises and changes, most of which Chapin planned to make anyway.

"Harry was willing to reorganize the board of this organization," said Broad. "He was willing to stand behind the deficit for a number of years, which is the key for any arts organization. He said he would stay three, four, five years, whatever it took to create a basis of outside financial support."

In addition, Chapin agreed to pay Broad a $30,000 salary and give him complete control over all artistic policy, including hiring and firing. Broad's basic purpose was to transform PAF's playhouse from a local community theater to a regional one by increasing ticket sales. For this, the playhouse needed a new identity, so Broad suggested a complete overhaul of the artistic policy. His idea, which had Chapin's full endorsement, was to produce only original plays, as opposed to the safe revivalist policy that had characterized the theater since 1966.

Broad told Chapin, "If people want to see old plays, such as remakes of *Arsenic and Old Lace,* they can go to Manhattan. The train service is great. But we have to offer the local people something they can't possibly get elsewhere. So an all-new policy becomes an inevitability. I just think if we're going to lose money doing old plays, we might as well lose money doing new ones."

At the same time, Broad liked the idea that PAF was close enough to New York (one hour) so it could attract major artists, actors and playwrights, yet far enough away to develop original works without media scrutiny. In addition, successful PAF plays could earn a future life on Broadway, and now Broad had a forum for his own works as well. That night, Jay canceled his trip to Maine.

In the weeks that followed, Broad's regime came down on PAF with all the subtlety of an iron fist. "The minute he took over you realized it had been a complete revolution in terms of professionalism," said one trustee. "Axes fell and heads rolled." Broad fired all incompetent personnel in key positions and replaced them with new, more experienced ones, often at higher salaries. He also scrapped the previously announced 1975–76 season of revivals for a collection of six new plays, including a musical cowritten by Harry and Sandy called *The Zinger.*

All of the changes meant that PAF's expenses ballooned from approximately $400,000 to well over $500,000, the highest ever. "Jay was really pretty damned expensive," said Peter Bellimen, PAF's former business manager. "He cost an arm and a leg. We used to produce shows for $12,000 or less. Even our strongest shows were under $16,000. But Jay's were between $50,000 and $70,000."

The main reason was that Broad demanded perfection. If an actor on stage was supposed to be dressed as though he were in Philadelphia in 1776, then he better not be wearing shoes that looked like they were right out of Florsheim's window. He made sure the costume designer bought the right pair, no matter the cost. And Chapin was all for it. So were PAF's approximately 4,000 subscribers. It meant that Harry would have to perform more benefits to keep pace with Broad's high standards, but at least the playhouse was attempting to enter the realm of respectability, and for that, Chapin felt, it was worth it.

In the meantime, Harry became more involved in the world hunger issue and increasingly found himself thrust into the political arena. On April 30, 1975, Chapin achieved his first "minor splash in Washington" when he testified in the first of three hearings before the House Agricultural Subcommittee on Oilseeds and Rice. The hearing concerned a bill that would eliminate a law that kept the price of rice artificially high in five states for the benefit of the growers. The bill was cosponsored by Arkansas Congressman Bill Alexander on the Democratic side and New York Congressman Peter Peyser on the Republican side. Peyser was Chapin's contact and invited Harry to speak before the subcommittee as a representative of WHY. "But I, like most people," said Peyser, "didn't think he was seriously in there to keep pluggin'."

Said Ralph Nader: "That's because most entertainers or people in the public eye come down for one day, get their picture taken with a senator, and then disappear. It's good PR."

"But Harry was not that way at all," said Peyser. "He was significant primarily because of his consistency, knowledge and background, which were much more than just an entertainer who was interested. Any time I called on Harry to speak, over a period of eight months, he came down."

The debates were attended by numerous rice growers and beer brewers (the better beers use rice in their brewing process) who were highly volatile (especially the growers) and who claimed the new legislation would ruin them. The USDA heard their case. But as Chapin soon found out, the debates were incredibly one-sided. The only proponents of the bill were its cosponsors and Chapin. No consumers were represented. In fact, Chapin was the first person from a hunger/consumer group to ever testify on rice legislation before the subcommittee.

"I remember sitting there thinking, where is everybody?" said Chapin. "Here we've got a major situation. America has a surplus of rice and we've got false limitations on our production. Why? Well, there are two things about that. One, it's terribly depressing, and two, it's terribly exciting. Because if you go down there and stew, it's like one man shouting in an empty gymnasium. It sounds really loud. It echoes and does all kinds of weird things. But many of us choose to be sheep, giving people who do act an inordinate effect."

The hearings tended to involve those directly concerned, because the subjects were not glamorous, nor were the hearings. There were no television cameras. But there was a lot at stake. House hearings served as a vital reference source for congressmen and senators, who often based their legislative votes upon them. Transcripts of the hearings were printed in the *Congressional Record* and made available to the general public in every library nationwide. This meant that congressmen and senators who wanted to appear tremendously involved used the *Congressional Record* as a puppet piece, and in the process further accelerated the one-sided hearing debates. Politicians frequently came to the hearings, gave a short speech to get their names on record, and left ten minutes later. This left industry spokespeople virtually unopposed, sitting face-to-face with government agencies. The outcome of the hearings, then, was predictable.

However, this was not the case with Chapin before them. Dressed in a conservative light brown summer suit and tie, he gave his speech with didactic vigor, plus two more over succeeding months, and after two defeats of the rice bill, the legislation was finally passed into law. It was Chapin's first major accomplishment in world hunger issues. But more importantly, it inspired him to realize that if WHY lobbied for its cause, he could have an awesome impact on American hunger legislation which affected billions of dollars in foreign and domestic aid. The final inspiration came when he heard another story, this one about little children.

In 1972 there was a television program about wild mustangs being captured and killed by dog food manufacturers. In response to the program, one fourth-grade Maryland boy wrote his congressman a letter asking that the mustangs be saved. The congressman then sent a "Dear Colleague" letter to all members of Congress and enclosed the boy's letter. "While this was happening," said Peter Peyser, "it seemed like every third- and fourth-grade teacher in the country decided this would be a wonderful project for their classes."

Inside of three weeks, every congressional office was deluged by thousands of letters from children. Within one month's time, legislation to save the mustangs was out on the floor of the House and Senate. Three weeks later, the bill was signed into law by President Nixon.

"The whole damn bill moved on the basis of these children," said Peyser. "In fact, the legislation was so effective that four years later the mustang population reached such proportions that the Department of the Interior had to relocate them to different sections of the country."

Chapin kept that story in mind, especially during Thanksgiving weekend, 1975, when he cohosted, with Father Bill Ayers, the first of what turned out to be three, live, annual radio-hungerthon broadcasts on WNEW-FM in New York. During the hungerthons, the station suspended all commercials and regular Sunday programming for twenty-four hours to publicize the world hunger crisis. Chapin and Ayres conceived the idea hoping it would educate the public and arouse at least a vocal minority of Americans to help change the nation's food policies.

Chapin approached WNEW-FM with the idea partly because of its progressive history. It was not a "hit singles" station that confined itself to Top 40 playlists. Disc jockeys were free to play whatever records they chose, regardless of length, and that meant, over the years, the station frequently played Chapin's music. It also meant that Harry was friendly with most of the disc jockeys, like Peter Fornatale, Scott Muni, Allison Field and Julius LaRosa. The station had aired public affairs programs with entertainers in the past, such as Janis Ian and the group Renaissance on two live benefit performances for cerebral palsy.

In September 1975, Chapin met with Muni and WNEW-FM station manager Mel Karmazin and discussed the hungerthon idea over lunch. Harry was asking for a rather unusual and bold commitment. Most stations, for fear of losing audiences, would never devote twenty-four hours of air time to one single issue.

"Harry wanted to do a fundraising program and education program combined," said Karmazin, who had recently been made station manager and who was at first suspicious of Chapin's sincerity. "However, the entire staff at WNEW vouched for Harry's integrity and said there was no selfish motivation.

"As it turned out, Harry was one of the few artists I would ever get involved with, and the only reason I did was because of Harry being the kind of person he was and because of the idea. It had no benefit to him at all. It wasn't connected with any of his music. It wasn't connected with whether we would play more of his records. It was totally unrelated. Harry knew that his involvement in a station for world hunger had no benefit to him professionally. In fact, he probably left himself open for some criticism by those people who would criticize any somewhat controversial subject."

The hungerthon, besides occasional live music performances by Chapin and guests, was an all-talk format which functioned as an educational clearinghouse for hunger information, much like Jerry Lewis's Muscular Dystrophy Telethon. During the program, Chapin informed the public about the basic causes of hunger, its effects, and what individuals and groups could do to help solve the problem. He told listeners where they could make financial contributions. But more importantly, remembering the story about the mustangs, he urged listeners to write their congressmen.

Besides Chapin and Ayres, all the station disc jockeys participated in the program, as well as a number of experts on food, nutrition and developmental agriculture, and celebrities such as broadcast journalist Geraldo Rivera and Columbia Records president Clive Davis. Even old camp friend, Bob Mullevaney, who'd become the head of the Department of Pulmonary Medicine at New Jersey's Englewood Hospital, spoke at Chapin's request. Ralph Nader had promised he would call in on Monday morning for a live interview, and Chapin prized him the most. But Nader was on a plane flight when he remembered his promise.

"So the following day, I had the unusual experience of having Ralph Nader call me and apologize for half an hour," said Harry proudly. "He was kidding me about all these unreliable rock stars, so I started kidding him about all those unreliable public interest activists."

The hungerthon was a triumph, tangibly measured by more than 15,000 letters and telegrams that were sent to local congressmen and senators. The hungerthon reached an estimated audience of more than one million people. Station manager Karmazin was delighted. "I don't know if the hungerthon made people listen who weren't listening before," he said. "But the program really helped our station. The mail we received was absolutely fantastic. I question what it did for Harry."

The fall of 1975 also saw the release of Chapin's fifth album, *Portrait Gallery.* Unlike *Verities and Balderdash,* the album was a completely new collection of ten story songs recorded by Chapin's brothers and band, plus studio musicians. The record offered several potentially fine numbers in "The Rock" and

"Bummer" (about unsung heroes), "Babysitter" and "Someone Keeps Calling My Name" (about Chapin's past), and "Star Tripper," "Sandy," "Dirt Gets Under the Fingernails" and "Tangled Up Puppet" (about family relationships). Of the collection, "Tangled Up Puppet" was the most poignant, with lyrics written by Sandy as a companion piece to "Cat's in the Cradle." But in this song, instead of the parent ignoring the child, the child ignores the parent.

Still, none of the songs achieved excellence, because Chapin recorded them during his Broadway show (from midnight to noon) and was simply too involved in too many projects to allow time for creative contemplation. Most of the songs were written during plane or car trips, en route to the Bridgeport studio. Once there, Chapin recorded his first versions immediately, without going back to polish, perfect and rewrite the new material. He also wanted *Portrait Gallery* to be a double album and he recorded twenty-four songs. This further reduced the quality of any one recording. His voice was gruff, the production tired, and some of the songs, by theme, were excruciatingly painful, like "Shortest Story," Chapin's first (and last) story song about world hunger. In it, Harry described the slow-motion death of a starving child. Alan Schwartzberg, the studio drummer, couldn't bring himself to play it. "My wife is having a baby," he told Paul Leka, the producer. "I can't think. I can't play this song." Finally he appealed to Chapin. "Harry, don't put that on the album. It's a turnoff."

Chapin didn't. But it was part of his twenty-four-song presentation to Elektra who, not surprisingly, rejected his double album idea. They also told him that for his sixth album they wanted to put together a "greatest hits" package. As far as Harry was concerned, it was the perfect opportunity to involve his brother Steve and Fred Kewley in the production and sever his relationship with Paul Leka. Harry was enormously disappointed with the outcome of *Portrait Gallery,* so before the album was mastered, Kewley took over the production to try to improve it.

"Fred just sort of rubbed me out," said Leka. "Fred took what he thought were the best cuts, edited the album, and it turned out to be an abortion. It was terrible."

Ann Purtill thought so, too, especially when it came to "Stop Singing These Sad Songs," a last-minute addition to the album and a tongue-in-cheek attempt by Chapin at self-criticism.

"After I heard it," said Ann Purtill, "I thought it was the worst song I ever heard. So I wrote Harry a letter and said, 'Stop singing those bad songs!'"

As one might imagine, reviews of the album from the critical rock press were particularly scathing, best typified by *Rolling Stone,* which wrote: "*Portrait Gallery* finds Chapin at the peak of his powers with a collection of story songs as mundane, vacuous, overblown and cliche-ridden as any he's ever written."

Nevertheless, the album, at first, did seem to have a hit single in "Dreams Go By," a bouncy, rhythmic song with a contagious melody built around the theme of broken dreams. "If I were to bet on one of my songs ever being a hit, I would've bet on that one," Chapin said. Executives at Elektra felt the same way. However, the production of the song was too glib, contrived and upbeat, which tended to mock the downbeat nature of the lyrics. The song began with a melody reminiscent of what Chapin described in concert as "the theme from *Godfather II.*" It was Harry's attempt at adding what he called "some funk factor" to his music, and in performance it worked beautifully as audiences joyously clapped along. But on record it created a circus atmosphere, a sense of funkiness Chapin always wanted but could only pull off in concert.

"Dreams Go By" received limited airplay and once Elektra saw there was no big single, they released *Portrait Gallery* with minimal promotion content with the sales of Chapin's approximately 250,000 diehard fans (which was what *Portrait Gallery* sold). This scenario became a standard routine for the rest of Chapin's albums at Elektra. One key reason was that by the fall of 1975 both Jac Holzman and Ann Purtill had long since left the label, and with them went Chapin's chief supporters at the company.

For the moment that put Harry in the unsympathetic clutches of Elektra chairman David Geffen, a consummate wheeler-dealer Harry neither liked nor respected. (Geffen later became one of the wealthiest men in the music business when he sold his company—Geffen Records—to MCA for more than $500 million.) On the day they met, Harry wanted Geffen to hear the final mix of *Verities and Balderdash.* Geffen told him, "Harry, I'll listen to the album. I will. But I've got to tell you, I don't like music." That album, of course, was a big success, but his latest record, *Portrait Gallery,* was not. Geffen was very disappointed. When Harry called Geffen and asked him to participate in the WNEW hungerthon, Geffen responded, "Harry, what are you getting involved with hunger for? Why don't you do something useful like writing yourself another hit single like 'Cat's in the Cradle'?"

Instead, that November, Harry recorded his *Greatest Stories Live* album. "Elektra felt it was time for a greatest hits record," said Chapin, "and during the past four and a half years, fans had approached me at concerts saying I didn't capture the same excitement on record that I did in concert. 'When are you going to do a live album?'"

Harry decided to combine the two, rather than release recycled versions of hits from older LPs, which he felt "had grown and improved through frequent concert appearances over the years." In addition, Chapin felt a live album would not be complete without such long concert pieces as "Thirty Thousand Pounds of Bananas" and "Circle" and, from his perspective, that necessitated a double album.

"For the first time, Elektra agreed," said Harry. "In part because it was mostly a greatest hits album, but also because it was live. Elektra was constantly frustrated that I was a larger live act than a record act. In other words, I could consistently draw

15,000 people at Pine Knob in Detroit, or Aerie Crown Theatre in Chicago, but not necessarily sell the same number of records the average act that pulls 15,000 people could do."

A live double album also gave Harry the opportunity to record two of his brothers' songs; Steve's beautiful ballad "Let Time Go Lightly," and Tom's "Saturday Morning," plus three studio-recorded songs that were culled from the *Portrait Gallery* album, which Chapin felt made important social statements: "Shortest Story," "She is Always Seventeen," and "Love Is Just Another Word."

These songs marked the first appearance of political writing in Chapin's albums. In "She Is Always Seventeen," Chapin wrote about America, recounting the turbulent events of the sixties, from Camelot to Kent State to the fall of Nixon, and how the "love generation" was so much a part of those events. In many ways, the theme of the song was a recycled version of "What Made America Famous?" That theme was further developed in "Love Is Just Another Word," a bitter, pseudo-disco rock song that scorned the love generation for having sold out its conscience in the 1970s at the very time when social improvement was needed, particularly in regard to the world hunger issue.

The *Greatest Stories Live* album was slated to be recorded during Chapin's first major tour of the West Coast, an eleven-concert swing starting in San Diego, on up through Seattle, Washington, and Boise, Idaho. Like most music groups, the plan was to tape each concert and afterwards choose the best recorded version of each song. But at the last minute Elektra decided it didn't want to go to the expense of recording eleven concerts and cut it down to three: at the San Diego Civic Auditorium, Santa Monica Civic Auditorium and the Berkeley Community Theatre on November 7, 8, and 9.

The sudden change in plans caused numerous audio/recording mishaps that forced the band to rerecord most of the songs in Elektra's L.A. studios. Michael Masters replayed all his cello parts and Doug Walker his guitar leads. Steve Chapin then remixed the album (the live sound with the recorded parts) at Phase I Recording Studio in Toronto.

"I was pissed," said Walker. "Here I was making a live album and I was in the studio redoing everything I'd done live. I was feeling horrible for weeks afterward. Any time anybody mentioned the live album I would say, 'Yeah, live, right!'"

Despite all the makeshifting and patchwork, *Greatest Stories Live* turned out to be a well-produced record and Chapin's biggest selling album. Released in the spring of 1976, the album sold (over the years) at a pace of 10,000 copies per month (800,000 overall) and even had a semiturntable hit in "A Better Place to Be," which became the number-one request song and single off the album despite its running time of 19:17. Chapin's only disappointment was that Elektra did not promote the single more.

"It might have gone somewhere near the Top 40," said Harry. "But it still would have been a piece of news. It wouldn't have sold the teenyboppers, but it would've been more like a 'Taxi' or 'W*O*L*D.' I mean, a Harry Chapin song that reaches twenty-four or thirty-six on the charts is a major success. First, because it's more of a story than a song and people notice. And secondly, the story, because of its length, has to be of high quality for it to reach those numbers in the first place. Most people think 'Taxi' and 'W*O*L*D' were number one songs. Promotionwise, Elektra shouldn't have approached my career with the same logic they reserved for other artists. A Harry Chapin song at thirty-six is like a number-one hit. Elektra never realized that."

Despite this, the *Greatest Stories Live* album brought national attention to Harry's brothers, but, more important, offered a whole new dimension of Chapin to the general public and a far truer one, that of the entertainer. Wrote a reviewer in the *Massachusetts Daily Collegian* ". . . while his studio material has at times presented itself as being too serious and overly melodramatic, hearing him in live performance enables one to see him for what he really is; an outstanding performer with a unique

way of incorporating humor and spontaneity into his show . . .
Harry Chapin's true home is on the concert stage."

The perfect example of this was Harry's performance of
"Thirty Thousand Pounds of Bananas," his tongue-in-cheek disaster song about a banana-truck driver that Chapin used as a tool
for audience participation. It was a surefire hit with fans, especially when Chapin gave his legendary lesson in the difficulties
he had in coming up with an ending (of which he had three and
eventually added a fourth).

For the rest of his career, the participation became a kind of
cult piece ending with an encore of his classic "Circle," in which
he challenged the cellist and road crew to sing a few verses, as
well as the audience, of course, who sang the song in four-part
harmony at Chapin's coaxing and whom Harry identified, depending on the city, as the ___ Memorial Choir. Crowds ate it up.

"Harry did those good shows and that was the secret of his
success, I think," said Steve Chapin. "People felt they were getting their money's worth. His performances were always better in
concert than on record. In the studio Harry got all caught up in
the moment of it all; that THIS version was THE version for posterity and he tried to get real fancy with it. He didn't get cranked
up in the studio the way he did for a live performance because
nobody was there."

*　*　*

During the winter of 1976, Harry immersed himself in a number
of creative and personal projects. In January, he took off a couple
of days from his busy schedule to help his brother Tom shingle
the roof of the main house in Andover, part of a modernization
project Tom had begun two years before. Each brother contributed $40,000 toward the effort and, except for electric and
plumbing installations, they did all the construction work themselves along with Phil Forbes, the ex-drummer of The Chapins,
who worked full-time on the project. The remodeling work
included a new upstairs extension replete with loftlike bedrooms

and stained-glass windows (a favorite hobby of Tom's), as well as a chestnut beam door that connected the old and new sections of the house, which Harry described as the "Alice-in-Wonderland door" because it rose no higher than the shoulders of the average person. Downstairs, the extension included a large living room and modern tiled bathroom, which replaced the outhouse on the hill. "The best part of the place has been ruined," Harry often joked.

Also that winter, Chapin hosted two television specials. The first one, "Conscience of America," aired on ABC one Sunday afternoon and was narrated by both Chapin and news correspondent Frank Reynolds. The program was a historical view of the United States, from the Declaration of Independence to the present, along with music performed by Chapin. However, Harry had a far deeper message to communicate. Since 1976 was both a bicentennial and an election year, he wanted to resensitize the American public to the unsung heroes—our forefathers—who created the dream we live for, a dream requiring an active involvement in the political process, which, though 200 years old, meant more than a commercial charade that Chapin described as the "Buy-centennial."

"I think we're celebrating the fact that we haven't had a revolution in 200 years," said Chapin on Tom Snyder's *Tomorrow Show* that February. "The whole idea of this country was that we were going to have a constant revolution . . . that we were going to be public citizens, not private citizens. But we've all gotten to the point where we say, 'Well, we'll vote every two years and every four years and that's enough.' Well, it's not enough! There's a natural perversion process in politics so it's naive to expect elected officials to represent our concerns."

A few weeks later, on March 12, Harry hosted a ninety-minute program on NBC called *Friends,* an offbeat talk show in which Chapin interviewed, one-on-one, comics Bill Cosby, Peter Sellers and "The Fonz," Henry Winkler. The program's opening and closing scenes were filmed in L.A. showing Chapin strolling along a stretch of beach doing a short narration with the music of his song "Friends" (written for the program, but never recorded) in the background. The interviews—three half-hour chats—took place in the homes of each of the stars; Sellers' flat in London, Winkler's modest L.A. apartment, and Cosby's plush penthouse atop Harrah's Hotel in Lake Tahoe. Of the three, Harry told me he liked Winkler the most and Cosby the least. He said Cosby— whose dramatic television success would come a few years later—disappointed him the most because in between takes he "found his behavior a little bit disgusting, because he had these white showgirls hanging all over him. But also the way he was treating them . . . He acted like a king."

"My ideal vision of the show was to have three comics," Chapin said. "One person who was beginning, desperate for his first shot to express himself and what his drives and feelings were—Winkler. The second person would be a superstar, some-body who was literally at the top—Cosby. And the third person would be someone who was a major star a while ago, but still holding on a little bit—Sellers."

Though the program was not a ratings success (it was broad-cast in Tom Snyder's one A.M. time slot), the show illustrated Chapin's versatility and the reviews were glowing. On March 17, 1976, *Variety* wrote: "The find of the show . . . was composer-singer Harry Chapin as the interviewer. Possessed of enough fame of his own . . . Chapin was quite obviously accepted as an equal by his subjects and this led to the kind of penetrating ques-tions and answers that are extremely rare on talk and interview shows. . . ."

Such positive reviews did not follow Chapin's only other major project that winter, a musical he cowrote with Sandy called *The Zinger,* part of PAF's first season of six all-new pro-ductions under the direction of Jay Broad. *The Zinger* was a vaguely defined futuristic rock musical set in a recording studio sometime around the year 2000. For the most part, it was little more than Chapin's own determined attempt to succeed in the theater art form, an opportunity to redeem himself for his "Broadway bomb."

From January through March 1976, Harry and Sandy spent every available hour writing and rewriting the script, along with a man named Brother Jonathan, a Franciscan monk and theater veteran who worked for PAF. *The Zinger* was slated to open long before its eventual debut on March 19, but due to Harry's hectic schedule, the show was delayed. In fact, when rehearsals began, the music wasn't even ready.

"It was terrible," said Steve Chapin, who worked with Harry on the music. "The show was a total collaboration, yet nobody was involved. Harry and I never got a chance to write the music and words together. He, Sandy and Brother Jonathan were the script. They would rewrite various chunks and then sandwich them together. The dialogue was awful."

As opening night approached, problems compounded when Brother Jonathan tried to infuse his own personal interpretations into the play, which created a hopeless rift with his collaborators. Jonathan saw himself as the brain trust of the three and could not accept Harry's part-time presence and full-time comments. So one night at a rehearsal, Jonathan ripped into him.

"I was on stage and all of a sudden this explosion took place," said Bill Gensel, who became PAF's stage director. "Jonathan yelled, 'Now listen, Harry, I'm a professional . . .'"

Finally, four days before opening night, Brother Jonathan quit the play (and PAF) as Chapin made a futile last-ditch effort to salvage the musical. "Night after night, Harry fell asleep in a chair at the playhouse," said Susan Gensel, who had become Harry's personal secretary three months earlier. "He rested for an hour and then went back to work. It was his Manassas Mauler approach."

On March 19, *The Zinger* did open, and not surprisingly, reviews in local papers were poor to mixed. The show did survive a one-month run and even played to sell-out crowds, mainly because most of those in attendance were members of Long

Island's corporate community and their families with whom Chapin had become heavily involved in his attempt to build a new power board at PAF.

The process of building such a board first began in the fall of 1975 when Chapin began amassing lists of Long Island power brokers, representing a community of more than three million people whose major industries were electronics, aerospace and high technology. Chapin's quadruple requirements for his new board were "energy, enthusiasm, clout and money."

Susan Gensel, in addition to working part-time as Chapin's secretary, was also a trained librarian who headed the library at Cold Spring Harbor Laboratories, a research institute run by Dr. James D. Watson, the pioneer of DNA. Each week, Chapin showed up at Susan's home in Huntington with lists of names which she then cross-referenced with companies and put on a master list. Then, one by one, Chapin called them. With his typically well-rehearsed monologue, he tried to "seduce them" into joining PAF's board. He spoke of the importance of the organization's role in their children's education and how corporations have a personal responsibility to help support the arts in the communities they profit from. Harry closed his conversation by inviting them to a cocktail party at his home.

"But maybe one out of five was interested," said Susan Gensel. "Harry would say, 'I've talked with more cultured accents in the last three and a half months,' and then go on and imitate their snobby voices."

For Harry, this was a completely new experience in communication. He was trying to relate to the Gold Coast, the bankers and up who inhabited Long Island's North Shore and who never even heard of Harry Chapin, much less listened to his music. But there was the possibility they might have heard "Cat's in the Cradle" on their car radio, so sometimes Harry sang a few bars over the phone. If that didn't work, their secretaries occasionally knew who he was. Often Chapin paused on the phone while they went to find out more.

"I've spent a large part of my life trying to be in situations where I wouldn't have to deal with such people," said Harry, "but I also found it very exciting because here I was dealing with businessmen, bosses, leaders, all of whom I would've probably had to work for if it hadn't been for the stardom of my singing career."

By mid-January 1976, Harry had persuaded enough Gold Coast leaders to "hear more," so for the next three months he and Sandy hosted what Susan Gensel fondly described as "dog and party shows"—cocktail parties—at the Chapin home. Attending were some of Long Island's leading corporate kings and their well-groomed wives. However, Sandy—and Harry especially—were hardly polished socialites. In fact, the Chapins didn't even have a bar. So Susan and Bill Gensel helped prepare one, and ordered the food from a local deli (at Chapin's expense).

"Meanwhile, Bill tended bar at the parties, and I was going around introducing people to keep everything very social," said Susan. "And also, to make sure that Harry's children didn't run in too prematurely, but that they were running in and out so he looked very normal. My two kids were there too. Harry wasn't about to hide all our kids in the upper stories of that house while he entertained."

Said actor Don Murray, who attended one of the parties: "The Chapins were quite an extraordinary family because they weren't the typical show business family at all. You got the feeling that Harry could have been a farmer and Sandy a farmer's wife. Or this could be a professor of sociology and his wife. They were very unpretentious and untheatrical type people. He never made a big deal of himself. He had a natural, unassuming way about him, both in his work and in person."

During the parties, numerous speeches were made, with Chapin the first to talk. He spoke about the arts and education and their relationship to the business community, about PAF's deficit and what would be expected of each board member. Then Jay Broad stood up and gave an overview of theater in the

United States, followed by a speech from the head of the Huntington Arts Council.

But the purpose of the parties was not only to screen and inform prospective trustees but also to raise funds. At the time, PAF had a deficit of $120,000, was living hand-to-mouth and was completely dependent on Chapin's benefit income. So once the speeches ended, Chapin "worked the room" as many businessmen wrote checks.

However, Chapin wanted more than a donation. He wanted a commitment. So the following day, he called them back with personal appeals. "If you give a thousand dollars this year," he'd say typically, "you'll be expected to give a thousand next year." Chapin raised $60,000 that way.

"It wasn't enough," said Susan Gensel. "But at least it got us through the '75–'76 season."

During the winter of 1976, the Chapins gave approximately forty cocktail parties (sometimes three and four nights per week), but they weren't always successful. "Some nights it would snow and only half the people would show up," said Susan. "And then we'd have to cancel and rework it. Other nights, we'd take our dog and pony show and go to someone else's house. An old opera singer had us at her house once, and a lot of Sandy's friends. But nothing came out of those financially or boardwise."

So Chapin pushed harder. He held continuous meetings with Broad and picked a committee to help interview potential members on days when he was out of town, performing concerts. On two occasions he was the keynote speaker at a Long Island businessmen's breakfast, and to those who met his quadruple requirement of energy, enthusiasm, clout and money, he made personal appeals, making appointments at their offices. "His pitch was we need the prestige, we need you," said Susan.

"Harry was a very persuasive person," said Jay Broad. "And he was not easily put off once he was in your office. He was a pest. Once he was in your office, you listened!"

But Chapin also had some indirect help. By the spring of 1976, PAF's season of all-new works was the recipient of several rave reviews (except for *The Zinger*). NEW PLAYS BRING NEW THEATERGOERS TO PLAYHOUSE IN HUNTINGTON, was the headline of an article by Mel Gussow in the *New York Times*.

Such articles helped persuade the corporate community Chapin was trying to impress. But they were impressed also if they saw Harry on *The Tonight Show* or a television special such as "Friends" or "Conscience of America."

"The industrialists, who were financially and socially established, were both bewildered and intrigued by Harry's background; entertainer, singer, strolling minstrel," said Broad. "They made their money logically through investments and business expansion and here was this strange guy with a guitar."

"There were other factors too," said Clint Marantz. "It wasn't just a question of this very charming person knocking on your door to tell you to be involved. He had a track record behind him. He was backed by Jay Broad and an organization that had been around for more than ten years with a significant arts-in-education program. He had supportive evidence to back him up."

By 1976, the arts-in-education program was servicing 122 schools in 27 school districts educating more than 130,000 children in both elementary and high schools throughout Long Island. It was that kind of impact that drove Harry to save PAF, as much for that program as the theater, if not more so. He felt it was the education of the future. His motivations were no longer an attempt to prove his humanistic worth to Sandy. He was doing it for himself. PAF had taken on its own momentum and become a personal obsession with him.

Said Broad: "I think Harry sensed himself as a social activist. There was something in him which drove him to feel that what he did at PAF went beyond . . . I mean, he didn't just write a song. He wanted the song to have social reverberations. He truly believed that what the arts-in-education program did had a cosmic effectiveness. And being a part of that, I think, gave him a sense of self. It was part of the activism. In the sixties we were marching on the White House. But in the seventies it was more organized."

On June 29, 1976, PAF held its first annual board meeting with all the newly chosen members, twelve in all (which totaled twenty-four by October). The meeting took place in a conference room in the Huntington Public Library with a broad spectrum of political and personality types, from superconservatives such as Kennedy Middendorf, president of United Mutual Savings Bank, to ultraliberals like Chapin. In between, there were presidents and vice-presidents from the financial community such as Citibank, Chemical Bank and European-American Bank. There were heads of industrial corporations as well as executives from brokerage and accounting firms and Sandy Zimmerman, the head of A&S Department Stores. They were all responsible for "giving or getting $10,000" except for actors Don Murray and Jose Ferrer, who were elected to PAF's board in name only, to lend credibility to the organization. However, those who did attend did so in common cause, having been convinced by Chapin that their involvement was worthwhile to achieve a "higher quality of life on Long Island."

"It's true that most of them did not represent the most enlightening institutions," said Chapin, "but all of them had a consistent history of being on boards. It was exciting because some new board members were naturally opposed to each other in their outside business concerns, but were now working together for a good cause. For instance, Edward Barrett, the general counsel of Long Island Lighting Company, was on the board, but so was James D. Watson, a major foe of nuclear plants. It was a marriage of different kinds of people. I believe the genius of America is a collective genius of all different kinds of people working together, maybe having to make some compromises, but arriving at decisions on an open basis rather than have small groups of leaders sit in board rooms and make decisions for all of us."

So, while the mucky-mucks were learning how to be liberals, Chapin was learning how to be chairman of a board. In fact, he'd already learned quite a bit during his first year in office. In the past, under the old board, meetings were chaotic, zoolike. Agendas were not followed, discussions wandered, and members were not held accountable for commitments at prior meetings. There was occasional shouting, and sometimes half the trustees were absent. In many ways, it was a typical portrait of a nonprofit board.

"Harry ran very informal sessions during his first year," said board member Elizabeth Lindsay. "People were free to speak up. He knew nothing of Roberts Rules, without which the United States Congress couldn't function."

But now, with his handpicked board, Chapin ran a very orderly meeting. The new members sat around a long rectangular table with PAF annual reports in front of them, neatly packaged in baby-blue folders, and by occasionally pointing his finger, Harry calmly recognized people from the floor with all the style, verve and panache of a young Kennedy.

"It was a new role and Harry was playing it," said Lindsay, who attended that first meeting. "I thought he did it very well. He had become very nervously correct. He had an agenda in front of him and he'd look down and say, 'And now we'll have the financial report from our treasurer . . . Now we'll have . . .' He was a real chairman! He was very careful to keep his mouth shut. The whole idea of being chairman was to pull the information you needed from others, and Harry was doing it."

Chapin also looked like a chairman, although that was something else he had to learn. For instance, at Harry's very first board meeting in 1974, he wore corduroys while everyone else wore suits. At one point, Chapin was about to cross his legs when Sandy leaned over to Susan Gensel and whispered, "Watch, he won't have any socks on."

Said Gensel: "Lo and behold, he had no socks."

But now, Chapin looked distinguished. He puffed a big fat cigar and wore gold-trimmed glasses as well as a dark suit, white shirt and tie, even socks!

Said Gensel of that board meeting: "It was the most incredible thing. Harry really accomplished it! I mean, he could be quite bumbling, you know, but he got all those businesspeople on his bandwagon. And the culmination of seeing them all in one room in their suits and ties sitting around and talking about something that had been nothing but a slipping dream for five years was incredible. He saved it!"

A few days after the board meeting, the Gensels took the Chapins out to dinner. "We really wanted to do it," said Susan. "We wanted to take them out for a change, and it was the first night we had a chance to be together in a long time. Just the four of us."

They went to a Mexican restaurant in Huntington called Pancho Villa's, there was a strolling guitarist. His name was Roberto. At the end of the meal, Harry decided to join him in the music festivities. Harry collected all the water glasses on the table and, like a chemist, started adding and measuring water until he had a perfectly tuned scale. Then Harry began tapping the glasses in rhythm while Roberto sang and strummed. Everyone at the table joined in as the entire restaurant looked on. By the time they finished, people were beginning to recognize Chapin. At one table someone called out, "Hey, that's Harry Chapin!" and the person sitting next to him said, "Harry who?" Chapin overheard the exchange, and they all began to laugh as Harry went through his routine of not being recognized. "Harry can't stand to be somewhere more than an hour and a half and not be recognized," Sandy told Susan.

Finally, the maitre d', who was a good friend of the Gensels, came over to the table. "Would you play for us, Mr. Chapin? There are many of your fans here."

So Harry borrowed Roberto's guitar and sang "Nobody Loves You When You're Down and Out." "It was the first time I ever heard him play someone else's music," said Susan. "Then, for an encore, he sang 'Corey's Coming' in a marvelous resonant tone, and he brought the house down!"

*   *   *

While Chapin was busy mobilizing the Long Island corporate community into supporting the arts, he was also trying to mobilize the entertainment community into social causes. He wanted to create an organization called PIE, Public Interest Entertainment, whereby major entertainers (far bigger than he) would perform one FSO (for services of) benefit per year. The concert money would go into a general fund and be distributed directly to social organizations who needed it most.

"The administration of some charity organizations is atrocious," said Chapin. "By setting up an organization like this, we can make best use of the money. If the top fifty or one hundred entertainers performed just one FSO concert per year, it would generate millions of dollars for charity. I mean, most performers make an inordinate, almost criminal amount of money in this business. We should pay something back to society."

Chapin's idea was originally triggered by Ralph Nader who, for years, had tried to convince entertainers of the potential impact they could have in citizen causes. During the previous four months, Chapin and Nader had several meetings to map out the details for PIE. Linda Ronstadt and other performers attended such meetings on the West Coast.

"What we discussed was hiring professionals to work full-time on the projects we care about," said Chapin. "Instead of doing flash-in-the-pan things like bullshit Hurricane Carter concerts or Bangladesh concerts that don't change anything, and where the money is either ripped off or put into short-term solutions."

However, PIE wasn't the only organization of its kind. Actor Robert Redford, who was also committed to social issues, had already formed an organization called CAF (Citizens Action Fund) which supported various consumer, solar energy and environmental groups. One day Ralph Nader, who was a good friend of Redford's, arranged for Chapin to meet him in Washington, D.C. Harry's goal, in part, was to convince Redford to team up with PIE and also to find out more about CAF and its organizational structure.

Said Redford of Chapin: "I had been aware of his records and public appearances, but I was not aware of Chapin as the public-interest figure. I was boggled by his incredible energy and his full commitment to what he said he wanted to do. A lot of people had energy and were hyper, but very few people were able to channel that energy into goodwill plus their careers."

Most performers also had no desire to channel their energy into goodwill, which Chapin soon found out, despite their interest and promises, and his PIE idea quickly fell by the wayside, although Harry made numerous failed attempts to resurrect it over the years. He also became very bitter toward his peers. This was reflected in a conversation with his activist-mentor Pete Seeger (one of PIE's few supporters) at a benefit backstage at Lemoyne College in Syracuse, New York. Chapin had just completed thirteen concerts in nine days; eleven of them were benefits. He told this to Seeger, who started to tune his banjo.

"You know, you meet the best people in the world," Seeger said, occasionally stroking his thin gray beard. "I don't know if any benefit, march or demonstration I've done has ever made a difference, but I can tell you one thing. When you work together with the people who care, you're working with the live hearts, live eyes, live minds, the good people. People who knock themselves out trying to do something important, and I just hope the whole idea spreads."

There was a pause in the conversation. Chapin, who was leaning against a wall, listening intently, could no longer hold back his disgust.

"You know, Pete, it's absolutely impossible to get the so-called counterculture involved. They are more hypocritical. I mean, Bob Hope and Frank Sinatra, God bless their fascist souls, do more benefits—not that it matters because they do 'em for the wrong causes—than the Rolling Stones, Bruce Springsteen and Bob Dylan. You should hear Ralph Nader talk about Dylan. He says they're raising hundreds of thousands of dollars for [Rubin] 'Hurricane' Carter [the heavyweight boxer, who, in 1976, was accused, and eventually convicted, of a triple murder in Paterson, New Jersey], but the fact is, if they were really interested in helping the Hurricane Carters of the world, instead of spending it on $200-dollar-an-hour lawyers, where the money gets chewed up in two months, that money should go into a fund helping hundreds of Hurricane Carters and hire young lawyers who work at a pittance. But most people don't understand institutionalized change. They look for the glamour issue rather than the ongoing thing like Clearwater or WHY. Change doesn't occur through one march or one demonstration. It occurs because of people like yourself who are here today, tomorrow, next month, next year. That's the disheartening thing. The only people you get to do benefits are Mary Travers, Peter Yarrow, Arlo Guthrie, yourself, Don McLean, Harry Chapin—you know, the old folkies . . ."

Seeger: "Richie Havens."

"Exactly. The ones who have been there all along. You call up Paul Simon and talk about a benefit? Melanie may do a thing now and then for UNICEF. But in terms of being available on a regular basis?"

Harry paused. "That whole crew," he resumed bitterly. "That whole Rolling Stone crew is just unreachable."

Chapin was particularly dismayed that so many performers from the sixties had lost their social conscience. He felt like the Japanese soldier who continued to fight World War II, and then, one day, rose from the jungles of Japan only to find that the war had been over for thirty years. "I thought, where is everybody?" said Chapin. "Most of them had sold out. They had become pampered entertainers who behaved like medieval royalty."

Harry was particularly stewed when he read about Bob Dylan in an airline magazine. Dylan was quoted as saying that in the sixties he was very socially active and paid his dues, but in the seventies he was into larger issues, like self-realization. Chapin bristled. He talked about it for months. "I mean, who is he trying to kid, us or himself?" Chapin said. "I think Dylan's ego is unbelievable. It's saying that I'm realizing myself is a larger issue than worrying about the state of the world. Well, my basic message is involvement. Selfishness doesn't score. History isn't changed by a bunch of people sitting safely in their rooms. It's always been made by an active minority."

Chapin addressed his disillusionment with his peers in the song "Parades Still Passing By," a tribute to Phil Ochs who, from Chapin's perspective, had never sold out to change and who, in the later stages of his life, became an alcoholic, until he finally committed suicide in May 1976 by hanging himself in the garage of his Long Island home. In the song, Chapin compared Och's social commitment to those who had long since forgotten the phrase when he wrote:

> You went to hell and
> Even when you weren't selling
> You never ever sold out.

"Here was a guy," said Harry, "who was going through a tremendous amount of personal pain. But despite that, he could always care. The last line in the song says, 'And your greatest gift and the curse you lived with was that you could always care.' And an awful lot of the people from the sixties have moved away from that kind of concern. But Phil was still worried about Allende, the Vietnam War, the Cambodian bombings, Kent State and so many injustices. As well as his incredibly high-quality writing in the early sixties, he should be remembered for that kind of consistency."

Chapin was not merely bitter toward his peers. He also slammed the whole of society in the title song of his album *On the Road to Kingdom Come,* which he recorded that summer in Los Angeles. Uncharacteristically of Chapin, the song was a political propaganda piece written during the presidential primaries at the time of the Wayne Hays/Elizabeth Ray sex scandal, and Chapin was feeling very cynical. He took potshots at political figures (Nixon and Edward Kennedy), the military, the music business (managers and sundry rock stars), American values (grandpa at an orgy), and religion (the Pope, choirboys and Billy Graham).

"Hypocritical attitudes was the key message," said Chapin at the time. "I wrote it during a three-and-a-half-hour layover at Kansas City Airport after doing a Nader benefit in Manhattan, Kansas. It was an eleven-verse song cut down to six verses. And I read about disaster after disaster in the morning paper and how our politicians had such holier-than-thou attitudes which were being exhibited by both Ford and Carter. And I just thought I should write an ode to all our hypocrisy."

Chapin also tried to do something about it by getting involved in the political process. That summer Harry was elected as a delegate for Morris Udall to the Democratic National Convention at Madison Square Garden in New York. He was elected from the Third Congressional District on Long Island and was among twenty-nine other Island delegates who included House Representatives Otis Pike and Thomas Downey.

For Harry, politics was a complete departure from the intellectual heritage of his family, except perhaps for Aunt Happy who'd been a Maoist and an active politicker. "His grandfather, Big Jim, drew paintings of what he thought about social issues," said Sandy Chapin. "He never got into a march someplace and demonstrated. But Harry broke from that because he became a political activist, which probably had more to do with me."

It also had a lot to do with his brother James, who was not only a college professor of America politics but in 1974 also worked on Tony Oliveri's campaign for lieutenant-governor in New York. In addition, James's wife, Diane, was Oliveri's campaign manager and, in this election year, ran Ed Koch's successful mayoral primary in Queens, where James was head of the

NDC (New Democratic Coalition) and later served as treasurer of that organization.

So while Sandy served as Chapin's political impetus, James served as his political instructor. For instance, Harry was originally registered as a Fred Harris delegate at the suggestion of James. James thought Harris was the most progressive of all the Democratic candidates. Then, due to some alteration in the New York election laws, he switched Harry over to the Udall ticket.

"Harry was not a political person, but he did understand persuasion," said James. "He was also naïve about himself. He was naïve about the way other people acted. In other words, he really didn't understand other people's self-interests and how they tied in to his own, so as a politician he still had one huge blank spot."

Though Mo Udall was badly defeated by Jimmy Carter at the convention, Harry didn't think his vote was wasted. He thought Udall's strong following helped urge Carter's selection of liberal Vice-Presidential candidate Walter Mondale. "I was impressed when Carter chose Mondale because he has a consistent record on social issues," said Chapin. "I'm not an old-style, beat-the-wool liberal. Liberals got us into Vietnam. They did all kinds of dumb things. What I'm saying is, I'd much rather make mistakes in the name of doing something good."

By the end of July, Chapin completed the recording of his seventh album, *On the Road to Kingdom Come,* but not without numerous delays and production problems. As usual, Chapin's frenetic schedule was a key factor. He recorded his collection of nine story songs on and off during the months of June and July, in between benefits, group concerts and the Democratic Convention. That meant he made five trips to Los Angeles and spent a total of only eighteen days in Elektra's studios, but not more than four or five days at a time. During most of these trips, Sandy and the kids joined him.

Said Doug Walker: "We were feeling very up about the album at first. But it was a question of getting Harry in the studio and keeping him there. And with Sandy and the kids out in Hollywood, forget it. They were going out to dinner. He was taking the kids to Disneyland. They were playing football at eight in the morning. He was going to lunch with Sandy. It got to be a really frustrating thing. I know that John Wallace and Steve said that as soon as Harry lost interest and wasn't there every moment overseeing what was going on, they lost interest."

So Fred Kewley took over the album's production, but that only created friction with Steve Chapin, who was the producer of record, and a man named John Stewart, who engineered the album. Stewart had been a friend of Kewley's and was promoted to the position after his successful remix of *Greatest Stories Live*. But Stewart was unfamiliar with Elektra's newly expanded twenty-four-track studio and had trouble working the control board.

"It was a fiasco," said Walker. "With Stewart doing one thing, Fred wanting another, Steve not knowing what to do, and Harry either not there, or when he was there wanting to do things that the other guys didn't like."

An enormous infight developed over how the album should be produced. Stewart thought Chapin should have a greater rock sensibility without losing the lyrical feel, while Kewley, who'd always been partial to the folky, a cappella sound, wanted it more low key, with an emphasis on vocals. Steve Chapin, on the other hand, who was by far the most musically talented of the three, was never allowed to fully utilize his skills; he was constantly overshadowed by Kewley. In the end, Kewley won out and perhaps too much so. The album's sound (recorded without studio musicians) was thin and weak, the music lost in the production.

"When I heard the final pressing of *Kingdom Come,* my electric guitar wasn't even there," said Walker. "In addition, Harry's acoustic guitar wasn't there and he's the main man. You didn't even hear the cello. You heard Harry's voice, the bass and drums."

Elektra was disappointed with the record. There was no single, and that meant promotion would be kept to a minimum. "They said they'd literally go out and kill for *Kingdom Come* if it was another *Verities and Balderdash,*" said Chapin. "But they didn't think the production was that good. They thought it was another representative Harry Chapin album, but nothing truly special." When *Kingdom Come* was released in September 1976, it met the same fate as *Portrait Gallery:* anonymity, and approximately 250,000 sales.

Chapin had grown tired of this fate, and, before the summer ended, made several major moves to change it. The first thing he did was to fire cellist Michael Masters, whose unhappiness in the band had been festering for months, mostly because of Masters's insatiable appetite for the limelight, which caused conflict with Chapin, the center of that limelight.

"Masters was a great musician," Steve Chapin explained. "But he kept seeing himself as Don Quixote doing battle with the windmill, the windmill being Harry. The reality of the situation was that Harry cut out most of the work for himself and Masters was just a tool of Harry's. John Wallace understood this—that's why he lasted as long as he did. But Michael kept on expecting to be treated as an equal."

In Wallace's view, "The most important thing at a Harry Chapin concert was Harry and his guitar. Everything else that went on was secondary. We were the tonal colors for Harry. But he wanted everybody in the band to have a persona, so he certainly wasn't trying to keep any of us down. The more we did on stage, the happier he was. It was another example of his head being in the right place."

Masters's unhappiness displayed itself in numerous incidents of disrespect and divisiveness toward Chapin. "He started getting drunk at gigs," said Harry. "Sometimes he wouldn't show up for an important benefit. And he was overpaid. He was earning upwards of $75,000 a year, and for that much money I expected some loyalty and innate putting out, which I wasn't getting."

Harry had brother Steve hire a new cellist named Ron Evanuik, who was twenty years old and had trained at the Cleveland Institute of Music. Remarkably, Evanuik learned all of Chapin's material within three days (Masters trained him), and because of this he was able to record with them on a few selections for the *Kingdom Come* album. Masters's last concert with the band was on August 4, at the Dr Pepper Music Festival in New York's Central Park.

In late August, Chapin made his second major move when Kewley's five-year personal contract expired. Harry decided not to renew it. Many factors contributed to his decision, not the least of which were Chapin's disenchantment with Kewley's production work on *Kingdom Come* and Sandy's dislike of Fred, particularly after the black book incident. But there were also deeper differences between the two men. Kewley wanted a different image for Harry than Harry wanted for himself. In the past, Chapin exuded a rugged, counterculture kind of image, but now he'd become a true family man. He cultivated an available, nice guy, philanthropic image, through all his benefits, PAF and WHY. Kewley wasn't against any of this. He felt only that Chapin went overboard, and in the process, his benefits destroyed markets for paid concerts such as New York, where Chapin was oversaturated.

Benefits were a low priority on Kewley's agenda, partly because he didn't get paid for them. Chapin often had to remind him to book them. It was a question of emphasis, and that led to disagreements over the phone, with Fred telling Harry he thought "he was making a mistake" and Harry concluding, "Well, this is the way it's gonna be."

"Fred felt I made too many decisions against money and not enough decisions for career," said Chapin at the time, "and he felt being so available, having my phone number listed and things like that, were counterproductive. Indeed he was right, in the last couple of months we had to get the number unlisted because of all the ridiculous calls that were coming in. But Fred's point was that if I became as big as Elton John, I could really have an impact on social causes. So, according to him, I should spend my time getting my career up to that level. But then I started realizing that, like anything else, you have to do things and not assume there's going to be one moment when it all falls into place. It's an effort if I'm going to be a person who wants to do things, and that when things are not easy I still do 'em and not find execuses.

"It's just like the Nixon analogy. By the time he became president, even if he wanted to be a good human being, he had already made so many compromises over twenty-five years that he wasn't able to change himself. Unless you get involved in the process early on, you can't suddenly put a halo around your head after years of ignoring things. In that sense, I made a lot of decisions that will make it more difficult for me to become a superstar. A superstar maintains a veil of mysticism, but I've got an image where people go, 'Aye, Harree!'"

Of all their differences, it was Kewley's laziness that bothered Chapin most. For example, all the press kits that Kewley was responsible for were, according to Chapin, "second rate." One promotional bio still talked about Tim Scott and Ron Palmer. "It was absolutely insane," said Chapin. "Fred really didn't understand hard work. He would work hard at times in the studio, but I mean, he was playing more golf than I was playing. Yet he was the manager, I was the artist. In his last year he made $150,000, and every time we had big meeting, big decisions, big crisis situation, he'd fuck up. Fred achieved the Peter Principle: he progressed to the level of his own incompetence. He didn't have enough internal security as a human being to have an intense sense of worth.

"He was a good guy, but he wasn't an original. He wasn't a person who had a deep core of belief so that when the pressure was on, he had something to fall back on. He was a loyal guy, an honest guy, and he wanted to manage me for the rest of my life. But in the final analysis, Fred Kewley was getting paid all that money to answer the phone and be a good friend, and for that amount of money, I should get top-notch professionalism."

Chapin hoped to find that professionalism in Jerry Weintraub, who owned a Los Angeles-based artist-management firm called Management Three. Chapin had considered hiring Weintraub for several months. At the time, Jerry Weintraub was one of the most powerful and successful managers in the music business. He sported an all-star roster of clients: Frank Sinatra, John Denver and Led Zeppelin, among others. Weintraub was big business personified and he looked the part. He was a cross between Neil Sedaka and Pat Boone, a sharp dresser who wore fine European-cut suits, Gucci shoes and had gold-bedecked fingers. In short, he was a symbol of everything Chapin and Kewley weren't. Chapin, then, hoped to join forces with a management company that represented the "Rolling Stone crew," the very "club" he detested, yet longed to be accepted by; but he also saw a potential marriage. His dealings with PAF's power board, congressmen and senators proved to him that embodiments of power and prestige could be utilized toward achieving positive goals. So if PAF and WHY benefited from the power structure, why not his music career?

"Weintraub needed a little more credibility from my side of the world and I needed his power and connections," said Chapin a few weeks after he signed with Weintraub. "Plus the fact I liked him. He was a nice dude. He was not a bullshitter. His trip was power. But there's nothing wrong with power theoretically if it doesn't pervert you and if you're willing to use it in the right ways. The whole story of Lord Acton's dictum. *'Power corrupts; absolute power corrupts absolutely.'* The problem is it's seductive and addictive. Yet powerlessness has no virtue at all."

Chapin's new manager, on a day-to-day basis, would not be Weintraub but an employee of his named Ken Kragen. Chapin was delighted. Kragen was an accomplished music manager with solid folk roots, having handled such artists as The Limelighters and Chapin's teenage idols, The Kingston Trio. Kragen was also the man who eventually made a superstar of Kenny Rogers, whom he was also managing at the time.

Chapin hoped to use the power of Management Three to organize, diversify and expand his career. He had always wanted to adapt some of his dramatic ballads to film, and lately, it seemed, several TV movies, programs and feature films were inspired, in part at least, by Chapin's story songs. It was speculated in several magazines that the movie *Taxi Driver* and the television program *Taxi* were influenced by Chapin's ballad. There was also a TV movie about Charles Whitman that some press reports surmised to have been based on "Sniper." Chapin also wrote a screenplay called *The Sweet Ascension of Charlie* about a violent rookie hockey player. He sent the script to actor Paul Newman, and though he couldn't prove it, Chapin believed it eventually materialized into the movie *Slapshot*. In addition, Harry felt that many of his songs, such as "The Rock" and "The Mayor of Candor Lied," could be turned into cartoons like the *Legend of Sleepy Hollow* or *Fantasia*.

"Jerry Weintraub and Management Three create things you haven't planned on," said Chapin at the time. "Before, most of the surprises were coming from my side. I always felt there were cinematic possibilities to my songs, and I feel they can help bring them out."

Chapin also hoped Management Three would mean larger municipal concerts, since Weintraub owned and ran Concerts West. Chapin hoped this would allow him to perform fewer concerts for more money and give him greater lead time in planning benefits. This included Harry's PIE idea, which he hoped to breathe life into with Weintraub's blue-chip artists and contacts.

But what finally decided Chapin on Management Three was Ken Kragen's suggestion that Harry could raise money for WHY at his concerts through concession sales of T-shirts, souvenir booklets and Chapin's book of poetry, *Looking, Seeing* (which Harry first published through a subsidy publisher and later by the Thomas Y. Crowell Company). Kragen told him that many country artists went into the lobby after concerts to autograph and sell concession items for profit, so why not do it for a good cause? The idea was merely a more efficient way of fundraising, which made terribly good sense to Chapin and sealed Kewley's fate.

"These things could have been sold all along," said Harry somewhat angrily. "I mean, the money is going toward something worthwhile. It's not like I'm ripping off people. It's just that Fred Kewley didn't think of it. It wasn't going to make money for him. And also, he didn't have much experience with those kinds of things."

Kewley was bitter about his dismissal. "Harry and I had talked on the phone and he told me of his interests in Jerry Weintraub and making changes. But he never said he was going to. He never said he made a decision. And then one day I received a letter of termination in the mail from his lawyer, Monte Morris. Harry thought it was time to make a big power play and go with somebody who knew a whole different side of this business. Weintraub was not in this thing because he liked music, as far as I know. He was more interested in buying a circus and things like that. It became a political thing and what was best for Harry Chapin, with little thought of what would be best for me. He was a user. I haven't talked with him since."

"It was slow," said Paul Leka of the situation. "It was creeping. And it was just a matter of time. I think everybody knew it. Fred had the opportunity to make Harry into a bigger guy and he didn't do it. Fred was all of a sudden a hit manager in 1974, regardless of whether he was capable or not. But he didn't milk it, either for himself or his act. The reasons were obvious. Harry's career was going downhill and Fred wasn't doing anything. I think Fred was trying to conduct Harry's life from the basement of his house, and you can't do that. You've got to be out there hustling. Harry was hustling. Fred wasn't."

In the end, Kewley sued Chapin for all the income he lost through Harry's charitable dates and benefits, approximately $50,000. There were also contractual complications that connected Kewley to Chapin's royalties. Over the years the attorneys for both men tried to arrange an amicable out-of-court settlement, but without success. Finally, in 1980, Kewley took Chapin to court and won. Harry also had to pay another $50,000 to cover Kewley's legal expenses.

"I wanted to pay off Kewley immediately," said Chapin. "But Monte Morris said no. It was the only bad legal advice Monte ever gave me."

All the changes meant that Chapin's career became more organized and better managed with Susan Gensel as his personal secretary, Ken Kragen his career manager, Magna Artists his concert booking agent, and, most importantly, Jebbie Hart in charge of benefits. After Harry's experiences with Kewley, he wanted to keep his social concerns "in-house" and believed Jebbie would have his best interests at heart. Chapin was also confident of his stepbrother and his abilities. For the past six months, Jebbie and Bob Hinkel (formerly of the group Mount Airy) had been managing Tom Chapin and successfully set up a $100,000 college concert tour for Tom as opening act for Janis Ian. The tour called for 114 performances in 120 days, which Jebbie and Bob arranged to promote Tom's first album called *Life Is Like That* on Fantasy Records.

In September 1976, Ken Kragen and Management Three began the task of organizing Chapin's career. For starters, Kragen hooked Chapin up with a large publicity firm in an attempt to reverse Harry's adversary relationship with the "cool-school rock press." The firm, Solters and Roskin, also handled John Denver, Don McLean, and Hall and Oates, among others. Kragen also made arrangements for Chapin's first major European tour in mid-October and suggested that Chapin compose "response letters" to the bundles of fan mail he received (usually from the city of his last performance). So Harry had stationery printed (on recycled paper) and wrote three different drafts; one as a general thank-you-for-writing; a second for those who were interested in getting involved with World Hunger Year; and a third for fans who sent him their music material, which Chapin politely explained he did not have time to review. Finally, Kragen made plans to have T-shirts printed with Harry's name and bio-souvenir books for concert concession sales.

But there were some things Kragen could not possibly organize, such as Chapin himself. He was, after all, a disorganized person, his mind constantly juggling a dozen different projects and personal goals. He often did things in the fury of a last-minute rush and was habitually late for meetings, concert appearances and plane flights. For instance, on September 2, Chapin was slated for an eight P.M. outdoor concert at Pine Knob Theatre near Detroit. As usual, the band arrived early and, as usual,

Chapin was late. He missed his scheduled New York-to-Detroit flight and took the next one. The promoter, meanwhile, planned to escort Chapin by car to the concert. But seeing he was late, and with the concert hall located several miles outside the city, the promoter had a helicopter waiting at the airport to whisk Chapin to the outdoor arena. It was quite a scene. Harry made a dramatic James Bond entrance before a packed house of 15,000 people. "It was the first time," a Pine Knob spokesman said, "that an act started late in five years."

Chapin's preoccupation of mind also left the daily deliberations of life unattended, and often in total chaos. "Harry was not conscious at all about anything," said Susan Gensel, whose job it was to tie up all the loose ends. "His checkbook was rarely balanced and he constantly lost credit cards. I canceled credit cards every other week. You never knew whether it was his charges or someone else's."

Chapin also had a suspended driver's license because of dozens of unpaid parking tickets and speeding violations. "We paid more tickets and late fees than it would've cost to fly him around the country in a helicopter," said Susan. "So I told him, if you just parked in the right place, you wouldn't get a ticket."

She also suggested, and frequently, that Harry hire a chauffeur. But every time the subject came up, Chapin quickly rejected the idea. "Oh, no, that's too fancy," he'd tell her. "Look, if I'm going to have my license revoked and they really push me and put me in jail, I'll just tell the judge all the wonderful things I do for people. My livelihood is my car!"

So Chapin continued to drive, primarily outside New York State where there was no way to check the validity of his license, but also because he was sometimes rewarded for his automotive misconduct. There was the time that year when he was driving through Iowa en route to a concert in Oskaloosa when a cop pulled him over for speeding. Harry handed him his license and registration.

"Are you *the* Harry Chapin?" asked the cop, starstruck, in a thick midwestern accent.

"What Harry Chapin?" he answered, surprised, more used to people asking, "Harry who?"

"You know, the singer . . ."

"Yeah, it's me."

"Well, I can't give you a ticket, Mr. Chapin. But I'd really appreciate if I could take a picture with ya. My partner over here has a camera in the car and . . ."

The next morning, the photograph wound up on the front page of the local paper, the biggest news to hit Oskaloosa in twenty years.

However, on September 7, Chapin was finally caught for speeding. He was late for a nine A.M. flight to Los Angeles to tape Don Kirshner's *Rock Concert* TV show. So he jumped into his Chevy van and headed directly for Kennedy Airport, speeding seventy-nine miles per hour in a fifty-five-mph zone on the Seaford-Oyster Bay Expressway on Long Island. He was pulled over by an unmarked police car. The officer ran a routine computer check which revealed that Chapin not only had a suspended license, but also an incorrect birth date on the registration of the vehicle. Apparently, when Harry bought the '76 van, the automobile dealer wrote down his own birth date by mistake. But the cop didn't know this, so Chapin was frisked, handcuffed and shuttled off for arraignment at police headquarters in Mineola, Long Island. "The officer thought he had nabbed a crime kingpin," said Chapin at the time.

In the past, Chapin had done numerous benefits for the Nassau County PBA (Police Benevolent Association). When he was brought into the station house, a group of policemen recognized him, shouting, "Hey, Harry, what happened to you?" Despite this recognition, Chapin was handcuffed to a wall while one of the officers asked him if he was available for another benefit.

Thirty minutes later, Chapin was released in his own custody, pending a court appearance, and within an hour the news had reached the press. By nightfall the incident had made the network news via the wire services, and by the following morning, it was in practically every newspaper in the country.

Three days later, at a New Jersey concert, Chapin told the audience what happened. "They let me out of jail to come sing tonight," Chapin teased. "I tell ya, I've never been arrested before and I prided myself in getting out of the Air Force and not getting killed in Vietnam. But I got more publicity out of that speeding ticket. I've been trying to get that kind of publicity for years. Now I'm famous . . ."

But Chapin's license was revoked. His humanitarian speech to the judge did not work. In fact, at the court hearing, Chapin was also cited for falsified registration of three other family cars (all secondhand), one of which was in Sandy's name. She also had a suspended license. Finally, after Harry's brother James and his wife, Diane, tried in vain to get him off the hook through their political ties, Harry decided to hire a man named Don Ruthig to drive him to and from local concerts and airports. Ruthig, in his mid-twenties, was a friend of Susan Gensel's. He eventually became her assistant and later replaced her. For out-of-town concerts, Susan arranged transportation for Chapin through promoters, friends and his biographer.

* * *

By September 1976, PAF, like most art organizations in New York State, was suffering cash-flow problems due to delays in funding from the New York State Arts Council. In addition to Chapin's regular PAF benefits (an average of two per week), he and Sandy hosted a series of fundraising barbecues at their home, a practice which began the year before. CHAPIN BEGINS BENEFIT BINGE, was the headline of one *Newsday* article.

The barbecues were held in the Chapins' sloping seafront backyard. For $25 per person, anywhere between fifty and one hundred Chapin fans dressed in T-shirts, jeans and sneakers participated in an informal feast of grilled hot dogs, hamburgers, and beer and a game of touch football. Later, a short Chapin concert followed, the guests sitting in a circle around Chapin and his "benefit guitar," an old nylon Ovation six-string. On one occasion, Chapin played for two hours in the rain. Nobody left. "I could never get enough of him," said one fan typically to *Newsday*. "I'm a thirty-year-old groupie with three children."

Often, Harry advertised his barbecues at his concerts. Once, he casually invited an entire audience of some 30,000 people.

"What if they all come?" someone asked him later. "Well, we'll just have to buy more burgers and beer," he said.

In addition to the PAF fundraisers, the November elections were approaching, so Chapin added another fifteen to twenty benefits to his concert schedule for political candidates whose social views reflected his own. Though he was a registered Democrat, Chapin supported candidates across a broad political spectrum, from socialist Michael Harrington to conservative Robert Dole. There were, of course, Chapin's usual favorites: Al Lowenstein, Peter Peyser, Tom Downey, Howard Metzenbaum, Mo Udall and Ramsey Clark. Most of these candidates lost in the November election, so Harry performed more benefits to help pay their campaign debts.

"It was Harry's way of making contacts for World Hunger Year and the hunger cause in general," said Tom Downey. "He had developed a reputation as being an easy touch for benefits. He had become known as the 'Benefit King.'"

This largesse also extended to any organization seeking financial support. Chapin was bombarded with requests. Besides PAF, WHY, politicians and Nader's PIRGs, Harry did benefits for environmental causes, arts organizations and health organizations that fought multiple sclerosis, muscular dystrophy, cancer and cystic fibrosis. "I wanted to show that I was willing to be responsive to other causes besides my own pet areas," said Chapin.

In 1976, Chapin performed 230 concerts, of which 130 were benefits. He earned approximately $1 million that year but close to 60 percent of it was donated to charity. Of that $600,000, only 30 percent was tax deductible. That meant Chapin actually donated approximately $350,000 out of his own pocket.

In the meantime, as the requests came in, it was Susan Gensel's job to screen them before turning the booking arrangements over to Jebbie Hart.

"Specifically," said Susan, "Harry was interested in serving—I know it sounds trite—sick and dying children and hungry people. Those kinds of things came first rather than benefits for women's clubs. We wouldn't do that. I said yes to almost everything. He wanted to help people. He wanted to do something for everybody."

Chapin once did a benefit for the wives of eight dead Kentucky coal miners and a Presbyterian Church that could not afford to buy a new church organ. Another time he allowed his musical talents to be auctioned off for a private party to benefit the Huntington Arts Council.

"I'll never forget when I spoke to a child in New York University Children's Hospital on 34th Street," said Harry. "The kid had ten percent function of his kidneys and didn't know whether he was going to live. So I started talking to him and all of a sudden this flow of humanity starts coming in and I finally ended up agreeing to do a concert. It was for maybe thirty-five kids and probably half of them were going to be dead within a month or two and their parents were there. God! What a freaky feeling!"

Most of Chapin's benefits were on Long Island where, due to his overexposure, he sometimes had to enlist the services of other performers, like Pete Seeger, Don McLean, Oscar Brand, Josh White, Jr., Richie Havens, Steve Goodman, Bob McGrath (of *Sesame Street*), and one time, in 1977, Kenny Rogers, who was about to ride the crest of his hit song, "Lucille," his stepping-stone to superstardom. All these performers appeared with Chapin for PAF at Huntington High School over the years. And in exchange, Chapin performed benefits for their causes, such as Seeger's *Clearwater*.

"I think in terms of time spent on citizen causes, Harry has no peer," Ralph Nader said that year. "The difference is not only in the quantity of his benefits but also his attitude in doing them. Harry looks for them to do rather than wait for the telephone to ring, duck seven, and do one."

But sometimes Chapin was forced to be selective in his benefits, only because of the absurdity of some of the requests. A teenager once called Harry and asked him to perform a benefit, but was "acting a little bit dumb."

"He wanted me to appear at his senior prom at Walt Whitman High, which is located in one of the most privileged congressional districts in the country," said Harry. "Well, I thought the request was ridiculous and wound up spending half an hour on the phone suggesting things he should be thinking about. I did it because I wanted to make sure that the people around me were not just saying, 'Screw you, kid.'"

Despite the volume of Chapin's benefits, he was still under-recognized for his commitment to social good. For instance, on September 18, he was nominated for forty world hunger concerts in the category of Outstanding Public Service at the second annual Rock Music Awards in Los Angeles. It was the first official recognition of Chapin's social concerns by the music industry. However, the magnitude of the social commitment of the other four nominees was almost an embarrassment when placed next to Chapin's. None of them had performed more than four concerts for their respective causes: Bob Dylan, for Hurricane Carter; Crosby and Nash, for environmental improvement; Paul Simon, for the New York Public Library; and Lynard Skynyrd, for trying to save the Fox Theatre in Atlanta, Georgia.

Lynard Skynyrd won the award.

Chapin felt betrayed and he voiced his betrayal three weeks later with Ken Kragen in a telephone conversation long distance to California. On that day, October 5, Chapin was in a lonely Holiday Inn room in the backwoods of Batavia, New York, stretched out on a double bed. It was eight P.M. In one hour Chapin had a solo benefit for WHY at Genesee Community College. After talking with Kragen for ten minutes the subject of benefits came up, and Chapin went into a monologue, his voice mounting with anger:

> The irony of all these benefits is what pissed me off a little about those public service awards. Lynard Skynyrd or Paul Simon does one benefit a year and gets the same recognition as me. It's

ridiculous! I'm going to generate $500,000 this year for various charities and do you realize how many mornings, afternoons and nights that represents?

Sure, it would be nice to be in John Denver's earning bracket and generate a million dollars a week. But I'm not John Denver. And the problem is, sadly enough, there aren't very many people in hunger and consumer issues.

I mean, let's talk facts, Ken. Chapin is out here in the battle lines, without paying an agent, without bringing his group, and working because he's personally committed. In these gigs I've been paying my own goddamn expenses too!

So the point is, I'm a whole different ball of wax. And if I'm, in a sense, going to be crucified careerwise because of it, the people who are doing it should have that tossed right back in their faces!

Thirty minutes later, Chapin stood alone in the student activities room of the college, huddled over the latest copy of *Billboard* magazine. He checked for his name and the chart position of his new album, *On the Road to Kingdom Come*. Nothing.

He sat down in a chair beside his beaten brown leather shoulder bag and benefit guitar, his only road companions. He took out his spiral notebook and pencil, set them to one side, and began to play his guitar. He closed his eyes, feeling his way through the chords of a new song, "I Wonder What Happened to Him." His mind directed his fingers to find the emotion. He sang two verses. He stopped. The sound didn't match the feel. He crossed out some chords in his notebook and replaced them with new ones.

At this point, a group of ten students entered the room and asked for autographs. Chapin obliged them. A blind girl named Kathy Johnson and her golden retriever Flicker appeared at the door and quietly waited for his fans to finish. Of all Chapin's fans, Kathy was one of his biggest, and he felt a special warmth toward her. In fact, three days earlier Chapin had performed a concert in upstate New York and made sure that Kathy and Flicker were admitted free. He had told her weeks before that he wouldn't sing unless he knew she was safely backstage.

Chapin finished signing the autographs and looked up. "Kathy!" he bellowed, jumping up. He gave her a kiss and helped her to a chair.

"Harry, I want you to have this," she said earnestly, and handed him a note written in braille, expressing her gratitude for free admission to his last concert.

All the students cheered.

There was a knock on the door. It was time for the concert to begin. Adam O'Keefe, an old washed-up comic, had just finished his opening act. Chapin grabbed his guitar and headed for the gym, filled four hundred strong. He stood at the back, off to the side. Then came the announcement: "Ladies and gentlemen . . ." (Chapin walked slowly toward the stage in the dark, his guitar at first limp at his side, then flipped over his shoulder Woody-Guthrie style) . . . "Harry Chapin!" The room erupted with applause and cheers as Chapin bounded for the stage until he and the oval spotlight on the stool where he'd sit became one.

Then, pretending his band was with him, he introduced each member one by one as the spotlight pointed to the empty spaces on stage. And then he proceeded to sing his fourteen-song set of story songs.

Chapin was not in top form this night. Occasionally his fingers missed a chord; his voice, a note; his mind, a few of the words. His head was somewhere in Huntington with Sandy and the kids. It was difficult to get it up for a small crowd, in a small college, for a benefit that would net perhaps $1,000. He knew his efforts would go unappreciated. The Rock Music Awards proved that, and he felt one of those momentary flashes of futility. "What the hell am I doing here?"

But with bravura and professional finesse, Chapin never gave up on having fun. He pressed harder, reaching back into that well of talent which earned him the right to be there in the first place. He straightened up on his stool and drove through the raspiness in his voice with gutsy determinations.

Finally, near concert's end, he invited Kathy on stage to sing the high part in "Mr. Tanner." She took Flicker with her and stood beside Chapin. Behind them, on the gymnasium wall, their shadowed images were a poetic contrast: the big, burly minstrel with his guitar, the small, plump figure of Kathy, and the wag of Flicker's tail. Kathy had a beautiful voice and she and Chapin timed the last note in perfect harmony.

The crowd jumped to their feet. Kathy cried in joy. Harry kissed her cheek.

"Truly, Batavia," he called out, "this is a better place to be," and immediately went into "A Better Place to Be," closing with an encore of "Circle." He invited a chorus of fans on stage as the audience huddled close together, singing, clapping, until finally—on the last verse—Chapin improvised again. "Our love is like a circle, Kathy, let's go 'round one more time."

The crowd jumped to their feet again as Chapin made a clenched fist with his right hand, raised his guitar with his left, and trotted proudly offstage, into the darkness, to deafening applause. . . .

CHAPTER XIII

Dance Band on the Titanic

In mid-October, Chapin embarked on a ten-day concert tour of Europe, specifically England, Ireland and Scotland. This, like most of the nine European tours Chapin made during his career, was low-key and low-budget. The trips lasted anywhere from two days to two weeks. He performed in small clubs and concert halls, and to generally good acceptance and reviews. The concerts were not blockbuster events. But Chapin did have a small but dedicated following, primarily in England, and mostly because of the success of "W*O*L*D" there in 1974. The only non-English-speaking countries where Chapin performed were Spain, Holland, Denmark, Italy and Germany. In Germany, Chapin also played for American servicemen at the military bases there. However, the language barrier in those countries prevented him and his lyric-based ballads from achieving any appreciable acclaim. Chapin's European tours were not big money makers, and some-times even lost money. Chapin looked upon them more as "an attempt to have fun and combine work with a vacation" (he dis-liked vacations), and an opportunity to see the world with Sandy and the kids (who often joined him) as well as brothers Tom and James, whom Harry invited on two occasions.

Said Harry: "It was exciting to plug into places I heard about, but hadn't been to, that sense of unifying audiences. I mean, everybody hears about what's going on in Belfast, but it's nice to go there and actually see it and do a good concert."

When Chapin returned from Europe on October 21, he immediately immersed himself in the world hunger issue—twenty to thirty hours each week—as the crisis began to take on new meaning. There were two inspirations. One was a new hunger book called *Food First,* written by Joe Collins and Frances Moore Lappé, the latter also the author of the best-selling *Diet for a Small Planet.* In *Food First,* Lappé and Collins subjected various hunger myths to careful analysis by examining the causes rather than the symptoms of the problem, and in so doing were able to offer constructive solutions.

The book became Harry's new hunger bible. Often at his concerts he told his fans to read it. "It was the first book I ever read, irrespective of the subject matter, that made the whole world make sense," said Chapin. "The book is a system of looking at the world and the hunger problem where you can see why things happen and where you can apply some pressure."

The second major inspiration came from new U.S. government statistics on domestic hunger. Chapin was already aware that "over twenty-five million Americans suffer from malnutrition," which was "a significant cause of mental retardation." But what he didn't know, and found out, was that "one out of every four cans of dog and cat food sold in the United States is purchased by senior citizens who eat it themselves."

"That's wrong!" he often told concert crowds. "Downright wrong! It's the best definition of obscenity I can think of. Here you have old people, who have worked hard for twenty, thirty, forty years, expecting to retire in some dignity, but suddenly find themselves living alone on fixed incomes. After they pay their basic expenses—rent, heat, utilities—they have practically nothing left over for food and they have too much pride to ask for help, to be a burden. I mean, it really is a silent scream, a silent crisis, and it's happening all over this country."

Chapin did his very best to publicize that "silent crisis." During Thanksgiving week of 1976, he tried to enlighten newly elected politicians by sponsoring, along with Representative Tom Downey and Senator Hubert Humphrey, a congressional harvest dinner in Washington, D.C. The dinner, an all-vegetarian, natural-food meal of black bean soup, vegetable stew with dumplings, whole-wheat macaroni casserole and sauteed vegetables with soy protein, was held in the Sam Rayburn Cafeteria on Capitol Hill and was attended by seventy-eight congressmen, six senators and their staffs. There was a panel of speakers, as well as a short, two-song concert by Chapin, including his stark (and totally depressing) hunger ballad "Shortest Story."

"It was a great event," said Downey. "It made people aware of some alternative foods that were available to people besides turkey, stuffing and sweet potatoes—and that some of us are not so fortunate during Thanksgiving time."

"Some guys got their heads changed a little bit," said Bill Ayres. "And a lot of congressmen got to know what we were—World Hunger Year—who Harry was, and hopefully got a little better perspective on food and hunger."

Three days later, on November 28, Chapin continued his anti-hunger fight when he cohosted WHY's second annual 26-hour hungerthon on WNEW-FM in New York. Once again, the program was a success, with numerous phone calls and guest appearances from a wide variety of people such as Tom Chapin, Ralph Nader, Ramsey Clark, Frances Moore Lappé and Pete Seeger, who sang for forty minutes. The event ". . . stirred up some of the ancient spirit of the sixties," wrote *Rolling Stone* magazine in its "Random Notes" section, which included a group picture of Harry, Tom and Pete Seeger at the station.

"I keep remembering Gandhi's words," Seeger told *Rolling Stone*. "To the millions who have to live on one meal a day, the only form in which God can appear is food."

The only down moment in the hungerthon (which *Rolling Stone* did not fail to mention) was the behavior of guest-singer Patti Smith. She had just completed the last in a series of fourteen concerts at the Bottom Line in Greenwich Village and arrived at WNEW's studios at four A.M. in, according to Mel Karmazin, the station manager, a "miserable, nasty mood." This mood took a turn for the worse when Smith, who like all the guests had been warned to watch her language on the air, decided she didn't "like being censored." Thus, at the beginning of Chapin's interview with her, she proceeded to say "fuck" to "prove the station can't censor the people's slang," going off into a long and vacuous tirade.

When she finished, Harry (who had never met Smith before) downplayed it. "Well," he said after a pause, "that is our classic Patti Smith monologue," and went directly to the next guest.

Despite the incident, Chapin received an award for Broadcast Excellence for his hungerthons from the International Radio Programming Forum at its annual convention in New York on December 2. Chapin was the first performer to ever receive the award. The recognition of his efforts was not only for his work at WNEW but also at WASH-FM in Washington, D.C., which followed the lead of the New York station and broadcast its first hungerthon on September 25.

In addition, three days after the awards ceremony, WNEW's sister station, WMMR-FM in Philadelphia (both owned by Metromedia Corporation), decided to jump on the hungerthon bandwagon as well. This included (through the auspices of WNEW's microphones) the broadcast of two live benefit concerts for World Hunger Year that Chapin performed at the Westchester Premiere Theatre in Tarrytown, New York. The concerts were simultaneously aired on both stations.

In the meantime, ever since Chapin's return from Europe, he had tried to reconnect with the emotion in his songwriting; that sense of intimacy that characterized his first four albums but was conspicuously absent in his last one, *On the Road to Kingdom Come*. For instance, three love ballads, "Roll Down the River," "Fall in Love With Him," and "If My Mary Were Here," were all exercises of craft rather than feeling.

The same was true of the song "Laugh Man," a by-product of his TV special "Friends," which attempted to reveal the emotions of a fading comic. But as music critic Michael Schumacher wrote, when "placed next to Anthony Newley's classic, the number is embarrassing."

Other songs failed on different terms. The title song, "On the Road to Kingdom Come," was a deeply felt personal statement, but it tended to, as Chapin would say, "propagandize" rather than "sensitize" the listener. "Caroline," another love ballad, with beautifully understated lyrics written by Sandy, had a soft, subtle melody that was far too bland for Chapin's gruff vocal style.

The only songs that saw a marriage of music and lyrics were "The Mayor of Candor Lied" and, to a lesser extent, "Corey's Coming" and "The Parade's Still Passing By." And that's because all of the songs were a direct slice from Chapin's emotional past. "The Parade's Still Passing By" was about one of Harry's longtime folk heroes, Phil Ochs, and "Corey's Coming," which had numerous influences, was "emotionally based" on Chapin's friendship with Zeke Marsden. "The Mayor of Candor Lied," the album's jewel and one of Chapin's best pure story songs, was about his first love, Clare MacIntyre. So naturally, the ballad was emotionally true to form and proved that Chapin's finest melodies emerged with his best lyrics.

As a collection, though, the songs on *Kingdom Come* lacked a sense of believability because Chapin was cranking, not creating, and his fans told him so. "I got more letters from people who loved me but said, 'Harry, I'm not so sure the emotional commitment is in this new album,'" he said. "The story songs really didn't make that connection, the pressure points, where you feel like the writer is giving a chunk of himself. Ironically, the criticisms of various critics and people in my past could be applied to this album where art was craft, not art."

Schumacher accurately concluded his review of *On the Road to Kingdom Come* by saying of Chapin, "Maybe he's tired of taking chances. Self-analysis and evaluation are answers easily attempted by critics, and maybe Chapin has some of his own. . . . Roads are meant to take people to and from places. Hopefully Chapin can make use of his own metaphor."

Said Chapin at the time: "I've been so active in my own life for the last couple of years, with causes and benefits, that I've been too much of a participant and not enough of an observer [of life]. People who are creators hear the whispers and are aware of what's happening in other people's eyes. They hear the rustlings and send in a report, but the problem is that the sound of success is a different kind of sound. It's jet planes, fast cars, crowds going crazy, and that tends to drown out the whispers. So I've got to find a balance.

"Having finished my seventh album, I'm in a position in my life and career right now where it relates to something Cus D'Amato, the old boxing manager, said recently of Muhammed Ali. He said Ali's doing a poor imitation of himself, and I'm at a point now where I could do poor or good imitations of myself. I am having to say, 'Harry, you're exploring a song form virtually no one else has explored, with extended lyrics and strange subject matters. But now there's a need to reconnect to something, because when art turns to craft it's not communicating.'

"There's a real tendency for successful people to protect their fiefdom. And the important thing is that Bob Dylan line: 'He who is not busy being born is busy dying.' I mean, you've got to fight the tendency when you've got a successful formula to just hold on to it. So I think my job for the next album is to rediscover where the emotional commitment to my music lies, to rediscover the roots—the things that made me successful in the first place."

Chapin tried to "rediscover" those roots by going back to basics and putting himself in situations where he had to articulate the songwriting process. For instance, late that fall of '76, he taught several music classes, one as a guest speaker at New York University. The others were six songwriting workshops as an artist-in-residence for PAF. And always Chapin told his students that he wanted to have a dialogue with them and be challenged so it would force him into new ideas. "The only way I know what I'm really thinking," he'd say, "is when I speak."

As a result of these classes, Chapin went on a torrid writing streak, composing twenty-seven story songs, thirteen of which appeared on his eighth album, *Dance Band on the Titanic*. These songs formed the basis of a concept album in which Chapin communicated his discontent with the "me generation." Their lack of social concern, he felt, was further perpetuated by the music industry.

At the time the industry was in its prime, experiencing the largest financial growth in its twenty-five-year history. It was a time of punk, and disco, and dance the night away. It was a time when middle-management executives were earning upwards of $100,000 and even second-rate disco bands were selling one and two million albums at a pop. In short, music was America's most popular art form, but from Chapin's perspective, it was not its most vital. In his opinion, disco especially was "little more than an opiate for the masses," and unlike the music of the sixties it did not attempt to reflect America's social problems. Instead, it wanted us to forget them. Sooner or later, Chapin thought, this "lack of quality" would also be perceived by the American buying public.

In *Dance Band on the Titanic*, Chapin tried to warn the industry of this, and, indeed, his warning turned out to be prophetic. Beginning in 1978, after the sales explosion of the Bee Gee's *Saturday Night Fever* album (more than 30 million copies sold), the music industry slowly began to disintegrate. By 1980, the music business had dropped from a $4 billion to a $2.5 billion industry.

Of the album's concept, Chapin said: "I believe the music of the seventies, the music industry and most of the art world is functioning like the dance band on the *Titanic*. Planet Earth is the *Titanic* and there are icebergs all around of our own making. The music industry's job is to divert attention in the ballroom so that people aren't worrying about the icebergs outside and promote business as usual. I think the theme song for the 1970s is Paul McCartney's 'Silly Love Songs.' What's wrong with that? Well, there's nothing wrong with it except that great art, at its best, should appeal to the popular consciousness but at the same time talk about ideas and sensitize us to the kinds of things that are compelling about our times. We seem to be purposely avoiding those issues."

To communicate his theme, Chapin wrote two songs that functioned as the album's bookends. One was the title song, or "short version" at five minutes and eleven seconds, "Dance Band on the Titanic," which described the sinking of the ocean liner. Chapin researched the disaster before he wrote the song. The facts were these: On April 14, 1912, at 11:40 P.M., the "unsinkable" *Titanic,* carrying 1,502 passengers, struck a massive iceberg in the North Atlantic that peeled apart six bulkheads in the ship's side like a can opener. Despite the impending doom, the dance band on the *Titanic*'s deck continued to play as the ship submerged in the icy waters, reflected in Chapin's lyric: "The iceberg's on the starboard bow/Won't you dance with me?"

"First they played ragtime, then waltzes, then 'Londonderry Air' and 'Nearer My God to Thee,'" said John Eaton, historian of the Titanic Historical Society. "Finally, while the last lifeboat was being lowered into the water at 2:02 A.M., they played 'Autumn.'"

During the evacuation, passengers from the third deck raced to the upper salons to get into lifeboats, but were instructed to go back down to the third level and get their own. "Except there were no lifeboats on the third deck," said Chapin. "And that's what's happening now. The rich on the top deck are getting richer and richer, while the bottom two-thirds are in worse shape than ever."

The album's other bookend, the "long version" of the title song (fourteen minutes, six seconds), was called "There Only Was One Choice." It was the longest song Chapin ever recorded and perhaps his most ambitious. Harry called it his "clean-out-the-notebook song" because it was created from bits and pieces of lyrics he liked and saved over the years. The lyric sections were so diverse that Chapin composed and incorporated twenty-one different melodies in the work. But it wasn't always easy. So in the studio, his band often joked, "Call Dial-A-Riff."

In the song, Chapin commented on the larger concept of how music and people should interact with society, not hide from it. The song, unlike any other, truly summed up the life, beliefs and fears of Harry Chapin. It was, in short, his autobiography set to music. It even predicted his own death. Harry was thirty-three now. In the song, he reflected that Jesus Christ, Percy Shelley, John Keats, Wolfgang Amadeus Mozart, and Charlie Parker all died at that age, concluding: "And I fantasized some tragedy'd be soon curtailing me."

The other songs on the album served as counterpoint to the larger theme, being stories of male-female relationships, as though they were the people in the ballroom and cabins of the ship.

The only song that did not fit the theme of the album was a three-minute spiritual written in 1922 by Harry's grandfather, Kenneth Burke, called "One Light in a Dark Valley." It was the only song Chapin ever recorded that he didn't write. "I put it in because it represented loneliness and yearning for a better world," said Chapin. The spiritual begins in a slow, somber tone as one man (K.B.) watched a light in a dark valley (Andover) fade to black. But then, at the end, the melody turned jazzy and joyous, expressing a sense of rebirth.

Dance Band on the Titanic was the pivotal album in Chapin's career, and with it he hoped to make his comeback, especially since two of his last three records, *Portrait Gallery* and *On the Road to Kingdom Come,* were both commercial and artistic failures. Although his popularity continued to grow because of his frequent touring and superb concerts, he hadn't had a hit record in more than two years.

"Harry wants to push for the big leagues," said Don Ruthig, an assistant to Susan Gensel at the time. "He can't sit back in the comfort of his old albums. He can't stay small-fry. He has to show some kind of trend. He went to a hump with 'Cat's in the Cradle' and went down after that. Now he has to build momentum back up again, or Elektra isn't going to be interested anymore."

Chapin desperately needed a hit single. In the wake of the dissatisfaction with Steve Chapin's production of *On the Road to Kingdom Come* Elektra suggested Harry find a new "big gun" producer. "It's the one thing he hasn't tried yet," said Elektra president Mel Posner. "Harry needs a different stimulus. His first album was a big success with Jac Holzman, then he had Paul Leka and a big success. Now, Harry's challenges for '77–'78 are for him to get a hit single that will bring him to the next plateau."

The search for a new producer was left to Chapin, who did make a halfhearted attempt at finding one. He contacted Jon Landau, the ex-*Rolling Stone* critic who was now producer for Jackson Browne and Bruce Springsteen. With Landau at the helm, Chapin felt the critical rock press would look at him in a more positive light, but Landau declined the offer. "I did seriously consider it, though," said Landau a few weeks later. "I spent a day or so just talking with Harry and getting to know him. He's a fascinating guy, a great guy, and he had some great ideas for this album, I thought. But I had other things that prevented me from taking it on."

"So I ended up with Steve," said Harry, "partially because Elektra didn't do their job to get a new hotshot producer. But also because Steve was an in-house situation. I'm a great believer in not counting on chance, but trying to be professional and craftsmanlike and in charge of my own destiny. I mean, if I was counting on other people's material and glitz or whatever the sound of the day is—disco, punk—my career would be less stable than it is. My career isn't based on any contextual thing like a hit single. Sure, it makes my career jump. But at every level I do jump to, I can pretty much hold that level. It would be more stable if I had a gigantic album with Steve than with Jon Landau. If I need Steve, I can count on him. I can't count on Jon Landau. So although the record company didn't want Steve, they also didn't do very much about it. Besides, I don't think Landau is that good a producer anyway."

Chapin's relations with Elektra were further strained when he informed Management Three that he wanted *Dance Band on the Titanic* to be a double album. Jerry Weintraub met with newly hired Elektra chairman Joe Smith in L.A. Smith, of course, was ardently against the idea. "Why not have Chapin put out one great single album?" Weintraub agreed. To induce Chapin, Smith told Weintraub that he'd give Harry "two hundred thousand dollars' worth of promotion for a single album, no matter what!"

Weintraub informed Harry.

"I said I'd be willing to go along with it," said Chapin a short time afterward, "except there were certain artistic considerations. I had this long song, 'There Only Was One Choice,' and if it turned out well, I'd want to put out the album the way it is because I couldn't fit the song onto a single record. It would take up one whole side. I also told Weintraub that Elektra is a knee-jerk operation in terms of me, that they have no sensitivity to the unique aspects of my career. I could come in with 'Alice's Restaurant' and they'd say, 'No, we don't want it.' So I said that my job is to come up with a mondo work of art with Steve and push them to do a mondo job. And give the album the kind of time and careful consideration I haven't been able to do in the last few albums."

In February 1977, Chapin began recording *Dance Band on the Titanic* at Secret Sound Studios on West 24th Street in New York. By this time he had hired his fourth cellist, Kim Scholes, to replace Ron Evanuik.

"Ron was the worst cellist we had," said Steve Chapin. "He was about the same level as Tim Scott. When he first started he was great. He made a tremendous leap over all the material, but a month later he was still playing the same way he did after the first three days."

Chapin chose Secret Sound Studios partly because his brother Tom recorded there a few months earlier (for his album, *Life Is Like That*), and also because Harry wanted to remain in New York. As usual, the pressure came from home. "We were having another of our annual marriage crises," said Harry. Also as usual, the crisis centered on Chapin's frenetic schedule and inability to say no to benefits that kept him on the road. In January, for example, Harry worked twenty-eight out of thirty-one nights, over 60 percent of them benefits (mostly for WHY). In addition, ever since the October European tour, Harry had promised Sandy that Thanksgiving Day, Christmas Day, the week after Christmas, and February school recess would be "family time." For the most part, he kept his promise, further agreeing that Easter week would be taken off the itinerary. When he informed Management Three of this, they promptly turned it into a European tour; nine days in nine cities.

This annoyed Sandy to no end. She commented at the time: "They said, 'Aha! Ten whole days in a row! This is the perfect time to do a European Tour!' Everything is the next critical stage—in building a European market, in adding a new dimension—so that record sales and reputation will be increased and Harry can finally become an international Jacques Brel. There's always some terribly good reason that one should be terribly responsible and unselfish. So I scream, I yell, or I cry, and we come up with some kind of change, but then it doesn't happen. In a certain sense, nobody is very responsible. It gets to a point where I say, 'Harry, look, I know you have lied to me in some ways and I know there are a lot of things you're committed to, and we have a calendar. There's time on the calendar for PAF, WHY, awards dinners, making money for the group and political benefits. But the time for family and for me is whatever's left over.'

"You can be sure that every morning there'll be six calls with six requests for one thing or another, here or through Susan. So I say, 'Time for us can be written in black and white on the calendar just like anything else. I'm not even asking for a list or a rank order of priorities.' Then Harry will say, 'Of course, I agree with you.' He'll call the manager, freeze the schedule, call Susan and say this is personal time. But what happens is that family time becomes an opening for all the other people to come in for a chunk. Susan will finally get to sit down and straighten out matters. Jay Broad will arrange a meeting. And Ken Kragen will say . . ."

Chapin settled the matter of the April European tour and temporarily doused the flames of another of their annual marital flare-ups by making arrangements for Sandy and the kids to join him, something they were unable to do for his October trip because the children had school. In the meantime, "Harry's relationship with Sandy was shaky and he was really down," said Don Ruthig. "Susan and I couldn't approach him for weeks. We couldn't get business done because he didn't want to deal with us and we didn't want to deal with him."

During those weeks, in addition to recording *Dance Band on the Titanic,* Chapin spent a lot of time at home. He began building an enormous treehouse for his kids and played tennis with them on a large concrete court that was built several months before, off to the side of the house. He also appeared on the children's program *Wonderama* with Joshua (four years old) and Jenny (five) and occasionally took them to his concerts, a practice he continued through the years.

Once there, Josh often joined his father near the end of the performance at center stage, and rocked back and forth while Chapin strummed and sang, usually a *Make a Wish* tune called *Stoopid,* Josh's favorite. "He thinks he's Rudolph Nureyev," Harry said once. "He's got it all figured out. He says, 'Daddy sings, I dance and the people clap.' When I call him on stage he starts bargaining with me. 'Can I do four songs, Daddy!' Then we usually bargain down to two."

Before the final encore of "Circle," Chapin began another new practice, a short speech on his commitments to the world hunger issue where he asked his audiences to support WHY's efforts through a donation or the purchase of his poetry book, T-shirts, or souvenir programs. Then, once the concert ended, he went out into the front lobby and autographed the items for fans, who generously supported the cause and swarmed Chapin, who stood behind a small table, answering questions. In fact, he was frequently the last person to go home.

Harry also tried to improve his relationship with Ruthig, Gensel and others. He had a Huntington jeweler make a dozen silver-chained medallions in recognition of those people who were part of what he called "the early-Chapin-believers club." The medallions were molded in the form of a taxicab. Inscribed at the center were the initials of the people he gave them to, such as Ann Purtill, Manny and Janet Castro, a few family members plus Don and Sue and this biographer.

By late March, a series of events occurred that made Harry realize the futility of doing so many hunger benefits when he could have a far greater impact lobbying his cause in Washington. "There's so little going on there," said Chapin at the time. "During one three-day period, I met with various congressmen and senators, and the level of debate is that hunger is caused by overpopulation, which is flat-out not true! This whole issue is really an open book, a tabula rasa."

Chapin was further inspired by the idea when the White House began to show an interest in the issue. One day Chapin got a call from John Denver saying he had seen a hunger film Chapin appeared in and was deeply moved by it. Denver was going to meet with White House officials and tell President Carter how he could end world hunger. Chapin found this rather amusing, and a few days later told his staff at WHY's Garden City, New York, office, "Okay, folks, you're out of a job. Two weeks' notice. John Denver has solved world hunger!"

A few days later Chapin got another call, this time from Paul Drew, head of the RKO radio chain. He said he and Denver met with Chip Carter, the president's son, and Tom Beard at the White House. Denver's plan was to donate 20 percent of his concert revenues toward ending world hunger. He also said he told Chip Carter "the one person who really knows what they're talking about in this issue is Harry Chapin. He's been involved in it for a long time, and he's got that kind of commitment. Before you make a move on this issue, you should sit down and talk with Chapin."

Two days after his return from Europe on April 13, Chapin met with Chip Carter at the White House. But prior to their three o'clock meeting, Harry spoke with Ralph Nader "about the best way to use the White House connection." As a result of the meeting, President Carter and his staff watched the hunger film in his office, and afterward the president sent a handwritten memo to the National Security Council, asking them "to come up with possible initiatives." He also instructed his son Chip to be in charge of the proceedings.

The final incentive for Chapin to reduce his concert and benefit schedule came after two absurd concerts, the first one a group date in Murray, Kentucky. "I thought, 'What am I doing here?'" Chapin said. "It turned out to be a good concert, but if I had a choice of either being home that day, in Washington working on world hunger, fundraising for PAF, writing songs, or being in Murray, Kentucky, Murray would come fifth. Yet there I was, in Murray, Kentucky. I suddenly realized my investment of time is important, that it comes down to the bang for your buck, because my time is money anyway. Every time I do a concert I can generate money. But it's not even the money. Things like this aren't productive for my career. Frankly, writing one really good song is worth far more. I mean, I played Murray, Kentucky, for $7,500. Who gives a shit?"

Then, six days later, Chapin found himself in another backwater town, Ferrum, Virginia. It was a last-minute solo benefit for Robert Redford's CAF (Citizen Action Fund) at Ferrum Junior College. But the benefit was poorly organized and it turned out to be one of the worst performing experiences Chapin ever had. The concert was held in a gym. Fire regulations demanded the lights remain on during the performance, creating "a horrible focus problem" compounded by an especially rowdy crowd of students. They wandered aimlessly in and out of the gym because the concert was free (CAF was paid from the school's concert budget). For the first time in four years, Chapin had to lecture his audience.

Said Chapin: "I told them, 'listen, for Christ's sake—I do two hundred concerts a year. I think I'm pretty good at getting people to interrelate with me and have a good time; otherwise, people wouldn't be hiring me. Give me a break! If you want to go out and talk, get stoned, screw—go out on the lawn and do it. I'm not telling you to stay in here. But if you're gonna stay, please give me a shot at doing what I do."

They all shut up.

Harry had had enough! He made up his mind that from then on he'd perform perhaps four or five benefits per month instead of per week, plus ten group dates per month instead of fifteen. He decided to become more directly involved in the politics of world hunger. For the moment that meant more hungerthons, which had become increasingly successful and even attracted several big-name stars, such as actress Valerie Harper, John Denver and the rock group The Moody Blues. But all Chapin did was replace one obsession with another. During one four-week period, he cohosted three hungerthons; at KSWD-FM in Dallas on April 17; KMET-FM in Los Angeles on May 1; and KSAN-FM in San Francisco two weeks later.

"He was torn between a music career and politics," said Jim Lipscomb, who spent a whole day with Harry in Los Angeles the day before his KSAN-FM hungerthon. "He said, 'You know, I realize if I quit the music business and went to Washington, I could save 250,000 people who are going to die of starvation.'"

Lipscomb, who cared for Harry as a father would a son, was not so much startled by Chapin's goals as by his means. Harry's frenetic pace reminded Jim of the days they worked together. "When he came out there, he was going faster than ever," said Lipscomb. "He was planning more things than ever and didn't leave enough time for any of them, and didn't sleep. It was a horrendous experience."

That day, May 14, Chapin had flown to California early in the morning after performing two concerts the night before in Omaha, Nebraska. He had not slept except for three bumpy hours on the plane and had a bad cold. When Lipscomb picked Chapin up at the airport, he looked forward to a quiet day with Harry, whom he hadn't seen in more than a year. Instead, Lipscomb found himself inexorably caught in Harry's nonstop activity.

Said Lipscomb: "As human beings, we were not really connecting. I felt on the edge of a whirlwind. I was sort of following along, and the whirlwind knew I was there. Sometimes you can be with somebody you care for and you almost don't have to talk and there's something going on between you. But that wasn't happening. He was interested in his life and I was interested in what he was doing. But there were all these other forces impinging, and he was sort of planning it that way."

Immediately after Chapin's arrival, they rushed to Ken Kragen's house. Harry wanted to play tennis. Some friends of Kragen's were already playing, so Harry and Jim got into a game of doubles. It was 11:00 A.M. and Chapin had a 1:00 P.M. benefit at a school an hour-and-a-half's drive from Los Angeles. "When it got to be 11:30, I didn't want to be rushed," said Jim. "So I quit tennis and got dressed. Then I waited until he was through playing at 12:30, which meant he knew we were going to be late."

They were late by an hour. Then Chapin sang for two hours, drove back to L.A., ate dinner and went to a performance of a musical called *Chapin* at the Improvisation Theatre. It was a simple, musical revue based on Harry's story songs. Chapin had yet to see the show, which had opened on January 30, 1977.

Chapin was conceived by its coproducer Joe Stern, who had been a longtime fan of Chapin's and got the idea for the musical after seeing Harry on Broadway in *The Night That Made America Famous*. The show "didn't do well," Stern said at the time. "But I thought there was a special magic to it—to this guy. I think what makes him important is that he transcends the record."

Stern believed Chapin's musical stories lent themselves to theatrical productions and were so powerful in and of themselves that a show could be based on them alone, without the eclectic razzmatazz that marred . . . *America Famous.* He and actor William Devane, who coproduced *The Changing Room,* teamed up again for *Chapin,* a cabaret-style production that resembled *Jacques Brel Is Alive and Well and Living in Paris.* The show was cast with five singers: Scott Jarvis, Wings Hauser, Barbara Illey, Jennifer Darling and George Ball (who was in the New York cast of *Jacques Brel . . .*). Together they sang twenty-one of Chapin's story songs, most of them standards such as "Taxi," "W*O*L*D," "Better Place to Be," "Cat's in the Cradle," "Mr. Tanner," plus selections from *On the Road to Kingdom Come* and an unrecorded song from Chapin's Broadway show.

For Harry, the production was a major compliment. *Chapin,* wrote the World Rock News Service that year, marks "the first time that a contemporary American artist has been honored with a theatrical presentation comprised entirely of his own compositions." Unlike *The Night That Made America Famous,* the presentation was also blessed with a much shorter title. Still, Chapin continued to be jinxed with the curse of those who could not remember his name. After one performance of *Chapin,* a sixty-year-old man, evidently a little hard of hearing, said to Joe Stern, "You know, I love Chopin. I didn't realize he had so much range."

Chapin was a critical success. It eventually ran for more than seven months. "Even so, after the performance, Harry had a meeting with the cast to give them some tips," said Lipscomb. "Very strong tips—'You've gotta sing it this way. Don't sing it that way. Play this chord this way'—and just talking as fast as he could."

Afterward, one of the singers asked Harry if he would listen to his girlfriend's songs. So the three of them drove half an hour to a studio on the outskirts of Los Angeles. There the girlfriend sang for an hour as Harry helped her with improvements on her music.

By now it was 12:15 A.M., and Chapin had a one o'clock flight to San Francisco, where he was to go on the air for twenty-six hours straight as host of a hungerthon on KSAN-FM. Lipscomb rushed Chapin to the airport barely in time for him to catch his flight.

Lipscomb said of the day's experience: "I've never seen anybody do anything like that in my life. To me that would be punishment. He couldn't say no to anybody about anything. There just weren't that many opportunities when he was younger. But now there were dozens of them. At the same time, it was hard for me to imagine Harry growing old, or even into middle age at the rate he drove himself. It seemed so frantic. You'd think, this man can't stand to contemplate! He can't stand himself! Yet, if that were true, how had he written all of these songs and poems? He obviously reflected sometime, somewhere. But I've never seen him. Those things took time, hours. But I've never seen those hours. I never saw him contemplative. He was always turned outward."

The following day, Lipscomb—out of true love, concern, even fear—wrote Harry a six-page handwritten letter. In it he tried to analyze on a healthy level what he saw, and the sense of doom he felt.

It's a Sunday morning. I'm listening to quiet music and watching the early morning surfers, pleased today at my solitude and this time of repose. In a few minutes you will have to be running for breakfast if you are to have one before the talkathon begins. The idea that you, after your Saturday, face 26 more hours with your little sleep and a runny nose and throat leaves me in head-shaking wonder or concern. I'm not sure which emotion is appropriate, but this letter is inspired by concern, and I hope you will hear what I say without being angry with me or a knee-jerk rejection.

You have always run harder than other people, and it was always kind of charming and funny. But to me yesterday was, as I think back on it in reflection, not funny. I'm of two minds actually. Maybe you are a superman. The trappings of your life would suggest a shallow man who is obsessive about work and movement. But your poetry shows you are a reflective man who carefully weighs both personal and social concerns, so you cannot be that shallow man, and may be a superman. The story is half told. You are 35.

I am concerned that you may not be a superman and that it may take some desperate shock—if you are lucky—to awaken you to a mortality you share with the rest of us.

There are other drugs than heroin. Work, movement, living on the edge, can become a habit. They can also become so closely tied in with one's sense of self that they have a strength, a possessiveness greater than habit. I don't know whether you would like yourself if you were not pushing harder than anyone you know.

If you are not a superman, but are instead captured by this picture of yourself as a superman, then your life has to be exacting a terrible toll. Think about this. One-half of those who suffer from fatal heart attacks have no warning. I remember that you said yesterday that in setting up your schedule you never take into account that you may be under the weather. But you also do not take into account that the body needs rest, the mind needs repose, and your pressure toward motion is self-imposed. The boy in the parking lot said, "Why are you hurrying?" and there was no real answer because we were not pressed then for time, but you were galloping anyway.

Sometimes the best thing that can happen to a young man—if he is not a superman—is a warning . . . Harry, you seem to me to be treating your body almost as an antagonist. You are organized toward jet lag, to few hours of sleep, to shouting over a crowd in a smoke-filled room when your voice is already breaking with fatigue. It seems that you are out to exhibit that you do not have to worry about your body machine like the rest of us. Is that part of the act? Or is that just the off-hand view that observers get when they are close to a superbeing? I truly don't know the answer, but I suspect it is a bit of both—both an extraordinary human being and a showboat . . .

So I found myself watching you, not knowing what I was feeling or sure what I should be feeling. Should I be aghast or awed?

Was pity or wonder more called for? Surely I know I was watching an extraordinary exhibition, which was both attractive and wearing. I found myself wondering what it was like to live with you. Would one feel the excitement of being on the edge of a hurricane? To survive it, would one have to have a kind of worship or the ability to turn off the mind as one does in a room with a loud TV that is fascinating to watch but goes on very well by itself with no attention at all?

So I left bemused. My every instinct cries out, "That way leads to disaster," but my mind says, "What the hell, at 35 he has already accomplished more than many men at the end of their lives. A superman cannot lead a life which mere mortals consider normal or logical. Or maybe he is destined to die young. Who's to tell a candle how fast it should burn? Or is he a long-lasting candle that just burns brighter than those around him—and will burn as long or longer than all the rest?" You gave me a fascinating and confusing day, you see.

> Love,
> Jim

In a letter dated June 25, 1977, Harry replied to Jim, thanking him for his concern but ignoring the letter just the same.

CHAPTER XIV

I Wonder What Would
Happen to This World

In July 1977, Harry Chapin took Washington, D.C. by storm. During that summer and early fall, Chapin spent three and four days each week trudging through congressional offices from early morning until late afternoon. His goal was to gain both advice and support for a Presidential Commission on Domestic and International Hunger, a commission that he hoped would create a cohesive food and hunger policy for the United States. By early evening, Chapin taxied to National Airport and flew off to perform a concert in some distant city.

The idea for a Presidential Commission came from Sandy. "My best ideas always did," Harry once said. Two months earlier, Congressman Tom Downey and Father Bill Ayres met at Chapin's home to discuss world hunger and the sad reality that twenty-three government agencies spent $9.5 billion a year on hunger-related programs, yet the problem continued. They conceived the idea of a hunger impact statement to be presented to Congress every two years to gauge the general effectiveness of these programs. The statement, though, would not have any real influence. So at one point, Sandy interrupted them and said, "What you guys need is a Presidential Commission."

At first Chapin scoffed at the idea. In the past, most Presidential commissions turned out to be little more than window dressing for administration study groups who filed reports soon forgotten. "But the more I thought about it, it made sense," said Chapin. "They had commissions for every douche-bag thing you could think of, and here was a gigantic issue being namby-pambied about and I couldn't come up with a better idea, so I said, 'Let's try it.'"

In order to create a Presidential Commission, Chapin first had to find cosponsors for the idea (one from the House and one from the Senate), and then put that idea in the form of a bill or resolution. The resolution would have to pass both congressional bodies, and if it did, it would be sent to President Carter's desk for his approval or rejection.

Downey recommended two politicians who might agree to become the "godfathers" of such a resolution: Senator Patrick Leahy of Vermont and Congressman Rick Nolan of Minnesota, both young, liberal Democrats who had a consistent (though short) history of skepticism regarding the efficiency of presidential commissions and U.S. food aid programs. Their support would add credibility to the resolution.

Chapin met with each man. "He told me about World Hunger Year and his ideas for a hunger commission," said Nolan. "He said that it could be the beginning of making our domestic, international and agricultural policies more effective because most of the studies on hunger had either been domestic or international, and the hunger problem many times fell through the crack. At first, I must admit, I was a little skeptical of Harry's sincerity."

So was Leahy. "We were besieged daily by someone in the entertainment field. People who suddenly decided, 'Well, this week I'll be into feeding Bangladesh, or snail butter. That'll be my crusade for the week and maybe I'll get a spot in the newspapers.' I think most of us got a little bit wary after a while."

But, within a few days, both men saw that Chapin was committed and agreed to cosponsor the resolution. "I refused to sponsor any such resolutions in the past," said Leahy. "This was my first. I didn't want to sponsor any unless I thought they were extremely meritorious. And I doubted very much if I'd see another one anywhere near as meritorious as this one. A great deal of my reaction to it was also based on Harry's enthusiasm. He was willing to pound the halls day after day. He was also extremely knowledgeable. In fact, in a number of areas, he was far better versed than I."

Chapin's next mission was to gather the necessary technical expertise to draft the resolution, that is, what it would say and how it should be written. Leahy and Nolan recommended that Chapin talk to agriculture and nutrition expert John Kramer, perhaps the most important man in his field in Washington. He was also exceedingly savvy about Presidential commissions. Kramer was an assistant to Representative Thomas Foley, President Carter's personal advisor on farm and agricultural policy and chairman of the House Agriculture Relations Committee. Kramer, then, was an indirect advisor to the President. So if anybody knew how the resolution should be drawn, Kramer did.

On July 28, Chapin took the seven A.M. shuttle flight to Washington. At the airport, he was greeted by WHY's new codirectors, Geri Barr and Wray MacKay (who replaced Steve Spinola, and who frequently joined Chapin during his intensive days of lobbying). Geri Barr was an attractive blonde in her early thirties with an impressive knowledge of the hunger issue; and MacKay, in his early forties, sported a thick brown beard, glasses, and receding hairline, and had the quiet reserve of a country butler.

During the past year, the trio had regularly lobbied Congress to increase the visibility of World Hunger Year, and share information on the hunger issue. On a typical day, they fit in as many as fifteen appointments with various congressmen, senators, and their aides, who advised their bosses. For such occasions, Chapin transposed himself from concert corduroy to his light brown, three-piece "lobbying suit," his neat appearance betrayed only by his overstuffed, hippielike leather shoulder bag. The appointments were scheduled thirty minutes apart as Chapin rushed frantically from meeting to meeting, with Wray and Geri hopelessly trying to keep pace.

By two P.M. that July day, after a series of twelve meetings, the WHY connection found themselves in the Longworth Building on Capitol Hill in the office of John Kramer. Kramer was twenty minutes late. Chapin hated to be kept waiting. But today he didn't mind so much and was in particularly fine spirits because Congress had unanimously passed his hunger impact statement the prior afternoon. The legislation had been presented by Congressman Downey as a trustee member of WHY, one of seven members including Harry's uncle, Michael Burke, and Harry's brother James.

Finally John Kramer arrived. He was a heavyset, brown-haired man with a thick mustache and a garrulous sense of humor. In many ways (except for the mustache), he resembled James. After more small talk, Chapin switched to automatic pilot and began his typical five-minute monologue, speaking so rapidly and with such intensity that a listener was left with the feeling there was nothing left to be said.

"Well, what I wanted to acquaint you with is we're zeroing in on a Presidential Commission on hunger and we need your sophistication . . . The whole idea of this commission . . . There's a consortium of twelve corporations . . . So . . . $17 million of taxpayer money . . . In Honduras and Haiti . . . I mean, it's death on the land . . . In 1776, there was a war network. The sugar crop . . . Then the hillsides eroded because all the topsoil . . ."

By meeting's end, Kramer told Chapin exactly what he needed to know, specifically that he should pattern his commission resolution after the one for International Women's Year. "Just take every single power they have and make sure yours has the same ones," said Kramer. "They have totally broad power and you don't want to have any limitations on the use of your money."

Then Kramer paused.

"You know, a lot of cynics will think of the commission as a buyoff," Kramer added. "They'll think, 'Oh, that'll keep the hunger groups quiet. Quick, give 'em a commission.' That's what Nixon tried to do in '69."

He paused again.

"It's a locker room down there," he continued, referring to Congress. "I've been on that floor for twelve hours in the last two days and it's a very cynical bunch. They'll make fun of the commission idea and at the same time sign it. They're a funny group. If you get 300 supporters, 150 are going to be skeptical and sign it with no real belief."

"Well, as long as they sign it," said Chapin, unfazed. "That's what counts! Besides, when I get done with them—they may not believe—but they'll sure be listening!"

Chapin kept the rest of his appointments, then met with Senator Leahy and Congressman Nolan to see if they approved of Kramer's suggestions. They did, so at six o'clock, wasting no time, Chapin began the creation of the resolution, Nolan allowing the threesome the use of his office. Geri and Wray sat behind Nolan's desk drafting the resolution, while Chapin, having no concert that night, sat in the adjoining room, editing and typing it.

By ten P.M. the four-page resolution was finished. It began as Kramer said it should, with a series of short general statements pointing out the need for a Presidential Commission preceded by the word *whereas,* for instance: "Whereas the United States has at present no clearly defined and/or universally understood Food and Hunger Policy . . ." Eight such statements were concluded by, "Therefore, let it be resolved that . . ." The resolution then delineated the commission's duties, composition, goals, powers, administration, and cooperation with other government agencies. It specified that the commission last two years, the first year to analyze and collate all existing government hunger studies and programs. At the end of the first year, an interim report was to be sent to the President. The second year, the commission was to devote itself to public education and the preparation of a final report with conclusive recommendations. The proposed cost was $5 million.

When it was all over, Harry telephoned his triumph to Sandy. "We wrote a little bit of history today, hon." By eleven P.M., he was back on the shuttle to New York, the last flight out of town. Wray MacKay and Geri Barr joined him, sitting bleary-eyed at the rear of the plane. But Chapin stood jubilantly in the aisle, his arms spread-eagle against the overhead baggage racks, his mind racing, plotting which politicians he could persuade to support the resolution. Nervously he shouted instructions to Geri and Wray, who desperately tried to stay attentive and take notes.

"What made it difficult working with Harry," said Geri, "was that when he got excited about something, he talked nonstop and spun off a thousand ideas which nobody else could keep up with. He'd make statements and plans, and dream and dream and dream until I found myself in a position to say, 'Hey, slow down! Go slow. We can't do all that.' I remember once talking to him in a car where I actually had to reach over and put my hands on his knees to hold him still and say, 'Now, look, I want you to hear what I'm saying!'"

Twenty minutes later, Chapin was still shouting instructions. Then he paused for a minute and looked down at the aisle floor. "You know, I've slept two hours in the last two days," he finally said. "And I know that might sound crazy, but I could really go for a game of tennis!" He looked up at Geri and Wray for their reaction.

They were fast asleep.

* * *

On paper, the Presidential Commission looked like a superb anti-hunger strategy, if it could only get passed by Congress. In the weeks following, Chapin accelerated his commission campaign, often flying to Washington during early morning hours after his evening concert appearances. Then, having slept on the plane, he rushed off to the Capitol to lobby his cause. "During one seventeen-day stretch," said Chapin, "I didn't sleep in a bed."

To aid the effort, Congressman Nolan distributed more than two hundred "Dear Colleague" letters to persuade congressmen to support the resolution. But, such letters could only generate between 50 and 100 supporters at best, and Chapin needed at least 250. So Leahy and Nolan gave him a list of key congressmen and senators to approach. If Chapin had trouble convincing them, Leahy and Nolan made personal appeals. But that wasn't too often. Harry pestered political targets out of committee hearings and in washrooms to give them his impassioned speech. Once at a breakfast meeting with two congressmen in the House of Representatives' dining room, Chapin got so worked up that he pounded the table with his fist, accidentally spilling hot coffee in the laps of both men, whose cries of pain turned the heads of all nearby munching pols.

But Harry didn't restrict his antihunger crusade to Washington alone. He spoke out wherever he went, from concert halls to television talk shows. In fact, he became so obsessed with the topic that even after twenty *Tonight Show* appearances, he was rarely invited on the program and only when a guest host was present. "They looked at it as an entertainment show," said Ralph Nader. "That's why Johnny Carson for a while didn't have consumer people like me on. They don't want any bad news after 11:30 P.M., even if it came with how to make the news less bad."

"I told Harry," said Zeke Marsden. "His big fault was, once he got on a show, he started talking about the world hunger situation. I know how concerned he was about it, but people were there to be entertained. They don't want to hear about the fuckin' sad, sad world. They must have thought, 'Oh, shit, here comes Harry Chapin, the guy with the guitar, and he's gonna start talkin' about hungry kids.'"

Once, after a full day of lobbying the resolution in Washington, Chapin called Zeke and Peachy and invited them for dinner before a performance in Providence, Rhode Island. "We had a beautiful dinner," said Zeke. "Harry had just come back from thirteen appointments with senators. Well, for Christ's sake, he thought he was still in Washington. He was using all them fifty-dollar words. I didn't understand a fuckin' word he was saying. After we got him to slow down, he must have looked across the table and thought, 'Oh, shit, I'm with Zeke and Peachy.' But that was also the beauty of the guy. He could put himself in any situation. At my house, I had a cross-section of friends, and Harry could talk fifty-dollar words with fifty-dollar-word people, or swear out of the side of his mouth."

By late September, the resolution was shaping up well. Chapin already had the support of all the key politicians such as Majority Whip Jim Wright of the House Agricultural Relations Committee, Senator Frank Church of the Foreign Relations Committee, and senators such as John Anderson, Tom Clark, Robert Dole and Ted Kennedy (Chapin particularly enjoyed lobbying him). The resolution was also endorsed by Senator George McGovern, who was the principal architect of the Food for Peace Program under President John F. Kennedy, and Hubert Humphrey, who was Pat Leahy's mentor and a firm believer in Presidential commissions. Unfortunately, Humphrey died a few months later of cancer.

But the most important person Chapin did not have was Representative Thomas Foley, John Kramer's boss, who abstained from endorsement, not because he "didn't think the resolution meritorious, but because, as a rule, I never supported resolutions before my own [agriculture] committee." But Foley's support would almost guarantee that of President Carter, even Congress.

So to rally him to his corner, Chapin flew to the state of Washington and gave a benefit for Foley in his district. A few days later, Foley endorsed the resolution. "That was a major coup," said Congressman Nolan. "At that point, everything looked pretty well set."

But Chapin took no chances, as a congressional by-law prohibited more than twenty-five congressmen from sponsoring a bill in the House. "So we introduced bill after bill," Chapin told *Rolling Stone* magazine. "No one had ever seen so many bills."

On the day the bills were presented, Chapin made sure politicians did not forget their promises of endorsement. He stood with his guitar at the top of the white marble steps of the Capitol and gave a free concert for congressmen and their aides. Ironically, there was a film crew nearby producing a documentary on the energy crisis, spearheaded by Chapin's old boss from Drew Associates, Don Pennebaker. Pennebaker immediately had his crew shift their positions and film the entire concert rally, unbeknownst to Harry. "It was really something," said Pennebaker. "Harry had the whole Capitol buzzing."

It was reflected in the voting. By day's end, the resolution had 258 sponsors in the House and passed that body by a vote of 364–38. In the Senate, the vote was unanimous. It was then sent to President Carter's desk for his verdict (which would not come for five months). However, everyone agreed, from Ralph Nader to Rick Nolan, that Chapin's amateur politicking was truly extraordinary.

"I've never seen anything like it," said Nolan. "The traditional Washington lobbyist was well paid for the job he did and worked much slower and more casually. So to have a private citizen work the halls of Congress as effectively and comprehensively as he did was truly remarkable. In fact, he not only worked the halls of Congress effectively, he worked the administration effectively. He tried to nip any possible source of friction by anticipating the obstacles that might emerge and went after them before they reached the budding stage. He had everything covered, from the Secretary of Agriculture to the Secretary of State, the White House staff and all the key congressmen."

To supplement his antihunger campaign that September, Chapin started a bimonthly magazine called *Food Monitor*. It offered news updates and feature articles on food, agriculture and the hunger crisis in general. Chapin wrote several pieces for it over the years.

On October 15, Chapin performed a benefit to raise funds for the creation of the Food Policy Center, WHY's lobbying arm in Washington, D.C. The concert was held at Detroit's Olympia Stadium and featured John Denver, James Taylor and Gordon Lightfoot. From it, Chapin raised $156,000; $56,000 to WHY and $100,000 toward the purchase of a Washington brownstone to house the Food Policy Center, which subsequently hired a small but full-time staff.

In the meantime, Chapin fought and won his fight with Elektra that *Dance Band on the Titanic* be a double album, but not without considerable struggle. After five months of recording, Chapin was delighted with the final mix of the album, especially his autobiographical epic, "There Only Was One Choice." In addition, the title song (and the album's single) also appeared strong and Chapin made up his mind. "I'm just going to say this is going to be a double album," he said at the time. "I'm not even going to play any games with it."

Chapin informed Elektra chairman Joe Smith of his decision. Smith sent Ralph Ebler (then in charge of East Coast artist relations) to the Manhattan studio to hear the final product. Chapin's booking agent, Ed Rubin of Magna Artists, was also present, and they all seemed impressed. Harry asked Elber, who'd always been a die-hard fan, to be the album's cheerleader. "I asked him to spread the word with all the Elektra people on the West Coast," Harry said. "To start ticklin' 'em that this was going to be a motherfucker."

But Smith didn't think Chapin's "artistic considerations" were worth the merchandising expense of a double album, which was confirmed a few days after Elber's visit when Ann Purtill showed up at the studio. "I was supposed to talk Harry out of a double *Titanic*," said Purtill. "Elektra told me I was the only person he listened to, which of course was a lie. Harry didn't listen to anybody."

"In a lot of ways," said Don Ruthig, "Harry threw his middle finger up at all of them and said, 'Screw you, guys. I'm putting out a double album. The music is good. The production is excellent. The album's right there. And I'm not going to let you butcher it up and just give a little bit of it. You've got to take all or none.'"

In quite another way, Chapin did not feel he was being obstinate. His only double album, *Greatest Stories Live,* continued to sell at a pace of 10,000 copies per month. And in 1976 and 1977, other artists scored big hits with double albums such as Stevie Wonder, Peter Allen, Nils Lofgren, Santana, Paul McCartney and Wings and Peter Frampton (whose album *Live* sold more than six million copies). Chapin knew he was not in their sales league, but he also knew that in 1977, the record-buying public was the largest in the industry's history, an industry that generated more than the combined income of all three major television networks, the film industry and trade book publishing. In short, he felt the market would bear a Harry Chapin double album.

"Finally, Elektra did give in," said Chapin. "But I think they felt a little bit screwed." Harry's main worry was that Elektra would retaliate by not promoting the record, although at first it didn't appear that way. On June 11, Chapin was given the Humanitarian Award by the Music and Performing Arts Lodge of B'nai Brith at its thirteenth annual awards dinner in New York. The dinner was emceed by WNEW-FM personality Allison Steele and attended by more than 600 people, including several Elektra executives like President Mel Posner. Chapin accepted the award by giving his "Dance-Band-on-the-Titanic speech," asserting that people, like music, should be more involved in social concerns; that music alone is not enough. "If all we're going to do," he said, "is dance the night away and ignore our problems like those patrons in the Titanic's ballroom, then we shouldn't be surprised when the iceberg hits."

Afterward, Chapin received a standing ovation. Posner congratulated Sandy on her husband's speech. "You know, I really pray for the day when Elektra is going to come around and recognize what Harry Chapin is all about," Sandy told him. "Everybody wants a million seller. But I don't think you know what an important contribution Harry is making to the industry as a whole."

"Oh, we really do," Posner protested kindly. "As a matter of fact, with this next album, we're going all out! For the first time, we really are."

Shortly thereafter, Elektra threw a lavish $10,000 advance press party for the release of *Dance Band on the Titanic,* on a fifty-foot yacht that sailed around the tip of Manhattan's summer skyline. But that was where the promotion began and ended. When the album was released in late August, Elektra already knew they did not have a hit single in the album's title song or short version, and once again it met the same old fate.

"They figured they'd just merchandise my usual quarter-of-a-million die-hard fans," said Chapin. "And they did. That's what it sold. But I was pissed off for Steve because I wanted it to be a big success for him."

The album was reviewed favorably on an artistic level. In *Billboard* magazine's September 3 issue, *Dance Band on the Titanic* was chosen as the week's "Top Album Pick" and "There Only Was One Choice" was described as "the album's shiner." They also advised music dealers: "Chapin is at his best here."

The album was surprisingly well received in England, where Chapin happened to be during the first week of September on a two-week European tour. London's *Sunday Times* tabbed *Dance Band* as the number-one album of the year. "Randy Newman and Yes came close," wrote *Times* music critic Derek Jewell. "But the best album of the year had, ultimately, to be Chapin's. . . . There can't be better songs about the way we live . . . nor better flights of documentary imagination . . . nor apter, more original instrumental arrangements. . . . A work of absolute inventive artistry."

But as usual, Chapin also drew strong negative reaction. The same week he was in London, another local paper concluded a less than glowing piece on *Titanic,* saying, "No wonder it sank!"

And because the album's single (like most of his recent works) received marginal airplay, *Rolling Stone* magazine in its year-end issue dubbed its "worst single of the year" category as the "Harry Chapin Award."

For the most part, Chapin overlooked the failure of his commercial comeback because the social activist side of his life had progressed beyond his wildest dreams. This included not only the commission resolution and WHY (which had become one of the largest and most respected hunger organizations in the country), but PAF as well. By October 1977, Chapin had convinced twelve owners of forty-one McDonald's franchises on Long Island to give the foundation a grant of $25,000 to transform a defunct grammar school in Centerport, New York, into a children's theater, which was subsequently named the PAF-McDonald's Youth Theater.

Chapin also obtained a five-year $334,753 Challenge Grant from the Ford Foundation to subsidize PAF's Playhouse. The Challenge Grant meant that if PAF matched the sum of the Ford grant through fundraising, the money was theirs to keep. If it did, it also meant that at the end of the grant's five-year period, PAF would have balanced books for the first time in sixteen years. So Chapin immediately kicked off a $700,000 fundraising drive to meet the terms of the grant, wipe out PAF's existing deficit ($250,000), and double the size of PAF's present 253-seat theater (at a cost of $200,000), this to meet the ever-increasing number of subscribers (then 10,000) due to the success of Jay Broad's productions.

The significance of the grant was far-reaching. It signaled a major step in Chapin's quest for PAF's financial stability and immediately turned it into Long Island's largest cultural and educational tax-exempt foundation. But more importantly, the grant marked the Ford Foundation's "biggest single commitment to the development of American theater in its fifteen-year history." In fact, during that period, only about sixty such grants were approved, and only two organizations were able to "meet the challenge." The grant was further remarkable in that it came from an organization with rigid acceptance codes, and at a time of severe grant cutbacks.

But the Ford Foundation was confident "in the theater's current leadership," and that "necessary matching funds can be raised." At a press conference that October, Roger Kennedy, the senior financial officer and vice president of the Ford Foundation, said, "After carefully studying PAF Playhouse for the past twelve months, we feel it has an excellent chance to become economically viable if it can retire its current debt and move into a larger facility. The theater promises to be one of the country's leading professional theaters."

The failure of Chapin's music comeback was further minimized by the sudden recognition he received for his social activist efforts. Besides B'nai Brith's Humanitarian Award and a bevy of honors bestowed on him by various charity organizations over the years, Chapin won the 1977 Man of the Year Award from both the Junior Achievers of New York and the Long Island Advertising Club. He was also honored by the United States Jaycees as "one of the ten most outstanding young men in America," of whom past recipients included John F. Kennedy, Nelson Rockefeller, Gerald Ford, Henry Ford, Joe Louis, Orson Welles, Howard Hughes and Leonard Bernstein. From contemporary music, the only other recipient besides Chapin was Elvis Presley.

At these awards functions, Chapin wore a distinguished black tuxedo, and once at the podium, put on his gold-trimmed glasses and gave what often was a dynamic address.

"It was a whole different personality," said Sandy, who often joined her husband for such functions. "It was like a metamorphosis, as though he just pressed a button. He was definitely an actor. I used to think he could only act Harry Chapin. But now he had a lot of roles."

Said Chapin, in a familiar speech at one awards ceremony: "If these awards serve to give a small bit of attention to the fact that this is a participatory democracy, then they are truly worthwhile. It is a wonderful feeling to be honored for doing things I deeply believe in. On the other hand, successful performers have the responsibility to show they care about the millions of people who care about them, people who need more help than just music can bring."

Chapin was able to address those performers directly on September 15, 1977, when, on national television, he was finally presented with an award for outstanding public service during the third annual Rock Music Award show. In total, there were six winners, and Chapin was the last to speak. Dressed in his "award outfit," Chapin waited for the splash of horns to die down, and then jumped right in, offering an aggressive monologue. He chided his peers for their snobbism and, after a long description of his typical weekly schedule, emphasized that benefit concerts were part of the natural ongoing order of his life.

Chapin, he was trying to say, wasn't there for good PR. He was always THERE. He continued in this vein long after he was motioned to end his speech, and finally did when the network cut him off and shot a commercial.

* * *

By 1978, for the first time, the frenetic pace of Chapin's life began to subside as he paid increasing attention to his family. In the fall, Chapin's oldest daughter, Jaime, now eighteen years old, would be leaving for Hamilton College. He realized it was the last opportunity for the whole family to be together. So on his concert itineraries, Sundays and Mondays were now reserved as "personal time," and from Christmas 1977 through most of the month of January, 1978, Harry enjoyed his family in Hubbardton, Vermont, where he had recently purchased a new vacation home. It was a small, wood-framed house located along a gorgeous, spring-fed lake and was previously owned and built by Eva and Allan Breckinridge, friends of Sandy's who lived in Teaneck, New Jersey.

"The Breckinridges also had a house in Vermont, and for four years we used to visit them and go skiing," said Harry. "They introduced me to skiing. They were also part of the first audiences at the Village Gate and helped Sandy and me when we went through our marital troubles.

"They bought some property across the lake from their house and built this new one. But they weren't able to sell it and convinced us to take it. It was not a bad real estate buy. Sandy had this vision of us being a ski family and anything Sandy wanted was fine with me because she hadn't had so many money goals and I had been spending a lot of money with PAF and WHY and everything else. Also, the Breckenridges had three kids, so it was a good social thing for our kids. I put down $25,000 and mortgaged the rest (approximately $60,000)."

Chapin's family preoccupations were reflected in his ninth album, *Living Room Suite*. Most of the songs were written during his time in Vermont. Two songs on the album were based on his daughter Jenny ("Why Do Little Girls" and "Jenny"); one about his son Joshua ("Dancin' Boy), and one, about Sandy ("It Seems Only You Love Me When It Rains"). There was also a song called "Poor Damned Fool" about Sandy's ex-husband Jim Cashmore, who had died a few months earlier, and one about children's education, "Flowers Are Red." In addition, Chapin included an easy-listening tune called "If You Want to Feel" and two songs of social commentary, "Somebody Said," which spoke of the direction of American music and was a derivative of his *Dance Band* theme, and "I Wonder What Would Happen to This World," about social activist commitment.

Unlike previous albums, the songs on *Living Room Suite* were not story songs but "mainstream feel numbers," with the exception of "Flowers Are Red," the album's only single and the only song Chapin felt a deep personal commitment toward. In the story, Harry chastised the lack of creativity and self-expression in children's education. He was primarily inspired by a report card of Susan Gensel's eldest son, Robbie, whom Harry affectionately described at concerts (when introducing the song) as a "marvelous Huck Finn–type kid." In the report card, the teacher made one comment that boiled Chapin's blood: "Robbie started the year marching to a different drummer, but he is gradually joining the parade."

"I thought it was really disgusting," Chapin said. "If that's the goal of our education system, Robert Frost should've written, 'Two roads diverged into the woods and I took the one more traveled by.' The song was also partly triggered by a poem Sandy showed me by a first-grade teacher saying how things should be done, and I had been trying to write a song about teaching and education for years."

For the most part, "Flowers Are Red" was successful from a melodic and lyrical standpoint, but the same could not be said of the rest of *Living Room Suite*. None of the other songs impressed, and they lacked much of the "emotional connection" Chapin seemed to have regained with *Dance Band on the Titanic*. Part of the reason was that Chapin spent himself on *Dance Band;* he said most everything he wanted to say. Also, he had grown discouraged with Elektra Records. He felt he had "taken his best shot on *Dance Band*" and that "no matter what I hand in to them from here on," he said at the time, "it will be greeted with disinterest."

Chapin decided to let Elektra "take their best shot" and hire a "new big-gun producer." He was Chuck Plotkin, the head of A&R at the label and recommended to Chapin by Jon Landau. "On the album, Steve was relegated to arranger and keyboards, but it was Steve's decision," said Harry. "I told him that if he really wanted to produce the album, I'd tell Elektra to shove it. But Steve said, 'Let's make Elektra call their bluff.' What we were finally down to, if we were going to make a go of it with the record company at all, was to let them have their way."

In late January, Chapin went into Secret Sound Studios in New York and completed *Living Room Suite* in less than one month. Most of the songs were recorded in just a few takes, as producer Plotkin wanted to emphasize "freshness" over "slick, overplayed arrangements."

"We'd play a song a couple of times and if there was any problem he'd make everybody leave the studio and just work on the sound problem," said Chapin. "So that we never played a song more than six times. If there were any miniature mistakes, he wouldn't worry about it."

But perhaps Plotkin should have. Though the material was hardly Chapin's finest, the production also lacked imagination. The music sounded insufferably tired and thin and was, by far, Chapin's weakest musical effort to date, and he knew it. In fact, after the album was released in mid-June, Chapin went back into the studio to rerecord a few of the songs, but to no avail. By that time, "Flowers Are Red" was already rejected from AM airplay and *Living Room Suite* was a victim of poor promotion and poor reviews, best typified by *New York* magazine, which voted it "one of the top ten worst albums of the year."

Plotkin, then, was not the "big-gun" producer Elektra had hoped for, and soon after the album's release, he left the record company. The album left Chapin in a neglected and irrevocable position, and symbolically marked the end of his relationship with Elektra.

*   *   *

On February 3, 1978, President Carter scheduled a 9:45 A.M. meeting with the key sponsors of the Presidential Committee resolution. It was Carter's intention to hear their case and give his verdict. For Chapin, the zenith of his social activist career was about to come.

The night before, Chapin was in Hamilton, Ontario, for two group concerts at the Hamilton Place Theater. That night Chapin was more restless and hyper than, as Zeke Marsden fondly described him, "a half-fucked fox in a forest fire." During the sound check, Chapin sat alone in a backstage dressing room, rushing through his set of songs, practicing guitar chord changes and singing lyrics under his breath. When he finished, he jogged to the backstage lobby entrance and made his usual preconcert call to Sandy. He spoke for half an hour, saying everything and anything cuddled up in a corner under a wall pay phone. Harry knew that Carter could "nix" the commission he worked so hard to create.

At one A.M., after the second show, Harry gathered his belongings in anticipation of the big day ahead. He already had his hair cut to "Republican length," and now he collected his shoulder bag, "lobbying suit," toilet kit and hair dryer (Chapin never traveled with a hair dryer).

Outside was more than a foot of snow—a blizzard—as we drove through the bleakness of what came to be known as the blizzard of 1977 to Buffalo, New York, and Butler Aviation, where Chapin had reserved a small charter plane to take him to Washington since there were no regularly scheduled flights at that hour. But once in Buffalo, the blizzard intensified due to strong northeasterly winds whistling off Lake Erie. Buffalo Airport looked like a winter version of the famous airport scene in *Casablanca,* with heavy snow instead of mist creating near-zero visibility.

The runway was covered with a slick sheet of ice as Chapin placed one foot on the ladder of the fragile four-seat prop plane. His foot slipped. He turned to me, "Another Jim Croce special," he said half jokingly.

Twenty minutes later, after one abortive takeoff attempt, the plane was finally airborne, headed due south for Washington, but not without some tremulous moments. The flimsy aircraft was battered by high winds and swirling snow that froze the windshield wipers and tossed us into air pockets. We'd struggle up to previous altitudes only to be met by another fist of Mother Nature's wrath. In the meantime, Chapin, who was used to such flights, was scrunched up in the backseat, fast asleep; his head resting on his shoulder bag for a pillow, his apricot parka for a blanket.

We finally landed at Washington's National Airport at five A.M., the meeting with the President less than five hours away.

Chapin grabbed a taxi and instructed the driver to take us to the Hyatt Regency Hotel near Capitol Hill, one of the best in town.

"I just need a couple of hours' sleep," he said to me.

"But isn't the Hyatt a little expensive for two hours' sleep?"

"Yeah, but what the hell. It isn't every day you get to meet the President."

By 7:30 A.M., Chapin was properly attired as he walked out into the shiver of a gray Washington morning. He trekked the short distance to Senator Pat Leahy's office, where a quick strategy session was planned on how to present their case to the President. Rick Nolan and his farm expert, Randy Henningson, joined them.

"I've been to meetings with the President before," said Nolan, "where you have a number of people; you've got fifteen minutes. And they're all politicians and all damn good talkers, and unless your program's planned, you can get shot out of the saddle and suddenly find your fifteen minutes are up and never get a word in. So we weren't going to give the President an opportunity to respond, because I've also been at meetings with him where he did all the talking."

The four of them figured out a strategy to dominate the meeting. Leahy would introduce their purpose, quickly turn it over to Nolan, who'd discuss the political ramifications of the commission, and finally Chapin would relate the broad base of citizen interest. They allotted themselves two minutes each.

But Leahy also warned Chapin: "Carter might not give any commitment because he's been very reluctant to set up presidential commissions and has spoken against them. So he might be giving us the meeting to let us down easy."

Chapin didn't think so. Unlike previous Presidents, Carter was expressly concerned with human rights and related issues. For instance, the government program ACTION, which incorporated the Peace Corps, Vista, and Foster Parents, was disliked by Richard Nixon, who tried to eliminate it. And Gerald Ford, though he retained the program, sought only $6 million in appropriations for it. Under Carter, ACTION received $27 million.

By 8:30 A.M., all four men had a brief breakfast in the House of Representatives dining room with Senator Dick Clark, another resolution sponsor. Afterward, Chapin and Leahy piled into Clark's car (Nolan took his own) and headed for the White House. When they arrived at the front gate, Clark and Leahy flashed their identification. But Chapin had forgotten his. He had left it in his shoulder bag at Leahy's office. But Harry had been to the White House on so many occasions to meet with Chip Carter and other administration officials that one guard said, "Oh, that's Chapin. We know him," and let the car pass.

Inside, a hostess escorted them to a cabinet room adjacent to the Oval Office. The meeting was to be attended by eight congressmen, seven senators, and their aides. But it was still early, so only a handful of them were present: Congressman Ben Gilman of New York, Guy Herb of the National Security Council, and Allan Stone of the Nutrition Committee. They milled about, sipping coffee near a hospitality table. In the middle of the room was a long, oval mahogany conference table equipped with pads, pencils, ashtrays and, in front of the President's chair at the center of the table, a glass and thermal water pitcher atop a silver tray. But Harry was more interested in the Oval Office, and in between sips of coffee, occasionally glanced inside.

By 9:30 A.M., the rest of the troupe began to trickle in: Thomas Foley, George McGovern, Don Frazier of the House Foreign Relations Committee, and Robert Dole. Dole began shaking hands.

"Shake his left hand," Leahy whispered to Chapin. "His right hand was injured in the war."

Then Dr. Peter Bourne, the President's health counsel, arrived. "Well, we got this far," Chapin told him nervously. "Let's get over the hump."

At this point, they all started jockeying for seats. Leahy sat to the left of the President's chair, Nolan to the right. The rule was that cosponsors from the House and Senate sat to either side of

the President. Chapin sat in the Vice President's chair directly
across from Carter. They had planned it so that Carter would
have to face Chapin when he spoke.

At precisely 9:45 A.M., President Jimmy Carter marched into
the room. Everyone at the table stood up as he made his way to
his seat while shaking hands. At that very moment, a barrage of
photographers and reporters charged into the room. Cameras
clicked and flashed as the President made a two-minute opening
statement. At the end of his remarks, a tall White House staffer
in a dark suit ordered, "Okay, everybody out!" And they went.

The room fell silent.

Carter motioned to Leahy. And just as they planned it, the
relay started: Leahy to Nolan to Chapin, who, like a thoroughbred at the starting gate, plunged forward.

Mr. President, your campaign theme was a government as good
as its people. Well, there's no doubt about the goodness of the
American people and how they feel about this issue. Poll after
poll has showed they deeply care about doing something to affect
hunger. But they're very confused. They don't know what to do.
They've got major questions like why in a world where there's
enough food to feed everybody twice do half a billion people go
to bed hungry? And why in a country as rich as the United
States—the richest country in the world—do twenty million
people go to bed malnourished?

President Kennedy's Commission on Retarded Children
showed that of the six million retarded people in this country, half
have malnourishment as a significant cause. Americans are confused. They are confused when they see farm prices extremely
low and food prices in the supermarket so high and yet we are
losing our farmers.

But American public citizens are not the only ones confused. I
spent a lot of time talking to experts in the State Department,
Agriculture Department, Senate, and the House, and there's a lot
of concern. But there's very little agreement about which direction to go to solve this problem. Indeed, this confusion can be
seen even greater in that there's been study after study of all
kinds sitting in various cubbyholes all over Washington, but

there's been no attempt to collate these into a cohesive food and hunger policy.

At best, our programs are a bunch of Band-Aids. Some programs are good, but are not getting properly funded, while others are a complete waste of money and are getting far too much. I say it is time to give a clear-cut signal and collate. The problem with past commissions has been they haven't had effective follow-up. But the unique aspect of this commission is that during the first year we would study and disseminate the information to the public, and the second year help implement the recommendations of the commission in terms of the legislature. Now . . .

Chapin's two-minute allotment was already five minutes over. People stirred. There were coughs and nudges. Three minutes later, Chapin crossed the finish line and stopped.

"Well," said Carter in his soft southern drawl, "if this is the kind of enthusiasm that was brought to this resolution, I can understand why it's reached my desk."

Recalling the scene at the front gate, Senator Leahy added, "Yes, he's even infiltrated the White House."

Everyone chuckled.

"It's gotten so bad," Carter continued, "even Amy is asking me what I'm going to do about world hunger."

Carter flashed his famous smile. Everyone smiled. Chapin did not.

Then, with head slightly bowed, and in a voice so low it was barely audible, Carter murmured, "Yes, I think it's a good idea. Let's go ahead with it."

Chapin quickly glanced at Leahy, then Nolan, to confirm what he thought he heard. He heard it right. He began to smile, his eyes shone and widened. He'd done it! His populist dream had come true!

Two months later, another dream came true when Chapin's triumph was documented in a long article in *Rolling Stone,* but not without some coercion by Ralph Nader, who called up the magazine's publisher, Jann Wenner. "I told him that Chapin's lobbying job was the most effective I'd ever seen," said Nader. "I said, 'I know you people evidently don't like his music, but if you want to think of yourselves as involved in music and politics, you're really missing a story here.'"

So Wenner brought up the subject before an editorial board meeting and writer Dave Marsh, who was a friend of Bill Ayres, volunteered to write it. Later, in the liner notes of *Living Room Suite,* Chapin thanked Marsh for "having guts and a heart." The interview took place at Gaylord's, Chapin's favorite Indian restaurant in Manhattan. There he and Marsh and Bill Ayres talked for five hours.

"Later I also spoke with writers Chet Flippo and Chuck Young of the magazine," said Chapin. "It was amazing how positively defensive they were about the magazine's attitude toward me."

But the biggest surprise of all came to Chapin's fans, who were well aware of his adversarial relationship with the publication. In a letter to the editor in the following issue, one fan wrote: ". . . I knew the two of you would cross paths. Congratulations!" Another fan said: "Each year, one of your writers comes up with a piece that helps write that check for renewal. This year, please credit Dave Marsh with at least one renewal, mainly due to his piece on Harry Chapin."

However, the Presidential Commission did not get off to the auspicious start that Chapin expected. Dr. Peter Bourne, the President's health counsel, met with Chapin, Nolan and Leahy and asked them for a list of people they'd like to see on the commission, particularly, the name of a chairman. "Within a month's time," Bourne said, "the President will make a final decision on the list and sign an executive order."

Two weeks later Chapin, together with his staff at the Food Policy Center, drew up a list of names. "We didn't put any David Rockefeller– or Kingman Brewster–type names on it," Chapin said. "We put some nuts-and-bolts names on there because Allan Stone said the commission would be a disaster if the chairman turned out to be Carter's friend, who happened to be the head of Coca-Cola or General Motors."

Bourne submitted the list to Carter, who was dissatisfied with the results and asked to see more names. He sent a memo to the director of the National Security Council, Zbigniew Brzezinksi; Secretary of Agriculture, Bob Bergland; and head of the Democratic Council, Stuart Eizenstat, asking for their recommendations. When their lists were returned, the leading candidates for commission chairman were John David Rockefeller, David Rockefeller, Nelson Rockefeller and Dean Rusk.

Chapin boiled. "I'm not going to say anything, but they're names of the past," he said. "They're people of stature, but not of a willingness to grow. I mean, most of their careers are behind them. You can't expect those people to make any radical changes; they've done their bit. I'd much rather have a commission of live wires, people who have yet to be morally challenged."

Said Rick Nolan of Carter's initial list: "I was livid. Those names have simply come to symbolize excessive multinational power for too many people. I told Harry that if Carter goes and appoints somebody like that as head of the commission, I'm going to introduce legislation to destruct it!"

Finally, in early October, eight months after the White House meeting, President Carter signed the executive order for the Presidential Commission. He named a twenty-member panel and chose former Panama Canal negotiator Sol Linowitz as the chairman. The rest of the members were neither the "dignified honchos" Chapin wanted nor the Rockefellers and Rusks Carter first considered. Instead, the commission was composed of a wide variety of people, from Senator Robert Dole to 1970 Nobel Prize winner Norman Borlaug (father of the "green revolution") to Thomas Wyman (President of Green Giant Food Corporation) to singer John Denver and, of course, Chapin.

From October 1978, and for the next two years, Chapin concentrated his antihunger efforts almost solely on the commission's activities. Harry realized its success would have far greater impact on the hunger issue than anything else he could do, and that meant the end of his radio-hungerthons; his last one was on

KMET-FM in Los Angeles on Thanksgiving Day of 1978. Instead, Chapin attended the commission's bimonthly meetings (fifteen in all) in various cities throughout the country and regularly gave benefits for the Food Policy Center, whose main function was to oversee the commission's proceedings.

As the business of the commission heated up, Chapin tried to reduce his commitments, financial and otherwise, to PAF. For the moment, that meant securing PAF's financial future by matching the terms of the Ford Challenge Grant. In essence, PAF had to raise $575,000 by June 1978. But during the past six months, PAF's fundraising drive had netted only $325,000. So, in a last-minute attempt to raise money, Chapin scheduled a gala dinner and benefit concert for PAF at the Nassau Veteran's Coliseum on April 9, "the single largest glamour event in the history of Long Island," Chapin termed it.

"I've always been outspoken against such event-psychosis approaches to problems, but it was the only way I could raise that kind of cash in a short period of time. Besides, if I could pull this off, PAF would literally have a life of its own."

The dinner was a $125-a-plate celebrity affair of poached salmon and beef tenderloin at the Coliseum's Exhibition Hall. To cohost the occasion, Chapin already had commitments from actors Robert Redford and Jose Ferrer. He also lined up his father, Jim Chapin, and his group, Jazz Three, to provide the dance music. But it was the concert half of the evening that worried Harry. His overexposure on Long Island meant he would have to attract other performers far bigger than himself to fill the Coliseum's 16,000 seats.

So for two months, after the February Carter meeting, Chapin called every big-name artist he knew and asked them to join the effort: Jackson Browne, Elton John, Billy Joel, Kris Kristofferson, Stevie Wonder, Linda Ronstadt, John Denver, Bruce Springsteen and Gordon Lightfoot. But for one reason or another, none was available. The only performers who immediately consented besides Tom Chapin were Peter, Paul and Mary. They were staging a comeback after a six-year hiatus, and this was their first concert since being reunited. But to sell out the Coliseum, Chapin needed bigger drawing cards than Peter, Paul and Mary, which was what Paul Simon said when Chapin called him, and the only terms under which Simon would perform.

But as of two weeks before the concert, Chapin could find no one else. On that day, March 25, Chapin was home juggling the phone. He was not his usual hyper self. Instead, his movements were markedly slower. He was almost calm, reflective, even depressed. His face had a worried, discouraged look as he lay back on daughter Jaime's bed, his left hand behind his head, which was propped against a pillow. With his right hand, he fidgeted with a computer football game that looked like a calculator. His fingers raced swiftly across the face of the machine as he tried to press the right series of buttons for a touchdown. Then, suddenly, the machine flashed a bright red light to the three-note tone of what sounded like the old NBC-Westinghouse jingle.

"Ah, touchdown!" Chapin shouted childishly, his worried look replaced with a giant grin. At that moment the telephone rang. Chapin ran into the master bedroom to answer it. Another performer was returning his call, this time, James Taylor. Taylor turned him down.

Chapin's face resumed its sullen look as he stretched out on a love seat near his bedroom window overlooking Long Island Sound. "It's a discouraging business," he said. "Nobody ever wants to get involved in benefits. You've got to believe enough in what you're doing so that you're willing to humiliate yourself egowise with the people you're dealing with. A lot of these performers feel a little insecure about me because I push so hard. They're also afraid of being used because everybody in the world is after them. The music business is a bullshit business, so it's very hard for them to distinguish between the reality and the bullshit."

Chapin paused for a moment. He rubbed the thick lines of exhaustion under both eyes. Then, suddenly, he set his cleft jaw and resumed talking, almost lecturing himself. "You can't accept no for an answer," he said convincingly. "You can't have your ego battered down, which means you've got to start out with no ego to begin with. See, there's a functional ego which allows you to keep going and do what you care about, and the other kind of ego which always gets in the way because you're always getting insulted. So I'm refusing to operate on the second kind of ego. I mean, the minute you start talking down to these people, you've lost the battle. What you've got to do is almost like a Zen thing. You've got to find the level where you can communicate with them because they have a gift. They have something you want to use. But you've got to persuade them so they want to flow into that space you're offering. I tell you, these last two months have been a real experience."

Finally, at the last moment, the only other artist Chapin could muster was Kenny Loggins, who'd recently split from Jim Messina of Loggins and Messina, and who was promoting a new album. By April 9, Chapin went with what he had, and at first, the event couldn't have looked more promising. At the gala dinner, the hundred-and-ten table Exhibition Hall was filled to capacity with 1,100 of Long Island's top business leaders and their wives, who enjoyed the festive spirit of dance, food and drink, as well as numerous awards and speeches by, among others, Robert Redford.

"I don't come out for these dinners very often, but Harry is a stand-up guy who gives without equivocation," Redford told the audience. "That's one of the reasons I'm here today. Also because this is for a theater. There were not many regional theaters around when I was getting started. In the late 1950s, the only places you could go were California and New York City. There is a desperate need for this kind of program, and so I support it."

But for Chapin, the best part of the evening came when a representative of forty-one owner-operators of McDonald's franchises across Long Island pledged a multiyear grant of $170,000 for the PAF/McDonald Youth Theater. The grant was the largest single corporate donation in PAF's history. With the money, Chapin planned to create a PAF complex in Huntington Station Industrial Park, relocating the youth theater from Centerport, New York, into the old playhouse that would sit right alongside the new 526-seat theater, which began construction that summer.

However, the after-dinner concert was hardly successful. Only half of the 16,000 Coliseum seats were filled. PAF raised only $158,000, approximately $125,000 short of its intended goal. Later, Chapin asked all PAF patrons to endow a chair in the new theater. But despite the added revenues, by June 30, the Ford grant deadline, PAF did not "meet the challenge." The Ford Foundation modified the grant conditions and eventually gave the organization a $100,000 low-interest loan instead.

For Chapin, PAF's failure to meet the terms of the grant was a crushing blow, both to him and the organization. At PAF's annual June board meeting, Chapin stepped down from the chairmanship to become president (and one year later, vice president). David Westermann, the head of Hazeltine Corporation, took over as chairman of the board. With the new corporate involvement, Harry deescalated his annual financial commitment from a high of $114,000 in 1977, to $75,000 in 1978, then $50,000 in 1979, and on down.

"I fulfilled my three-year term as chairman and I felt it was time to rotate the leadership and urge other people to get involved, both financially and otherwise," said Chapin. "I wasn't there for glory. I was there to have an impact. I went through my period of being everything and all to the organization. But the ideal thing was to start severing the umbilical cord and allow other people to have a role. That line Pete Seeger had told me was stuck in my brain; that if *Clearwater* winds up being Peter Seeger's boat, it will fail."

"At that point," said Bill Gensel, "Harry wanted to walk away from the burden of PAF. He did his part. And I thought it was the best thing PAF ever had. We had some very good names on the board by then. We certainly had enough clout where we could raise money on our own."

However, Harry never stopped raising money and never fully cut the "umbilical cord" to PAF. During the last three years of his life, Chapin always remained on call as a fundraiser. He continued his benefit concerts at Huntington High School, attended numerous PAF fund-raisers, and carried on the tradition of annual gala concerts set forth by the impetus of the Nassau Coliseum affair. In fact, to the end, Chapin remained the organization's principal financial supporter.

But for PAF, Chapin's value went far beyond money, and though neither the foundation nor Chapin knew it then, his "reduced role," plus the Ford grant failure, signaled the beginning of PAF's demise. From the summer of 1978 onward, Chapin no longer involved himself in the foundation's daily operations and frequently missed board meetings. This hurt PAF's financial viability more than the money he raised. For although Chapin had assembled an impressive power board that could adequately steer PAF's future, none of the members, in the final analysis, could replace Chapin's leadership.

Chapin was a problem solver, a creature of crisis, who thrived on the self-drama of saving a hopeless cause, such as world hunger. He had that definable ability to overcome obstacles because, as Gilbert Price once said, "He wore an umbrella of hope around his spirit," a "hope" that somehow stared down the face of disaster and won. He believed in the best of all possible worlds, and he had an indomitable idealism that was reflected in the imperativeness of his actions and his attitude toward life: "We can do it! Let's do it! It's possible! Now!" It was that sense of possibility combined with the energy of Harry Chapin—to rock the boat and make things happen—that drove the engine of PAF. Chapin was the organization's inspiration, but in many ways he was also the organization. In the final analysis, PAF *was* Harry Chapin's boat. It was one problem not even Chapin could solve.

But for the moment he thought he had, and during the year that followed, he turned his attention to the larger dream of upgrading what he described as Long Island's "major cultural cornerstones," of which PAF was only one. The Long Island and Suffolk Symphonies and the Eglevsky Ballet were badly in need of funding and support. The bottom line of Chapin's "cornerstone" dream was to make all of Long Island's cultural institutions vibrate together by having the corporate and public community join hands as they had done with PAF. In this way, Chapin hoped to create a climate of concern and involvement on Long Island so that its arts could flourish.

Chapin had begun the cornerstone process a few months earlier, when representatives of both the Long Island and Suffolk Symphonies knocked on his door on separate occasions and asked him to do a benefit. Chapin agreed, but he also told them they were "bent on a collision course," since both symphonies were in direct competition for audiences and funding.

"It was basically ridiculous," said Chapin. "So I met with the chairmen of the boards of both symphonies and told them that if they want to talk about better quality symphony on Long Island, they had to start talking about getting together because the Long Island Symphony was considered a third-rate orchestra and the Suffolk Symphony second-rate."

Chapin initiated a series of meetings at his home to achieve something never accomplished in recent classical music history, the merger of two fairly large symphony orchestras. The meetings took place during the summer and fall of 1978, but as it turned out the symphonies could not merge since both had outstanding deficits. According to the New York State Arts Council, the only solution to the problem then was for both symphonies to pay off their deficits, fold completely, and have the new orchestra purchase the assets of the two old ones. "I did a bunch of benefits to pay off their debts," said Chapin. "I raised about $15,000."

Chapin also began the process of building a new orchestra, which he called the Long Island Philharmonic. Just as he had done at PAF, he put together a twenty-five-member board of corporate executives whose responsibility was to "give or get" $5,000 annually. Among others, the board included George Dempster, head of the Eglevsky Ballet, and Robert Keeshan, television's Captain Kangaroo. Chapin also persuaded Christopher Keene of the Syracuse Symphony Orchestra to be the conductor of the Long Island Philharmonic for its 1979 fall debut.

In the meantime, since the summer of 1978, Chapin had also been trying to improve another Long Island cultural cornerstone, the Eglevsky Ballet. At the time, the ballet's nineteen-member board was in complete disarray after the death of its founder, Andre Eglevsky, one of the premiere Russian-born dancers in America in the 1940s. Eglevsky had founded the ballet in 1975, and when he died, the board began a major fundraising drive in his honor. The drive failed, putting the ballet on the brink of bankruptcy.

Then, in August 1978, George Dempster, chief executive of the Transleisure Corporation and a major force in Long Island business, was elected chairman of Eglevsky's board. He refused to accept the position unless Chapin became a board member too. Over the years, Chapin and Dempster had become good friends through their involvements in Long Island's cultural affairs. Besides the Long Island Philharmonic, Dempster was a board member of PAF and chairman of the board of Hofstra University (where Chapin later became a board member). Specifically, Dempster respected and needed Chapin's "institutional fundraising know-how."

"He said he would get involved in Eglevsky if I came on and helped him," said Chapin. "So I came in and gave my usual request that anybody who can't give or get $5,000 should get off the board because they're taking up space. I cleaned out the old-lady concept of the old board, but on a day-to-day basis I wasn't that involved with Eglevsky. Eglevsky was George Dempster's baby. I was a key member of the operation in the sense I was sort of the resident guru for fundraising. I just helped them with high visibility when they needed money."

As he had for PAF's gala dinner-concert, Chapin put together a similar event for the Eglevsky Ballet on April 8, 1979, at the Nassau Veterans' Memorial Coliseum to help erase a $125,000 deficit. Chapin called it "Challenge '79." But this time Harry planned the event far in advance and had no problem finding performers. The concert featured Gordon Lightfoot, Dave Mason, Waylon Jennings, plus Chapin and his band, and they performed to a packed house. The gala dinner was also a success, cohosted by Frank Langella, then starring in the Broadway show *Dracula,* and Edward Villela, formerly of the New York City Ballet, who eventually became Eglevsky Ballet's artistic coordinator. In all, Challenge '79 raised approximately $90,000 and Chapin, along with Dempster, vowed to have a challenge night every year to benefit one of Long Island's major cultural cornerstones.

A few weeks before the Eglevsky gala, Chapin also helped one of America's cultural cornerstones, Pete Seeger. At the time, Seeger was approaching his sixtieth birthday and all three of his pet organizations, *Clearwater, Sing Out!* magazine and the Woody Guthrie Foundation, were in deep financial trouble.

"So I thought it was time to help Peter," said Chapin. "I mean, Pete had helped PAF every year and he was turning sixty and nobody was paying any attention. Here's a guy who for forty years put his money where his mouth is and did benefits for everyone. A guy who made the industry look good when most of us had our heads up various bodily orifices. Also, I read a putdown of Pete in a review in *Rolling Stone,* I think, basically castigating him for being on call for every cause and cry. And it seemed to me that if that was the slam against Pete . . ."

"So Harry called me," said Harold Levanthal, Seeger's manager for most of those forty years. "Harry knew Pete's birthday was coming up in May and had the idea of getting all the top performers together for a big tribute to Pete at the Felt Forum in Madison Square Garden. The money would go to Pete's causes. But Pete wouldn't agree to that. He didn't want any tribute."

However, the annual convention of NARM (National Association of Record Manufacturers) was coming up in Hollywood, Florida, on March 24, ". . . and Harry kept saying the music industry should at lest acknowledge the status of Pete," said Levanthal. "At the convention, there was a big dinner where they gave awards, and Harry felt a special tribute should be given to Pete."

Chapin persuaded NARM officials to give Seeger its first Presidential Public Service Award "in recognition and appreciation of a lifetime of dedication and service to humanity." But more importantly, Chapin "thought some money should be raised" and circulated letters to all the major record companies to contribute to a $100,000 kitty. Then Chapin followed up his letters with telephone calls. The first record company he contacted was Columbia, Seeger's old label.

"I talked to Walter Yetnikoff, the president of the company," said Chapin. "I said to him, 'Listen, you had Pete for many years. And you know he's been one of the best things in the industry. You may not agree with his every social stance, but he's done more for people and stood for more things, and you had a great year last year. So I'd like you guys to set the leadership role and put $25,000 in the pot for Pete!' Yetnikoff said yes right away."

But Chapin had a lot of hard selling to do with the other record companies, and although he received pledges totaling $108,000, only $70,000 was actually collected. To help make up the difference, Chapin performed a benefit for Seeger at The Dick Clark Westchester Theater in Tarrytown, New York, plus a benefit in Seeger's hometown, Beacon, New York. "I will say this about Harry," said Levanthal. "He was more consistent in supporting causes that meant something to him. I've known many artists who did one thing and dropped out of the picture. You had to pull teeth to get 'em to do things."

Chapin wrote about his admiration for Seeger in the song "Old Folkie." He told about Pete being there for everyone, for over forty years, never saying no and always caring. "Pete Seeger responded to every cause and every issue," said Chapin. "And a lot of people say he's ineffective, yet his name is on everything. So people ask, Why is he insecure? Does he have a big ego? Is he a bleeding heart? Well, after a while you start saying, 'Who gives a fuck? He's there!'

"One time that spring, I sang the song for him downstairs in a dressing room at a benefit up in Beacon. Pete didn't say anything. He studiously, in a sense, didn't react to it. When Pete got embarrassed, he got a little bit dumb. It happens to a lot of people; acting like you're not quite registering. My original version was 'Old Softie.' But I felt that would be a little tough for Pete to listen to."

That spring, Chapin recorded "Old Folkie" along with nine other new story songs on his tenth and final Elektra album, *Legends of the Lost and Found*. It was a double album recorded live at concerts in eight cities: Chattanooga, Memphis, Knoxville, Austin, Houston, Dallas, Phoenix and Tucson. Prior to the recording dates, Chapin knew his days with Elektra were numbered. According to music copyright law, none of his old songs could be recorded for at least five years if he signed with a new label, so on the album Chapin included six story songs from older LPs. Three of the songs—"Mail Order Annie," "Tangled Up Puppet" and "Poor Damned Fool"—were chosen because Chapin felt his concert versions were far superior to the recorded ones. The same was true of "Corey's Coming," "If My Mary Were Here" and "Flowers Are Red"—because on the recorded versions, Chapin edited out key music sections which he performed live, and wanted to "set the record straight" by recording "the definitive long versions."

"After *Living Room Suite*," said Harry, "I wanted to move back into story form and I felt my record-buying audience was very willing to have another live double album. Elektra was willing to do whatever I wanted because, in a sense, they felt they had taken their best shot on *Living Room Suite* and were completely immune to the fact I was probably going to another record company. I mean, they offered me a continuation deal, but they didn't make a giant effort to come up with giant bucks to hold me. They weren't in an argumentative phase. What they wanted was something that was relatively commercial that they could merchandise to my fans.

"As it turned out, and not surprisingly, Elektra put less promotion in this album than any other and barely got it out. In fact, it was released in October of 1979 and many of my fans weren't even aware the album came out. I mean, it didn't even sell 100,000 copies."

The album's poor sales was not so much the by-product of Elektra's nonpromotion, or even the album's questionable artistic quality, as a reflection of the music industry which, by 1979, was in a state of economic chaos. It began in late 1978, when America's economy sank into a steep recession. The 1979 congressional tax hike (the largest in the nation's history), coupled with a dramatic rise in OPEC oil prices, was just beginning to be felt, and it severely cut back the disposable income of the American consumer. "The eighteen-year-old who had a car was suddenly paying $1.50 for a gallon of gasoline," said one record executive. "He or she had less money to spend. So instead of buying two albums, they bought one."

Soon teenagers began taping albums and songs off the radio, which further crippled retail record sales. To offset losses, some stores began to purchase counterfeits of legitimate recordings. By published accounts, this became a $400 million business by 1979. The stores also began to abuse what was known as the "returns policy." In the past, most record companies allowed music shopkeepers to return a large percentage of their stock if it didn't sell. This meant stores ordered large volumes of albums and tapes and record companies continued to ship them because sales were phenomenal (an increase of as much as 25 percent a year). But by 1979, the growth stopped and stores had minimal cash flow. So when they ordered new records, instead of paying for them, they sent back the old ones in exchange.

"I remember Linda Ronstadt had a record out and her company shipped three million copies, but two million were returned," said Harold Levanthal. "It became a logistical problem. What do you do with two million records?"

Most record companies began to experience serious cash flow problems and some even a negative cash flow, in that more records were coming back than going out. But since the economic changes were gradual, all the excesses of the music industry continued.

"We were expecting to continue to grow," said Joe Smith, Elektra's chairman. "We were expecting to continue to add people, sign artists, ship records in a reckless way, have our parties, rent out limousines, shrimp cocktails, champagne, baseball jackets, T-shirts . . . And when somebody turned around in mid-1979 and realized at the other end that we weren't selling as many records and we were getting back records that we had shipped at the end of 1978 in expectation of growth, you suddenly realize that you're losing a lot of money."

The same was true of concert promoters. Their business was down an average of 35 percent, particularly those who handled the college market—Chapin's bread and butter. As consumers became more choosy with their entertainment dollars, big acts such as Fleetwood Mac, Linda Ronstadt and Peter Frampton could no longer fill ballparks and receive their usual $100,000 guarantees from promoters. So their booking agents turned to the college market to get those guarantees, usually large student campuses such as Michigan State, where the school's whole entertainment budget may have been $100,000. In the past, the policy of such schools was to hire several artists in the $10,000–$15,000 range (such as Harry Chapin), and over the course of a year, gradually use up the fund in a series of concerts. Some made money, some lost money, but there was no giant bath.

"But now these young college kids who had no experience promoting concerts were being hyped by the agents of these stars," said one veteran promoter. "The agents said, 'Of course you're gonna make your money back. This is one of the biggest acts in the world, and then you'll be able to do the rest of your concerts.' But what happened, of course, was that a college like Illinois State University would book Fleetwood Mac into their 18,000-seat basketball arena and only 8,000 people would show up, sometimes 12,000. But even with 12,000 people, once you started adding up expenses such as advertising, these green college kids were suddenly losing $30,000 to $60,000 in one show. As a result, there was no box from those school's entertainment budgets to book midrange artists such as Gordon Lightfoot, Kenny Loggins or Harry Chapin. In essence, the artists were killing each other off."

"I had to be a jimmyrigger and take the work where it was," Harry explained. "I mean, I was insecure about the whole business. I was insecure about whether I had a career that was going to be in trouble. Everybody was telling me the music business was in disaster. I knew there wasn't necessarily going to be a big-bucks record contract when we had not had a hit record in four years. I got very worried because I didn't want us to die off. I mean, if you're immensely hot and all you have to do is choose between alternatives, that's one thing. But if you're sitting in an industry that has lost its momentum and doesn't know where it's going, where promoters you had a relationship with for five years went out of business and those who were there couldn't book you sometimes or even pay you, it was scary. So that every concert that came up was like a triumph to me, a momentary stay against the night, in a sense. So I was saying to the band, 'Let's take the gig, any gig. Let's work!'"

But that often brought complaints from Chapin's band because of the inconveniences. It was not uncommon for the group to play in Massachusetts one day and Ohio the next. As a result, the group's sound and light crew—since they traveled by truck—

could not physically make every concert, and that forced the band to perform with inferior "house" systems.

"I said the reason was because we were survivors at a time when there was an awful lot of brutality going on," said Chapin. "What made us different was that we were flexible. We were not dinosaurs that could only eat one diet. But they felt I was not worried enough about their creature comforts such as the quality of their hotel rooms, their food, the sound systems. If we did a great concert but John Wallace's bass sounded shitty all night, John was in a bad mood. It's that simple. To them, the monitor sound was important, but to me it's meaningless. I was willing to put up with a lousy monitor if I saw the audience go bananas. But they weren't in it for audience reaction.

"They didn't understand or have any sensitivity for what was happening in the music business, the external pressures which I felt the industry was putting on everybody to see if we could survive. Most of what they were complaining about were external forces beyond our control. There were just a lot of things which came together at the time to give a negative flow."

The soft concert market meant that since January 1979, Chapin changed his concert booking agent three times. The first to go was his old standby, Magna Artists, "because I felt they no longer gave me their full efforts," said Chapin. That January, Harry hired the Home Run Agency, headed by Dennis Arfa, who booked all of Billy Joel's concerts. "They started out with a bang and did two great months," said Chapin. "But after that, Arfa had Billy Joel's career to worry about and didn't have the extra staff to handle us." In the fall of 1979, Chapin jumped to ICM (International Creative Management), one of the largest booking agents in the entertainment business, and remained with them for the rest of his career.

In addition, that fall Chapin's three-year contract with Management Three expired and he did not renew it. Jerry Weintraub had not lived up to all the glamour and promise Chapin expected. He was especially disappointed at Weintraub's failure to put his story songs to film. The closest Harry came was $25,000 that

NBC paid him to write a treatment for a TV movie based on "Cat's in the Cradle," but nothing ever came of the project. Ironically, a few days after Chapin left Management Three, five of his songs (including "Circle," "Woman Child," and "Tangled Up Puppet") were used as the basis of an ABC-TV movie starring Tuesday Weld about a divorcee's struggle to raise her daughter. The movie was called "Mother and Daughter—The Loving War" and aired on January 25, 1980.

Chapin even appeared in a bit part at the end of the picture. It was his first and only acting appearance. The scene took place in Los Angeles airport as Tuesday Weld returned to her former lover (Chapin), who greeted her at the gate. Harry's lines consisted of three words, "Welcome back, beautiful." At which point he took Weld in a strong embrace and kissed her.

"The only major question I had was what to do with my tongue and whether I was supposed to fake it," Chapin teased. "We did five or six takes, not fourteen as I sometimes joke in concert. At the end, I just kissed her naturally."

The only positive parts of Chapin's Management Three relationship were Ken Kragen and his idea to sell concession items for WHY at concerts. But Kragen was desperately overworked with other artists and had already left Management Three (with Kenny Rogers) when Chapin's contract expired. So, once again, it became a matter of trust and Chapin hired Jebbie Hart and Bob Hinkle to manage him "because they had done a good job booking my benefits."

All combined, these changes only created more tension between Chapin and his band, since members were not consulted on management moves and were dissatisfied by them. "They didn't understand me and my goals," said Chapin in self-defense. "They didn't understand what was happening with Jerry Weintraub, or why I would've gone with him in the first place, and then why I left. Why I went with the Home Run Agency and why I left for ICM. They didn't know what Jeb and Bob were doing. And they were unhappy with the record company situation. They were unhappy about everything. I mean, it was almost like I was working against the band while I was trying to save both them and me from dying. But it was also partially my fault because I hadn't done a good job in communicating with them. I insulted them in many ways because I made all these decisions myself."

In an attempt to calm the dissension, Chapin tried an experiment in democracy with the band. Now all group business was openly discussed before any major moves were made. "They couldn't come up with a better suggestion," said Chapin. "I was tired of hearing them complain, so I said, 'Okay, guys. You think you can do better? Fine. C'mon in. Get in the water. Join me.'"

The mounting conflicts came to a head one evening in November, when Kim Scholes, Chapin's cellist of two years, left the group. It occurred in Dallas, Texas, at a club called the Palladium, which, like many in the country, was in deep financial trouble. Chapin had performed there four months earlier, sold out two performances, so the promoter, in search of a "sure thing," rebooked the band at the last minute. And once again, that meant they performed without their own sound system.

During the show, Kim Scholes got a buzz out of his amplifier, which was connected to a harp-synthesizer on a stand near his stool and cello. Before the concert, Scholes was aware of the problem, but felt he didn't get the proper concern from the sound technicians or Chapin. So he stood up, pushed the harp-synthesizer off its stand, and walked out in the middle of the gig, never to return (not as the cellist anyway). The following day, the concert reviewer of the *Dallas Morning News*, Pete Opel, called the concert "the best performance of the year under duress."

"I was very mad at Kim because I felt it was very unprofessional," said Chapin. "But the band had different feelings about it. They were allied to Kim's dissatisfaction in some ways, especially Jeff Gross (the road manager and light man). Jeff thought it was wonderful. He hadn't the guts to face me down. He thought Kim's blowup was sort of a triumph. Well, to me, it was stupid. If you're gonna quit, you give notice and you leave."

Scholes had also been the group's travel agent, and the band wanted to continue with him. So as an act of diplomacy, Chapin kept him on. In addition, Scholes eventually wound up conducting two major Chapin concerts with symphony orchestras.

"I did it because he knew the music, he wanted to do it, and because he wanted to move into conducting and writing music," said Chapin. "Also, it was a great chance to show there were no bad feelings, because to me, it's meaningless to zap somebody after the connection is gone. I mean, I was mad. But I can't stay mad per se. Plus, I felt Kim felt a little guilty himself."

In the meantime, the band played two concerts without a cellist and began the search for a new one. Chapin put ads in the *Village Voice* and on the bulletin boards of Juilliard and the Manhattan School of Music. In the days that followed, Steve Chapin and Scholes auditioned forty-eight cellists; a woman named Yvonne Cable emerged as the best. Steve recommended her very strongly, but Chapin had his doubts.

"I felt having a woman would change the ambience of the group," said Chapin. "As it turned out, I was completely wrong. The thing that made it effortless was that Yvonne was an adult. She was mature, perhaps more mature than anybody else in the band, including me. She was thirty-three years old. She never had a shining position before and, though the cellist in our group was not a personality, she was grateful for the shot and was a virtual nonproblem. I paid her $30,000 a year. Also, she was attractive, and I don't mean this to sound like a chauvinist remark, but somebody said to me it was exciting to see a lady with her legs spread around a cello."

But of all the backbiting conflicts and fears Chapin experienced that year, it was the loss of a notebook that bothered him most. The notebook contained the impulses and ideas for twenty-two poems that formed the basis of a second book of poetry called *The Book of Eyes*. Chapin hoped to add the book to his other concert concessions to aid WHY and the Food Policy Center. The notebook disappeared on July 23 during a solo benefit at the Civic Theatre in New Orleans, a movie theater turned nightclub. The club seated 1,500 people, but the promoter admitted 1,900. Chapin agreed to let part of the crowd sit on stage for the performance. But that night, Chapin had a couple of new songs he wanted to try and, after intermission, brought out his notebook, which contained the chords and lyrics.

"After the concert," Chapin said, "I went out to the lobby to do concession sales and I came back and a stagehand gave me my guitar, capo, but no notebook. So I searched all around the place, and indeed, it was gone. At first I wasn't superpanicky because I'd been working on the poems and I figured I could somehow recreate them. Also, the inside of the notebook said 'important papers' and showed my telephone number and address. I figured someone would contact me."

Nobody did.

In the months that followed, Chapin tried to reconstruct the poems with no success. "I would start one, but I couldn't get the same energy I had before," he said. "And this became a greater and greater block. I wasn't able to write anymore poetry. It was literally a giant thing sitting on my head. And I kept hoping for the notebook's return until I finally gave up."

* * *

In the remaining twenty months of his life, Chapin tried to overcome the external forces around him, forces that affected not only his music career but, as he soon found out, his social causes as well. In many ways they were months of tragic disappointment; his only real consolation lay in the love of his family and his love for life. It was a life in which Chapin planned to build a new beginning, enter a new phase, and reach out for that peace and harmony his demons never permitted. It was an attempt not so much to eradicate as refine this mad marathon he was running. And to achieve his goals, he proceeded in the only way he knew: he increased the tempo and shifted his engine into overdrive. In doing so, he hoped to "save his world," and he almost did, until . . . he simply ran out of time.

CHAPTER XV

You Are the Only Song (Circle)

Chapin signed a one-album recording contract with Casablanca Records in November. Though it was a minor deal, no better than Elektra's continuation offer, it was with a new company that was excited about him, particularly Casablanca's vice president and general manager of East Coast operations, Irv Biegel, who persuaded Chapin to sign after several months of negotiation. In the early 1970s, Biegel had worked at Bell Records and was a Chapin admirer from the start. In fact, he persuaded the brass at the label to offer Chapin a contract during the 1971 bidding war.

"When I found out that Harry's recording contract was not going to be renewed with Elektra in March of '79, I went to see his attorney, Monte Morris," said Biegel. "I told him I'd like to make a deal for Harry."

Chapin and Biegel met that August to negotiate. The meeting was to begin at 10:00 A.M. at Biegel's Casablanca office on West 55th Street in New York. But by noontime Chapin had yet to show. "I called Monte Morris and he didn't know where he was," said Biegel. "Well, it seemed Harry had flown in very early that morning to LaGuardia Airport from a concert the night before.

Rather than come to my office early, he decided to get some sleep, so he went to the parking lot, found the backseat of somebody's car and overslept."

Eventually they met and the negotiations were satisfactorily settled. The main reason Chapin signed with Casablanca was its owner/chairman, Neil Bogart (who died of cancer a few months after Chapin's fatal car accident). Over the years, Bogart had built a reputation for being one of pop music's top creative merchandisers. He knew how to promote an artist, plan a career, and had a twenty-year track record to prove it. In many ways Bogart, like David Geffen, was another boy wunderkind. At the age of twenty-five, after appearing with Alan Freed and Dick Clark as a singer in the sixties, Bogard ran Cameo-Parkway Records, and in 1973, founded Casablanca Records.

Since that time, Bogart guided the careers of numerous stars: Donna Summer, Kiss, Bill Withers, Mac Davis, Robin Williams, and Gladys Knight and the Pips, among others. Bogart produced more than sixty records, of which twenty went platinum, and was called Mr. Disco because he created the "Superfly" phenomena in the 1970s.

Bogart was also in the film business via his company Filmworks, which produced the musical soundtracks of *Foxes, The Deep* and *Thank God It's Friday.*

"Neil Bogart and I always felt that Harry Chapin had nowhere reached the success he could," said Irv Biegel. "He was a troubadour, the classic storyteller. And I don't mean to sound corny, but he was a spokesman for the people. He was a pioneer. Prior to making the deal with Harry, I went to about five of his concerts and he had an incredible following. Unlike other artists, his audiences were incredibly knowledgeable. They knew all his songs, all the words. They knew when to be quiet and respectful and they knew when to make noise. I mean, the guy constantly sold out concerts. He booked more dates than any other artist.

"Somebody once told Harry, and I think it was Pete Seeger, that when things are bad in this country on a financial basis,

Pete's records and concerts would sell better. Maybe some people wanted a lift. I think Harry gave them a lift.

"Neil and I felt Harry was going to be one of the major artists of the eighties, someone who was going to write a song that would have an impact such as "Blowin' in the Wind." We felt America was ready again for that great singer-songwriter-storyteller. His social commitments were a plus too. I respected the man for being dedicated to what he believed in. I'm not saying he was a giant among giants, but I thought he was a giant of a man. Because, in one respect, he did the best he could."

During the first week in December, Biegel made arrangements for Chapin to meet his new record producers, brothers Ron and Howard Albert. The Alberts worked out of Miami, Florida, where they were minority stockholders in Criteria Recording Studios and the owners of Fat Albert Productions, Inc., a small independent music production company. As producers, the Alberts were seasoned pros. During their seventeen years in the business they had recorded such stars as Barry Gibb, Jeff Beck, Stephen Stills and Eric Clapton. Biegel had known the brothers intimately for years and felt their professionalism, plus their easygoing personality, would blend perfectly with Chapin's.

On the day Chapin was to meet the Alberts, Biegel planned to meet Harry at LaGuardia Airport for a 5:30 P.M. flight to Miami. But as usual, Chapin was late, so Biegel stood near the security check keeping a careful eye on the second hand of his watch. When it hit 5:30 precisely, Biegel, after his last experience with Chapin, figured he wasn't going to show. But sure enough, at 5:31, Chapin came charging toward security and tossed his bags on the belt shouting, "Irv, it's Harry! It's Harry!"

"Don't tell me, tell the pilot," Biegel shouted back, because the airplane was now taxiing away from the gate. So Chapin bolted past Biegel down the concourse. Irv stared after him. As Chapin ran past the National Airlines ticket counter, a reservations clerk called out, "Missed another flight again, didn't ya, Harry?"

But Chapin found one departing for West Palm Beach, so he rushed onto the plane without a boarding pass. "Harry's theory," explained Biegel, "was if you're going to Miami, the best thing to do was catch any plane going south because you're going in the right direction. Eventually you're gonna get there. He was an incredible guy. He had no monetary concerns. He went on these trips with no money. He'd hitchhike or ask somebody at a concert to drive him back to the hotel. I couldn't live like that. But he was probably right. He always got where he was going."

Said Ron Albert: "We stayed up that entire night with Harry and our only regret was that we had to go to sleep. We fell in love with him. If he was a chick, we would've fucked him. He was absolutely the most amazing human being we've ever been with. We couldn't believe that this man could be so incredible, not only as a talent but as a person, and be so unrecognized in many ways by the public. In all our years in the record business, there was no one as wonderful as Harry. I'll never forget something that was just so typical of him. We recorded some of the great guitar players, and to them, little minute details like the quality of their strings were very important. So at one point that night I asked Harry what kind of strings he used, and he said, 'Any ones that will fit!'"

From December 17 to 23, Chapin began recording his eleventh album, *Sequel,* at Criteria Recording Studios. It was a collection of ten new story songs that included the title song and single "Sequel," which continued the story of "Taxi." In it, the cabdriver—Chapin—seeks out his lost love Sue—Clare MacIntyre—ten years later. The idea for "Sequel" came from Sandy.

"For years she had been saying I should do a sequel to 'Taxi,' yet it's not that simple," said Harry. "She said that life keeps changing, people keep changing, and if you put them together again, you'll find there'll be a different reaction. But I was afraid the song would diminish 'Taxi.'"

At first, Chapin did not take the idea seriously. Then, during the winter of 1979, he wrote a long lyrical poem he sang-talked in concerts as an encore. The poem received strong audience reaction, so by late fall he tried to put some music to it, realizing he'd have to record soon for Casablanca.

"But I was in a real quandary about what to do melodically," said Chapin. "Whether I should go with the old melody, create a new one, or make a hybrid. I finally decided to make a hybrid."

Ironically, the key factor which spurred Chapin to complete the song was Clare MacIntyre herself. He had spoken to her several times over the years, but had not seen her since 1973, when he "sought her out to see how she'd react to my fame." That meeting was fairly close to the story line in "Sequel," but not his second meeting with Clare, which occurred that fall. This time, she tracked him down.

"I guess she saw me on TV, or heard me on the radio, and it triggered something," said Chapin. "Tom and Steve had also seen her at various clubs in New York. She called Don Ruthig and I got the message."

Since 1973, Clare had led a difficult life. She had fallen victim to numerous physical ailments that put her in the hospital on and off for extended periods of time. At one point she had a stroke and was in a coma. And she had long since divorced her husband, a proud Latino whose nasty temper and philandering drove them apart. On occasion over the years, Clare called Harry for support and reassurance. Harry always kept these contacts secret from Sandy for fear they would upset her. Harry did not speak to Clare while she was married, mostly because she lived in South America. But now she lived alone in an apartment on the Upper East Side of Manhattan and worked for an investment company, Drexel Lambert.

"I met her at her office and we had a quick snack and we talked," Harry said. "I didn't spend that much time with her because part of what she wanted me to do was talk to her father. She felt he was doing heavy numbers on his three kids. Clare was the most together. But her brother was crazy, literally schizophrenic, and her sister had a nervous breakdown. So she had this vision that I, by dint of my fame, could talk to him and make sure . . . She was worried he was going to write her out of his will and a whole bunch of paranoid things."

So one day Harry met Mr. MacIntyre for lunch in a mid-Manhattan restaurant, a man Chapin had not seen in nearly twenty years, since the days when he was "Harry, the boy with potential." Now it was particularly satisfying for Harry to "show up" one of the emotional villains of his past, in this case the "Mayor of Candor."

"I got a chance to impress him," said Chapin. "My own ego was nice. We talked about a bunch of things including Clare. I told him about the Presidential Commission and he said, 'Well, you turned out to be quite a young man.' He was very respectful, and in a final sense, put a closed chapter on that."

It also put a closed chapter on Clare. Chapin never saw her again, although he did speak to her a few times before he died. However, that deep burning love he once felt for her was now gone. "I think it got burned out during all the years of chasing the elusive butterfly of fame and fortune," he said. "She was only interesting intellectually. She was not an emotional issue anymore. I mean, I haven't fallen asleep nights for years thinking about Clare. Still, you always hope there's a romantic element to your past and coming back. But in the truest sense, this was fiction. There was just nothing . . . except for the fact she was once someone I cared for and I felt sorry to find out . . . I mean, I felt sad that she'd been fighting all these physical problems. She was very sick. The stroke left her partly damaged. She wasn't all there. So interestingly enough, she turned out to be 'Clare, the gal with potential' because she never had long stretches of time to utilize her abilities.

"So part of the reason 'Sequel' took so long to write was that I wanted to make sure it was true to itself, to the story, and not to me. Because if it were true to me, it would've been a dead issue. I mean, if I had finished college and hadn't broken up and made the mistake of marrying her, it would've been a disaster. In 'Sequel,' the implication is that it might have been something positive. But Clare and I were wrong for each other. We would've driven each other bats! We would've been divorced a lot quicker than the guy in the song. The only true verse in 'Sequel' was the last stanza, 'half the time thinking of what might have been/and half thinking, just as well.'"

From January 2 to 16, Chapin did a series of concerts in Ontario, Canada. Producers Ron and Howard Albert joined him for the tour and continued their production of the *Sequel* album at Nimbus 9 Recording Studios in Toronto. Then, on January 17, they returned to Miami and finished the album for projected release in late spring. But before the month of January ended, Neil Bogart decided to sell his financial interest in Casablanca Records to the Polygram Record Group. He and Irv Biegel decided to form a new label called the Boardwalk Entertainment Company and wanted to take Chapin with them. Both men already believed in Harry, but the clincher was the final mix of his *Sequel* album, which they had heard a few days earlier. They loved it!

Bogart told Chapman he wanted *Sequel* to set the tone for his new company by having Harry be the first recording artist on the label.

"He was a sure bet for us," said Biegel. "Not in sales, but that wasn't the most important consideration. He was a sure bet for us creatively. We felt he was going to give our label a new image, an image we didn't have at Casablanca, where we were known as the 'disco company.' Harry gave us a certain amount of credibility. He was unique. His music was unique, in the sense it told a story and it gave you hope. It was that musical fireside chat."

Chapin, of course, accepted their offer without much hesitation. He was concerned about being left at Casablanca without his "two rabbis," a situation he was well acquainted with from his Elektra years. Once Jac Holzman and Ann Purtill left, his relationship with the company was never the same. But with Boardwalk, Chapin would be the leading artist on the label, and that meant lots of attention, something he always craved, especially after being virtually ignored the last few years. Although signing with an unestablished company was a major risk, especially during a bad economic period, he had tremendous respect for Bogart, and especially for Biegel, who started and sold two successful companies of his own, Private Stock and Millenium Records.

Said Biegel: "Finally I went to see Bruce Bird, who was the president of Casablanca at the time, and said, 'Listen, Bruce, you have a product that belongs to Casablanca. And if, in fact, you don't really believe in it, why don't you sell it to Boardwalk?' He did. Bird liked Chapin, but the company was going through a restructure as part of the Polygram group. It was being scaled down and they were letting people go. I think Bird felt, based on the commitments he had, this was a project that could certainly come to us."

Chapin signed a simple one-album contract with Boardwalk. The company was still unsettled, so the release of *Sequel* was postponed for six months. Bogart and Biegel had yet to find office space for their New York and Los Angeles headquarters. And they still had to hire promotion people, a general staff, and secure production and distribution deals with other companies for their records. They also had to begin the search for other artists besides Chapin.

One of them, at first, was going to be Tom Chapin, who was in Toronto performing as the opening act in a few of Harry's concerts. Tom also had several new songs, so Harry convinced Bogart to sign up his brother. But Bogart wouldn't allocate the same production expense for Tom that he did for Harry. Ron and Howard Albert, out of deference to Chapin, agreed to produce Tom's music at no fee, with studio time the only real expense (approximately $30,000). The album was called *In the City of Mercy*. But Bogart hated it. The record was eventually released two and a half years later on Specter Records, a small outfit out of Miami.

More importantly, during his time in Toronto, Tom saw the dissension in Harry's band and voiced his distress to his brother.

It was clear the "democracy" was not working. "I told him it was crazy," said Tom. "I couldn't believe the amount of bullshit that was going on—the bad vibes, backbiting and everything else. I said to Harry, 'Why are you putting up with all this stuff? You're the boss, you might as well take charge.'"

A few weeks later, the democracy ended when Jeff Gross, Chapin's road manager and light man for five years, quit because of various drug and personal problems. "Most people can't take the pressure," said Chapin of Gross. "Most people couldn't be on the road for five years without being whacko, without being a druggie, or this or that. I wasn't looking to have a problem with Jeff. At the same time, his departure brought a certain stability into the group, because he was part of the cause of all the bad vibes that were happening."

For an interim period, at Steve Chapin's suggestion, Harry hired two members of his road crew to assume the responsibilities of concert lights and road management. But Harry felt neither made as good a first impression with promoters as Gross did and soon after hired a man named Richard Imperato. Imperato was a charter pilot Chapin became friendly with over the years when he rented planes from northeast gigs to get home at night. Harry was particularly impressed by Imperato's ability to "remain cool under pressure," especially after several rough, late-night journeys.

"One time we had a flight from Pittsfield, Massachusetts," said Chapin. "It was bad weather and for two and a half hours we were sitting on that plane bombarded by eighty- to ninety-mile-an-hour winds, snow, thunderclouds, everything! We were forced to land in Poughkeepsie, New York, because we couldn't get back to Islip Airport on Long Island. Watching him under that kind of pressure, and the fact that he was a diplomatic guy, and was available, I ended up hiring him."

After the failure of the "democratic experiment," Chapin learned some valuable lessons about himself and his band. "I learned it was absolutely silly to have to take them along on every step and every decision," said Chapin. "Ironically, in the end, they were glad I was handling all these decisions because of all the complicated questions involved. At the same time, it's naive of me to expect them to have any appreciation for my demons or goals. I'm not expecting that anymore. What I should do, though, in my own growth, is to try to become a better leader, to put my hand on their shoulder occasionally and say, 'How's it going?'"

The democracy also gave Chapin a greater understanding and appreciation of his band. "At certain moments in the past, I did take the group for granted," he continued. "But I started realizing more and more what their world is and the fact that as pissed as I can get at John [Wallace] and Howie [Fields] for their lack of big vision, they're sitting back behind me making sure the bass and bass drum are exactly right. They do a beautiful rhythm section; I mean, they really do work together. To have me say it's just audience rapport is naive on my part because what they're getting off on is the sound of their instruments, the professionalism. And also, they're trapped into having to play my music.

"In addition, I am very, very lucky to have my brother Steve the last six years, because he gives more crunch to my music and sets a criterion for excellence in the band that sometimes I don't even know what's going on. I mean, if there's a fuck-up in the back there and Steve gives them one look from his piano, they know what's happening. They straighten up. Steve has got a musical authority I don't have. All together, I've come to appreciate them in a way I haven't before. I've got a damn good band. Even the people who slam me admit the band is good.

"And then there's the road crew. They are the unsung heroes of the rock-'n'-roll generation. These guys do good jobs given the kind of nonlives they live. It's inhuman. They can't go home. They can't see their ladies. They get to the concert before we arrive and spend all that time setting up so there are no kinks. Then we get there and do the show. But they have to work during the show. And after we leave, they have to break down the set, put everything back in the truck and, while we are asleep, drive to the next town. The bottom line is, I realized, that a team is a lot of people with tough pressures I know nothing of. I don't know what it's like to be drummer Howie Fields. I don't know what it's like to be Doug Walker. I'm trying to be more sympathetic to them."

By spring of 1980, Chapin also realized he need not worry about the downturn in the concert business because he had a solid core of fans and promoters. In the past, most promoters went after the "home run," "the hot act," and booked Chapin as an afterthought. But now, in a time of economic crisis, they appreciated Chapin as a model of consistency, not only in his drawing power and the high quality of his shows, but his attitude in doing them. Over the years, Chapin had developed the reputation of being a "nice guy." He was professional, easy to work with and, most of all, reasonable. If Chapin earned $10,000 at a concert hall one year, but was only offered $7,500 the following year, he accepted the loss so he could gain the continued loyalty of his fans. He was not greedy. In fact, if a promoter lost money on one of his shows (which was rarely the case), Harry was more than happy to pay him the difference out of his fee.

These virtues became a tremendous selling tool in a declining market and were reflected in his concert earnings. In 1980, Chapin grossed more than $2 million (up 25 percent from 1979) and performed more than 250 concerts, the most ever, partially because he was nervous about the music industry, but also because he was being offered more gigs. And that showed in the attitude of promoters.

"Harry was a decent man," said Herb Fisher, a northeast promoter. "He was a good man. He was probably the only entertainer I actually looked forward to doing business with. Most stars were spoiled and arrogant and half drugged out of their minds. They tore up dressing rooms. I never had a problem with Harry. He really was an exception in this business."

As Chapin expanded and improved his music career, he tried to do the same with his social causes. Some of them were in good shape, such as the Eglevsky Ballet, which was no longer in financial difficulty, and the Long Island Philharmonic, which had successfully debuted its 1979–1980 season under the conductorship of Christopher Keene. Other causes were brand-new, such as Long Island Cares, a grassroots hunger organization he founded. In addition, Harry successfully lobbied Congress to pass the Good Faith Food Donors Bill, which opened the doors for food banking on Long Island. That bill inspired a second organization he created, the Long Island Regional Food Bank, whose job it was to work with local businesses and government agencies to distribute food to the needy. Finally, to coordinate these causes, Chapin opened an administrative office on New York Avenue in Huntington, which was run by his full-time secretary-assistant, Don Ruthig, Susan Gensel having relinquished her position to settle her divorce from Bill Gensel. Susan later became director of public affairs at Cold Spring Harbor Laboratory, and eventually remarried.

However, the organizations Chapin held closest to his heart began to flounder, such as WHY. So Chapin expanded its board of directors and replaced Bill Ayres with his brother James as chairman of the board. He fired codirectors Wray MacKay and Geri Barr. In their place, Marty Rogol, a lawyer who used to work for Ralph Nader, assumed the reins of both WHY and the Food Policy Center.

Said Chapin: "What happened was, the WHY office got into what I call a 'middle-class hunger movement.' They did a lot of traveling and went to a lot of conferences, but Wray and Geri really didn't have the political sharpness needed or enough goal orientation. They didn't do any fundraising outside of me and it just became a time to pare down the fighting lines and have the goals of both organizations merge into one, which was enacting legislation based on the final recommendations of the Presidential Commission."

Once again, PAF was in desperate shape, facing financial ruin. One principal cause was the bloated construction cost of the new 526-seat theater. The original estimate was $200,000. But eventually that figure ballooned to $557,000, more than a thousand dollars per seat. "We simply tried to expand too soon," said Chapin. "It really hurt us."

Another key factor was the lack of audience acceptance of Jay Broad's productions. Ever since PAF's most successful season (1976–1977), and the emergence of *Gemini* and *Vanities,* which went on to long runs both on and off Broadway, respectively, the organization hadn't had a hit play. Though few denied that PAF's productions were professional, letters to the editor in PAF's monthly newsletter also described its plays as "unbearable," "grim," and "shocking."

PAF's disgruntled audience showed its displeasure at the box office. Once the novelty of the new theater wore off, PAF's subscriptions plummeted from an all-time high of 14,000 (in 1978) to 8,500 in 1979, a loss of approximately $300,000. "The scripts chosen lead one to wonder if the course PAF has chosen is wise," wrote one subscriber of the new play policy. "A revival here and there would certainly make the season more bearable."

By the 1979–1980 season, Broad agreed and went to a half-and-half policy of old and new productions. He also extended the normal number of plays from six to eight. "I thought it was a mistake," said Chapin. "Because the income generated from six plays was not worth the added cost of eight, and indeed, as the season progressed, it was a mistake. Our subscription sales declined."

PAF was further crippled by the cost of the productions themselves. Chapin's "power board" was certainly not at fault. Over the years, in fact, they'd been remarkably consistent in meeting the $10,000 per member give-or-get requirement. According to Harry, the principal blame rested with Broad, who refused to compromise his projected production budgets when it became apparent (midway through the season) that there was not enough income to cover cost.

"Jay promised he would make some budget adjustments in terms of cashing each dollar in for each dollar out," Chapin said. "But when it came down to the crunch, he wasn't able to make those kinds of adjustments. I mean, Jay was known as an extraordinary theater man, but he was also know for having budget problems, overspending. So all of a sudden, we were back in a situation of survival again, not growth. I described the situation as a train going full-speed toward a mountain. Even though Jay knew there was a crash ahead, he kept on hoping we were gonna move the mountain. But that wasn't going to happen."

But Chapin tried. In January 1980, he asked Chemical Bank to loan PAF $150,000. The bank declined his request because it felt the foundation was a bad credit risk. So Chapin took out a personal loan for that amount and loaned it to PAF. The only problem was that Chapin had insufficient cash flow to back the loan. Most of what he earned he donated or spent. So he put up his home in Huntington as collateral. But the money made little more than a dent in PAF's deficit, which was upward of $350,000, the largest ever.

In February, several board meetings were held to come up with a solution. Chapin attended most of them, gradually finding himself back in the full-time role as PAF's savior. "There was talk of closing the foundation again," said Chapin sadly. "I felt the ramifications of PAF closing would be extremely negative for Long Island because PAF had been the leader of all the cultural cornerstones. If it did close, it meant it would be harder to raise funds for the Eglevsky Ballet and the Long Island Philharmonic because banks and corporations would feel Long Island couldn't support quality cultural organizations, and that included me. I had become so identified with PAF that my credibility would be destroyed."

PAF wasn't the only art-theater organization suffering financial woes. The problem extended nationwide because a recessionary economy produced severe grant cutbacks at both federal and state levels. Even private granting institutions such as the Ford Foundation had moved dramatically out of the arts. PAF's Challenge Grant, for instance, was the Ford Foundation's last significant expenditure. Everywhere, it seemed, the arts were dancing to a dirgelike tune. In San Francisco, for example, the

Act Theatre, one of the largest regional theaters in America, was forced to cancel two productions despite a $12 million budget. In Minneapolis/St. Paul, the prestigious Tyrone Guthrie Theatre fired its artistic director because of too many experimental plays and too many empty seats. And in New York, the Chelsea Theatre closed, the Circle-In-The-Square Theatre wasn't far behind, and the Vivian Beaumont in Lincoln Center, perhaps the country's premier house, reshuffled its play selection and brought in Woody Allen's *The Floating Light Bulb* to stimulate sagging sales.

Inevitably, Broad resigned as PAF's producer in April 1980, citing "budgetary restrictions and differences in artistic philosophy" as the cause.

"I didn't want to fire Jay or force him to leave," said Chapin. "But with the realities of a budget that was literally going to make us go bankrupt by the end of the season, I saw no virtue in that kind of integrity. The PAF board was awash wondering what to do."

Bill Thompson, the head of the arts-in-education program, was selected to replace Broad for the 1980–1981 season. "He had a very strong relationship to the community," said Chapin. "He didn't quite have the directorial credits and stature in the theater industry we would've liked, but he knew PAF intimately. And we didn't have the time or money to go through an extensive talent search. I wanted minimal disruption and Thompson was very willing to watch the budget realities."

By July, the Boardwalk Entertainment Company had finally established itself, so Chapin took off two days from his concert schedule and supervised a final remix of his album at Criteria Recording Studios in Miami. There he also recorded a "shortened version" of his song "Sequel" (the version that eventually appeared on the album), as well as the "up-tempo version" of "Remember When the Music." The "Reprise," or "slow-tempo version," was recorded in January 1980, at Nimbus 9 in Toronto. It was part of what Harry called his "American trilogy," which included "Up on the Shelf" and "I Miss America."

Chapin first wrote "Remember When the Music" in 1977, during the time of *Dance Band on the Titanic*. Not surprisingly, it was another extrapolation of his anger at contemporary music, but done much better and with far more feeling. In the song, Chapin tried to reconcile, in a nostalgic tone, his idealistic longing for music to return to its former social relevance: "And as we sang the words/It would set our minds on fire/For we believed in things/And so we'd sing . . ."

"During the sixties, music was the place to go to find out what was going on in the world," said Harry. "You had to listen to the Beatles, Rolling Stones, Dylan, Paul Simon. . . . If you didn't, you didn't know what the hell was going on. Everybody then, from Leonard Bernstein to some pimply faced kid, was listening to the same kind of music. In those days, every six months it seemed, you'd hear a song that would knock your socks off. I mean, it sort of altered the way you perceived yourself; 'Hound Dog,' 'Blowin' in the Wind,' 'American Pie.' But today you can go away for six months, miss the music completely, and return to find you haven't missed anything."

Boardwalk president Neil Bogart agreed with Chapin and felt the song made an important social statement, but he also felt Harry should write a second version with a more "positive, hopeful" feel. And Harry did, but not until after March 14, 1980, when his longtime political idol, a man some people called the conscience of America during the sixties, Allard Lowenstein, was brutally gunned down in his New York law office by a former coworker. Chapin was greatly saddened by Lowenstein's death, not only because Chapin admired him, but because his passing seemed to symbolize the death of an era.

"Al's spirit was the 1960s," said Harry a few days after the murder. "It was one of moving forward, an ongoing dream. Along with Pete Seeger and Ralph Nader, he was one of my three heroes. I loved Al's passion for justice, his concern for the underdog, the oppressed, his willingness to respond as Pete Seeger does to almost any cause."

Chapin also saw parallels between his life and Lowenstein's, and that scared him. He knew the emptiness Lowenstein felt in the last few years of his life without his wife, Jenny, who divorced him. Lowenstein was so caught up in saving the world he forgot to save himself, and his marriage.

"He died a lonely man," said Chapin. "He was all by himself at the end, despite millions of acquaintances, living in an apartment in New York City. His wife and kids lived with somebody else. But he loved Jenny. He would make speeches and tell how much he loved her. That's what had become of their relationship. He just wasn't doing it on a day-to-day human basis and so she left him. That frightened me. Sandy was adamant about me not overpraising her from the stage because she didn't want to have the Al Lowenstein version of a relationship from the podium."

Chapin attended Lowenstein's funeral at a synagogue in Manhattan. Also attending was a throng of journalists and celebrities such as Ted Kennedy, Jacqueline Onassis, Andrew Young, William Buckley, Coretta King and Governor Hugh Carey of New York. Chapin gave a short speech and then sang "Circle."

"I was gonna sing 'Remember When the Music,'" Harry said, "but I wasn't that secure about the song. It was so new then."

For the rest of that summer, Chapin toured heavily, and expected to have a small break in September and October. But except for a four-day vacation with Sandy in the Caribbean, he was hardly home as he squeezed 24 senatorial and congressional benefits into his already packed schedule. In September, Harry performed 25 concerts of which 21 were benefits; in October, 33 concerts, of which 23 where benefits. The main reason was that most of the politicians he supported were Democrats. As the 1980 campaign progressed, they took a beating in popularity polls at the hands of Ronald Reagan's red-white-and-blue Republicanism, which had captured the country's imagination.

"When things started looking chancy, I did everything I could, not so much to shore up Carter but to help all the politicians I believed in," said Chapin. "At best, I came home for two hours and left. It's not that I didn't want to be home, it's just that in many cases I couldn't physically get home after concerts. Many of the late-night flights I used to take from the Midwest were canceled because of the gas shortage and the rise in oil prices."

One such flight, "Northwest 222," was the title of a song Harry recorded on his *Sequel* album. It was about a mail-run flight Chapin used to take forty times a year that was canceled in late 1979 when the airline lost the mail contracts. Typically, the plane started out in Minneapolis at one o'clock in the morning, arrived in Chicago at three, Detroit at five, and finally New York City.

"I often took little planes to get to that plane," said Chapin. "And it was cheap and I could sleep. It was a 747 with only twenty or thirty people on it and I'd stretch out across the seat. I was bitter at the airlines and the oil shortage. It really cut back on my flexibility. I mean, the song said it."

* * *

That fall, Chapin's life came full circle in many ways. For one, he rehired Ken Kragen as his manager. After Kragen left Management Three, he turned Kenny Rogers into the biggest music act in America, and, because of his newfound fortune, was willing to take on Chapin's multidimensional if less lucrative career. Kragen was also sympathetic to Harry's social concerns. But Harry was also loyal to Jebbie Hart and Bob Hinkel. So he decided to merge them with Kragen to work as a team. "Any doubt I had with Jeb and Bob was that they couldn't deliver the big one," said Chapin. "They could do the day-to-day. But that was solved by Kragen, who did deliver the big one and didn't have time for the small ones, so it was a marriage made in heaven."

Another full circle was the return of Chapin's long-lost notebook. That October, Harry returned to New Orleans for a group concert at the Saenger Performing Arts Center. A few days earlier he had done a live radio interview to promote the concert and he mentioned his "lost notebook," saying it was "the only down thing about the city," and he'd "pay $1,000 to get it back." But Harry didn't think anyone was really listening and forgot the matter entirely.

On the day of the concert, Chapin was in Houston for a speech at the World Hunger Conference as a member of the President's Commission. Afterward he hopped a flight to New Orleans, arriving at 7:25 P.M. for an eight o'clock show. Road manager Rich Imperato met Chapin at the airport.

"Everything looks good tonight," Imperato told him. "Good sales and . . . By the way, there was some creep who said something about a notebook and that he wants $2,250 for it."

"What?"

"Yeah, some guy said he's got your notebook and that you'll buy it back from him."

Once at the concert hall, Chapin met a half-drugged, scruffy little man, who looked like a down version of Ratso Rizzo in *Midnight Cowboy.*

"What's this about a notebook?" Chapin asked him.

"Yarr, I got your notebook," the man slurred. "I have it in an envelope."

"Well, let me see it," Chapin said. "I want to make sure it's mine."

Rizzo pulled out the notebook, showed it to Chapin, but held on to it. Chapin reached out to take it.

"Noo, noo, noo," Rizzo teased, pulling the notebook away. "If you want it, it's gonna cost ya $2,250."

"I said I'd pay a thousand bucks for it."

"Yarr, but I paid $1,250 to get it."

Then Chapin noticed two cops backstage, standing off to the side.

"Look, I don't care what you bought it for," said Chapin confidently, "because if you don't like the price, we can talk to those two gentlemen over there."

Chapin pointed to the cops. Rizzo turned around. He paused for a second, clearing his musty throat.

"Ahrr, noo, noo. Ahrr, I'll take the thousand."

"So I wrote him a check and got the notebook," Harry said. "I realized I could stop the check and screw the guy. But I was also really glad to have it back. I didn't want to tempt the fates in my head because the notebook did have an impact on my writing and I really did have a whole different tonality than the first book of poetry. It was kind of a progression. The incident was one of those wonderful chances and I was very grateful."

For the next nine months, Chapin worked on his poetry with a vigor he hadn't had in years. He completed approximately thirty poems and gave each one to Rob White for illustrations as he went along. One of the poems was about Henry Hart, Chapin's childhood nemesis. Harry had heard from Jebbie that his stepfather was sick and dying, perhaps of cancer. So Chapin wrote a poem called "Black and White Movie." The title referred to Harry's old feelings that Henry was the villain in black against the brothers in white. "But, of course, Henry survived," said Chapin. "It turned out not to be cancer. He even raped the rationale of the poem!"

Ironically, a short time later, Harry met Henry at Jebbie's wedding in Providence, Rhode Island, the first time they'd seen each other in twenty years. Henry didn't look at all like the "frightening villain" Harry imagined. Now, he saw a small, frail, slightly genteel, seventy-seven-year-old white-haired man.

"In a funny kind of way I thought, God, was this the big villain of my youth?" said Chapin. "I realized two things immediately. First, that I really was frightened and bitter during my childhood, hanging out there in the wind with no one to protect me. And second, that it was pointless to have anger or revenge against him or my mother, because I was really angry at both of them. But it was too late in a sense. I mean, it's amazing what time does. It removes. . . . The first couple of years you feel angry, the second couple of years you feel abandoned. But finally, after all is said and done, time does wash away old wounds. I mean, you can never go back and stare your stepfather in the eye and shout,

'I hate you!' or something. It means absolutely nothing because it's not the same, not the same situation."

So Harry just said, "Hello, Father," since Henry had always wanted to be called that. They talked. "He wanted to know what I'd been doing," said Chapin. "He wanted to talk about the Presidential Commission and a bunch of other things I was doing on Long Island. He also talked about my kids. He said he liked kids in the abstract. He thought they were beautiful. He saw Jaime, Jono, Jason, Jenny and Josh, and said how attractive they were, and he wanted to meet Sandy. So he did all those things. It was very pleasant, no pressure, no controversial subjects. He was purposely harmless. There was nothing to say about the old days. In a way, it was a triumph, though, because you gotta remember, his son—his dear, dear son—was making a living off Tom and I. . . ."

Soon afterward Sandy had a similar experience with her mother. Mrs. Gaston lived near Miami, Florida. During the previous four years, Jaime had stayed in contact with her grandmother, who was curious to see the rest of Sandy's children. In their conversations, Mrs. Gaston also told Jaime how she'd read about Harry in the newspapers and that it sounded like he'd become "a really decent young man."

Chapin had a series of Florida concerts in the middle of October, so a get-together was arranged. Sandy and the kids were willing to go down. Jaime had smoothed the way. "We decided not to put any pressure on it and just drop by one afternoon, which we did," said Chapin. "All of the kids called her Gampy or Grammy. I called her Mrs. Gaston. Sandy underplayed it. She kept on saying to me how old and frail she looked. When you look at your parents you have this vision of a very potent figure. Her mother was very frightening to her. She's not frightening to her anymore. But the point is, you can't keep blaming them, and if you can take off the anger or silence before they die, then you've done something!"

The Chapins stayed at Mrs. Gaston's home for a couple of hours. Afterward they all went out for dinner, but Harry had a concert that evening and left early. "Sandy later said the dinner kept going on and on," Chapin said. "She said she didn't want it to end."

Mid-October also saw the release of Chapin's *Sequel* album. Unlike Elektra Records, Boardwalk did not allow the product to go unnoticed. The company's promotion people hyped all the leading radio stations and, later that month, Chapin flew out to L.A. for a two-day media blitz, mostly interviews with reporters.

"I told them the news about Harry Chapin is no news," he said. "I was probably more political and less bendy than I've ever been. I talked about what I believed in. I said I've been doing this for nine and a half years and have been pretty damn consistent, more consistent than most people both artistically and in my social concerns. I said that despite record sales that have gone up and down, I made more money each year and have a growing career irrespective of what the media perceives."

By December, the single "Sequel" rose to number 23 on *Billboard*'s charts, one notch higher than "Taxi." According to a *Billboard* check, it was the first time a hit song had a hit sequel. The song even sold well in England where, according to *Musical Express* magazine, "Sequel" reached the low seventies on the British charts. The album remained on *Billboard*'s "Hot 100" chart for more than five months and sold in excess of 300,000 copies.

"I first heard 'Sequel' played on WABC in New York," Harry said. "I think it was disc jockey Ron Lundy who said, 'That's a shiver record.' Other than 'Sniper' and 'There Only Was One Choice,' I probably worked harder on that song than any other, and I think it paid off. I don't think it diminished 'Taxi.' And when I sing it, I really feel I've done something. It's funny, Sandy is now telling me I should write a sequel to 'Sequel' and call it 'Hearse' and have the guy carried away."

Before October ended, the Presidential Commission on International and Domestic Hunger handed in its final report to President Carter. The report predicted "a global hunger crisis is likely over the next twenty years that may pose even greater problems than current energy woes." The report also contained numerous recommendations to avert such a crisis, at least as it related to U.S. foreign policy. Among other things, the commission urged that the United States double its nonmilitary foreign aid (to $14 billion) since "countries most in need of development assistance seldom pose a direct military threat to national security." The commission also stated that the primary cause of hunger was poverty, and therefore the focus of that nonmilitary foreign aid should be "on self-reliant growth," to help others feed themselves through better farming methods and more equitable distribution of land ownership.

The final report was, in fact, the "dry, passive document" Chapin feared, and in many ways, then, the Presidential Commission was a failure. Most members spent the first six months arguing whether poverty was a cause of hunger.

"It was ridiculous," said Chapin. "They were trying to isolate hunger from poverty and from political and economic ramifications. It was just terribly naive. All the studies we reviewed over the last decade showed that poverty had a direct link to hunger. So we wasted a large part of our time and effort trying to justify why all the other major studies came to that conclusion."

What the twenty-member commission was missing was solid expertise in the hunger field. Most of the members fell into one of three categories. There were those who truly cared but were frustrated early on by the scope of the problem, such as Thomas Wyman, president of the Green Giant Food Corporation. Then there were those who were adequately knowledgeable about hunger issues but hopelessly political, such as the commission's chairman, Sol Linowitz. And finally there were those who never attended a single meeting, such as Senator Robert Dole. In fact, of the fifteen scheduled commission meetings, only Chapin attended every one!

The commission also had meetings with President Carter for the submission of its preliminary and final reports. "But at those two meetings, Carter simply made the standard statements and disappeared," said Chapin. "The commission and its recommendations got swept into the thrust of the Presidential election campaign and all the economic troubles. So, in the final analysis, both the commission and the final report turned out to be only 75 percent effective. But we [Chapin and The Food Policy Center] were able to correct some of the weaknesses of the commission by beginning the process of putting its recommendations, plus others, into legislation called the Hunger Elimination Act of 1981."

But Chapin's Hunger Elimination Act suffered a major blow when Jimmy Carter was defeated on November 4, and took half the Democratic Party with him, many of whom were key legislators who would have supported the bill. Several major names in American politics were ousted that night, including Senators George McGovern and Frank Church. Even Senator Patrick Leahy of Vermont, one of the few Chapin pols who survived reelection, won by the slimmest of margins, approximately 2,000 votes.

"I was heartbroken," said Chapin bitterly. "Six years of work went down the drain that night. I literally had enough allies in the House and Senate and all the key committees to get this legislation passed. Over the years I had built that kind of relationship. But now I had to start at practically zero and lobby all the new Republicans. Yes, we did have the commission and its recommendations and bipartisan support to an extent, but let's put it this way. It would have been easy. It would've been salutory. It would've been reaping the benefits of a helluva lot of work over the years if Carter had not been such a bad advocate of the human agenda. But pissin' and moanin' is not my strong point. I just move on."

Mostly, Chapin moved toward home. For the first time since 1973, he went through an intensive period of self-evaluation that lasted the rest of his days. One factor was the failure of his hunger dream. But the key reason was Sandy. During the months

Harry was off trying to save his world, she gradually found herself alone in hers, a single woman again, with all the disadvantages of being married and all the disadvantages of being single. As much as she admired her husband's goals and was sympathetic to the setback to his populist dream, she also had very real complaints of her own.

"Sandy blew up, in one sense," Harry explained, in this, another of their annual battles. "She said, 'Fine, maybe you're going out there to save your world, but we don't have a marriage. I am a single woman. I just happen to have a marriage degree. Yes, you are a great man, but if your goals are taking you away from me, where does that leave us? Because this isn't what we've been fighting so hard for. So if you want to chase after all those things, and if you are so insecure about all this stuff, then fine, go ahead, but you're not going to have me.'"

Suddenly, the "Al Lowenstein version of a relationship from the podium" became real for Chapin. "It was the 'Cat's in the Cradle' syndrome all over again," said Harry. "I imagined myself living in a small room somewhere in Huntington, because I never wanted a big house anyway. And occasionally visiting my kids, being an uncle-daddy, and them feeling a little bit funny about seeing me. I was afraid of winding up like Al, a very lonely man."

That November, Chapin's twenty-year-old daughter, Jaime, sat down and had a long talk with her father. She explained to him that he needed to slow down, organize his life and be more sensitive to the people around him. "You are no longer that frightened nineteen-year-old up at Cornell," she told him. "There is no reason for you to be such a controversial figure in your own milieu, because you're not a selfish person; you're a generous person. There is no need for you to continue this blind charge."

This message was brought home to Chapin on December 8, the day of John Lennon's assassination and the day after Harry's thirty-eighth birthday. That evening, the family had a birthday dinner because the night before Chapin was in Flint, Michigan, for a concert. Chapin's seven-year-old daughter, Jenny, said to him innocently, "Daddy, why don't you tell them you don't want to work on your birthday?"

"Well, hon, I gotta admit, there is no them. I am them."

"Well, you should tell them you are gonna be home on your birthday."

"I will," he said. "I'm gonna make a big change this coming year and not work so much."

But Chapin's son Jonathan overheard, and said, "Talk, talk, talk."

"I was working on the external agenda of being an institutionalized good guy," said Chapin. "But I realized I wasn't solving my personal questions. I realized you can be a hero to the world, profit the multitudes and still be a louse or nonfactor in terms of home. It's the participant-observer question again. Career, family, marriage—what's the right balance?"

In January 1981, Chapin tried to get some balance when he hired a public affairs coordinator to organize his social causes and their funding. He also wanted to reduce the "repetitive aspects of my career," which was understandable enough when he celebrated his 2,000th career performance that month at the Bottom Line in Greenwich Village.

So he made himself a promise. From now through the spring he would tour heavily (which he did), only so he could take time off during the fall to begin work on numerous creative projects he had started over the years and then "put up on the shelf." There was a musical about the late folksinger Phil Ochs, a screenplay about the revolutionary Che Guevarra and two novels he wanted to do. One of them was *The Flow,* a story about the chaos that would result if the food supply system from Midwestern states to Northeastern cities was disrupted. The other was called *Candor,* based on the story song "The Mayor of Candor Lied." For that project, in 1977, Chapin was paid $35,000 as an advance by Doubleday. Chapin, in turn, hired a young writer to interview him and write the book. But the initial draft, in Chapin's words, "was a piece of shit," and the project was abandoned.

Chapin also had reels of film footage of his grandfathers, K.B. and Big Jim, and wanted to make a documentary called *Legacy*. He first began it in 1969, and had since invested more than $30,000 in the project.

In another new project, Chapin wanted to collaborate with Edward Villela, the artistic director of the Eglevsky Ballet, in choreographing several of his songs in a presentation called *Ballads for Ballet*. He also wanted to complete the *Book of Eyes*, write a two-act play called *Goddess of a Woman*, adapt "Taxi" and "Sequel" to film and write a nonfiction book that summed up all his life's philosophy and beliefs. "It's about history, art, the Presidency, hunger, politics, America, power, values, ego, education, and what you do with your job," said Chapin of the book. "It's a whole bunch of practical thoughts I want to put down, a combination of things I thought about and my brother James thought about."

Harry also wanted Sandy to pursue her ambitions as a teacher. That May, she began teaching a course at Hofstra University called Creative Process/Social Issues. "I wanted her to begin living her own life," said Chapin. "I didn't want her to just be Harry Chapin's wife because she's a brilliant woman. She has a lot to offer. It was my way of letting her know that the next generation of our lives was not going to be just me chasing after windmills."

In the meantime, Chapin pursued support of his Hunger Elimination Act and adjusted his strategy to the new Republican-dominated Congress. In December, WHY's director, Marty Rogol, had the recommendations of the Presidential Commission drawn into legislation by the Washington law firm that represented the Republican National Committee. "In this way," said Chapin, "we wanted to show that the hunger issue was not a bleeding-heart, left-wing, Democratic issue."

Chapin formed an ad hoc group composed of Congressman Ben Gilman (D-N.Y.), Senator Patrick Leahy and Thomas Wyman to strategize the passage of the bill and lobby Congress. Chapin also had the legislation distributed to several hunger groups in an effort to gain their advice and support. Chapin himself gave visibility to the legislation when he staged a benefit concert on May 6 at the Capitol Center in Landover, Maryland. Among others, the concert featured Kenny Rogers, and for it Chapin distributed dozens of free tickets to Republican congressmen, senators and their aides. The event raised more than $150,000 for WHY and the Food Policy Center, and with it Chapin hoped to lobby the legislation into law. Unfortunately, it never got that far.

During the rest of May, Chapin became involved in a play called *Somethin's Brewin' in Gainesville.* The play was based on a book called the *Cotton Patch Version of Matthew and John* by Dr. Clarence Jordan, a theologian and minister, who created an interracial farming colony and religious utopia on Koinonia Farms in Americus, Georgia. Jordan's book was one of several "cotton patch" versions of the Gospels and Epistles in the New Testament, but this particular version asked what would have happened if Jesus Christ had been born forty years ago and had to deal with a modern South?

Jordan's book sold more than 300,000 copies and inspired a brilliant young actor named Tom Key, who began performing a one-man show based on Jordan's book throughout the South at divinity schools and colleges. In his shows, Key played thirty-three different characters, from Jesus to John the Baptist, aided by his persuasive, booming baritone.

Key was doing his show one night in Alabama in the fall of 1980 when Russell Treyz, a regional theater veteran (who eventually directed and coauthored the *Gainesville* play) saw Key's performance. Treyz was so enthusiastic that he asked Key to come to New York and perform it for some friends in the theatrical community. One of them was Phillip Getter (who became the producer of the play and had numerous production credits himself, including the Tony Award–winning drama *The Shadow Box* and the musical *A Day in Hollywood/A Night in the Ukraine*).

"I was completely stunned by it," said Getter. "So I approached Harry Chapin and asked him whether he would be interested in writing one or two songs with some lyrics for a backup singer onstage for Tom Key's show."

That spring, Chapin went to see a performance of the two-act play. "I loved it," he said. "I loved some of the larger morals and questions the play raised. Such as, what does a man stand for? What can he do with his life? What part of Jesus is man? What part divine? Heaven and hell are within us. It was a show about the power of belief. I was excited about the idea in a moral way, not a religious way. What I felt was that Jesus was one of the most charismatic men in human history. People have forgotten how much of a revolutionary he was, a genuine revolutionary. But today, the Moral Majority have made him into an almost negative, arbitrary person, rather than a gentle, seductive, forgiving one. When I saw Tom Key, there was no music to the play, but I thought there were some things about it that were not redundant in terms of all the standard biblical movies, or *Godspell,* or *Jesus Christ Superstar.* It just became intriguing."

Chapin was mostly attracted to the anachronism of it. According to the story, Jesus was born in Gainesville, Florida, grew up in Valdosta, Georgia, and wound up preaching in Atlanta, the contemporary Jerusalem. At the end, Jesus died much as he did some 2,000 years ago, murdered, in this case by a lynch mob. Along the way Jesus had to deal with the doubters and the cynics, such as the Georgia governor, the Ku Klux Klan, Jerry Falwell and the Moral Majority, plus all the greedy, quasi-religious television preachers who turned "belief" into big business.

Instead of writing one or two songs for the show, Harry wrote thirty, of which sixteen were used. And of the sixteen, four were old Chapin numbers such as "I Wonder What Would Happen to This World," "Everybody's Lonely," and two from his Broadway show: "You Are Still My Boy" and "When I Look Up." He also convinced brother Tom to be the musical director and changed it from a one-man show to a five-man show by adding a four-piece country western/bluegrass band called The Cotton Pickers. They were Scott Ainsle (fiddle, banjo, dobro, mandolin), Jim Lauderdale (banjo and guitar), Michael Mark (guitar and mandolin), and Jervis "Pete" Corum (bass fiddle). Chapin wrote parts for each of the band members and infused his songs into the story line of the show.

"I find it so outrageous that the Moral Majority people call *humanism* a bad word," said Chapin. "In other words, caring about other human beings is something you're not supposed to do. But that's ridiculous! It's much like the Spanish Inquisition or the Salem witch trials, where people tended to pervert the basic message for their own selfish goals. People should care about other people."

By late May, *Somethin's Brewin' in Gainesville* went into rehearsals at the Charles Playhouse in Boston. Six previews were scheduled beginning June 4. Opening night was June 10. The musical was slated for a five-week engagement. From there, Chapin hoped to bring it to Broadway. Ironically, the show that previously occupied the Charles Playhouse was none other than a production of *Jacques Brel Is Alive and Well and Living in Paris.* And like the Brel show, *Somethin's Brewin' in Gainesville* was a low-budget production with an emphasis not on props or staging (there was no set to speak of), but rather the actor/singer/musicians and their story.

Since the musical was staged in Boston, Harry naturally found some way to involve his old friend Zeke Marsden. Chapin hired a Boston publicity firm, Deedee Chereton and Associates, to promote the musical and attract customers to the 523-seat theater. But Harry was a great believer in safety devices and in this case that meant Marsden. Chapin flew up to Boston for a rehearsal (which he often did that month in between regular concerts and benefits) and, as usual, Zeke met him at the airport.

"I've got a common Harry Chapin problem," he told Zeke. "I want you to get involved in this and do the PR. I'm giving you the authority. We've already got this gal, but you tell her you're my Northeast publicity manager. I'm also giving you fifty free tickets for the first preview show. You can bring all the church friends, everybody!"

That was all Zeke needed to hear. He made a flurry of calls and within no time had his fifty theatergoers. But he didn't stop

there. On May 31, Chapin had two concerts at the Chateau Deville in Framingham, a wealthy suburb of Boston, and the last
performances of his spring tour. During both performances, Zeke
went out in the audience (1,500 people per show) and personally
invited them to the play by taking their names and addresses. "In
the meantime, I kept telling Zeke to cool it," said Peachy. "I was
afraid he was going to take one more step than he should've."

In fact, Getter was annoyed that Chapin had given Zeke fifty
free tickets, especially after making a big speech to the cast
about how their family and friends would have to buy their own.
In addition, Deedee Chereton promised to fill at least 225 seats
per night, more than half the house.

When the first preview night arrived, the seats of the Charles
Playhouse were bare except for the Marsden entourage, and the
following night (a show the Marsdens had no tickets for), the
Charles was virtually empty. "Maybe this Deedee Chereton was
good at publicity," said Zeke. "Maybe she was the greatest. But
she didn't put three people in that theater!"

Seeing this, Getter called Marsden and told him to invite
anyone he wanted, free! So Zeke pulled out the stops. He called
up everyone he knew, plus a lot of people he didn't. He started
with the list of names he'd collected at Chateau Deville. Then he
offered free tickets to all the local radio stations. He even invited
the entire crew of the U.S.S. *Constitution,* which was anchored
in Boston Harbor.

When opening night arrived on June 10, the Charles Playhouse was standing room only.

Unfortunately, Zeke's efforts went to waste. *Somethin's
Brewin' in Gainesville* was a progressive Christian play in a conservative Christian town, and, not surprisingly, was a victim
of mixed reviews. One theater critic from the *Boston Herald-
American* loved the show, reflected in his headline, GOSPEL SHOW
IS CHARMIN', but the *Herald-American* was much smaller, with
far fewer readership and less respect, than the city's leading
paper, the *Boston Globe.* The main theater critic at the *Globe* was

Kevin Kelly, a sort of Clive Barnes of Boston, who didn't appreciate the sacrilegious overtones in the musical. So he panned it. His disfavor was reflected in his headline, SOMETHIN'S BREWIN' IS REALLY SUMPIN' AWFUL. A few days later, the show closed.

In June, Chapin performed only two concerts. One was at the eighth annual Lively Arts Festival on June 7, and on June 24, he ushered in the sixteenth season of New York's Dr Pepper Music Festival on Pier 84 in Manhattan. The old location, the Wollman Skating Rink in Central Park, was undergoing renovation. At the Dr Pepper concert, Chapin performed before a capacity crowd of 8,000 people, including luminaries such as New York mayor Ed Koch. It was Chapin's last major public appearance.

That month, Chapin also organized the fourth, and final, PAF gala dinner. But not even the $100,000 fundraiser could help PAF now. Ever since the fall of 1980, the foundation's subscribership had fallen below 4,000. The growing deficit of $550,000 was now the largest ever. So Chapin decided to make a plea for public support by running two full-page ads in *Newsday,* the Long Island daily. Chapin didn't have any money to pay for the ads. He approached *Newsday* publisher David Laventhol and tried to convince him to run them for nothing. Laventhol turned him down. But Chapin persisted.

During the past few years, the men had become good friends, having intersected at various Long Island functions. In 1979 they both received honorary degrees from Dowling College, and met at one meeting of a business group called the Long Island Action Committee, which Laventhol described as the "Long Island Inaction Committee." At the meeting, Laventhol nominated Chapin as a member because he felt Harry would "stir the pot." They also met in December 1980, when Harry was inducted into the Long Island Hall of Fame.

Laventhol eventually agreed that Harry could have his ads if he paid for them over a six-month period. The ads were run that fall, and in them, Chapin stood with his pants pockets turned outward as he asked Long Islanders to "Please help!"

"As many people on Long Island know me for that as for anything else," said Harry. "It dramatized the fact I had given as much as I could. In the ad, I told them about the $150,000 loan to PAF. I told them about the benefits. . . ."

But Chapin's pleas fell on deaf ears, and in February 1981, PAF filed for voluntary bankruptcy under Chapter XI of the U.S. bankruptcy code. This allowed the foundation to continue operations for six months, provided no further debts were incurred. At the same time, PAF could barely meet its payroll. Chapin performed two benefits that spring at Huntington High School with Pete Seeger and raised $20,000. But that triumph was quickly minimized since it cost $20,000 per week just to keep the playhouse doors open.

One week after the concerts, PAF was forced to cancel the final two productions of the spring season and let most of its remaining personnel go. By June, the foundation's fate was already sealed and Chapin's annual gala dinner was little more than "an exercise in futility." In fact, within six months after Chapin's death, PAF closed its doors for good.

By the end of June, Chapin was spending several days a week at Secret Sound Studios in Manhattan recording his twelfth album, *The Last Protest Singer.* The most significant song from that album was a ballad called "The Last Stand." It was the very last song Chapin ever wrote. It was also a song that reeked with doom, as if Chapin knew of his impending death when he wrote, in the last four lines:

> It came down to the last day
> And then the last out
> And then the last play
> And you're alone at last

On the last day of June, Chapin took Sandy, his children, and more than twenty members of his family on a two-week vacation to Hawaii, something he had wanted to do since the summer of 1974 and the aborted trip to Australia. Chapin, of course, paid the bill. The timing of the journey was eerie. It was as though he wanted to see his entire family one last time—together.

While Chapin was away, the Marsdens had their own premonition of Chapin's death. There's an old Irish superstition that when a picture falls off a wall, someone close to you will soon die. And although Zeke and Peachy never believed in such things, it happened once, on April 23, 1973. That was the day Zeke's father died. The picture was a Sacred Heart of Jesus, a ninety-nine-cent reprint Zeke's mother, Mame, purchased at Woolworth's twenty-five years earlier. But the picture was close to the heart of the family, especially the prayer at the bottom, which read: "Christ is the head of this house. The unseen host at every meal. The silent listener to every conversation." The picture hung in the kitchen.

"I came out to the kitchen that morning," said Peachy, "and looked up to the Sacred Heart of Jesus I always prayed to and it was gone. It had fallen off the wall. At first you joke and say, well, who could it be? And then, of course, we found out, and I thought, well maybe there's some truth to the superstition. That picture hadn't moved in years!"

Neither had another picture, a wood-framed poster given to the Marsdens by a friend who had made Chapin his first corned beef and cabbage dinner in 1972. The picture hung at the entrance to the Marsden home. At the bottom there was an inscription: "To a friend's house, the road is never long."

On July 11, five days before Chapin's fatal car accident, that picture fell off the wall too.

Chapin returned from Hawaii on Monday, July 13. He planned to begin a late-summer tour with an 8:00 P.M. concert on July 16, a benefit with his band at the Lakeside Theater in Eisenhower Park on Long Island. On that day, Chapin awoke early as usual, made his dozen or so morning calls, and at noon got into his blue Volkswagen Rabbit and headed for Manhattan, where he had a couple of business appointments. On the way, he stopped, as he often did, at the Harbor Delicatessen on New York Avenue in

Huntington. He "offered to save me a front row seat at his concert . . .," said Philip Purpura, the owner, to *Newsday*. "He walked behind the counter and took his own coffee and custard, just like he always did. That was at 12:10 P.M."

Back in his car, Chapin took his favorite shortcut to the Long Island Expressway, Woodbury Road, a winding country drive that led directly to exit 45A. He hit the ramp and headed west toward New York, driving in the left-hand lane at approximately sixty-five miles per hour. "That's the story of my life," Chapin once said. "Always driving in the fast lane."

But not for long. Either because of engine failure or some physical ailment, speculated to be a heart attack, Chapin flicked on his emergency flashers near Exit 40 in Jericho, New York. He slowed to fifteen miles per hour. Then, in what must have been a desperate attempt to get off the highway, Chapin veered into the center lane. There was a near collision with another car. So he swerved left, then right, this time moving directly in front of a flatbed tractor-trailer truck. Unable to brake in time, the truck rammed the rear of Chapin's car, climbed its back, ruptured the gas tank. Sparks . . . explosion . . . fire . . .

> the taut shriek
> of rubber on the road,
> the shattered windshield
> and blood.

Epilogue

I found out about the car accident—Harry's death—at 5:45 P.M. that Thursday, July 16, 1981. I was supposed to meet him that night at his home in Huntington and drive him to an 8:00 P.M. benefit concert at Eisenhower Park on Long Island. Along the way, I was going to interview him for the final chapter of the book. I was gathering my questions and tapes and tape recorder when the telephone rang. I didn't recognize the voice of my old college friend Art at first because it was barely audible, choked with tears: "He's dead . . . Harry Chapin's dead."

"Look," I said indignantly, "if this is some sort of joke . . ."

It wasn't a joke.

I immediately called the Chapin home in Huntington. Don Ruthig answered the phone and confirmed the fact.

The news jolted me. I remember dropping the phone and collapsing along the kitchen wall. I remember the rhythmic drone of the telephone. I remember turning on the television in my den, sitting on the floor, leaning against the base of a club chair with a remote control in one hand, a glass of whiskey in the other, as I clicked from station to station for news of Chapin's death. I remember waking up some time later to a cartoon of a witch on a broomstick and the mockery of her surreal laughter. I was convinced I was living a nightmare. This was another time zone—warped and bizarre.

Then I found myself driving to Chapin's home. In one sense, the fact that Harry had been killed in a car accident was not surprising—car accidents were a consistent metaphor throughout his life. And yet—that he had died at all was incredible: Harry was the essence of life. He was also reckless. I had always had the feeling that something could happen, but not that it actually would. There had to be some sort of mistake, I kept thinking . . . and then I got to the Chapin home. Dozens of people passed in and out of the kitchen door off the driveway: Bill Ayres, Susan Gensel, Harry's father Jim Chapin, neighbors, friends, and members of Harry's band, who came from the canceled concert. I was convinced Harry was going to pop through that door any minute with his big cockeyed grin. He had a habit of disappearing.

But he never showed.

Three days later, on Sunday, July 19, 1981, my wife and I attended a private open-casket viewing of Chapin at the A. L. Jacobsen Funeral Home on Route 110 in Huntington. It seemed like everyone I interviewed for my book was there, including Manny and Janet Castro, and Zeke and Peachy Marsden. It was like the encore of a play, with all the cast marshaled for the final curtain call. It was all very eerie.

When I reached the casket my whole body ached. But I did not cry—that came later—as I whispered a prayer to Harry. Then all I wanted to do was get out of there.

Another three days passed, and on Wednesday, July 22, friendly relations with Sandy Chapin were severed: I received a letter from her attorneys saying I did not have the rights to my own book, and that if I did not return (to attorney Monte Morris) everything related to the book (transcripts, tapes, manuscript) within one week, Sandy would sue me.

She never sued me. But she did make numerous attempts over the years to block publication of this book. For her interference, I sued her in 1983 in Manhattan Supreme Court—for $9 million. Seven years later, Sandy Chapin—rather than go to trial—settled with me out of court.

* * *

Meanwhile, Harry Chapin would have been amazed to find out that shortly after his death, and in the years that followed, the antihunger cause took on a life of its own, spearheaded by—of all people—music entertainers who were always "unavailable" when Harry was alive. The cause became a global movement, as entertainers came together in an unprecedented display of unity and purpose that eventually raised more than $200 million. The response was so swift and so strong you might have thought hunger started overnight, because these entertainers were suddenly championing the cause as their own.

In a word, hunger became "chic."

The momentum began in 1982 when Bob Geldof, lead singer of the Boomtown Rats, organized a group of British superstar rockers to record the single "Do They Know It's Christmas." The group included Paul McCartney, Sting, Phil Collins, Culture Club, Duran Duran, among others. They called themselves Band-Aid, and their single became the biggest seller in the history of the British record business, eventually raising more than $10 million for African hunger relief.

The news spread to Canada, where that country's best musicians—Gordon Lightfoot, Neil Young, Joni Mitchell, Anne Murray, etc.—came together to record the single "Tears Are Not Enough" which sold nearly 200,000 copies.

Finally, the momentum reached the entertainment capital, Los Angeles, and specifically Chapin's former manager Ken Kragen. Kragen had gotten a call from Harry Belafonte, who had received his hunger education from Chapin, suggesting that something be done for African relief. Kragen, who managed the careers of Kenny Rogers and Lionel Richie, agreed. An organization was created—United Support of Artists for Africa, or as it became known, U.S.A. for Africa. The office of Kragen and Company became its headquarters. Marty Rogol, the former head of Chapin's Washington lobbying organization, the Food Policy Center, became its executive director. Lionel Richie then teamed up with Michael Jackson to write the title song of the album *We Are the World,* which became an instant hit single and video.

Soon the movement spread worldwide, but there was plenty of hunger in America, too. So there were events such as Farm Aid with Willie Nelson, and the mega-media event of 1986, Hands Across America, in which Americans held hands in a line from California to the Statue of Liberty. Kragen, who also organized this event, was there at the finish line when the last hand was clasped. There were tears in his eyes. When a local television reporter asked him why, he said, "Because Harry Chapin is not alive to see this."

In fact, the sad part of this great eruption of stars and events was that Chapin—who lobbied Washington for the better part of a decade, who convinced President Jimmy Carter to authorize a Presidential Commission on world hunger, who donated millions of dollars in time and money to the cause and cleared the path for these stars—was being paid scant attention by them and the media.

I remember watching the video "We Are the World," witnessing Quincy Jones fervently conduct a chorus of forty-seven of mainstream rock 'n' roll's biggest stars, from Dylan to Simon to Springsteen—all joyously rocking in rhythm with arms wrapped around one another—and thinking Harry would have been at the center of this movement. He probably would have been the ringleader. He would have been in that video. And he would have asked these performers to make their enlightenment a permanent thing, a part of their regular work, and not some one-shot mega media event in which they shine to the masses and then withdraw into their beefsteak estates. He would have asked for a commitment. The irony of this great star-studded, event-driven movement is that, today, there is more hunger and homelessness in this country, and around the world, than ever before. It takes more than working from a concert stage; it takes working in the trenches.

Chapin knew this.

The only public recognition of Chapin by his peers came at the 1986 Grammy Awards. Harry Belafonte, accepting the public service award for his U.S.A. for Africa efforts, spent nearly his entire speech reminding, even chastising, the music industry audience that "it was Chapin who started this whole thing when nobody was listening."

It wasn't until December 7, 1987, that Harry received formal recognition—on what would have been his 45th birthday—at a memorial concert at Carnegie Hall hosted by Belafonte. The highlight of the show was the posthumous presentation to Chapin of the Congressional Gold Medal for his hunger activism. The award placed Chapin alongside the likes of George Washington, the Wright Brothers and Thomas A. Edison—an elite club of approximately 200 Americans. Senator Patrick Leahy presented the award to Sandy Chapin.

On hand to perform were many of Chapin's old supporters— mostly "old folkies": Richie Havens, Pete Seeger, Kenny Rogers, Judy Collins, Harry's former band, brothers Tom and Steve and Peter, Paul and Mary. Ralph Nader and Senator Edward M. Kennedy, among others, gave speeches. Bruce Springsteen— besides Pat Benatar the only representative from mainstream rock 'n' roll—sang "Remember When the Music," commenting beforehand that Harry was always pestering him to see the big picture—to return something to society—"but I just wasn't ready yet."

But the irony of the evening was the surprise appearance of Paul Simon, who was invited to come, then couldn't, then showed. He sang his song "America" (every other performer sang a Chapin song). Still, it seemed too good to be true that the most unreachable "old folkie"—Simon—was there on that concert stage commemorating Chapin.

In the end, Harry had reached even him.

In the aftermath of Chapin's death, there were two Off-Broadway revues of his music. In October 1981, the show *Somethin's Brewin' in Gainesville* opened at the Lamb's Theatre on West 44th Street in New York. It was retitled *Cotton Patch Gospel* and went on to both critical and financial success. The musical lasted over seven months. Then, in April 1987, there was *Lies & Legends,* a theatrical staging of Chapin's most popular songs, which did equally well, and opened—appropriately—at the very spot where Chapin's music career began, the Village Gate.

In the meantime, Chapin's band tried to keep the magic going by renaming themselves The Strangers and adding a live-wire Paul McCartneyesque keyboardist and guitarist named Malcolm Ruhl. But without Chapin's songwriting—his original material—they were just another slick commercial band. After a few Greenwich Village appearances the group disbanded.

In the years since Harry's death, four albums of his work have been released. The first was the *Anthology of Harry Chapin,* which was put out by Elektra Records in 1985 and was entirely made up of previously recorded songs, primarily Chapin's greatest hits. *Remember When the Music* was next. It was released in 1987 by Dunhill Compact Disc Classics and was also a compilation of previously recorded material (most of it taken from the double album *Legends of the Lost and Found*) except for two previously unreleased and forgettable songs, "*Hokey Pokey*" and "*Oh Man.*" Then there was the *Gold Medal Collection,* a double compact disc that was issued in the spring of 1988 by Elektra Records. Except for one previously unreleased song, "*Dirty Old Man,*" this was another compilation of old Chapin tunes plus voice clips from Harry's hunger speeches and interviews. With few exceptions, none of these records offered anything new or interesting.

The only album of completely original material was *The Last Protest Singer,* which was released in the fall of 1988 on Dunhill. Chapin was recording the album weeks before he died, and as a result the record's production was never completed. Most of the songs were rough cuts later remixed with overdubs by Chapin's band, and the results were predictably disappointing. Embarrassing is more like it. The production was awful, and Harry's voice sounded so tired and hoarse it was almost as if someone coerced him to get up on a stool and sing. Though there were the usual flashes of superb lyrics, few, if any, of the songs were melodically interesting. The album's only single, "*I Don't Want to Be President,*" received no airplay, and for good reason: it was terrible. *The Last Protest Singer* literally sounded as if Chapin had run out of gas; that he had said everything he had to say; that he felt death's lurking shadow—all of which he wrote about in the song "*Last Stand,*" which was the last song he ever wrote and the only semblance of a gem on an album that was—at best—a sad punctuation to a brilliant career.

Equally sad was that, with Chapin's death, most of his pet causes and organizations floundered or folded. PAF was the first to go. It closed its doors in 1982. So did the Food Policy Center in Washington, D.C. And though World Hunger Year is still alive, it's hardly kicking. Still headed by Bill Ayres, it sorely misses the vision, vitality and funds Chapin gave to it. "After Harry died," said Ayres, "the organization almost fell apart."

Kenny Rogers saved it when he donated $100,000 a year (for six years) toward the annual World Hunger Media Awards, which went to journalists who wrote on hunger issues. But when that infusion of cash stopped, Ayres—more than ever—had to rely on revenues generated from occasional concert benefits and events. "It has not been easy," said Ayres. "Now we're in the position of having to do more with less money."

Perhaps the money will come from Chapin's widow, Sandy. She won a $12 million decision in a negligence lawsuit against Supermarkets General, the company that owned the truck that killed Chapin. Incredibly, Sandy's attorney managed to convince a jury that despite Chapin's hellacious driving record, the truck driver was at fault.

The victory was even more amazing in that Chapin's driver's license was revoked at the time of the accident. He had no right to drive his car—any car—in the first place. In fact, this was the main reason that I, and others, drove Harry to and from concerts when he was alive. Ninety percent of my taped interviews with Harry were done in a car with me driving . . . always.

After the trial, Sandy stated at a press conference that she would donate $2 million of her winnings to World Hunger Year and further her husband's most heartfelt cause. But to my knowledge, that has yet to occur. It would seem that Bill Ayres could certainly use the money.

* * *

When I think of Harry Chapin I'll always hold special value for December 7, his birthday, and July 16, the day he died. I'll remember traveling with him to the farthest reaches of New York State, his beguiling, cockeyed grin, his hurricane determination, his corny sense of humor, his brown leather shoulder bag, his constant use of the world "tonality" to define things he couldn't define, his need to be noticed.

I'll remember the gray bleakness of Green Bay, Wisconsin, in January 1981. There were two feet of snow on the ground outside as Harry and I sat in a hotel room talking—my last road trip with him. I could feel a sense of death hovering everywhere—what John Irving called "the Undertoad" in his novel *The World According to Garp*—as he talked about Clare, who had recently suffered a stroke, and how he wouldn't be surprised if she died before the end of the year because of all her physical problems. The irony, of course, being that it was Harry who died before the end of the year; Clare outlived him and eventually married for a second time.

I'll remember the electricity—the feeling of immortality, of being backstage at a concert on any given night—listening to the cheers and applause of a standing ovation, wondering what it must be like to be at the center of that attention. I'll remember Kathy and Flicker, and Flicker's shadow. And the night we drove through Watertown, New York, at four in the morning and Harry pointed out the bar that was the setting of *Better Place to Be*. I'll remember getting on that prop plane in a blizzard to fly to Washington, D.C., to see President Carter the following morning.

I'll remember driving my beat-up Mustang on some back-woods road, in some backwoods town, with Harry fast asleep in the backseat, scrunched up like a child. I'll remember Harry crying—the only time I ever saw him cry—in the parking lot of Smith College Auditorium after finishing a whole taping on Cornell, and his describing the loneliness and pain he felt. I'll remember Clare, visiting me at my father's apartment in 1980. I played Harry's songs for her on the stereo and, in particular, the sequel to "Taxi"—almost as if I was trying to get them back together.

Most of all, I will never forget that innocence, being young, living on the crest of a dream. The sense of mission. The sense of living on the edge. And the sense of fighting the good fight, of being good-tired, which Chapin's grandfathers gave to him and which he gave to me. And that's when I'll think of my college years in Buffalo, New York, and its stark, bleak, lonely landscape. Buffalo had that kind of edge. The perfect setting to Chapin's music; as real as a late-night subway train, an early morning bus station, or an empty midnight barroom. I'll remember all the nights I sat behind my desk and typewriter, staring out my boarding-room window to a blanket of winter snow, transcribing tapes to an early morning sunrise, wondering if this project would ever end.

Those were wonderful years.

The years after Harry's death were not. The most chilling moment came when I stood at his grave for the first time—eight years after he died. It was the summer of 1989. I had never been to his grave before because I didn't want to see it. He was so alive in my mind, in my memory, my being. I just wanted to keep it that way. I didn't want to spoil it. I didn't even know exactly where the grave was, and then someone gave me directions.

As I stood on that cemetery hilltop in Huntington, I just stared at the name Harry Chapin inscribed in granite, and the notation 1942–1981. I cried then as I could never have cried at his funeral. And I thought about all the miles, all the years—that after everything—life came down to *THIS!*

In some spiritual sense, I wondered if he knew all of the things that had occurred since his final day. Thinking that he might, I prayed to him . . . for him. I asked for his help. And then I walked away feeling more cleansed than I had in years. I got into my car and drove off. . . .

And to think all of this began because a teenage fan wrote a letter to a music star, wanting to write his life story. Sometimes I think I would have been better off if that letter had never been delivered. Sometimes I wonder what would have happened if "Cat's in the Cradle" had never come over the car radio that Christmas of 1974. How different my life would have been if my father, or I, had leaned over and changed the station.

Ode to Harry

He was a city man,
The kind where I came from,
Who saw truth in concrete land
And feelings when they were numb.

His music found the emotion
People feared to find.
His lyrics were the condition
Of fears we allow to bind.

In him I found a friend
Who understood where I came from.
He was a reflection of my feelings
And a refraction of the sun.

In his life I sought understandings
Of all that I was not.
Like a teacher in his teachings
I learned more than most had got.

I learned that life means loving,
Of reaching out to feel
That happiness will be coming
By living truths we may conceal.

That truth lies in our baseness,
In our needs and right to breathe.
From our dreams of glowing greatness,
To the hatred in those who seethe.

And that there's nothing like a good meal,
And there's nothing like a smile,
And there's nothing like the freedom
In the laughter of a child.

That a kiss can last a lifetime
Like a book of love poems on a shelf,
That a helping hand is the only hand
And is beautiful in itself.

And if we can be all that we can be
And do it with an open heart
We'll go farther than the eye can see
And maybe leave a mark.

PETER MORTON COAN
Buffalo, 1976

Discography

Albums

Chapin Music (1966, Rock-Land Records): (Side A) Baby Let Me Walk with You (2:40) / The Rains Come Down (3:05) / *When Do You Find Time to Breathe (3:40) / *Someone Keeps Callin' My Name (2:53) / Thinking of Tonight (2:45) / Ground Hog (2:20) / Foolish Games (2:25) / (Side B) Another Man (2:35) / *Stars Tangled (3:05) / Come Back Strong (2:50) / *Blood Water (2:45) / Going, Going, Gone (2:45) / Let Me Down Easy (2:48) / On the Road (3:05). (*Signifies songs written by Harry Chapin)

Heads & Tales (1972, Elektra): (Side One) Could You Put Your Light On, Please (4:30) / Greyhound (5:45) / Everybody's Lonely (4:07) / Sometime, Somewhere Wife (4:58) / Empty (2:57) / (Side Two) Taxi (6:44) / Any Old Kind of Day (4:56) / Dogtown (7:30) / Same Sad Singer (4:12).

Sniper and Other Love Songs (1972, Elektra): (Side One) Sunday Morning Sunshine (3:30) / Sniper (9:50) / And the Baby Never Cries (5:00) / Burning Herself (3:45) / (Side Two) Barefoot Boy (2:30) / A Better Place to Be (7:35) / Circle (3:20) / Woman Child (5:15) / Winter Song (2:30).

Short Stories (1973, Elektra): (Side One) Short Stories (4:35) / W*O*L*D (5:15) / Song for Myself (5:00) / Song Man (3:13) / Changes (4:32) / (Side Two) They Call Her Easy (4:03) / Mr. Tanner (5:08) / Mail Order Annie (4:52) / There's

471

a Lot of Lonely People Tonight (3:39) / Old College Avenue (4:25).

Verities & Balderdash (1974, Elektra): (Side One) *Cat's in the Cradle (3:44) / I Wanna Learn a Love Song (4:19) / Shooting Star (4:02) / 30,000 Pounds of Bananas (5:45) / She Sings Her Songs Without Words (3:31) / (Side Two) What Made America Famous? (6:53) / Vacancy (4:00) / Halfway To Heaven (6:10) / Six String Orchestra (5:25). (*Written by Sandy and Harry Chapin)

Portrait Gallery (1975, Elektra): (Side One) Dreams Go By (4:44) / *Tangled Up Puppet (3:42) / Star Tripper (4:17) / Babysitter (4:34) / Someone Keeps Calling My Name (6:21) (Side Two) / The Rock (4:15) / Sandy (2:47) / Dirt Gets Under the Fingernails (3:45) / Bummer (9:57) / Stop Singing These Sad Songs (2:53). (*Written by Sandy and Harry Chapin)

Greatest Stories Live (Double Album) (1976, Elektra): (Side One) Dreams Go By (4:43) / W*O*L*D (4:46) / Saturday Morning (3:01) (written and sung by Tom Chapin) / I Wanna Learn a Love Song (4:52) / (Side Two) Mr. Tanner (4:45) / Better Place to Be (9:17) / Let Time Go Lightly (4:34) (written and sung by Steve Chapin) / (Side Three) Cat's in the Cradle (3:51) / Taxi (6:37) / Circle (6:54) / (Side Four) 30,000 Pounds of Bananas (10:45) / She Is Always Seventeen (4:19) / Love Is Just Another Word (4:37) / The Shortest Story (2:27).

On the Road to Kingdom Come (1976, Elektra): (Side One) On the Road to Kingdom Come (5:28) / The Parade's Still Passing By (3:23) / The Mayor of Candor Lied (8:21) / Laugh Man (3:31) / (Side Two) Corey's Coming (5:38) / If My Mary Were Here (3:26) / Fall in Love with Him (3:50) / *Caroline (3:38) / Roll Down the River (4:26). (*Written by Sandy and Harry Chapin)

Dance Band on the Titanic (Double Album) (1977, Elektra): (Side One) Dance Band on the Titanic (5:11) / Why Should People Stay the Same (4:44) / My Old Lady (3:48) / We Grew Up a Little Bit (5:07) / (Side Two) Bluesman (5:12) / Country Dreams (4:44) / I Do It For You, Jane (5:04) / I Wonder What Happened to Him (4:06) / (Side Three) Paint a Picture of Yourself (3:49) / Mismatch (4:57) / Mercenaries (5:40) / Manhood (3:46) / (Side Four) *One Light in a Dark Valley (3:21) / There Only Was One Choice (14:06). (*Written by Grandfather Kenneth Burke)

Living Room Suite (1978, Elektra): (Side One) Dancin' Boy (3:40) / If You Want to Feel (5:03) / Poor Damned Fool (4:35) / I Wonder What Would Happen to This World (3:28) / Jenny (4:45) / (Side Two) It Seems You Only Love Me When It Rains (4:41) / Why Do Little Girls (5:03) / Flowers Are Red (4:28) / Somebody Said (5:13).

Legends of the Lost And Found (Double Album) (1979, Elektra): (Side One) Stranger with the Melodies (7:09) / Copper (5:12) / The Day They Closed the Factory Down (5:47) / Pretzel Man (3:09) / (Side Two) If Mary Were Here (4:50) / Old Folkie (5:00) / Get On with It (5:19) / We Were Three (5:29) / (Side Three) Poor Damned Fool (4:24) / Flowers Are Red (5:01) / Mail Order Annie (5:56) / Odd Job Man (5:18) / (Side Four) Legends of the Lost And Found (4:15) / Tangled Up Puppet (4:39) / Corey's Coming (8:08) / You Are the Only Song (3:59).

Sequel (1980, Boardwalk Records): (Side A) Sequel (6:35) / I Miss America (5:20) / Story of a Life (5:15) / Remember When the Music (3:50) / (Side B) Up on the Shelf (3:50) / Salt and Pepper (4:15) / God Babe, You've Been Good for Me (3:20) / Northwest 222 (3:45) / I Finally Found It, Sandy (4:35) / Remember When the Music—Reprise (3:50).

Anthology of Harry Chapin (1985, Elektra): (Side One) W*O*L*D (5:15) / Any Old Kind of Day (4:40) / Cat's in the Cradle (3:44) / 30,000 Pounds of Bananas (5:45) / Taxi (6:44) / (Side Two) She Is Always Seventeen (4:19) / Circle (3:20) / Sunday Morning Sunshine (3:45) / I Wanna Learn a Love Song (4:19) / A Better Place to Be (8:32) / Song Man (3:30)

Remember When The Music (1987, Dunhill Compact Disc Classics): Remember When the Music (3:50) / I Miss America (5:20) / Story of a Life (5:15) / Sequel (6:35) / Up on the Shelf (3:50) / Salt And Pepper (4:15) / God Babe, You've Been Good for Me (3:20) / Northwest 222 (3:45) / I Finally Found It, Sandy (4:35) / Remember When The Music—Reprise (3:50) / Hokey Pokey (previously unreleased) (3:20) / Oh, Man (previously unreleased) (4:05).

The Gold Medal Collection (1988, Elektra): (Compact Disc One) Taxi (6:44) / Sunday Morning Sunshine (3:30) / Dirty Old Man (1:25) / I Wanna Learn a Love Song (4:19) / Cat's in the Cradle (3:44) / Tangled Up Puppet (3:42) / Dancing Boy (3:40) / Thanksgiving Hunger Drives (0:47) / Flowers Are Red (5:01) / She Sings Her Songs Without Words (3:31) / Shooting Star (4:02) / Winter Song (2:30) / Story of a Life (5:15) / Commitment and Pete Seeger (1:47) / There Only Was One Choice (14:00) / (Compact Disc Two) A Better Place to Be (7:35) / Mail Order Annie (4:52) / Performing (0:30) / W*O*L*D (4:46) / Mr. Tanner (4:45) / Corey's Coming (5:38) / A Child Is Born (0:30) / Sniper (9:50) / Calluses (0:41) / The Rock (4:15) / Dance Band on the Titanic (5:11) / I Wonder What Would Happen to This World (3:28) / Sequel (6:35) / My Grandfather (1:45) / Remember When the Music—Reprise (3:50) / Circle (7:30).

The Last Protest Singer (1988, Dunhill Compact Disc Classics): (Side One) Last of the Protest Singers (4:41) / November

Rains (3:46) / Basic Protest Song (4:28) / Last Stand (4:38) / Sounds Like America to Me (4:27) / (Side Two) Word Wizard (4:14) / Anthem (3:48) / A Quiet Little Love Affair (2:48) / I Don't Want to Be President (4:00) / Silly Little Girl (3:26) / You Are the Only Light (4:11).

Bottom Line Encore Collection (1998) (Recorded live at the Bottom Line in New York in January 1981): (Disc One) Taxi / Story of a Life / I Miss America / Mercenaries / A Better Place To Be / I Wanna Learn a Love Song / Mr. Tanner / W*O*L*D. (Disc Two) Cat's in the Cradle / Mismatch / Old Folkie / Let Time Go Lightly / Remember When the Music / Thirty Thousand Pounds of Bananas / Sequel.

Harry Chapin—Story of a Life [Box] (1999): (Disc One) Taxi / Someone Keeps Calling My Name—The Chapin Brothers / Could You Put Your Light On, Please / Empty / Greyhound / Any Old Kind of Day / Sunday Morning Sunshine / Sniper / A Better Place To Be / They Call Her Easy / Mr. Tanner / Mail Order Annie / W*O*L*D / Old College Avenue / Circle. (Disc Two) Short Stories / Cat's in the Cradle / I Wanna Learn a Love Song / 30,000 Pounds of Bananas (live) / Shooting Star / What Made America Famous? / Vacancy / Dreams Go By / Tangled Up Puppet / The Rock / She Is Always Seventeen / The Mayor of Candor Lied / Caroline / Laugh Man / Taxi (live). (Disc Three) Corey's Coming / If My Mary Were Here / Dance Band on the Titanic / Mismatch / I Wonder What Happened to Him / Dancin' Boy / Flowers Are Red (live) / Poor Damned Fool / Jenny / I Wonder What Would Happen to This World / Old Folkie (live) / Remember When the Music (reprise) / God Babe, You've Been Good for Me / Story of a Life / November Rains / Sequel / Last Stand.

Books

Looking . . . Seeing (1977, Thomas Y. Crowell Company): (Poems) Rising Tide; Changing of the Guard; The Royal Kingdom; The Great Divide; The Summer of '64; An Admission; The Rain Bridge; Chauvinist Prayer; A Double-Edged Rib; Baptismal; Plains Crossing; Somersault for My Daughter; Butterflies; Peace Teachers; Double Image; Counterpoint; Revelry; One Simple Question; Spectator Sport; Consummation; The Quiet Answer; Seascape; Pandora's Box; Skirmish; Curses; Collision; Departure; A Child at Night on a Country Road; Service; Missed Connection; Transition; Convergence; Irrigation; Dissonance; Calling Card, Daily News; Postscript; Self Portrait; Droplets; The Shortest Story; (Song Lyrics) Taxi; Greyhound; 30,000 Pounds of Bananas; Halfway to Heaven; Dogtown; Womanchild; Pigeon Run; Better Place to Be; The Baby Never Cries; Any Old Kind of Day; Mr. Tanner; Mail Order Annie; What Made America Famous?; Sniper.

VHS

Harry Chapin—The Book of Chapin (1974)
Harry Chapin—Cotton Patch Gospel (1988)
Legendary Champions (1989, Big Fights, Inc. / HBO Video

DVD

An Evening with Harry Chapin (1998)

Harry Chapin Web Sites

Compiled by Tom Carpenter

Major Sites or Sites With Significant Information

New official archive site under construction:
www.harrychapinfoundation.org

Harry Chapin Appreciation Society:
members.madasafish.com/~chapintouch/chapint.htm

Biography:
www.tacademy.freeserve.co.uk/harbio.htm

World Hunger Year:
www.worldhungeryear.org

Rhino's info on the box set:
www.rhino.com/features/75875p.html

Home of the Harry Chapin Circle Webring, stories, links, collectables:
www.geocities.com/Paris/Palais/9900/

Liner notes from the box set:
rhino.com/Features/liners/75875lin.html

Images, articles, interviews, links, biography:
members.tripod.com/MrsSheep/grid1chapin.html

Homepage of John McMenamin—THE Chapin tribute artist:
members.aol.com/mcmen/hclinks.html

Pictures, articles, promoting Harry's charities and food banks:
www.ghgcorp.com/tgederberg/chapin/remember.html

FAQs from the newsgroup:
www.geocities.com/SunsetStrip/Alley/1878/chapnfaq.htm

Lyrics and comments, letters, biography, tribute essay, discography:
freespace.virgin.net/peter.steward/harry.htm

Stories, concert dates, links, Harry's charities, Steve Chapin Band:
www.harrysfriends.com/

Biography, links, audio clips, poll, message board:
www.harry-chapin.com/

News, drawings, discography, pictures, interviews, stories, links:
www.harryitsucks.com/

Listing of rarer tapes and documents:
www.tandet.freeserve.co.uk/tom/chapcoll.html

News, biography, lyrics, discography, poetry, pictures, links:
www.littlejason.com/chapin/index.html

Fantastic site of just about all links to sites that feature Harry Chapin:
www.netfx.com/~mansion/chapin.html

Articles, news, chords, tabs, lyrics, pictures, stories, links, FAQs:
www.harrychapin.com/

Analysis, lyrics, tabs, and chords to some of Harry's songs:
oak.cc.conncoll.edu/~bgbie/chapin/songs/

A roadie remembers Harry:
www.roadie.net/harry.htm

Covers in MP3, guitar and piano chords, rare audio files, pictures, links:
www.purgatory.com/scott/ChapinMusic/index.htm

Announcing a 1998 tribute concert:
www.billboard.com/daily/0713_05.html

The real story behind "Sniper":
members.nbci.com/towertragedy/

Hunger And Similar Sites Associated With Harry

Founded by Harry in 1980:
www.longislandcares.org (New Site)

Founded by Harry in 1980:
www.harrysfriends.com/licares/index.htm (Old Site)

Listen to Harry's "The Shortest Story" in Real Audio:
www.starvation.net/

Cofounded by Harry in 1975. WHY's 25th anniversary site:
www.worldhungeryear.org/

1997 winners:
 www.iglou.com/why/app97.htm

Sign up form for the 2000 Harry Chapin Memorial run in Huntington, NY:
 www.glirc.org/applications/pdfs/harry_chapin.htm

Homepage of the Food Bank in southwest Florida named in Harry's honor:
 www.harrychapinfoodbank.org/harry.htm

1996 winners:
 spj.org/contests/1996/harry.htm

A listing of US based community oriented charities . . . including Harry's:
 www.grass-roots.org/links.shtml

Chapin Family, Band Members, And Associates

Ron Palmer's Web site:
 www.ronpalmer.com

Biography, concerts, recordings, his band, FAQs, Steve Chapin and more:
 members.aol.com/chapinfo/tc/index.html

A Nova Scotia campsite owned by Steve and Angela Chapin:
 ovenspark.com/

Profile of Tom Chapin:
 www.music-tree.com/chapin.html

Singer/songwriter friend of Harry's:
 www.hepcat.com/mulvenna/index.html

Jen is Harry's daughter:
 www.jenchapin.com/

Biography of Harry's drummer from 1975 to 1981:
 idt.net/~rockpapr/hfields.html

Bio of the congressman recruited by Harry to fight hunger:
 www.house.gov/gilman/bio2.htm

A listing of charities supported by Bruce Springsteen . . . including Harry's WHY:
 oeonline.com/~trico/charities.html

About the Author

Born in Cleveland, Ohio, Peter Morton Coan is a graduate of the State University of New York at Buffalo and Boston University. He was editor of several magazines including *World Tennis* and wrote the travel book *World Tennis Magazine's Guide to the Best Tennis Resorts.* His work has appeared in many publications, including the *New York Times, Newsday, Time* magazine, *Tennis* magazine and *Travel & Leisure.*

Most recently he is the author of *Ellis Island Interviews: In Their Own Words,* which has become the definitive work on Ellis Island and the immigrants who passed through it. The book was a selection of the History Book Club, Book-of-the-Month Club, and QPB (Quality Paperback Book Club). Mr. Coan was honored by his home state of Ohio and Governor Robert Taft when *Ellis Island Interviews* was selected the 1999 Ohioana Non-Fiction Book of the Year.

He lives in New York.